D0933825

FIFTH EDITION

PSYCHOLOGY
HUMAN RELATIONS AND MOTIVATION

DONALD A. LAIRD

Late Industrial Psychologist
American Board of Examiners in Professional Psychology

ELEANOR C. LAIRD

Former Research Librarian
University of Dubuque
Dubuque, Iowa

ROSEMARY T. FRUEHLING

Associate Professor
County College of Morris
Dover, New Jersey

W. PORTER SWIFT

Professor of Psychology
Broome Community College
Binghamton, New York

GREGG AND COMMUNITY COLLEGE DIVISION
McGRAW-HILL BOOK COMPANY

New York   St. Louis   Dallas   San Francisco   Auckland   Düsseldorf
Johannesburg   Kuala Lumpur   London   Mexico   Montreal   New Delhi
Panama   Paris   São Paulo   Singapore   Sydney   Tokyo   Toronto

The sponsor of this book was Gerald O. Stoner. The senior editing supervisor was Sylvia L. Weber, and the editing supervisor was Carole Chatfield. S. Steven Canaris was production manager, and Charles A. Carson supervised the art and design. The book was designed by William E. Frost, Dimensions, and illustrated by Frank C. Smith. Photo research was done by Helena Frost, Dimensions, and Mitsy Kovacs.
The book was set in Helvetica Light by John C. Meyer & Son, Inc. It was printed and bound by Kingsport Press.

Library of Congress Cataloging in Publication Data

Main entry under title:

Psychology: human relations and motivation.

Fourth ed. by D. A. Laird and E. Laird entered under
Laird, D. A.
1. Psychology. I. Laird, Donald Anderson, 1897-1969
II. Laird, Donald Anderson, 1897-1969 Psychology:
human relations and motivation. [DNLM: 1. Psychology
Industrial. HF5548.8 P973]
BF139.L3 1975 158 74-22348
ISBN 0-07-036015-4

PSYCHOLOGY: HUMAN RELATIONS AND MOTIVATION, FIFTH EDITION

3456789 KPKP 78432109876

PREFACE

More than twenty years ago, the late Dr. Donald A. Laird and Mrs. Eleanor C. Laird wrote *Practical Business Psychology* to help students and business readers develop personal efficiency and leadership qualities. These goals remain the central themes of this latest edition of the Lairds' text. To assist the contemporary reader in achieving personal efficiency and leadership qualities, *Psychology: Human Relations and Motivation,* Fifth Edition, has been revised and expanded in light of the significant changes and developments that have occurred in career education during the past two decades.

In preparing the new edition, the authors were mindful of the ways in which career development bears on occupational work adjustment. Choosing a career and committing oneself to a career-preparatory course of study can be problematic for students who must confront the various and complex occupational fields in existence today. Because of this variety and complexity, and the pressures and tensions of contemporary society, today's students have a critical need for career maturity. In the fifth edition, new material on self-awareness, on career awareness, and on decision making is designed to develop this maturity.

Psychology: Human Relations and Motivation, Fifth Edition, is designed as a developmental tool. It provides a foundation in the psychological principles that influence the behavior of people toward one another. Human relations in work continues to be the critical factor in career maturity and has been the heart of the Laird psychology books from their inception. The new edition preserves this tradition while adding and analyzing several recent scientific studies on human behavior. Thus the book helps students achieve self-fulfillment and harmonious interpersonal relations in their work.

ORGANIZATION

This book is organized around five closely related parts. The four chapters of the first part introduce students to the field of psychology by discussing its history and development and its modern application to life and work. In Chapters 5 through 10, the second part, the students are directed toward self-improvement. This part covers learning and memory development, reading, aural comprehension, written and oral business communication, and work organization. New material on the physiology of sight and hearing relates to the efficient use of these two senses. The third part, Chapters 11 through 16, seeks to help students discover their personal values and aptitudes and guide them in making the decisions and adjustments that job-seeking and working will require. The fourth part, Chapters 17 through 20, delves more deeply into the area of human relations and deals with communication, interpersonal relationships, motivation, and the morale of individuals and groups. Chapters 21 and 22, the fifth and final part, explore the techniques of successful leadership and outline the ways in which students may develop their own leadership potential.

TEACHING METHODS

The authors believe that the most effective way to present and teach psychological principles and theories as they apply in business is through the concise and down-to-earth words of business leaders and through concrete examples. Thus histories of individuals and organizations are explained in detail. For example, the changes brought about by industrial expansion and the consequent increase in human relations problems are presented not in abstractions but in terms of what happened at the Seth Thomas manufacturing company.

The authors also believe that visual presentation of research findings is more effective than simple tabulation. Studies and surveys from business, industry, and government have been incorporated into the text, but they are also explained visually. More than 40 illustrated graphs present data in a manner that enlivens and clarifies research findings.

END-OF-CHAPTER MATERIALS

The end-of-chapter materials provide an opportunity for enrichment and creative activity. The bibliographical section, "Suggestions for Further Reading," a new feature of the fifth edition, lists both recognized seminal works in psychology and important recent studies. "To Help You Remember" consists of questions that will enable students to review the entire chapter. "Working With People, Data, and Things" introduces students to problems and situations that challenge them to think creatively and incisively. Students are asked to consider situations in terms of principles of human behavior discussed in the text. "Things to Do" suggests outside projects and assignments that give students an opportunity to develop skills in research.

INSTRUCTOR'S MANUAL AND KEY

The instructor's manual and key provides teaching suggestions for each chapter and answers for end-of-chapter questions and problems. It also offers guidelines for organizing the course and suggestions for projects and activities that will further enhance the learning experience.

ACKNOWLEDGMENTS

The authors acknowledge the following people for their assistance in revising and preparing the manuscript for publication: Dr. George C. Beamer, Mr. Charles Beamer, Mr. William B. Klein, and Dr. Bobbie Wilborn. Thanks are also given to the psychologists and sociologists who checked the interpretation of research findings presented in the illustrated graphs.

The Editors

CONTENTS

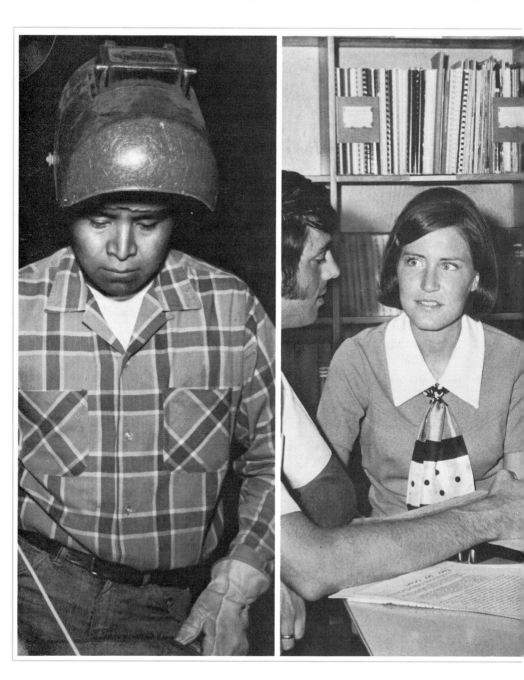

PART 1

ORIENTATION

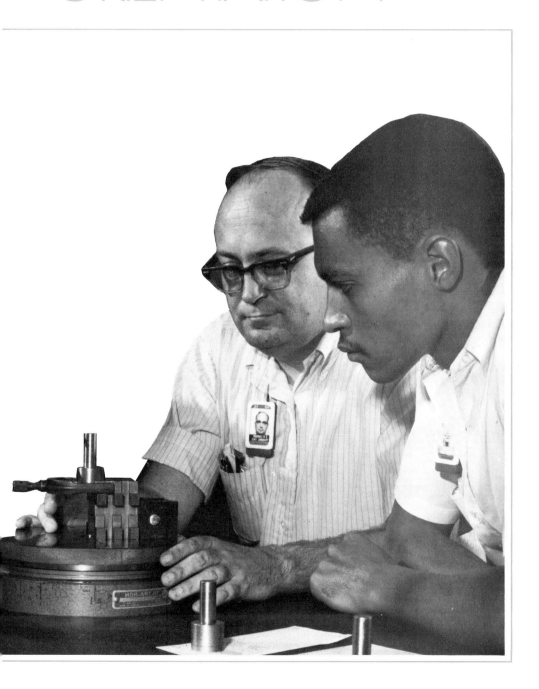

WHO, WHAT, AND WHERE IN PSYCHOLOGY

1

What This Chapter Is About

1 EARLY SCIENCE

The ancient Greek thinker Socrates (470?–399 B.C.) said, "Know yourself." Since his time people have tried to find out more and more about themselves, especially in terms of their behavior. And this interest in human behavior, which continued and became greater as time went on, eventually led to the development of the field of *psychology,* the study of human behavior. Modern psychology, as an independent field of study, really began toward the end of the nineteenth century. Psychology is considered a science because psychologists develop their theories and ideas on the basis of facts learned from experiments and carefully regulated observation.

There was no single word for the study of human behavior until the sixteenth century, when the word "psychology" was coined by a German scientist named Rudolph Gloclenius, and it appeared in a book on anthropology (the science of man) written by him and published around 1590. Psychology actually comes from a Greek word, *psyche* (sīkē), meaning "life," "spirit," or "mind," which is combined with *-ology,* meaning "science," "theory," or "doctrine." The word "psychology" first appeared in a dictionary in 1693, where it was spelled "psycology."

For centuries, man has been trying to understand himself and the world around him. He has been chiefly interested in finding the best ways to deal with other people and organize his environment. In every age, people have used the best available knowledge in order to find out why others behave the way they do, to explain unusual events, and to predict the future, for by doing so they could provide more security for themselves and their children. Since the "unknown" is somewhat frightening for all people, men found that they could reduce their anxiety or fear about the unknown by supplying logical or reasonable explanations for it. They felt that if the world could be explained, it would be a safer place in which to live.

In the light of modern science, many of the earlier explanations may seem superficial or even ridiculous, although man's access to facts was, in former times, very limited. Today, people are much more fortunate in that they can take advantage of the many discoveries of the modern sciences. It might be thought that by now man would have solved most of his behavior problems, but it seems apparent from current news reports that there is still a long way to go before this will be accomplished. Even though science has progressed more rapidly in this century than at any time before, there are still many explanations about things and events that are needed, and many ideas exist that are not supported by facts.

Many centuries ago, it was believed that if a person's behavior seemed disturbed, or strange, his brain was inhabited by evil spirits that affected his thoughts. Thus, ancient people reasoned that behavior could be improved or brought back to a normal condition by removing those evil spirits. It was thought that this could be accomplished by boring holes in the skull of the disturbed person through which the evil spirits could leave the person's body. Patients of this crude method of cure have been discovered by archeologists (scholars who study the ancient world). Clearly, when this method was used, the death rate must have been higher than the number of cures.

In the ancient world, there were three important figures who were primarily interested in human beings and in the environment in which they live: Hippocrates (450–356 B.C.), Aristotle (384–322 B.C.), and Galen (A.D. 130?–200?). They represented the beginning of science in the Western world.

Hippocrates is today revered as "the father of medicine," and every candidate for a medical degree must take the "Hippocratic Oath," a sworn statement that he will uphold the ethics of his profession.

Hippocrates tried to determine the symptoms or characteristics of a disease by observation, for many of the customary pieces of equipment in a modern doctor's office, such as the stethoscope, thermometer, sterilizer, and X-ray machine, were unknown in his time. He was the first to try to find out the causes of a disease and to formulate a prognosis (future course) for it. Epilepsy was considered a sacred disease, but Hippocrates wrote about epilepsy, "It is not any more sacred than other diseases, but has a natural cause, and its supposed divine origin is due to man's inexperience." He further wrote that "every disease has its own nature, and arises from external causes." In his book *Airs, Waters, and Places,* he considered the effects of food, work, and climate in causing diseases. He used drugs very sparingly and stressed natural cure. Accordingly he said, "Our natures are the physicians of our diseases." He studied his patients as whole beings in their environments and described the results of his studies briefly and clearly, recording his failures as well as his successes.

Aristotle is still considered one of the greatest geniuses of all time. His curiosity about the world of nature was endless, and he had a priceless knack of arousing curiosity in others. He is probably best known as a "naturalist" for his studies of plants and animals; his written descriptions of some 500 kinds of animals constituted the only source of such information that was so complete for ten centuries.

How was Aristotle able to accomplish so much? He had a combination of assets: a strong will to do things, the mental ability to accomplish them, and the ability to get along with others and to arouse their enthusiasm to work with him. These qualities are musts in any job or business venture.

Aristotle set up his own school and research center near Athens in ancient Greece. It was the first such center of any consequence in the world. With financial help from wealthy people, he was able to expand

As early as the fourth century B.C., Hippocrates was seeking answers to questions about human beings and the world in which they live.

The Bettmann Archive

his work, set up libraries, and employ assistants to help him gather information about nature.

The success of Aristotle's accomplishments can be attributed to his ability to learn how to make careful observations and logical deductions to support his observations. He avoided making conclusions based on current superstitions (ideas based merely on hearsay and imagination). Unfortunately, however, Aristotle was unable to perform experiments as scientists do today because much of the equipment used for experimentation, such as microscopes, telescopes, X-ray machines, and the like, was not available until the seventeenth century. Nevertheless, in spite of these drawbacks, Aristotle was able to glean an amazing amount of information through observation and reasoning.

One important discovery made by Aristotle was a result of his observation of how people see things. (Psychologists call this *visual perception.*) He noted that light-colored objects appear brighter when they are placed on a dark background. Salesmen and decorators frequently apply this principle, and jewelers, in particular, make practical use of it when they display diamonds and other bright gems on dark velvet cloth. This principle is also commonly applied in the design of traffic warning signals and dials on an automobile's dashboard so that they can be seen more readily.

Some of Aristotle's observations on human nature can be applied to modern business psychology. He observed, "No one loves the man whom he fears." This statement certainly applies to supervisors who threaten workers in an effort to get more work out of them. Aristotle also said, "All that one gains by telling a lie is not to be believed when he speaks the truth." In modern times, if an employee has a habit of lying, this trait may be noted on his employment record. Other frequently quoted comments made by Aristotle are "Bashfulness is an ornament to youth, but a reproach to old age," and "There is a foolish corner, even in the brain of a sage." An example of this last statement can be taken from the life of the famous nineteenth-century railroad magnate, Cornelius Vanderbilt. He was said to have been afraid of evil spirits, and so to keep them away from him at night while he slept, he supposedly set each leg of his bed into a dish of salt.

The last of our three ancient scientists, Galen, lived in the early part of the Christian Era. He was a Greek physician, but he went to Rome to seek his fortune; he lived there during most of his life as a doctor. Galen was greatly indebted to Hippocrates, whose works he had studied, and he followed the procedures prescribed by Hippocrates, which are generally called the "Hippocratic Method." He emphasized the importance of studying anatomy (the science of the body), and he is acknowledged as the founder of experimental physiology, which is the study of bodily processes. He accepted the "doctrine of humours," which holds that the human body contains four major fluids: blood, phlegm, choler (yellow bile), and melancholy (black bile). It was thought that a person's physical and mental character was determined by these four fluids. Galen realized that the arteries contain blood as well as air and that the heart acts as a pump in circulating the blood. Much of Galen's knowledge is based on results of his experiments with dissected apes and pigs because in his time it was against the law to dissect human cadavers. Galen was a prolific writer, and for many centuries after his time he was regarded as an unchallengeable authority in the fields of medicine and physiology.

2 MISBELIEFS IN MODERN TIMES

In spite of the development of science, many people still hold onto misbeliefs, or beliefs that are not based on facts. Some common misbeliefs, found among the superstitions, involve special types of behavior, such as knocking on wood or throwing salt over one's shoulder; or they might involve an idea, such as the belief that the number 13 is unlucky or that bad luck will come to a person if a black cat crosses his path.

Curiously enough, some important results have come from misbeliefs. One such result was the discovery of hypnotism in the late eighteenth century by Franz Anton Mesmer (1733–1815). Mesmer, in keeping with popular beliefs about the power of magnetism over human behavior, filled his bathtub with a secret potion in which thin iron rods were suspended. One day he found that the iron rods were missing, so he conducted his séance without the usual equipment. He was surprised to find that he was able to control his subjects as well by speaking more forcefully while glaring into their eyes. Thus, he concluded that the power was within himself. He called this power "animal magnetism." Other early hypnotists, naming their practice after him, called it "mesmerism." It is a technique that some silent movie stars later developed for their tense, romantic scenes. Today, hypnotism has many important applications in medicine and dentistry.

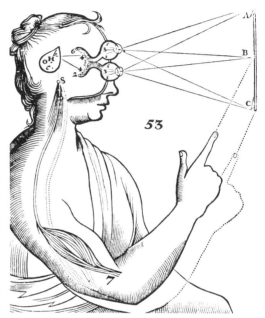

Some modern theories stem from earlier beliefs. According to Descartes, visual information was received by the eyes and transmitted by "strings in the brain" to the pineal gland which would then tell the muscles what to do. Today, there is evidence that the pineal gland is responsible for hormonal messages.

The Bettmann Archive

Another strange idea was developed by Franz Joseph Gall (1758–1828), a German biologist and physician. It was a method for evaluating personality by fingertip readings of the location, size, and shape of various lumps on the human skull. This method is known as "phrenology." If Gall's theory were tested on a person who had suffered a head injury, the phrenologist might think that the bumps caused by the accident were signs of a strange personality. Nevertheless, Gall's charts of the human brain gave later scientists the idea of mapping out special brain functions.

Many people today prefer simple explanations about their lives, such as those provided by astrology, which teaches that the positions of the stars and planets influence human behavior, and numerology, which holds that our lives are influenced by numbers. Unfortunately, however, there are still many misbeliefs about human nature that can interfere with our getting along with people and doing a good job at work.

Here are some examples of widespread misbeliefs of this type. Perhaps you can think of some other examples.

1 It helps sales if prices are in round numbers, that is, just dollars and no cents.
2 Good mechanics are likely to do poorly in jobs where mechanical ability is not needed.
3 People are born with their personalities, so these personalities cannot be changed.
4 Tall men work better than short men in jobs where a wheelbarrow is used.
5 Gossip can be stopped by telling gossips the truth.
6 More men than women look at ads with pictures of pretty girls.
7 Fear of being fired motivates good work in a job.
8 People who don't look you straight in the eye are all liars.
9 Long-time employees are smarter than short-time employees.
10 The best way to learn to do a job well is to watch an expert.
11 Hard study wears out brain cells.
12 If a person has enough initiative, he can do anything.
13 A good leader can tell how much ability a person has during the first interview.
14 People try harder to improve themselves when they are humiliated.
15 ˙ People do a better job when there is unfinished work for them to do.

3 ORIGINS OF PSYCHOLOGY

The first significant notion of modern psychology was proposed by Johann Friedrich Herbart (1776–1841), a German philosopher. He developed the idea of an "unconscious mind," and this idea was later to become the central theme of Sigmund Freud's theory of human behavior. The study of human behavior shortly after Herbart's time was considered a branch of philosophy, which is the search for wisdom in general, but today it is confined to the field of psychology, which is acknowledged as a separate field in its own right.

Perhaps the most important of the early psychologists was Wilhelm Wundt (1823–1920), who established the first psychological laboratory at Leipzig, Germany, in 1879. This is usually regarded as the beginning of modern psychology, especially because of Wundt's wide influence on experimental psychologists throughout the world, particularly in the United States. And, indeed, "Wundtian" psychology flourished until the early part of this century.

A landmark in the history of psychology is the founding of the school of "behaviorism" by John B. Watson (1878–1958), a noted American psychologist. Behavioral psychologists emphasize the point that human behavior is the product of responses to environmental conditions. The theory of the behaviorists was strengthened by the discovery of the "conditioned reflex" by the Russian scientist Ivan Pavlov (1849–1936). He conducted the now famous experiment in which a dog was given a signal, a ringing bell, just before it was served food. Pavlov noticed that the dog would salivate each time the signal was given. Then he had a bright idea—he gave the signal, but no food. He saw that the dog still salivated when it heard the signal in spite of the fact that no food was served. Thus, Pavlov concluded from this experiment that the dog had been "conditioned" to salivate by the signal. Salivating is just one example of a "reflex," an action that does not require any forethought but which happens automatically as a result of some kind of *stimulus* or external agent that causes a response.

Another landmark in the history of psychology was the development of the first intelligence test by Alfred Binet (1857–1911), a French psychologist. This first test laid the groundwork for the development later of *psychometrics,* the measurement of intelligence and aptitude as well as of emotional disturbances.

Perhaps the best-known of all those involved with the study of human behavior is Sigmund Freud (1856–1939), the famed Austrian psychiatrist and founder of the school of psychoanalysis, which holds that human behavior is guided and controlled by unconscious thoughts and motivations. According to this theory, painful experiences, especially those of early childhood, are "repressed" or put into the unconscious mind where they remain throughout adulthood, when they are responsible for disturbances of the mind and emotions, called *neuroses.*

Two of Freud's better-known theories are the Oedipus (ēd ĭpŭs) and Electra complexes. The Oedipus complex occurs in a boy between the ages of four and five, when he is supposed to compete with his father for his mother's love. According to an ancient Greek legend, the hero, Oedipus, slew his father, Laius, and later unknowingly married his mother, Jocasta. The Electra complex is similar and appears in a young girl who competes with her mother for her father's love. The name "Electra" was also taken from a Greek legend; the heroine, Electra, helped her brother, Orestes, avenge the murder of their father, Agamemnon, by killing their mother, Clytemnestra.

Freud had his patients lie down on a couch and say anything that came into their minds. This procedure is called "free association." Freud also analyzed his patients' dreams. By analyzing his patients' remarks in free association and their recountings of their dreams, Freud was able to discover their underlying motives for their behavior. The "Freudian slip," an accidental substitution of one word for another or a mixing of words in a sentence, was also used as a clue to unconscious feelings. Freud categorized basic unconscious human urges as life urges, or *libido,* and death urges, or *mortido,* and theorized that all human behavior could be explained in terms of these two conflicting forces.

Freud has been criticized because his theories were not tested by experiment, which is one of the demands of scientific procedure. In spite of this, he has had the widest influence of anyone in the field of psychology. And today he still has many followers. Two prominent men associated with Freud were Carl Gustav Jung (1875–1961) and Alfred Adler (1870–1937). Both of these men worked with Freud in Europe but later started their own schools of psychiatry.

A school of psychology called Gestalt became popular in the 1920s. This school was founded by Kurt Koffka (1886–1941), a psychologist who was born in Germany. The word *gestalt* (ge shtahlt) is a German word that means "shape." The Gestalt psychologists look at a person as a whole being and study his behavior in terms of how he sees objects in the world around him. Gestalt psychology has had a very important influence on learning theory and on theories about the individual's personality. This school promoted educational psychology and group therapy, in which people are helped by sharing in each other's problems.

World War II brought with it the rapid growth of industry in many nations, especially in the United States. During this time psychologists began to be interested in workers' on-the-job problems, such as how the worker can best get along with others on the job, and in how occupational choice occurs. Various tests were devised. The field of psychology that deals with workers' relations and job problems is called "industrial psychology." Today, many colleges and universities offer extensive training in this field.

Modern psychology investigates nearly every aspect of the human being. Therefore, there are now very many specializations in this behavioral science, and hence there is a wide range of opportunities for those interested in this field as a vocation.

4 PSYCHOLOGY AS A PROFESSION

The present-day need for psychologists has led many people to enter the field of psychology. In fact, membership in the American Psychological Association now numbers over 37,000. However, this represents only a small part of the country's total labor market. The field of psychology can be divided into over thirty subdivisions of specialization, such as clinical psychology, experimental psychology, evaluation and measurement, industrial psychology, and community psychology. Even within these general categories, there may be further specialized areas; also, a psychologist may be involved in more than one field of work.[1]

1. Anne Anastasi, *Fields of Applied Psychology,* McGraw-Hill, New York, 1964.

There are very few life situations that do not call for the work of a psychologist. For example, every school—from kindergarten through graduate school—employs psychologists as teachers of courses in psychology or as counselors who are asked for their advice concerning various school procedures. Also, virtually every large business or industry has one or more psychologists on its staff; these psychologists study human factors on the job, and they often work in the personnel departments, where they choose the right person for a job or counsel employees who have problems. Many psychologists work for the government in personnel departments, in the military, and in hospitals. Or, psychologists may be in business for themselves as counselors, giving people advice on problems at home or on the job, or as therapists, helping people with mental disorders to work out some of their problems so that they can live more useful and happier lives.

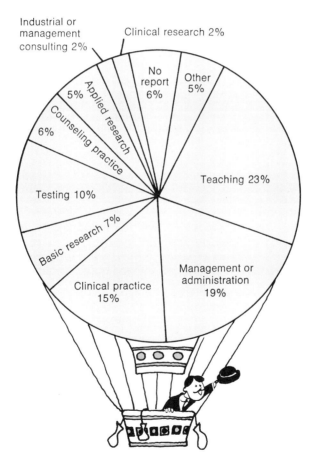

Psychologists have many choices of specialization and opportunities for careers in varied environments such as schools, laboratories, and businesses.

Clinical psychologists, or therapists, are referred to by many people loosely as "head shrinkers," or just "shrinks." Actually, their work has the opposite effect of "shrinking" because they try to "broaden" a person's view of himself and his environment. Therapists listen to, assess, and diagnose (characterize) a person's problems; then they engage in actual *therapy,* or a method of cure, in order to improve a person's attitudes so that he can better deal with his problems. The therapist assists a person in exploring his personality so that he can find out the cause of his difficulties and select better alternatives in coping with life situations.

The clinical psychologist is trained to specialize in emotional problems and mental illness. Since most people have had a long-term experience with their difficulties before visiting a psychologist, the process of cure naturally takes a considerable length of time in most cases. Clinical psychologists often are specialists in certain classes of problems and take only patients with these particular problems.

Clinical psychology accounts for nearly half of the total number of psychologists in the United States, and when counseling, rehabilitation, and school psychology are added, the total number of specialists exceeds sixty percent of the psychologists in this country. Any of the psychologists in these groups may teach psychology, conduct research, or perform therapy.

One of the most important areas in psychology is working with people who are handicapped by a bodily injury that prevents them from living normal lives. Such an injury might cause blindness or deafness or result in the amputation of an arm or leg. The job of the psychologist dealing with handicapped people is to prevent emotional problems that could result from the injury. Perhaps the most common problem of a physically injured person is a feeling of "inadequacy"; the person thinks that he is not as good as he used to be or that he cannot perform as well on the job as others who do not suffer from his disability. Psychologists who work with people who have suffered physical disabilities are known as rehabilitation psychologists because they help the injured person adjust to his new life situation. Part of this adjustment might involve learning a new job because the disability might prevent the person from continuing in the work he had before the injury. The training of a rehabilitation psychologist therefore must include courses in medical subjects such as human anatomy (the structure of the body) and physiology (bodily processes) as well as courses in occupational training.

A school psychologist works in the public school system, so most states require that he be licensed by the state. Usually he must pass an examination and complete certain courses that are concerned with his specialization. The school psychologist's duties include testing individuals or groups; counseling; engaging in research; and advising parents, teachers, and school administrators.

A counseling psychologist may be a rehabilitation psychologist or a school psychologist, but his work may have a broader scope. He may work for an agency or business or be called in as a consultant. His job will include, among other things, administering aptitude tests and interpreting their results. A counseling psychologist may advise a businessman how he can improve his personality for his particular job; he may be a marriage counselor; or he may deal generally with social problems.

The Experimenters

Many psychologists do research in addition to their other duties. The job of the research psychologist often involves performing experiments dealing with human behavior in order to find out why people react as they do to various situations. For example, he may try to advise a business firm why people prefer a certain combination of colors in the packaging of a product. Again, he may find that a certain room temperature or lighting is best for employee productivity. The research psychologist may study the behavior of animals as well as human behavior because animals provide a simpler mechanism for experimentation. Experiments with animals are performed in psychological laboratories, which are provided by an agency or firm.

In the early years of modern psychology, around the turn of the century, G. Stanley Hall reported some of his experiments dealing with the sensitivity of human skin to gradual changes in pressure. He found that such changes in pressure may not be noticed until the pressure has become great enough to injure bodily tissues; therefore he concluded that human senses cannot be relied on as guides. This is illustrated by the fact that people often bring about actual deformity on themselves by wearing ill-fitting shoes for long periods, according to orthopedic (bone) surgeons. Hall's conclusions still have important applications—in work with astronauts, in designing clothing for arctic wear, in planning good working postures, and so on. He also claimed that a frog could be boiled alive without trying to escape if the temperature of the water was increased so slowly that the poor creature could not sense the rise in temperature.

Another experimental psychologist, Christine Ladd Franklin, who lived at the same time as Hall, performed experiments dealing with visual illusions; these occur when people get a false impression of something they are looking at. She found that at certain points in the field of vision two objects look like one object and that at other points one object looks like two objects. These illusions, known as "horopter" (ho rop' tr) illusions, are common to normal vision and occur very often throughout the day.

Here is a way of seeing how a single object seems to become two objects. Hold one index finger straight up about 10 inches in front of your nose so that you can see it with both eyes. Focus your eyes on the middle joint of this finger, and continue to stare at this joint intently. While doing this, take a pencil in your other hand, and hold it vertically directly behind the index finger you are looking at so that the pencil is parallel to the finger. Slowly move the pencil away from you in a straight line behind the index finger, all the while keeping your eyes fixed on that finger. As you move the pencil away from the finger, you will see it through the corners of your eyes at first as one pencil, then as two pencils at a certain distance farther on; as you continue to move the pencil away, it will again appear as one pencil. This ability of the human eye to produce such illusions is probably the cause of a good many automobile accidents because it can impair the driver's judgment of road conditions.

Many research psychologists today are concerned with people's ability to learn and retain information. They perform experiments in order to learn how people can improve this ability. Through such experiments, it has been found that brain cells themselves are changed following a learning period. Therefore, it seems that memory depends on thorough learning followed by long periods with few interruptions, allowing the ideas to "sink in." If there are too many interruptions, the brain cells do not complete their change, and thus the information is not fully learned.

5 FROM ASTRONAUTS TO JAYWALKERS

Groups of people who have special skills or who live in special kinds of environments are often studied by research psychologists. The astronauts make up one such group. Many questions for psychologists to analyze came up concerning man's ability to exist for a time in outer space, as astronauts must do. Actually, the psychological study of the problems that astronauts encounter under the conditions of outer space had been going on for several years before flight time. Some of these problems were: Would the astronauts be able to watch their instruments and know what they had to do after the great strain of acceleration during the launching? How could the dials and indicators in the spaceship be made easy to see? How would weightlessness affect the astronauts' ability to work during their flight? What could be done to keep the astronauts from going "stir crazy" in their cramped quarters? Millions of dollars were spent in the attempt to answer some of these questions.

Most questions are not so unusual and can often be answered on the basis of inexpensive research projects that can take place right in a business organization without disturbing normal activities. Such research projects might be concerned with normal relations among workers and the effects of their ongoing relations on the business. In the home office

The astronauts have provided psychologists with a wealth of questions concerning man's ability to perform tasks in outer space. This device simulates the effects of lunar gravity on human beings.

of an insurance company, for example, some supervisors were mainly interested in work production, while other supervisors showed much consideration for the workers. This was a natural situation in which the effects of different approaches to the employees could be compared and analyzed. Contrary to what one might expect in business, the most efficient offices had the least pushy bosses.

Special situations are sometimes set up in order to study human behavior. Harry Helson's studies of influence and imitation are an example: He wanted to find out how personal grooming (personal appearance) affected an individual's ability to influence people and cause them to imitate him. He decided to use jaywalking as an experimental situation. Of course, he obtained permission from the local police department to carry out his experiments.

Helson's first jaywalking experiment was done on a university campus. This experiment was carried out a number of years ago. On the first day of the two-day experiment, he had only neatly dressed young men jaywalk, and he observed that their jaywalking practices were followed by many other students. On the second day, his jaywalkers were sloppily dressed. This time, he observed that they were followed by considerably fewer people. Of course, when this experiment was done, neatness was admired; today, neatness is not a trait that is likely to be imitated, and it may be that the sloppiest dressers would be the ones that are followed. In any case, it is the respected trait that people are likely to follow. Then Helson performed a similar jaywalking experiment in the downtown area of the university town, where there were mostly older people—business people or shoppers. Again, he found that the neatly dressed jaywalkers were followed by the greatest number of people. This experiment would probably be valid today, since neatness is still a trait that is respected by older people.

TO IMPROVE THE MESS

Although much present-day research is not available to the public, much of it is in the public domain. Not all government research in applied psychology must be kept "hush-hush." An Army study designed to help with the planning of meals that would keep soldiers happy and satisfied is a case in point. The studies of food preferences made by teams of psychologists are not confidential, and the information derived from these studies is of value for civilians as well as for military diet planners. The dietitian in a plant cafeteria can now know what foods the workers will like, and the homemaker can get some hints about what to serve when her husband brings his boss home for dinner.

From the 400 or so foods that have been studied, the ten best-liked and the ten least-liked foods are listed in the table on page 19. This preference survey provides a good starting point for an acquaintance with some of the research methods used by psychologists. The numerical score value listed for each food entry is the average; it is based on actual questionnaires, like the one on page 20, filled in by thousands of soldiers. The rating schedule, or questionnaire, was developed originally by Louis L. Thurstone (a psychologist who started as an electrical engineer with Thomas A. Edison). It provided nine degrees of liking each food, as shown in the samples taken from the scale. The percentile rank shows how much the food is preferred to all other foods rated. For example, the percentile rank of 98 for fried chicken means that it was preferred to 98 percent of the foods asked about.

If a boss happens to be a woman, these might not be the best lists to follow, since they show the preferences of men in their early twenties, on the average. No comparable research has been done on women's food preferences, but everyday observations indicate that there are differences in food preference according to one's sex. Nor may these lists be reliable guides for the preparation of meals for young men from a foreign country, such as France or Spain; these men have been used to food that is different from that served to soldiers in the United States Army. (And, as far as entertaining a boss is concerned, it might be wise to inquire about individual preferences.)

BEST-LIKED FOODS

	Score	Percentile Rank
Fresh milk	8.6	100
Hot rolls	8.4	99
Hot biscuits	8.3	99
Strawberry shortcake	8.3	99
Grilled steak	8.3	99
Ice cream	8.3	98
Ice cream sundae	8.2	98
Fried chicken	8.2	98
French fried potatoes	8.2	97
Roast turkey	8.1	97

LEAST-LIKED FOODS

	Score	Percentile Rank
Mashed turnips	4.5	4
Broccoli	4.5	4
Baked Hubbard squash	4.5	3
Fried parsnips	4.5	3
Creamed asparagus	4.5	3
Baked cabbage, cheese sauce	4.3	2
Asparagus, hollandaise sauce	4.2	2
Iced coffee	4.2	2
Cauliflower, cheese sauce	4.1	1
Candied parsnips	4.1	1

When it comes to quantity feeding, however, such as in a restaurant or cafeteria, the average preferences shown here are valuable guides and may be taken seriously. It would be foolhardy, for instance, to feature candied parsnips in a drive-in restaurant, no matter how much you personally happen to like them.

For all practical purposes, there is not much difference in popularity among the ten best-liked foods; all are in the "like very much" category. Likewise, there is not much difference in unpopularity among the ten items at the bottom; all are in the "dislike slightly" category. Some of the soldiers, we can be sure, rated a few as "dislike extremely," but their votes were offset by the votes of others who did like candied parsnips, and thus the average was raised.

Food	9 Like extremely	8 Like very much	7 Like moderately	6 Like slightly	5 Neither like nor dislike	4 Dislike slightly	3 Dislike moderately	2 Dislike very much	1 Dislike extremely	Not tried
Buttered broccoli	Like extremely	Like very much	Like moderately	Like slightly	Neither like nor dislike	Dislike slightly	**(Dislike moderately)**	Dislike very much	Dislike extremely	Not tried
Chili con carne	Like extremely	Like very much	**(Like moderately)**	Like slightly	Neither like nor dislike	Dislike slightly	Dislike moderately	Dislike very much	Dislike extremely	Not tried
Fried fish	Like extremely	Like very much	Like moderately	Like slightly	Neither like nor dislike	**(Dislike slightly)**	Dislike moderately	Dislike very much	Dislike extremely	Not tried
Roast beef	Like extremely	Like very much	Like moderately	Like slightly	Neither like nor dislike	Dislike slightly	Dislike moderately	Dislike very much	Dislike extremely	Not tried
Stewed apricots	Like extremely	Like very much	Like moderately	Like slightly	**(Neither like nor dislike)**	Dislike slightly	Dislike moderately	Dislike very much	Dislike extremely	Not tried
Corned beef and cabbage	Like extremely	Like very much	Like moderately	Like slightly	**(Neither like nor dislike)**	Dislike slightly	Dislike moderately	Dislike very much	Dislike extremely	Not tried
Buttered turnips	Like extremely	**(Like very much)**	Like moderately	Like slightly	Neither like nor dislike	Dislike slightly	**(Dislike moderately)**	Dislike very much	Dislike extremely	Not tried
Hot griddle cakes	Like extremely	Like very much	Like moderately	Like slightly	Neither like nor dislike	Dislike slightly	Dislike moderately	Dislike very much	Dislike extremely	Not tried
Potato chowder	Like extremely	Like very much	Like moderately	Like slightly	Neither like nor dislike	**(Dislike slightly)**	Dislike moderately	Dislike very much	Dislike extremely	Not tried

(From D. R. Peryam and associates. Food Preferences of Men in the U.S. Armed Forces. Department of the Army, Quartermaster Research and Engineering Command, 1960.)

Excerpts from the rating scale of nine categories that were developed under the guidance of Dr. Louis L. Thurstone to measure the popularity of foods. The circles indicate one person's preferences.

SUGGESTIONS FOR FURTHER READING

Capretta, P. J., *A History of Psychology in Outline,* New York: Dell, 1968.
Coopersmith, S. (ed.), *Frontiers of Psychological Research,* San Francisco: Freeman, 1966.
Evans, Richard I., *B. F. Skinner: The Man and His Ideas,* New York: Dutton, 1969.
Kohler, W., *Gestalt Psychology,* New York: New American Library, 1967.
Marks, Robert (ed.), *Great Ideas in Psychology,* New York: Bantam, 1969.
Peters, R. S. (ed.), *Brett's History of Psychology,* Cambridge, Mass.: M.I.T., 1969.
Schultz, D. P., *A History of Modern Psychology,* New York: Academic, 1969.

TO HELP YOU REMEMBER

1. Why did people in early times try to find explanations for human behavior before they knew about psychology?
2. What did people in ancient times think caused disturbed behavior?
3. What did Aristotle notice about the way people see things; that is, about how objects appear to people?
4. What influence did Mesmer and Gall have on later psychological research?
5. How did Pavlov and Watson influence modern psychology?
6. What was Alfred Binet noted for in the early development of psychology?
7. Name three sources of information used by Freud to discover unconscious feelings in his patients.
8. How many fields of psychology can you name? Where would you find psychologists working?

WORKING WITH PEOPLE, DATA, OR THINGS

Prepare a table like the one shown below, and fill in the required information based on your observations of automobiles at a fairly busy intersection in your city during a 30-minute period. Use a short, vertical line to indicate each car. Summarize groups of five as follows: 卌.

Car's Movement	Color of Traffic Light		
	Red	Yellow	Green
Straight			
Turn right or left			

For example, if a driver drove straight through the intersection when the light was red, place a short, vertical line in the "Red" column, adjacent to "Straight."

When you have completed the survey, answer these questions:

1. Did you find it difficult to keep track of the vehicles at the intersection?
2. Was it difficult to see both the light and the way in which a given vehicle was moving at the same time?
3. If you had marked down the license number of each car going through a red light, would you be able to testify accurately about each case in a traffic court?
4. From your observations, can you give any reasons why some drivers go through red and yellow lights?
5. If you saw any people drive through a red light, what facts can you give about them?

THINGS TO DO

1. Look in the *Bibliographical Dictionary* published by the American Psychological Association for the names of several psychologists, and see what kinds of work they have been doing. Also look at the back of the dictionary for Divisional Memberships (of the Association), and notice where psychologists live by state and city and where they are employed. Your school or local library might have a copy of this dictionary.
2. Follow your horoscope in a daily newspaper for a week. How accurate are the predictions? Is your day's forecast precise, or is it described only in very general terms? Is the amount of detail in your horoscope related to its accuracy? Compare your horoscope with those of your classmates for accuracy and amount of detail. If possible, compare your week's experiences with those of someone who shares your astrological sign (and therefore has the same forecast).
3. Go to your local public library and look through some of the journals of psychology. Look at some of the articles in these journals—notice the title, purpose, and conclusion or summary of each article. Then look at the *Psychological Abstracts* and see which of the journals you looked at also have articles in the *Psychological Abstracts.*
4. Choose an article that might interest you in *Psychology Today,* and read the article. Did you feel that this article could be understood by a person not trained in psychology? Did you gain something from reading the article?
5. Interview a psychologist in your community. You can probably find a psychologist in your school or another school—a public school or college—or perhaps in some business or government agency. Find out the psychologist's opinions about the many applications of psychology and about trends in the future of psychology in general.

PSYCHOLOGY IN BUSINESS AND INDUSTRY

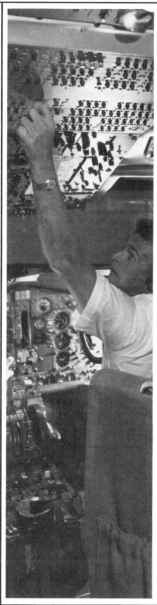

2

What This Chapter Is About

1 THE NEED FOR INDUSTRIAL PSYCHOLOGY

One of the most important jobs of the business and industrial psychologist is to promote the efficiency of workers. The psychologist is interested in learning the best ways to motivate people to do the best possible job over a long period. If a worker is happy and healthy, he will be able to work more efficiently. The measure of a worker's efficiency is called *productivity.* A person's productivity depends on how well he adjusts to his job situation and how well the job situation suits the person. Therefore, an important duty of the psychologist in business is to help the worker to relate to the job situation and to see that the job situation is best for the worker, as well.

The rapid growth of business and industry during this century has resulted in important changes in the relations between employer and employee. For example, in the last century the employer usually knew his workers personally, and the employer and worker took a personal interest in each other. But today the employer is often a large corporation, and if the employer is an individual, the worker may never see him or even know his name.

In the early part of this century farming was still the major industry in the United States. As a result, when other industries began to develop, there was a severe shortage of manpower, and so it was necessary, in most cases, to produce goods with the smallest possible number of workers. This, in turn, brought about the need for maximum efficiency on the part of the worker. Thus the psychologist began to make his way into industry as an "efficiency engineer."

Two pioneers in efficiency engineering were Frederick W. Taylor and Frank B. Gilbreth. Taylor introduced most of the production controls and planning methods that are still used today. Nevertheless, his revolutionary work did not become generally known until a congressional investigation of alleged inefficiency on railroads took place in 1911. Taylor was the star witness at the hearings, and the term "scientific management" came into use at that time. Those hearings and the widespread publicity given scientific management stimulated much interest in planning and organizing work.

One interesting study was made by Taylor before World War I. This study had to do with the amount of pig iron that could be loaded onto a freight car during a normal workday. Taylor found that a man's productivity in loading could be increased from 12½ tons to 47½ tons per day. Each chunk of iron weighed 92 pounds; thus, carrying such heavy pieces of iron made the laborers tired so that as the day wore on, they were able to do less and less work. Taylor found that if the workers were given rest periods at various times during the workday, the efficiency of each worker could be increased by close to four times.

Gilbreth had started in efficiency work a few years later and had been working independently of Taylor. He became interested in what he called "motion study," and so he devised laboratory methods for finding the most efficient ways to manipulate machines and parts. He studied workers at work to find better ways for them to do their jobs, and he was the first to use motion-picture cameras for this purpose. He even extended his studies to the management of his own household, and his efforts are recalled by two of his children in their book, *Cheaper by the Dozen*. Every really sizable firm today has a methods department that uses many of the devices that Gilbreth developed to find better ways of working.

In addition to Frederick W. Taylor and Frank Gilbreth, two other early pioneers in industrial psychology were Hugo Münsterberg in the United States and H. M. Vernon in England. These people studied various problems concerning human behavior in business and industry, and their successes proved the worth of the psychologist in this area.

In the beginning of this century, more and more people began to leave the farms (in 1790, 96 percent of the population of the United States lived on farms, in contrast to 37.5 percent in 1900), and so they became available for industrial jobs. Even so, they were untrained for those jobs, and in addition, they were for the most part poorly educated. In 1900, only 5 percent of the youth of this country had attended any type of school beyond the sixth grade, and vocational education (job training) at school did not become established until the 1920s.

More and more new work skills were needed, and businessmen and industrialists had the difficult task of training unskilled, poorly educated people to operate complicated machines and to use new ideas that the average person was not accustomed to thinking about. Thus, the need for the industrial and business psychologist grew.

The growth in importance of business and industrial psychology is indicated by the increase in the number of publications in that field. Before 1920, there were about ten each year; in the 1920s the number increased to about three hundred; today there are more than a thousand per year. Although the world of business and industry has been greatly helped by psychological methods, as well as by automation and computers, at the same time human work problems have changed and in many ways have become more complex.

2 ENERGY AND EFFICIENCY

Efficiency is the key word connecting psychology with industry. Whatever a psychologist looks for in any type of business, he is ultimately trying to find some possible improvement in human efficiency. This improvement in efficiency may be related to equipment or machines, work methods, work environment, or the skills and personalities of the workers. The results of any study might call for changes in tools or machines, the work area, the selection of workers for a particular task, and so on. *Efficiency* does not mean that a worker must keep producing until he collapses; rather, it means that the greatest amount of work should be done in the easiest and least expensive way.

The measure of efficiency is the ratio of input to output—the input being the worker, his tools, and materials; the output being the product, which is the thing to be done by the worker. Efficiency can be measured for most machines. Consider the automobile engine. For every hundred units of power put into it, the average engine puts out 20 to 25 units of power. The efficiency of the engine thus ranges from 20 percent to 25 percent, depending on the design of the engine. For example, steam engines are less efficient than automobile engines, and diesel engines are more efficient than automobile engines.

The efficiency of people can be measured in a way similar to that of engines or other devices. The energy exerted by a human being's muscles can be measured, but the equipment needed for making such measurements is very complicated. The efficiency of human muscles is almost the same as the efficiency of an automobile engine—25 percent to 30 percent in the average person. The efficiency of athletes' muscles is higher, about 40 percent. The reason is that athletes do special exercises that are designed to improve their particular skills; also, they follow special diets designed to provide the most vitamins, proteins, and minerals needed for developing and maintaining the health of their bodies. Thus, they avoid consuming candy, fats, soda pop, and alcohol; they do not smoke cigarettes or cigars; and they get a good night's sleep. They try to avoid conditions that cause sickness. The body of an athlete is like a special machine—it must perform a task in the most efficient way possible.

Energy input in everyday tasks varies quite a bit; it depends largely on the method of working. Pushing a heavy load on a smooth surface, for instance, requires less energy than pulling it. Walking three miles per hour (about ninety steps per minute) is the most efficient speed for a person of average build; running and walking slowly are both less efficient than this three-mile-an-hour rate, in addition to being more likely to cause a fall or slip. This shows that working too fast or too slowly both bring about inefficiency. The goal of efficiency studies is to find the best possible rate of speed and to maintain this speed, except, of course, for slowdowns and work breaks.

People are often surprised to see how little energy is needed for most work. Many people think that unpleasant tasks use up more energy, when actually it is the unpleasantness of the work that makes it seem that way. For example, dishwashing seems to be a tiresome job, but it actually uses very little energy. The table on page 27 showing optimal (best) work levels gives some examples of work and the energy (in calories) used up in performing the work, along with other pertinent

THE OPTIMAL WORK LEVEL*
— as determined by physiologists

How Hard	Pulse Rate per Minute	Breaths per Minute	Calories Used per Minute	Work Examples (Numeral Shows Calories per Minute)	How Long You Can Safely Keep It Up
Light work:					
1. Mild	Under 100	14 or less	1 to 4	Typing 1½, clerical 1½, cooking 1 to 2, ironing 2, light assembly 2, washing windows 3, driving truck 4	Indefinitely
2. Moderate	Under 120	15 or less	5 to 8	Scrubbing on knees 5, assembling 25-lb. parts 5, hand printing 5, shoveling 9-lb. load 8	8 hours daily on job
Heavy work:					
3. Optimal	Under 140	16 or less	9 to 10	Walking 5 mi. per hr. 10, hand riveting 10, blacksmithing 10	8 hours daily for a few weeks
4. Strenuous	Under 160	20 or less	11 to 12	Shoveling 14-lb. load 11, rowing boat 3 mi. per hr. 11	4 hours, two or three times a week, if special training
Severe work:					
5. Maximal	Under 180	25 or less	13 to 15	College football 13, hard stair climbing 14	1 or 2 hours, on scattered occasions
6. Exhausting	180 and up	30 and up	16 and up	Shoveling wet snow, 23-lb. load 18, crew rowing 19 to 30	Few minutes only, on rare occasions

*Adapted from research of Dr. J. Gordon Wells and colleagues in the U.S. Air Force School of Aviation Medicine.

information. Work at the optimal level uses approximately half of the average adult's capacity for physical work and should not deplete the energy of an adult who is in good physical condition.

Advances in mechanization and automation have almost entirely eliminated hard, physical work in most jobs. Even truck driving is light work because it does not require much energy. It seems that the truck driver, as well as the desk worker, can become overweight without realizing why.

Dr. Edgar S. Gordon of the University of Wisconsin studied the effects of mechanization on the exertion of energy in a job situation. He found that a farmer working with a tractor that had an old-fashioned steering mechanism used up 157 calories an hour; that is, his job demanded no more energy than light factory assembly work. When power steering was later installed on the tractor, the farmer used up only 126 calories an hour. This means that he used about 250 fewer calories during an eight-hour day, and therefore it was reasoned that he should accordingly cut down his meals by an equal number of calories.

Gordon also studied the effects of mechanization in an office. This time he used as his subject a typist who weighed 120 pounds. She used up 88 calories an hour when working with a manual typewriter but only 73 calories an hour when using an electric typewriter. If she ate the same amount of food when she worked with the electric typewriter as when she used the manual typewriter, she would gain one pound every ten weeks, assuming that her other activities did not change.

The brain uses very little energy. Dr. Francis G. Benedict, who was a pioneer in measuring metabolism, or energy conversion, found that one salted peanut supplies a person with enough energy to work on his income tax forms for two hours. While it is difficult to measure how much energy is used by a person in work that does not require the use of muscles, specialists have developed ways to find out how much energy can reasonably be expected to be used by a worker on each kind of job.

Efficiency in productivity depends on a worker's total environment—both outside and inside his body. Thus, the good health of a worker, as well as a safe, comfortable work area and a suitable job, are of great importance to an employer. Every employer knows that a worker cannot do his best if he is ill, if he is not suited to his work, or if working conditions are dangerous and unhealthful. These circumstances lead to absenteeism, unemployment, and high employee turnover rates, all of which are costly to any company.

3 YOU, THE WORKER

Psychologists have been studying the problems of the worker from every point of view, and they are continuing to do so. They study the worker's ability to learn, his sources of motivation, his habits and attitudes, and his emotional responses to the demands of his job. Psychologists are also very concerned with how the job affects the worker in terms of health, safety, fatigue, nervousness, boredom, and possible deterioration, disability, or death. Often the way a worker *feels* about his complaint is more important from a psychologist's point of view than the actual complaint itself. For example, in one factory, workers had been complaining about both too much heat and too much cold at the same time. Changing the locations of certain workers, opening and shutting some windows and doors, and making the sources of heating and ventilation more evident resulted in greater worker satisfaction. In some cases, the fact that the employer was really concerned with the worker's comfort was enough to diminish the worker's complaints.

The physical health of a worker is of primary concern to an employer. Most companies, especially the larger ones, have an infirmary with one or more nurses and even a doctor to handle the medical complaints of workers. Frequently an employee is given a complete medical examination before he begins his new job. Such an examination may reveal a health problem that could affect the selection of a job for an employee or his employment with the company.

Sebastian Milito

The worker's good health is of great importance to the employer. Many companies have an infirmary to handle medical complaints and to give new employees a complete medical examination.

Many big companies have cafeterias that are directed by a dietitian whose job is to select the best foods for a good all-around diet and to see to it that these foods are properly prepared. Salt tablets are frequently available to workers whose jobs cause them to perspire a great deal.

In spite of the efforts of government agencies, unions, and the companies themselves to protect the workers from danger and illness, there are still accidents and occupational diseases. Some people are "accident-prone"; that is, they tend to have more accidents than others. Psychological studies have shown that about 20 percent of a working population have about 80 percent of the accidents. Accident-prone workers are often inefficient in their movements because they are emotionally troubled. This, in turn, causes them to act impulsively—they perform certain job activities without first thinking about what they are doing and the dangers involved in the activities. Many young male drivers must pay higher automobile insurance liability premiums because of their record of having the highest frequency of accidents. Although many accidents are caused by inexperience or lack of training, young men have a greater proportion of accidents when driving than young women. The reason for this is of great interest to psychologists; hence, many of them are carrying on study programs to examine the personality traits and personal motives of young men and young women to find out why the men are more accident-prone behind the wheel of an automobile than the women.

The way a person lives his life, on and off the job, affects his health and his tendency to have accidents. Not enough sleep and rest, poor diets, the use of too much energy in physical activities, sensitivity to unimportant things, alcohol, cigarettes, and, of course, drugs all affect a person's attitudes. Even though many workers are aware of protecting their health and safety on the job, there are still many elements in the working situation that need to be studied to reduce dangers and conditions that lead to poor health.

4 WORK AND FATIGUE

Fatigue may be caused by any number of things that a person does during his waking hours. It can be caused by overusing one's eyes, ears, or mind. Boredom and monotony can result in fatigue. For example, too much loud rock music over a long period of time can be monotonous, as well as hard on one's hearing mechanism. Spending too much time doing homework (a rarity among most students) can cause both visual and mental fatigue. Even a person whose job is to taste coffee in order to determine the best blend may get a tired tongue, which will eventually become insensitive to taste if the person works continuously over a long period without a break.

Length of the Workday and Workweek

Years ago, many people worked six or seven days a week and sometimes ten to fourteen hours a day. Psychologists have found that such long hours of work lead to tension, ill health, and a shorter life span. Today such long hours rarely exist, but still, there are other factors that must be considered to improve working conditions. Improved equipment, better medical care, and time-saving devices such as computers all help the employee of today. Many psychologists are now concerned with the effects on the worker of the shorter workday, longer lunch hours, and rest periods and coffee breaks.

Early industrial psychologists, such as Münsterberg, Poffenberger, and Vernon, began watching workers' productivity by the day and by the week. They noticed that a worker's output was only fair on Mondays and best on Tuesdays and Wednesdays and that it declined steadily from Thursday to Saturday. These studies led to the acceptance of the five-day workweek. In fact, it was found that the five-day week yielded productivity as good as or better than that of the six-day week. For example, Vernon found a 15 percent gain in weekly output by workers when the workweek was reduced from 60 to 50 hours in certain British industries. Today, the usual American workweek consists of 35 to 40 hours spread over five days, but the four-day workweek is appearing on the horizon.

A few years ago, the employees on the Staten Island Ferry, which crosses New York Bay to Staten Island, were offered a choice of more money or a four-day week, and they chose the four-day week. In this particular case, the hours of work each day were not increased to obtain 40 hours a week, as is the case with more recent four-day-week proposals. This four-day week, that is, the 40-hour four-day week, has been initiated by some organizations, mostly manufacturers in the Northeast, and in some municipal government bureaus, particularly in the Southwest. There are now about 75,000 workers in four-day-week programs, but this number represents only one in every thousand workers. Necessarily, the 40-hour four-day week requires lengthening the workday from eight to ten hours. Accordingly, some unions have renounced this increase of working hours as a return to the "sweatshop" practices of the last century. Most of the concerns that have instituted the four-day workweek have been small organizations with nonunion workers.

Some police departments in smaller communities have been able to increase the effectiveness of their manpower by using the four-day week on a ten-hour-per-day basis. Service organizations, such as banks, hospitals, and government bureaus, have found that the four-day workweek on a ten-hour daily basis has improved their ability to provide extra services and normal services over longer periods.

Naturally, as with any innovation, the four-day workweek will present some problems to solve. For example, will the extra hours that a worker must spend on the job affect his health or safety? That is, would it affect him over a long period? Is the kind of work critical so that it would be affected measurably by the extra two hours in terms of a worker's being fatigued? Also, changes in the laws that specify pay requirements for overtime work would have to be made. Then, too, there is the question of automation, which poses an entirely different problem — namely, too little work. In this case, more than likely, a worker will be needed actually fewer hours per day, and so he will work perhaps a 32-hour (or less) week. Nevertheless, his paycheck must be adequate to support him and his family in their accustomed way of life, at least. The four-day workweek will doubtless become more and more important as a "way of work" in the coming years.

The four-day workweek is gaining popularity. What are some of the problems and advantages that it presents?

Another innovation in the workweek schedule is *gliding time,* developed in 1967 in West Germany by Christel Kammerer, a management consultant. She suggested that workers be allowed to schedule their own 40-hour workweek within the time the plant or office is open. For example, a company might be open from 7 a.m. to 7 p.m. An early bird could choose a 7 a.m. to 3 p.m. schedule, and an employee who preferred to sleep late could work from 11 a.m. to 7 p.m. The gliding time system of scheduling work hours has been shown to decrease lateness and absenteeism and to increase productivity.

Warm-up Periods, Rest, and Efficiency

Everyone has a few minutes or more at the beginning of his workday known as a warm-up period. The length of such a period varies from person to person: it depends on his physical well-being, his psychological frame of mind, and the type of work he is doing. For example, a typist may putter around a bit, type rather slowly at first, and then finally reach a chosen pace that is somewhat faster and that may be maintained more or less uninterrupted for an hour or two. Once a worker has overcome the slower pace of the warm-up period, he will come into a period in which he will probably reach his best rate of production. Of course, this rate cannot be maintained for too long a period, especially if he does fast work. If there were no rest periods or breaks and lunch hours, the pace of work would decline steadily throughout the day following the early hours of greater energy output.

The lunch hour, together with morning and afternoon rest periods or coffee breaks, interrupts this decline in productivity. After each such break, productivity picks up to such an extent that it well makes up for the loss of working time during the breaks. Therefore, except for very short warm-up periods that occur just after each break, productivity throughout the day tends to remain at an even level as a result of breaks, barring other distractions. Of course, it is also important that these breaks be separated by the best possible time intervals and that the worker really take these break times for relaxation to support his work efforts in the best possible way.

The workers in highway construction crews, for example, are often seen resting by leaning on their shovels or lying down on nearby grassy areas. Their particular work demands a lot of muscular activities, such as standing, vigorous motion, and lifting heavy weights. Because of these elements of the work, more frequent rest periods are essential. Also, in this type of job, where much physical effort is necessary, each worker must take a break when he feels tired. Thus the breaks cannot be regularly scheduled as they are for office work.

5 PLAIN AND FANCY

Psychologists have found that different jobs bring about fatigue in many different ways. As shown above, highway workmen become physically fatigued. A scientist may become mentally fatigued because he deals with problems that require a great deal of mental effort. An executive under continual pressure may suffer emotional fatigue. A night guard will become fatigued by the boredom of his job.

Workers are often selected for jobs that may be too simple and repetitive. Such jobs lack challenge for their particular abilities. The worker will soon become bored with his job, and as a consequence, he will look for another job. This condition will cause a high turnover rate in the job, which in turn will be costly to the employer in terms of the expense of training time. In one case, a bottle-capping job in a soft drink company was vacated fifteen times in one year until a worker was finally found who enjoyed this simple, repetitive task.

There has been a tendency in some businesses to simplify jobs in an effort to speed up the rate of learning for a worker on a new job. One consequence of this work simplification is that many jobs make use of only a fraction of a worker's capabilities. It is also true that such simplified jobs generally produce more worker dissatisfaction than other jobs that are more challenging. (This problem is discussed further in Chapter 3, Section 2.)

Nancy C. Morse made a study of white-collar workers in the same company relative to the variety of tasks on a job and satisfaction with the job. The table below shows the results of her study.

	Percentage of Clerks Reporting High Satisfaction With Their Jobs
On jobs having variety	41
On jobs lacking variety	8

Job simplification has been mostly a characteristic of mass-production, assembly-line operations. The effect of simple tasks on blue-collar workers' interest in their jobs is shown in the illustration on page 35, which represents workers in a modern automobile factory. These workers all receive about the same wages. But one-third of them did only one operation that took about two minutes, such as using the same tool on the same part over and over again as the conveyor line passed their stations. Another third of the workers did two to five operations, and the remaining third did five or more. The illustration shows that those who had a larger variety of tasks had a greater interest in their work.

Many surveys have shown that workers on skilled jobs derive the most satisfaction from their work. Qualifying for a skilled job gives a person a sense of self-realization over and above any increase in earnings he may receive.

If a worker's abilities are not fully used in his job, he will not operate at his highest efficiency level, even though his actual productivity may seem to be high. Some personnel departments search for hidden talents among employees and try to find jobs for them in the company that make better use of their abilities. Job supervisors, who observe workers very closely, can often determine if a worker is in a job that makes the best use of his abilities.

 ## ENRICHMENT PROGRAMS

In many companies, especially the larger ones, where assembly-line operations are the mainstay of production methods, workers are becoming more and more frustrated by their dull and boring jobs — jobs in which a worker performs one simple operation repeatedly for days, months, and maybe years. This frustration, in turn, is revealing itself in self-defeating forms of behavior, such as absenteeism, insubordination, bickering, and low morale in general. Hence, the tedium of assembly-line work is beginning to affect the worker's productivity. To counteract this trend, many companies are establishing "enrichment programs" that are

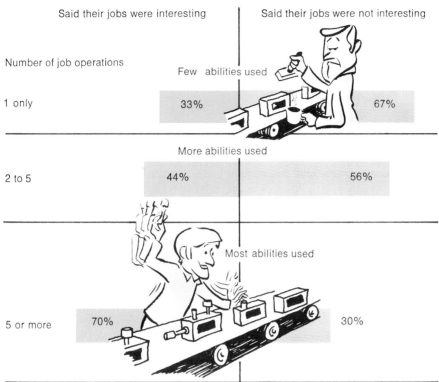

Said their jobs were interesting | Said their jobs were not interesting

Number of job operations

Few abilities used

1 only   33%   67%

More abilities used

2 to 5   44%   56%

Most abilities used

5 or more   70%   30%

Data from Dr. Charles L. Walker and Dr. Robert H. Guest, Yale Institute of Human Relations

The opportunity to perform a variety of tasks and use a number of abilities makes a job more interesting. A study of assembly-line workers showed that they reported the greatest interest in their jobs when five or more job operations were performed.

intended to give the worker a sense of accomplishment and satisfaction with his work—the feeling that he is making an important contribution to the product that he is helping to manufacture. As an example, in a new General Motors plant experiments are being done in which teams of from three to six workers are involved with the production of an entire automobile. Similar operations are now being tried at Ford and Chrysler plants. These production experiments are still in the early stages, and there are as yet no conclusions that can be drawn from them. Another example of an enrichment program comes from the Monsanto plant at Pensacola, Florida, where dull and dirty jobs are being eliminated by automation. Also, at this plant the workers are their own managers— this gives them a chance at decision making. The results at Monsanto are encouraging: waste has dropped to zero, and production is up by 50 percent.

Lyman Ketchum, a manager of organizational development for General Foods, has been pioneering with an enrichment program at the company's Gaines Pet Food plant at Topeka, Kansas. One of the things that he has done there is to remove the traditional barriers between the workers and management that have often been a source of grievance among workers in many companies. He has eliminated time clocks, special parking areas for management, and the special dining room for management, to list a few of his accomplishments. The managers have their jobs to do, and their jobs are no more important than the jobs of the workers. The emphasis is on cooperation and team effort. The old military elitist system, which draws a sharp division between the officers and the foot soldiers, is gradually but surely being broken down. Similar programs are under way at the Corning Glass plant at Medford, Massachusetts, the Travelers Insurance Co. headquarters at Hartford, Connecticut, and the Motorola plant at Fort Lauderdale, Florida.

Robert L. Kahn, who has studied job boredom among industrial workers, describes what he terms a "work module." According to Kahn, the work module is "a time-task unit—the smallest allocation of time that is economically and psychologically meaningful."[1] A work module consists of two hours at a certain task. For example, a stock clerk in a supermarket would have a choice of tasks available throughout his workday, each task lasting two hours. He might stamp prices on items, man a cash register, take inventory, and so on. These tasks would not have to be performed during the same times each day; they could be varied according to need or choice, so long as employees could coordinate their schedules to complete the tasks that needed to be done.

Kahn defines the humanizing of work as

> . . . making work more appropriate and fitting for an adult to perform. By this criterion, humanized work:
> 1 Should not damage, degrade, humiliate, exhaust, or persistently bore the worker;
> 2 Should be interesting and satisfying;
> 3 Should utilize many of the valued skills the worker already has, and provide opportunity to acquire others;
> 4 Should enhance, or at least leave unimpaired, the worker's ability to perform other life roles—as spouse, parent, citizen, and friend, for example;
> 5 Should pay a wage sufficient to enable the worker to live a comfortable life.

 IMPROVING THE WORK AREA

If a job is repetitive or boring, and job enrichment is considered impractical, working conditions can be improved at least somewhat by a pleasant work area. If you were in charge of improving the physical surroundings in a company, probably the first thing you would do to a work area would

---

1. Robert L. Kahn, "The Work Module—A Tonic for Lunchpail Lassitude," *Psychology Today,* February 1973, p. 36, © Ziff Davis Publishing Company.

be to clean it up and put it in good order. If space were limited, you might remove unnecessary furniture or equipment, or possibly you might look for a larger area.

When a psychologist begins his study of a work area, most of the obvious faults have probably been taken care of. He begins by making observations and taking notes; he interviews workers or uses an attitude questionnaire and examines productivity records of the past and present. He will probably have the results of earlier research studies of similar situations to help him make comparisons.

Some typical things the psychologist will study are ventilation, temperature, humidity, and air movement. For example, in one office it was customary to have the long-time employees, who were mostly older women, sit near the windows, while the newer employees, who were young women, sat near the wall away from the windows. The women who sat near the windows often complained of cold or drafts, even when the windows were opened only a few inches. There were three possible solutions to the problem: (1) The young women and old women could be put into separate rooms. (2) Air conditioning could be installed. (3) The young women could exchange places with the older women. The first two solutions were impractical; the third solution, however, could have presented a morale problem because the window locations were a privilege of seniority. To solve this problem, the psychological consultants suggested that the older employees be given new desks and equipment away from the windows and that the new employees be given older desks and equipment near the windows. Thus, the privilege of seniority was changed from location to quality of equipment. In offices and factories where most of the jobs are similar in nature, workers can be transferred from one department to another according to their seniority preferences or for particular working conditions.

Illumination

The lighting in a plant or office is another important factor in the work area that has been studied by psychologists, engineers, and other specialists. Poor lighting can make a worker tired by causing unnecessary eyestrain, which in turn results in loss of productivity. It has been found that increasing the intensity of the lighting up to a certain level is effective in jobs requiring the visual examination of small parts of equipment and that less intense light is better for jobs that do not require the use of sharp vision. It has also been found that the color of the lighting has an effect on eyestrain and fatigue. The daylight lamp (unsaturated yellow light) has been found to cause the least eye fatigue in continuous operations. Also, reduction of glare and shadows reduce fatigue and improve productivity. These principles that were applied to indoor lighting also apply to outdoor lighting. For example, psychologists and engineers are working on better designs for automobile lights and highway and street lights. These efforts will lead to safer driving and less fatigue. Thus, patterns of colored lights, which are easily distinguishable, are used to warn drivers of sharp turns, blind intersections, bridge abutments, and similar hazards of highway driving.

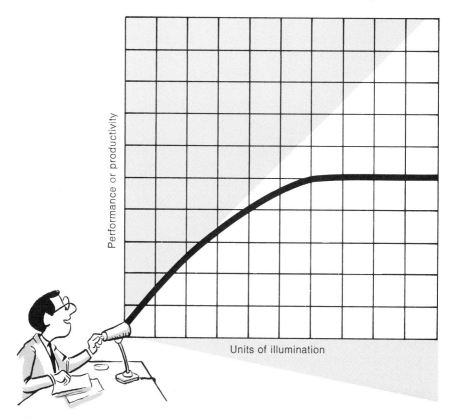

A fixed group of workers on one given job will show increased productivity with increases in illumination up to a point. Beyond this optimal point, increased illumination appears to have no effect on quantity of performance.

Color

Psychologists have found that colors affect the mood or feelings of people and often influence their judgment and behavior. Henry Ford is supposed to have said, "Customers may have a car in any color, so long as it is black." Nevertheless, automobile manufacturers since his time have disregarded his theory and presented to the buying public a wide assortment of colors for their cars. Car buyers choose colors that they feel will give them a sense of individuality and status.

Attractive color schemes enhance a person's dress or personal possessions. Experiments have supported this by showing that a person appears to be more attractive according to the colors he is wearing and that merchandise is also made more attractive by the use of color patterns. Furthermore, Hallmark Cards, Inc., found, through psychological surveys, that certain colors, sentiments, and sizes of their cards were the most suitable for different people and occasions. Dark green and brown shades, for example, were associated with rough, gruff masculinity.

Color even has some psychological relationship to speed of movement and one's desire for motion. A gaudy red, orange, or yellow car appears to move faster than one of a duller or darker shade. A cafeteria whose business requires a quick turnover of customers is usually brightly lighted as well as brightly colored, while a cocktail lounge relies on dim lighting and soft colors to keep customers for longer periods and reduce turnover.

Noise

In the rock music age, it was a bit difficult to define noise! A few years before, noise and music could be fairly well defined. Sound levels are usually measured in units called "decibels," and they have a certain effect on a person's productivity. Older people, in general, do not seem to be able to tolerate as much loud sound as the young, even though their hearing is less acute.

Hope Bagenal, writing in *Practical Acoustics,* found that a sound level of 30 to 40 decibels is satisfactory for most offices; a noisy office may have a 70-decibel din. By comparison, a past newspaper account of live rock-and-roll bands credited them with a blast of better than 100 decibels. The threshold of pain is in general about 130 decibels.

A pioneer experiment by Donald Laird showed that noise greatly affects personal efficiency in a job even though productivity appears to suffer very little. He found that during a work period with higher sound levels, the workers used 71 percent more energy than they did during less noisy or silent periods. On the other hand, the same type of work performed with acceptable sound levels raised the energy expenditure of the workers only 51 percent above that used during a typical rest period.

Although some individuals are affected more than others by loudness or pitch of sound, over long periods employees in a given work area become used to the customary sound level. If an unusually large change in the sound level should occur in a work area, it may be noticed, but small changes in the sound level usually go unnoticed. However, intermittent or abrupt changes in sound appear to be more disturbing than continuous noise; such changes in the sound level often startle workers and cause brief drops in productivity. Almost everyone has experienced a brief period of shock after hearing the loud bang after someone has burst an inflated paper bag.

The graph on page 40 shows that after the introduction of a sudden increase of noise in a work area, production drops sharply right after the noise, but then it increases and may even reach a slightly higher level. This higher level of production is more likely to remain if the noise is continued. However, although the worker makes up for production loss, he must exert more energy to overcome the effect of the noise.

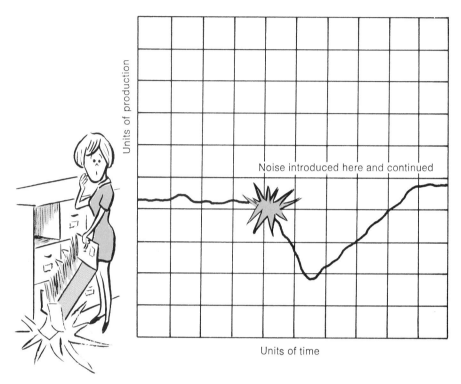

When a loud noise is introduced in a work situation, it will cause an immediate and sharp decrease in production, then a slow gain up to or beyond the production level at the time of the noise. However, production is maintained at this new level only by a greater expenditure of energy on the part of the workers.

The loudness of sound, or its pitch, has the least effect on routine types of work, but it can be very disturbing to someone whose job requires him to think about difficult problems. Experiments have been carried on that support this contention.

Certain types of music piped into a work area will have a beneficial effect on production, especially where a job involves a monotonous type of work. In ancient times, the slaves who rowed vessels, called galleys, maintained a steady rowing motion with the aid of a hammer beat on a block of wood with a steady tempo. Today, oarsmen who row college racing boats maintain a steady pace from hearing the rhythmical strains of the steersman's voice. Music was probably first introduced into industry in the manufacture of sugar in the West Indies, where the workers sang calypso tunes as they stamped out sugar from cane.

8 HUMAN ENGINEERING

The first automobiles did not have a convenient way to turn on the ignition with a key or pedal; it was necessary to "turn over the motor" with a crank, a tool that was connected to the front of the car. It was like starting a modern motorcycle with a pedal; several turns of the crank were necessary before the car was started. The first cranks were difficult to use, but as time went on, the shape and size were improved to make the job of starting an automobile easier. The improvement of a piece of equipment so that it can be more easily operated by a person is called *human engineering*.

Since World War II, more and more psychologists have been giving their time to the investigation of human factors in the work environment. One important aspect of this investigation has been the study of the design of equipment that a worker needs in order to perform a task. Such equipment must be designed to help the worker make the best use of his abilities and thereby increase his efficiency and productivity. In recent years, the rapid advancement of technology has placed a continuing strain on the worker, who must keep up with it by learning to adapt to new equipment.

By way of illustration, a manufacturer of business machines found that his typewriter would function better if it were built so that the typist had to push the keys down an extra twentieth of an inch. It was feared that this extra distance, even though very short, would require extra energy and thus reduce productivity accordingly. Nevertheless, it was an easy matter for this manufacturer to get a trustworthy answer to this question because there were a number of full-time psychologists working as a team on this problem. The result of the psychologists' study was that the typists would not notice the difference, and so the manufacturer continued with the new design. Other pieces of equipment, such as space-flight simulators, space suits, and control panels on jet planes, which are much more complicated than typewriters, require painstaking testing and research over a period of perhaps several years. In any event, any piece of equipment designed for human use should be thoroughly tested and studied until it is suitable for efficient operation.

9 OPINIONS FOR SALE

Businessmen are interested in studies made by psychologists that can tell them how human behavior can be predicted and influenced. This information is useful not only for improving employee relations and thereby improving productivity but also for influencing customers. Therefore, psychologists are often consulted or asked to make studies of human factors involved in buying and selling products and services. If you were producing and marketing goods, you would want to know how much demand there is for the particular item, who would buy it, how much of it people would buy, and in what areas people would be most likely to use it. The question of exactly what it is that influences a customer's choice would be equally important to a manufacturer. In the area of influencing customers, the psychologist would be concerned with how the potential customer feels about a product in terms of packaging, advertising, pricing, and how it should be displayed.

A. T. Poffenberger, one of the early industrial psychologists, was interested in advertising. He emphasized the importance of "market research," the measurement of human reactions to marketing procedures. Since the marketing, or distribution, of goods accounts for about 60 percent of their total cost, results of psychological studies in market research can be crucial to the successful acceptance of a product.

For example, the manufacturer of a detergent for washing dishes might want to know which of the advertising media he uses is the most effective. He may consult a psychologist or have a psychologist as a permanent member of his organization in order to investigate this and other questions about his products. The psychologist then prepares a survey in which homemakers are asked various questions about product advertising. They might be asked which of the advertising media they prefer: television, radio, magazines, direct mail, and so on. Another question might involve the package design or the color of the liquid. These surveys usually take the form of telephone interviews or personal interviews. A survey might also be in the form of a questionnaire that is mailed to the potential customer. In any case, the results of the survey are analyzed, and the psychologist makes a report of his conclusions.

Another important factor in the marketing of a product is knowing how potential customers arrive at their decisions to make specific purchases. Psychologists call the study of why people buy things *motivation research.* The job of the motivation researcher is to learn about the mental processes that lead to a purchase. He tried to find out why a customer selects one brand of merchandise over several similar brands.

Donald Laird was one of the first psychologists to do work in motivation research—more than forty years ago. He asked a large sample of housewives to select one of four pairs of stockings that were similar in price, weave, texture, durability, color, and weight. The only difference was in odor. About three percent of all these women gave odor as the reason for their choice of stockings; the others mentioned the other factors, which they thought varied for each pair, as reasons for their choices. This result might be explained by unconscious motivation, that is, behavior that cannot be explained in terms of conscious reasoning. Some psychologists feel that unconscious motivation could

The mental processes that lead to a purchase are a subject of prime interest to the motivation researcher.

Courtesy of *Chain Store Age*© General Merchandise/Variety Editions

consist of a group of processes that are so mixed up with other processes that they cannot be analyzed directly.

SUGGESTIONS FOR FURTHER READING

Berrien, F. K., *Industrial Psychology*, Dubuque, Iowa: Wm. C. Brown, 1967.

Blum, M. L., and James C. Naylor, *Industrial Psychology: Its Theoretical and Social Foundations*, New York: Harper & Row, 1968.

Ely, L. D., *Space Science for the Layman*, Springfield, Ill.: Charles C Thomas, 1967.

Gilmer, Beverly V., *Industrial and Organizational Psychology*, New York: McGraw-Hill, 1971.

Robert, C., *Human Engineering & Motivation*, Englewood Cliffs, N.J.: Prentice-Hall, 1969.

Siegel, Laurence, *Industrial Psychology*, rev. ed., Homewood, Ill.: Irwin, 1969.

TO HELP YOU REMEMBER

1. Why are psychologists employed by businesses to study worker efficiency? How is the worker likely to feel about these studies?
2. When did business and industrial psychology begin to be important in this country?
3. What factors in the work environment can help to improve worker efficiency? What are some physical and psychological conditions of the worker that affect his efficiency?
4. What is accident-proneness, and what causes it?
5. What are some causes of fatigue? Why is a person's perception or feeling of fatigue important?
6. What psychological facts have been found out about working hours, fatigue, and productivity? How can rest periods for workers benefit both worker and employer?
7. What effect does good lighting have on behavior?
8. How can the colors of the environment affect the speed of human activities?
9. What is motivation research? How is it used to boost sales?

WORKING WITH PEOPLE, DATA, OR THINGS

Search through a popular magazine that is no longer in use. Find and cut out a half dozen full-page advertisements, some of which have color illustrations. Now, check each of your chosen advertisements against the following criteria:

1 Ability to get attention. What is the most striking factor in this ad? What single feature has the appeal to catch the eye?
2 Consumer appeal. Who is being appealed to? Describe the primary type of customers who are sought by this ad. What traits of individuals are being related to by the illustrations?
3 Effectiveness. Does this ad appear likely to influence the target customer? Would he think more, or differently, about the product than he did before seeing this ad?
4 Readability. Pick out the most important ideas of this ad. Do they catch the eye? Can you read the entire ad easily? Are there parts of this ad that you are likely to skip because they demand more effort to read them?
5 Emphasis. How does the ad emphasize important points? By location, color, size of print, underlining, change in type, human figures, or eye-catching designs?

When you have completed your study of these advertisements, try to list any principles of human behavior noted in your text that appear to be applied in them.

THINGS TO DO

1. Interview several workers, one from each of several jobs, to find out their reactions to the workweek, the hours of the workday, rest periods, and their choice of pace in attempting to produce steadily.
2. Study a local business or industry that has been operating in your community for some years. Try to determine what changes have occurred in the nature of jobs, selection of workers, daily and weekly work schedules, and the total work environment. How have psychologists assisted in the changes made?
3. Read about a worker complaint or job grievance that has been noted locally. Try to find out all the facts you can about it. Check the various possibilities suggested in this chapter to see if you could assist with a solution for greater worker satisfaction.
4. A. H. Maslow and N. L. Mintz performed experiments which found that people were rated more beautiful in an attractively decorated room than in an ugly room. Also, people tended to report more fatigue, headaches, sleepiness, discontent, irritability, or hostility when they were in the ugly room. Discuss the significance of these findings for either individual improvement or changes in the business environment.

PSYCHOLOGY AND THE INDIVIDUAL

3

What This Chapter Is About

The psychologist in business or industry has an important role in matching jobs to employees and employees to jobs. To the worker, it may often seem that management and the psychologist consider the matching of employees to the job to be the more important function. A new employee may be hired on the basis of skill in operating a certain type of machinery or talent in performing a particular job. Then, when he is introduced to his new position, he may be given training or instruction in the rules and procedures that the company has set up. Time-and-motion studies are conducted to determine the most efficient way to perform an operation, and workers are educated to follow the established procedure.

However, it is not enough to mold the employee into a form determined by the boss. The sensitive employer realizes that workers have their own needs and desires and that the quality of their work is greatly affected by the personal satisfaction that the job provides. The personnel psychologist studies individuals working together. In addition to knowing the requirements of various jobs in the company, he must know about the organization and the work environment, and he must know about people—how they think and learn, and what motivates them.

As a worker, you can help the personnel psychologist to help you by learning to observe your own behavior. Observing human behavior is indeed a difficult and complex task, but it must be done before one is able to analyze the motives that cause behavior. Most people are not trained observers; they do not notice the fine points of all human activities. Nevertheless, most people are fairly accurate when observing routine, familiar, or meaningful activities. The baseball fan, for example, is more accurate in his observation of his favorite team than a casual spectator is. Still, the fan may see only certain elements and not others; he may be biased by his opinions and attitudes, and so he may often miss the reasoning behind an individual player's moves. Even if a person were able to observe as accurately as a camera, he would still need to make a careful analysis of his observations so that they would be meaningful for him. On the job, co-workers or a supervisor might observe a worker's performances and come up with some useful suggestions, but the psychologist, because of his training, is in a position to make a thorough scientific analysis of these performances.

If employees have been properly selected and thoroughly trained, and if little change has occurred in their work procedure, it is not a difficult task for the personnel psychologist to observe and analyze their performance. As changes are introduced to suit the job to the workers, new problems arise for the psychologist evaluating the changes and for the workers adjusting to them.

Although most people are not trained observers, they are usually accurate when observing activities that are meaningful to them.

Courtesy of Colgate-Palmolive Co.

One of the major problems in any industry is change. Two frequent types of change are reorganization of job procedures and modification of equipment. Change always tends to give a person some sense of insecurity because he has to adjust to something new and unfamiliar. It would be extremely difficult to create a job situation that completely satisfies a worker, but when an employee shows an excessive fear of new procedures, it is a sure sign to the personnel psychologist that this worker is experiencing an emotional problem. The well-adjusted worker recognizes change as a challenge rather than something to be feared.

2 JOB SATISFACTION

In the early years of World War II, the political situation imposed a major change on the working conditions of many Americans. Government and industry teamed up to meet the emergency needs of the military. Job simplification, the breaking down of complex jobs into simpler ones requiring less skill and training, was one way to speed up production. There were not enough workers to fill the skilled jobs, and there was little time to train the unskilled. Thus, reducing a complex operation into several simpler jobs enabled industry to train thousands of unskilled men and women to reach an acceptable rate of productivity in a short time.

After the war emergency, however, many workers became dissatisfied with what seemed to be dead-end jobs. As employees became more experienced, their jobs seemed less interesting. Monotony, boredom, and a lack of richer experiences began to weaken morale.

How would such a situation affect you? If you had a choice of job and work environment, what type of position would you look for? Which of your personal needs and desires would you expect to be satisfied by employment? Would you feel that a certain wage or salary would compensate you adequately for the time and effort you put into a job? If you were able to find a job in which you liked the work environment, if you had a sense of accomplishment and enjoyed your work, and if the salary were right, are the chances good that you would succeed? If these conditions were not satisfied to a reasonable degree, what would be your chances for success on that job?

An employee will be dissatisfied if his job is either too simple, so that it is far below his capabilities and lacks challenge, or too difficult, so that it is discouraging. Also, a worker's motivation may be dulled if he feels that neither his short-term nor long-term goals are attainable or if he feels that progress toward his goals is too slow or insufficient.

Another source of dissatisfaction could come from the supervisory policies of a company. A supervisor may be too watchful. This may make a worker feel that he is under constant pressure. The supervisor has to know how to criticize a worker as well as how and when to praise him; he must not expect too much from a worker too soon, even if he is directly involved in training the worker.

Most workers are happier when they can be involved to some extent in the planning of their own work. This makes them feel that they are in more control of their "destiny." While this is true for most workers, much more information about people is needed before the real meaning of job satisfaction can be understood.

3 THE STUDY OF EMPLOYEE BEHAVIOR

One method the personnel psychologist has for finding out about employees' attitudes is to conduct surveys. A carefully constructed survey questionnaire may be used with or without a personal interview. It is, of course, best if the survey involves the whole work group, but in cases where there is a very large work population, a sampling must be made; that is, the survey is conducted among a representative portion of the entire population of workers. This sampling is necessary because of the limitations imposed by cost, time, and effort. The results of the survey are analyzed and evaluated by the psychologist, who submits his report to management for action.

Another way to learn about employees' attitudes is to investigate their job situations, that is, to go down into the plant or office and conduct interviews directly. In this way, the psychologist can ask an employee specific questions concerning how he feels about various aspects of his job, such as the hours of employment, the rest periods, the lighting, and his co-workers.

These individual interviews are often useful to the psychologist in determining whether a problem involves an entire group of workers and is related to their working conditions or whether an individual's on-the-job behavior is being influenced by a personal situation.

After learning about the factors that influence a worker on his job, the psychologist can separately investigate each factor. For example, he considers the factor of interpersonal relations—how the worker gets along with others. If he does not get along with others, why not? Is the source of his problem at home or at work? It is up to the psychologist to isolate the most important factor and, having done this, to try to find a solution to the problem. Other possible factors in a worker's job situation that could be investigated by the company psychologist are lateness and a falling production rate. For example, a psychologist may have his attention called to a particular department where frequent absences occur. He can reasonably assume that there is discontent and that something is amiss in the department. The source of discontent may be an unpopular supervisor, unreasonable work quotas, or perhaps some physical hazard. On the other hand, if one worker is consistently absent, while the other workers in the same area are rarely absent, the psychologist can assume that there is a personal problem in the life of the individual that he does not share with the other employees.

There are many symptoms of discontent on the part of workers, any of which could be investigated to determine the cause. Some of these are accidents, carelessness and lack of order, low-quality workmanship, dishonesty, and unfounded grievances.

4 PRIORITY OF NEEDS

Even if he does not think so, the individual knows himself better than anyone else, including his family, friends, or company psychologist. He may not be sure where to find a vocation suited to his life style, but in the final analysis, it is this individual who must make his own choices.

In small matters, as well as when making major decisions, a person behaves according to the way he sees things. His actions are logical within the context of his own experiences. If a person's behavior seems illogical to you, it is because you do not know what is going on inside him; you see him only superficially, even if you are a relative or a

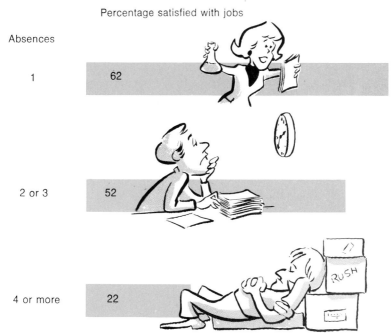

Percentage satisfied with jobs

Absences	
1	62
2 or 3	52
4 or more	22

Data from F. Mann and B. Baumgartel, *Absences and Employee Attitudes in an Electrical Power Company,* Survey Research Center, Univ. of Michigan, December 1952, p. 22

Frequent absences are often a symptom of discontent. Although absences may be caused by many factors, in groups where job dissatisfaction is high, there is a definite increase in the rate of absenteeism.

friend, for only a small part of a person's emotional life is visible to the outsider.

At any moment, an individual is involved in many bodily activities and is being exposed to many stimuli in his environment. Because a person is such a complex being, all these inner activities affect the entire person, even though he may believe he is reacting to a single influence only.

As long as a person is living, he may be said to be *motivated,* because as long as he is alive, he will have needs and desires and will act to satisfy them. A need may be a simple one that a person can satisfy without even being conscious of his response. For example, when his lungs need oxygen, he inhales. Motivation can also be a complex process involving many stimuli and an array of long-range and short-range goals, as in a business. The factory worker on the job may be satisfying needs for pride in his craftsmanship; for approval of his co-workers; for money for food, clothing, and housing; and so on. The employer, by giving the employee an opportunity to meet these needs, gains in return the fulfillment of his own needs that depend on the continuing operation of the factory.

At a certain time, a person wants to satisfy his most pressing need before all others. However, with many needs operating simultaneously, the individual must determine which ones have to be satisfied right away and which ones can be satisfied later.

In 1954, the psychologist Abraham H. Maslow developed a rank ordering of needs that are universal, at least within our Western culture. They are as follows:

1 Basic physiological needs
2 Safety
3 Affection
4 Esteem
5 Self-realization

Abraham Maslow ranked human needs in the order in which they must be satisfied. A job is an important source of need-satisfaction.

Basic Physiological Needs

The basic physiological needs are required to sustain life; they can be thought of as "survival needs." Hence, these needs must be satisfied before all others. Typical physiological needs include food, oxygen, and the elimination of waste matter. These needs are often automatically controlled by the body through breathing and body temperature.

Certain needs of man, such as sex and maternal activity, that are instinctive in animals have social or psychological implications. While these needs are still basic, there is some choice involved—they are not entirely automatic or built in. Human beings are able to postpone the satisfaction of these needs.

Safety

The safety needs may collectively be thought of as a general need to be free from anxiety and fear, to feel that one can cope adequately with one's immediate environment. Among the safety needs are the need for order in one's daily life, the need for routines that avoid sudden changes that would cause confusion, and the need to be in a physically balanced position (fear of heights is an extension of this need). A person may feel unsafe in a social environment; for example, a child may feel unsafe if his home life is disrupted by the inconsistent and confusing behavior of his parents. Adults frequently look for safety in marital adjustment, job security, protection from the aggressive actions of others, and stable government. Maslow says, "Other broader aspects of the attempt to seek safety and stability in the world are seen in the very common preference for familiar rather than unfamiliar things, or for the known rather than the unknown."

Affection

The need for affection includes the need to be loved, the need for friends, and the general need for a feeling of belonging with other people. Maslow stresses that love is not restricted to sex, although sex may be one form of expressing love; he also emphasizes the necessary capability of a person for giving and receiving love. Love in a more general sense implies "acceptance," and thus there are degrees of affection that are less intimate than sex. A pupil whose work is praised by his teacher or an employee who is given a merit raise by his boss receives satisfaction in the area of his love needs.

Esteem

The need for esteem is an aspect of self-evaluation. What do you think of yourself? How do you evaluate your abilities? What are your attitudes and values? How do you interact with others? Are you satisfied with your own perception of yourself? The feelings and emotions that result from self-appraisal are important to a person's life style. The esteem needs call for achievement and adequacy, recognized first by one's self and second by others, in the form of attention and appreciation. Esteem is vital to a person's confidence in himself as a worker and gives him a feeling of being useful and necessary for his job.

Self-Realization

The need for self-realization is the last need in Maslow's hierarchy because all the other needs must be satisfied before this one can be fulfilled. Self-realization implies that a person can say that he has had a "successful" life. If he had the opportunity to live it over again, he would choose to live it the same way.

There are many levels of self-realization for each individual. An office worker may feel that he has a wonderful life. He loves his family, his job, his friends; all his needs are satisfied. A movie star and a physicist may appear to have achieved self-realization, but they may also have problems with some of their lower-level needs that prevent them from attaining this highest goal. As Maslow has observed, "What a man *can* be, he *must* be"; that is, self-realization is within everyone's reach, but the form it takes varies according to a person's capabilities. The novelist may be poor and unhappy as an office worker, and the fulfilled office worker may not be able to write a good sentence.

The foundation of Maslow's hierarchy consists of the basic phys-iological needs, which he feels must first be satisfied before the indi-vidual can aspire toward the next-higher level, safety needs. Once a person has achieved satisfaction at a particular need level, he feels a strong urge to strive to achieve satisfaction at a still higher need level. Thus, a higher-level need will emerge only when and if all the lower-level needs are at least partially satisfied. A starving person or a person walk-ing in a dark street and fearing an attack is in no position to worry about receiving affection or satisfying the need for esteem or self-realization. The first need is to stay alive. But with these barriers removed, such a person might feel impelled to strive to satisfy a higher-level need.

A person's aspirations change in relation to his need-satisfaction. When aspirations rise far above what is being realized in need-satis-faction, tension and frustration result. This situation could impel a person to work all the harder to achieve or realize a higher level of needs. Another reaction is that a person might reassess himself and his abilities. Perhaps he is striving for something clearly beyond his abilities, in which case he may lower his level of aspiration. When aspirations and achievements are at the same level, a person is temporarily in a state of equilibrium. This equilibrium can be and usually is upset by a change, upward or downward, in the level of aspirations or in the level of needs.

5 MOTIVATION

Motivation begins when a person perceives a need that must be satisfied. This perception occurs when some form of stimulus attracts a person's attention to the need. The need, having been perceived, motivates action on the part of the person to satisfy the need. For example, hunger is a need; it is stimulated by nerves relaying to the brain a message of emptiness in the stomach. A person perceives his hunger and is then motivated to satisfy the need for food, and so he eats something.

Since there are many stimuli affecting a person at the same time, he must choose the order in which needs are to be satisfied. The most urgent needs, the physiological needs, will always come first. An individual can follow only one course of action at a time; for example, he cannot eat and sleep at the same time. He must decide which need is stronger, his need for food or his need for sleep. Having chosen the more urgent need, he will be motivated to satisfy it. A person may not always order his needs in the best way; for example, if he is crossing at a busy intersection and worrying about how he will pay his income tax, he may unintentionally expose himself to danger if he is too distracted by his thoughts.

The growing complexity of today's society makes it more difficult for people to deal with their needs and the motivations arising from these needs. The result of this condition may be that some needs are only partially satisfied, while others are frustrated or not satisfied at all.

6 INCENTIVES, GOALS, AND SATISFACTION

All individuals have the same needs, although the intensity of each need may vary considerably from individual to individual. Several employees in an office may feel a basic need, such as hunger, quite differently at a given time, and the feeling of hunger itself would be different for the same person at different times. One person may have no hunger pangs, while another may be ravenous. Some people usually feel hunger sooner than others.

The higher needs are more difficult to observe than the physiological needs, both in one's self and in other people. Accordingly, they are more difficult to evaluate. This is because obvious patterns of behavior do not show them off. For example, one woman worked in an office with a score of other people for twelve years before she dared to go out to lunch with them. Her desire for friendship and her wanting to belong, among other social needs (affection), were not strong enough to overcome her intense shyness and feeling of inferiority (safety). She claimed that she was not sure if the others wanted her to be with them or not, while the others, seeing that she brought her lunch every day, were hesitant to embarrass her by asking her out.

When an individual becomes aware of a need, he immediately has a desire to reduce it. This desire motivates the appropriate behavior for removing or reducing the need. The more experiences a person has in satisfying a particular need, the greater the variety of ways he has to satisfy the need. The first time a person experiences a certain need, he will usually deal with it in a haphazard way, which may be unsatisfactory. This type of behavior is often seen in very young children who use trial-and-error methods. But as they grow older and their needs are repeated, they learn how to deal with them more successfully. Of course, some needs are easily satisfied, while others are impossible to satisfy. In general, people will first try to satisfy those needs that can be satisfied more easily. Thus, a person directs himself toward ease and pleasure and avoids difficulty and displeasure, unless, of course, the need to satisfy a difficult problem is compensated by great feelings of accomplishment.

If a psychologist is to evaluate an employee's motivation, he must know a great deal about the employee's learning and experiences, which goals he is likely to select or avoid, and which needs he is intensely aware of. The incentives an employer offers to an employee must be recognized by the employee as possible ways for him to satisfy some of his own needs. The employee must evaluate the incentives made available by his employer before he responds to them, and he will respond to these incentives according to the value he attaches to them; he must weigh them carefully before he acts.

There are several factors that complicate the motivational decisions that a person makes. If he is limited in learning and experience, he has been exposed to fewer choices; if he has a less comprehensive perception or less intelligence than others, he may lack proper understanding of his experiences, and he may therefore shy away from new experiences. If a person experiences relatively little satisfaction for most of his needs, then he may find it difficult to perceive satisfaction in most new situations. The personnel psychologist can work with a person to determine the possibilities for placing him in a suitable job situation on the basis of these limitations. However, if these limitations are too severe, the worker should seek special help from a psychologist outside of his company who specializes in therapy.

 ## MOTIVATIONAL DISPOSITION

More often than not, everyone has a routine that he follows; that is, each person has an ordered set of duties that he must perform during the day. Each duty, in turn, must be performed in a certain amount of time and

What does this cartoon tell us about how employers and employees can accomplish differing goals?

at a certain location. For example, at home in the morning a person (1) gets dressed, (2) has breakfast, and (3) leaves to travel to work. (There are variations in the details of this routine from one person to another.) For each of these activities at home, so much time must be allotted. The person must then leave the house at a certain time because it takes him so long to get to his job; otherwise he will be late for work. The behavior that is involved in performing routine duties is almost automatic; the individual does not have to do much thinking about how to order them or how to perform them, and the question of choice is almost absent. Routines certainly make life easier—life would be slow and tedious if we had to think about and analyze every activity.

But there are other things that are interspersed with the routine duties. There are the special events, such as going to the movies, visiting friends and relatives, or bringing some work home that has not been finished at the office and that must be done by the morning. These special activities add interest and variety to one's life. The phone rings, and you hear the voice of an old friend who is just in for a few days from out of town. You will find the time to see him no matter how busy you are, especially if you are fond of him.

Although a person's outward behavior may not be directed toward satisfying his more intense needs, he will have a persistent tendency to fulfill his needs when he has a chance to do so. The possibilities of motivated action are called "motivational dispositions" by Ernest Hilgard and Richard Atkinson. Thus, a *motivational disposition* refers to a need that is put aside when a more urgent, simultaneous need occurs. For example, suppose that a shopper is looking for a pair of shoes for a special occasion. He has been to several shoe stores and has not found the style he wants. Then, suddenly, he feels strong hunger pangs. He must eat, and so he puts aside the need to obtain the shoes. A motivational disposition may occur before an activity has begun. Again, suppose a person wants to buy a pair of shoes. Another more pressing need may occur before he sets out to shop, and so he defers the need to buy the shoes.

John L. Fuller has noted, "If some block exists so that a specific action appropriate to a drive is not possible, the energy of the drive may be directed into another channel and displacement activities result." He calls this displacement activity *motivational displacement*; when a person is prevented from satisfying an intense need, he will indulge in less important tasks. People are always confronted with subordinate needs that require urgent satisfaction. For example, a person may have to interrupt his work on an important project because he has run out of an item necessary for completing his task. Thus, he is in a position of frustration because he is unable to finish his project and satisfy his need for fulfillment.

While sitting in the waiting room of a doctor's office just before an appointment, you are worried about a health problem. To lessen your tension while waiting to see the doctor, you might glance through some of the magazines, go through your pockets or purse to see what you have, study the pictures on the wall, look at some of the other people in the room with a critical eye, file your nails, or make up a shopping list. These types of behavior are clearly motivated by lesser needs; the energy created by your anxiety about your health is channeled into displacement activities until your turn comes to see the doctor.

 ## MOTIVATION ON THE JOB

The process of motivation on the job is the same as for other activities. It is part of a continuing series of actions during a person's waking hours, and it may even affect his sleeping hours in the form of certain types of dreams. Nevertheless, a person spends a third of his day, or half of his waking hours, on his job. This is a lot of time, indeed, when one thinks about it. In addition, it is the best part of his day. The average person gets up in the morning, has a bite to eat, and goes to work; he is still fresh from his long night's rest. When he leaves his job in the evening, around 5:00 p.m., he has the second half of his waking hours to do with as he pleases, except, of course, for the demands of family and friends. But he isn't as fresh as he was in the morning; he may be less enthusiastic about doing things. The element of fatigue has entered his motivational process, and this usually has a dulling effect. Therefore, the routines of people's lives affect their motivation. The routine of the average person is (1) sleep, (2) work, (3) personal time. But the routine of people who work at night is (1) sleep, (2) personal time, (3) work. In this case, a worker may be less ambitious on his job simply because he is not as fresh as the daytime worker or has become fatigued after eight hours or so of doing other things, even if they were exclusively to suit his pleasure.

Thus, the behavior of the worker on the job is determined by other phases of his life, as well as by job-associated problems. Factors in the job, such as the supervisor, job tasks, the working environment, or company policy, are often not the causes of need in a person, but they still may be important in terms of his ability to satisfy his job-associated needs. The question is: To what extent should the job be expected to satisfy the needs of the worker?

Even though a person may be in the process of satisfying one of his needs, which at the moment seems to him to be the most urgent, the others—all of them—are still in the background. A person cannot be divided up into different personalities for each of his needs; he is a whole being, and all his needs are acting on him at the same time. A person cannot give all his attention to satisfying one need and completely neglect all his other needs.

Maslow's order of needs may be applied to an employment situation. The physiological needs can be satisfied by the facilities in a plant or office. For example, food and beverages are available in a company cafeteria or in vending machines on the premises; most companies provide air conditioning and lavatories. Many of the needs, such as the basic physiological needs, of an employee and his dependents are satisfied indirectly by the employee's wages, salary, retirement and disability provisions, sick leave, and vacations.

The need for safety, in terms of finances, security, and health, is satisfied in the main by the worker himself—by his job performance and the knowledge that he is doing a good job—and by the work of unions, government agencies, and laws. Workers who have had some bad work experiences, such as being fired or demoted, may feel insecure in spite of a company's efforts to satisfy their needs for safety. Such persons must have stronger reinforcements of their sense of security because they are less secure within themselves. But for most people, security is reinforced by steady employment and knowing about future possible improvements in their work or status.

The need for affection is fulfilled for a worker if he is given recognition and support by his boss or supervisors. He needs to be told that his work is good. When a person first joins a company, he may receive much criticism during his training period or, if he is an experienced worker, during the time it will take for him to get adjusted to his new job situation. It is important during this period of adjustment that a worker receive

How can facilities such as a staff cafeteria contribute to a worker's job satisfaction?

praise to balance the criticism, and when the adjustment period is over, he must receive his share of praise, which will give him a feeling that he belongs. In this way his need for affection on the job will be satisfied.

The need for esteem is satisfied by recognition both from one's superiors and from one's peer group. Esteem also comes from knowing that one has good skills to offer to a company. To earn this esteem, the worker must continually reevaluate himself so that he can adapt himself to change. In a competitive society, such as ours today, workers are constantly being compared with others in similar circumstances. Thus, the worker is always concerned about how he measures up to his co-workers. If a worker is not doing something as well as another employee, he should be encouraged by his supervisor or co-worker to correct his behavior. He should under no circumstances be berated or harshly criticized, especially in front of his co-workers. Unfortunately, most supervisors are not trained in psychology; they often lack a good understanding of workers' problems concerning esteem. An alert and thoughtful supervisor, however, may realize that a certain worker has a low sense of self-esteem and also that the worker is capable of satisfactory work. Such a supervisor may try to help reinforce the worker's sense of self-esteem by praising certain aspects of the worker's work and personal habits.

Self-realization, Maslow's highest need requirement, depends on the prior satisfaction of the lower levels of needs in Maslow's list. The need for self-realization is satisfied in part when a worker feels fulfilled with his job, when he feels that his job is an essential part of his life so that he looks forward to going to work every day. Most people have all they can do to satisfy their other needs, so it is sad but true that most people do not achieve self-realization. This is the real tragedy of our society—one that could be avoided with just a little more thoughtful introspection and a little more real concern for the needs of others.

SUGGESTIONS FOR FURTHER READING

Ford, Robert N., *Motivation Through the Work Itself,* New York: American Management Association, 1969.

Hackman, R. C., *The Motivated Working Adult,* New York: American Management Association, 1969.

Irwin, F. W., *Behavior and Motivation (A Cognitive Theory),* Philadelphia: Lippincott, 1971.

McClelland, David C., and David G. Winters, *Motivating Economic Achievement,* New York: Free Press, 1969.

Maslow, Abraham H., *Motivation and Personality,* New York: Harper & Row, 1970.

Masterson, T. R., and T. G. Mara, *Motivating the Underperformer,* New York: American Management Association, 1969.

Neff, Walter S., *Work and Human Behavior,* New York: Atherton, 1968.

Vernon, Magdalen D., *Human Motivation,* London: Cambridge University Press, 1969.

TO HELP YOU REMEMBER

1. Why is it so difficult to observe and analyze human behavior?
2. Why are attitudes important in the study of employee satisfaction and productivity?
3. What are some of the industrial psychologist's means of studying employees' attitudes and behavior?
4. What is the basis of motivation? When is a person motivated?
5. Why must the "basic physiological needs," the first item in Maslow's list, be satisfied first?
6. How does a person select his goals in order to secure satisfaction?
7. What is meant by the terms "motivational disposition" and "motivational displacement"?
8. How are the needs for esteem, a feeling of adequacy, and achievement satisfied on the job?
9. Why is self-realization the least-urgent need in Maslow's hierarchy? Does the average worker achieve self-realization on the job?

WORKING WITH PEOPLE, DATA, OR THINGS

Select five or six workers to interview. Be careful to select individuals who have been employed for several years and who have different occupations and work at different levels of responsibility. You might interview an unskilled worker, a skilled worker, a supervisor, an office employee, and an administrator.

Make a check list of the several satisfactions that a worker may receive from his job. For each satisfaction, use a rating scale of one to five to indicate the degree of fulfillment for each interviewee.

From your scale, try to determine each worker's satisfaction with his job, the chief reasons for satisfaction, and the differences in satisfaction from one worker to another.

THINGS TO DO

1. Read several articles on psychological problems in business or industry. Make notes, and be prepared to discuss them. You will find articles in your local public library.
2. Look up the work of the American Management Association, the Society for the Advancement of Management, and the Industrial Conference Board, and compare their research activities. How well does their research contribute to the adjustment of the worker? Information about these groups can be found in your local public library.
3. Surveys of farmers tend to indicate greater motivation for them than for factory workers. List some reasons to account for the differences in motivation.

ON THE JOB

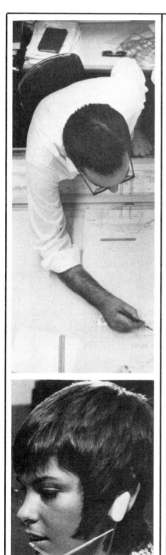

4

What This Chapter Is About

1 TRADING OLD PROBLEMS FOR NEW ONES

Before the Industrial Revolution, workers were concerned mostly with the basic needs of life: food, clothing, and shelter; they had little opportunity for anything else. The conflicts and frustrations they experienced related directly to satisfying these basic needs. In this environment, workers seldom moved or changed jobs, and as a result they were exposed to limited social groups. Also, *social mobility,* the movement from one class to another, was extremely limited; workers born into one class usually remained there for their whole lives. The need for adjusting to new situations rarely, if ever, occurred. For people in those days, life was almost entirely work-related, and so the higher-level needs, such as personal recognition and self-fulfillment, were seldom satisfied.

Today, because of technological advances, the average worker requires less time to satisfy his basic needs and enjoys greater occupational and social mobility. As we mentioned in Chapter 2, he usually works in a large company and deals with a wide variety of people. He may be employed as an executive, a manager, or a laborer (white-collar or

From *The History and Principles of Weaving by Hand and Power,* by Alfred Barrows, London, 1879

Before the industrial revolution, when work, such as weaving, was a family affair and was done in the home, workers were primarily concerned with the basic needs of life—food, clothing, and shelter.

blue-collar), and because he is socially mobile he may move up from one of these levels to another. A laborer may advance to a managerial position, a manager to an executive position. The new freedom of movement and the opportunity to advance have also set the stage for a wide variety of company-worker problems.

One function of a company is to serve the goals of different levels of employment—owners, executives, managers, and workers. Every company has conflicts among these levels that interfere with company goals and that also reduce efficiency and damage productivity. It is the job of the company psychologist to solve these problems. In a sense the psychologist is like a mechanic who oils a piece of machinery so that it will run more smoothly. The psychologist brings the insights of his discipline to bear on the specific problems of his company. Sometimes these problems reflect organizational shortsightedness, sometimes individual worker laxity, sometimes a combination of both. The psychologist is in a position to look at the operation of a company objectively because he is not intimately involved in production. He is free to study the behavior and attitudes of those who are directly concerned with production—at all levels within the company.

In order to study and resolve company conflicts, the psychologist has depended on research about worker attitudes and the revelations of general psychology. These areas of study have yielded several valuable insights into the strains and pressures the modern worker confronts in day-to-day experience on the job.

2 HARNESSING HUMAN ENTERPRISE

There are two basic types of management philosophy—two general ways that management deals with workers. These are the "traditional" and "democratic" approaches. Douglas McGregor, a well-known psychologist, analyzed these two organizational policies, which he labeled "Theory X" and "Theory Y."[1] According to him, Theory X, the traditional view of organization, is based on the following assumptions about human behavior:

1 The average human being has an inherent dislike of work and will avoid it if he can.
2 Because of this human characteristic of dislike of work, most people must be coerced, controlled, directed, threatened with punishment to get them to put forth adequate effort toward the achievement of organizational objectives.
3 The average human being prefers to be directed, wishes to avoid responsibility, has relatively little ambition, wants security above all.

1. Douglas McGregor, *The Human Side of Enterprise,* McGraw-Hill, New York, 1960, pp. 33-57.

McGregor emphasized that the assumptions of Theory X are based on long-term but outmoded managerial strategy rather than on the result of a scientific study of human behavior. William H. Whyte, Jr., criticized this approach as "that contemporary body of thought which makes morally legitimate the pressures of society against the individual."

To replace the traditional organizational assumptions of Theory X, McGregor proposed Theory Y. Its assumptions are based on a realistic appreciation of man's motivations, behavior, and goals. McGregor suggested that companies could develop more successful employee relations if they followed the principles of Theory Y:

1   The expenditure of physical and mental effort in work is as natural as play or rest.
2   External control and threat of punishment are not the only means for bringing about effort toward organizational objectives. Man will exercise self-direction and self-control in the service of objectives to which he is committed.
3   Commitment to objectives is a function of the rewards associated with their achievement.
4   The average human being learns, under proper conditions, not only to accept but to seek responsibility.
5   The capacity to exercise a relatively high degree of imagination, ingenuity, and creativity in the solution of organizational problems is widely, not narrowly, distributed in the population.
6   Under the conditions of modern industrial life, the intellectual potentialities of the average human being are only partially utilized.

Theory Y is based on a principle of organizational "integration"; it views a company as a means of achieving the employer's and the employees' goals. According to this approach, employees can satisfy their own needs in the process of realizing the company's organizational aims. Integration creates good company-employee communication and allows for some decision making on the part of the workers as well as the managerial staff and the executives.

The first four assumptions of Theory Y are directly concerned with motivation, behavior, and the influence of controls on the worker's activity. Although these assumptions may also apply to young children, they have a much greater impact on adults, who possess a wide range of individual behavior. And even though behavioral differences are great among adults, nevertheless, people are still quite similar to each other in how they are motivated and how they achieve their goals.

Assumptions 5 and 6 of Theory Y have not been put to use or even considered by many companies, and so employees do not come near to exercising their full intellectual and creative potential. This is often the fault of the company, or it may be caused by restraints imposed by workers on themselves. Many people are hesitant, or even afraid, to exercise their abilities in exploring new avenues or assuming greater responsibility. Some people in management have been known to ask for demotions when their positions put them under conditions of stress. Some employees develop psychosomatic symptoms when asked to take on new or larger assignments that require more personal responsibility and creativity.

The opportunities offered to the worker by modern technology and the levels of achievement to which he might aspire have created new pressures on him and new possible areas of discontent. Even companies that believe in the principles of Theory Y experience work dissatisfaction.

Jobs in 1976

Occupational groups in the U.S.	Number of jobs
Professionals, technicians	12,392,000
Managers, officials	9,612,000
Clerical and office workers	13,808,000
Sales workers	6,138,000
Craftsmen, foremen	11,920,000
Operatives	15,635,000
Service workers	11,359,000
Farmers	4,428,000
Laborers	3,795,000
Total	89,087,000

Data from U.S. Bureau of Labor Statistics

The diversity of jobs available today gives modern workers opportunities to meet their career needs, but it also exposes them to pressures and areas of discontent unknown to their ancestors.

3 UNDERSTANDING THE WORKER

Now, you may ask, "Why doesn't management recognize the problem of employee relations and make changes to benefit both the employee and the company?" Some companies have employed psychologists for many years to help employees develop their potential and cope with new pressures. Fundamentally, psychologists have attempted to guide the worker toward a greater understanding of himself and of his relation to his environment. They have also tried to use their insights about individuals as a basis for suggestions to management with regard to designing working conditions and incentives to motivate workers to achieve higher levels of productivity.

Workers' Needs and Aspirations

Carl Jung (yo͞ong), a famous psychiatrist who studied under Sigmund Freud, once wrote, "The supreme goal of man is to fulfill himself as a creative, unique individual according to his own innate potentialities and within the limits of reality." Security and freedom from financial problems alone do not satisfy this general goal. In the early 1970s several large corporations, including the major automobile manufacturers, experienced severe worker conflicts that were traced ultimately not to financial or security problems but to higher-level needs and aspirations. Psychological research helped these companies meet the crises by identifying the underlying problems involved and laying the groundwork for practical solutions to these problems.

Hygiene and Motivation Factors

Dr. Frederick Herzberg, a well-known industrial psychologist, has proposed that workers have two independent sets of needs. One set he calls the "hygiene factors," the other, the "motivation factors." The hygiene factors are worker needs that must be satisfied if worker dissatisfaction is to be avoided. When the hygiene factors are absent, workers rebel. The presence of hygiene factors keeps a worker on the job, provides security, or prevents complete unhappiness. The hygiene factors include a favorable work environment, financial rewards, benefits, good supervision, good administration, and company policies that support the employees.

The second set of needs, the "motivation factors," are intrinsic to worker tasks, according to Herzberg. These factors give the worker a feeling that he is extending himself beyond the simple needs of existence. The motivation factors give a worker a sense of self-realization over and above his basic need to support himself. Hence, the motivation factors are related to what a person does, not merely to the situation in which he does it.

Job satisfaction is most directly related to the motivation factors, such as the nature of the task, the type of responsibility, the opportunity for continued achievement, the expectation of recognition, and the probability of advancement. The hygiene factors can help to reduce turnover and prevent rebellion, but it is the motivation factors that have a direct relationship to worker enthusiasm, morale, and the quantity and quality of production.

Although Herzberg notes that "not all jobs in industry have the potential to be challenging and achievement-oriented," one must consider both the wide variety of occupations and the broad range of individual differences before accepting the application of his theory. We will have more to say about this theory in Chapter 19.

A favorable work environment is one of the hygiene factors that, if satisfied, will reduce worker turnover.

It is interesting to compare Herzberg's theory to Maslow's. According to Maslow's reasoning (see Chapter 3), the degree to which each individual has succeeded in satisfying low-order needs tends to determine how he applies himself to needs of a higher order. Those most deprived may be motivated to work for money alone, if they believe that money will provide for basic wants still unsatisfied. Although man is said to "work for bread alone only when he has no bread," the lack of bread will motivate until the need intensity is diminished. Furthermore, experiments have demonstrated that people who are deprived of basic needs early in life may attempt to amass a surplus of satisfaction in later years. While these observations limit the applicability of Herzberg's theories, there is some common ground between Maslow's insights and Herzberg's. Hygiene factors can be related to the basic physiological needs, and motivation factors to the higher-level needs. If the physiological needs and hygiene factors are not satisfied, there is discontent. If they are attended to, the worker becomes more concerned with his higher-level needs and with motivations provided by his job. A psychologist generally would not attempt to apply Herzberg's or anyone else's theories universally, since the range of individual behavior is much too broad to be explained by any single theory.

Realistic Goals

From time to time most people evaluate themselves, their goals, and their performances. A person's goals may change as he makes progress: one goal may be found too difficult to attain, while another one may be too easy to allow a person to satisfy his need for self-fulfillment. Ideally, one's goals should be realistic; that is, they should be possible to reach. The more care a person takes in assessing his potentials, the more able he will be to set realistic goals.

A student may have goals of earning high grades or playing on a varsity team. Or he may have a hobby, such as building model planes, that tests his ability to use his skills or create projects. Usually a person starts out with an easy project, and when he finds that he can succeed, he readjusts his goal toward a more difficult and challenging project. Each achievement encourages a person and thus helps to prepare him for his next project. One must be careful not to set unreasonable goals because these can be self-defeating and produce tension and anxiety, a condition that may further reduce the possibility of reaching one's goals. On the other hand, a goal that may be impossible now may be realizable at some future time when a person is better prepared to achieve that goal.

Although people periodically review their performances and set new goals, they rarely attempt to realize their full potential. Harry Helson expressed this insight in his "hypothesis of par or tolerance." He suggested that individuals tend to choose a satisfactory level of performance that is possible for them and that they seldom try to exceed their own standards of work. This implies that most people set levels of achievement below their actual potential ability. As with the Herzberg theory, Helson's generalization does not take full account of variations caused by individual differences in motivation. Some workers are more daring than others, and other workers are much too timid. Both of these conditions prevent a person from reaching his full potential.

C. N. Cofer and M. H. Appley described the positive effects of success on future performance and the negative effects of failure. Success and failure both affect the worker's motivation: success provides a strong reinforcement, while failure leaves a person insecure.

In earliest childhood, when a person begins to walk, he is confronted with small successes and failures. Even at this age, a well-adjusted child will not let small failures frustrate his goals: he will try to do something over and over until he finally succeeds. Gradually, as the child gets older and progresses to more difficult tasks, his failures and successes will become more important to him and will have a greater effect on his motivation.

Courtesy of Webster Division, McGraw-Hill Book Co.

Every child is confronted with small successes and failures; the well-adjusted child will do something over and over again until he finally succeeds.

On the basis of their personal successes and failures, people attempt to design a way to improve their status in life. While it is true that ambition varies from individual to individual, most people have some desire to "get ahead." This sense of *ambition,* the desire to improve oneself, is the direct result of a person's motivation.

4 HIRING AND PROMOTING

The well-motivated person is often the best worker. A company therefore should strive to maintain high positive motivation among its employees to keep productivity at a high level. When companies fail to notice the motivations behind employee actions, problems occur. Often difficulties could be avoided if managers understood the impact of the psychological theories discussed above. Sometimes, of course, solutions to employee problems require the professional advice of a psychologist. Sections 4 and 5 deal with common company-employee tension areas. Proper handling of these areas will bring about positive results; improper action will cause worker dissatisfaction and possibly other problems.

To anticipate and avoid worker problems and to ensure maximum worker satisfaction, most companies have established guidelines for dealing with employees. These procedures generally cover the major areas of possible tension from hiring to dismissal practices. These approaches aim to guide company officials in solving problems that arise and in preventing new problems, and often they involve the direct services of a company-employed psychologist.

The Company Psychologist

One major concern of industrial psychologists is company training programs. Often company psychologists are involved in the overall planning for the development of manpower and the organization of management levels. Both of these areas require the evaluation of groups and individuals to determine their needs for further training. Sometimes psychologists are concerned with large retraining programs when a company anticipates extraordinary change in the nature or methods of work. At other times, they experiment with methods of training to arrive at a most efficient procedure. Testing is often introduced at both the beginning and end of a training course to evaluate the true gains made by the participants.

Counseling plays a large part in both evaluation and training programs in business and industry, and psychologists are actively involved. Psychologists often plan for counseling as part of the overall personnel program and also directly assist employees with their problems. Some companies, such as Eastman Kodak and Prudential Life, have carried on counseling programs for many years. Their success encouraged other firms to develop similar programs and to advance into additional areas of counseling. Some years ago, F. J. Roethlisberger brought counseling right out on the plant floor, at a time when he was studying the employees of the Hawthorne plant of the Western Electric Company. Workers were pleased with the ready availability of the counseling service and felt they were talking on their own home grounds.

One important aspect of the psychologist's job is to show an employee those personality traits that hinder him in his effort to advance himself. A healthy person will realize his shortcomings and will accordingly try to help himself overcome them; an unhealthy person will not try to surmount them but will instead try to justify them. Changing a person's behavior is very difficult, especially since there are many subtle aspects of a personality that a psychologist may not observe unless he treats a person as a full-time patient. The company psychologist rarely has the opportunity to provide full-time counseling for employees.

Many employee problems originate outside of the work situation and have a negative effect on job performance. The willingness of management to help the worker is appreciated, and even though many problems seem difficult to solve, a greater understanding will develop between employer and employee as both attempt to find solutions. There are, of course, some disturbing factors in any work situation, but the *way* in which these factors are viewed by employer and employee is much more important than the factors themselves.

Job Recruitment

Even before you are hired by a company—in fact, even if the company decides not to hire you—employee relations will play an important role in your own relations with the prospective employer. The people who make the decision to hire need skill and information if they are to make wise selections.

Your family and friends might be willing to recommend you for a job. They have known you for a long time, and they know your likes and dislikes, your moods and attitudes, and your behavior in general. But when you apply for a job, you walk into your prospective employer's office for the first time as a total stranger. The employer will want some information about you—your experience as a worker, and some personal data as well. And generally he must find out in the shortest possible time if you are suitable for his company, if future relations will be to the mutual advantage of both you and the company. You may be asked to fill out an application as well as have a personal interview. The larger companies usually have personnel departments with trained recruiters whose job it is to find out if you would be a satisfactory worker in the position for which you are applying.

The personnel recruiter may be a trained psychologist, or he may be a specialist who has been trained in personnel work. In the latter case, his training has included many courses in psychology that pertain directly to his profession. In his field he may be thought of as a practicing psychologist.

To recommend the best applicant for a job the personnel recruiter first studies the training and experience requirements for the job. If a position does not require skill or experience, the recruiter investigates the personal life and work habits of the prospective employee. He contacts a previous employer to find out if the worker is dependable: Does he come to work on time? What is his record of absenteeism? Does he get along with others? Does he have any long-term illness that might affect his work? In the case of the skilled worker, the recruiter inquires about experience and training as well as attitudes and work habits. How long has the job candidate done this kind of work? How many companies have employed him?

For most jobs the personnel recruiter will have more than one applicant, all of whom have *similar* experiences. His job is to find which of these applicants has the experience that is *most* suitable for the available job. The skilled applicant usually has a résumé that lists the companies for which he has worked, the exact type of work he has done for each company, his schooling or training in his specialty, and some personal details.

Complete job processing generally involves one or more interviews, psychological and information testing, medical examinations, credit reports, and a follow-up on references submitted by the applicant. When an application form has been filled out and turned in, the recruiter often uses it as a basis for discussion. He probes more deeply into the training, experience, and background of the individual. In some companies, the personnel recruiter conducts a patterned interview using a standard form, prepared by psychologists, which can usually be scored to rank several applicants. In other firms, depth interviewing, which concentrates on the reactions, attitudes, and values of the applicant, is part of the job processing.

If a job is particularly difficult to fill, the personnel recruiter may seek the help of an outside employment agency for the preliminary screening of applicants. In general, the higher the salary offered for a job and the more experience required, the more elaborate will be the recruiting procedure. In these cases, a psychological test may be given to the applicant, as well as tests of job qualification.

State employment agencies, some private agencies, and about 70 percent of the major business firms use some form of psychological testing that makes use of standard scales of test items which have been pretested on individuals employed in similar positions or at similar work levels. The tests are administered to the applicant and scored, and then the scores are interpreted by comparing them with norms for the job. The results are not absolute, but they give the employer some idea of how a person will probably perform on the job in comparison with workers already on the job.

After all the interviews have been completed and all the information about each applicant noted, the recruiter chooses the applicant or applicants he thinks will be most suitable for the available position. He then gives his findings to the manager, who has the authority to hire an applicant.

If only one applicant has been chosen by the recruiter, that applicant will probably be hired, but if the recruiter has selected more than one applicant, the manager or executive must make the final judgment.

The job of the recruiter is therefore to "screen" the applicants to save time for the busy manager. As you can see, this job is very important. If several poorly qualified people are hired and then quit or are fired, the company loses money — the money that has been spent for the salaries and training of the unqualified workers.

New-Job Adjustment

When a person begins a new job and is learning to do the required work, he almost always feels some insecurity. But once the period of adjustment is over — and this period is crucial — an employee can begin to go forward, improve his productivity, and achieve successes. He will be in a position to realize his full potential. If new employees are dissatisfied, they will fail to survive the adjustment period. This failure will be costly for the company as well as the employee. A company should encourage the successful adjustment of its new employees not only out of kindness but also for the protection of its own investment of time, money, and effort.

Dissatisfaction is likely to occur in authoritarian companies where the officers and managers rule the workers with an iron hand. Even an exceptionally cooperative employee may have trouble adjusting to such treatment, and long-term maladjustment on a job increases tension for the individual. This tension is not generally relieved at the end of the workday. Usually the worker carries it with him in his personal life. His family soon becomes aware that something is amiss. In such cases, it may be worthwhile for the worker to change jobs, even though the move will require new adjustments.

Dissatisfaction caused by false anticipations about the job is more likely to occur among young workers, who have less experience with the world of work and, consequently, less background for realistic expectations about work situations. This kind of dissatisfaction can be corrected as the young worker matures and gains experience.

Promotions

Employees find it rewarding in terms of both salary and prestige to move upward within a company to a higher-level job. For example, a worker may move from a production job to a managerial job, or a manager may move up to an executive position. A worker may also move horizontally; he may change jobs at the same level of prestige and salary. Horizontal movement may often be as beneficial for a worker as vertical movement because the worker may move to a job that motivates him more even though he has not been upgraded to a higher position. The new job may also place the worker in a position of satisfaction where he will be able to advance himself; thus, the new job situation will be more favorable for him.

Many companies promote workers from within their organization rather than hire new people for the better jobs. This practice is more agreeable to the employees, since it offers them the opportunity for advancement and the personal and financial rewards that come with it. It also saves the company money because the employee being considered for promotion is probably familiar with some of the new work and the people who will be working with him in his new area. For example, if a worker is transferred to a managerial position in his department, he will know much more about how the department is run than an outsider who must learn its operations from scratch. Thus, training time is reduced, and this in itself is a great cost-saver for the company.

Once a worker shows complete mastery of all job elements, he may be ready for a promotion. A worker who has mastered his job may become bored; he may be dissatisfied because he is no longer learning, and he may feel that he has no opportunities for personal advancement. At this time the company faces major questions. How profitable is it, or when does it become profitable, to promote a worker who is finally doing his job well? If he is promoted immediately after he reaches his maximum efficiency, then someone else will have to be trained to do his work, and this amounts to the same thing as his being fired and replaced. On the other hand, if a worker remains too long at a particular job, his sense of self-fulfillment will be diminished, and his morale will be lowered. This can lead to a reduction in efficiency and result in poor productivity. For a time, salary increases may give the worker a feeling of being appreciated, but only for a time; he must have other rewards, which are in the long run more worthwhile than money.

After a worker has served in a particular job successfully and the company has profited by his work, to what job should he be promoted? That is, will there be an opening where he can be most useful to the company and at the same time find the work personally rewarding? Suppose, for example, that a managerial position is found for the worker, but it turns out after a short time that while he was excellent at his previous job, he will make a very poor manager. When this occurs and the worker must be demoted, obvious damage is done to the worker's morale and self-image.

In a sense, a worker being considered for promotion must be treated as a new applicant. In much of public service, a person advances only after he has been thoroughly tested and his qualifications reviewed. For example, a school principal must take a test before he can become a superintendent. In government offices, one does not automatically receive a promotion just by doing satisfactory or even excellent work in the present job.

It is clear, then, that before a worker is promoted to a higher position requiring different tasks and responsibilities, he must be equal to the promotion. His qualifications for the new position must be studied by both his supervisor and those in the personnel department.

 **IMPROVING THE JOB**

There are a number of programs and policies that a company can use to make the work atmosphere and the tasks of the individual worker more pleasant. In Chapter 2, we discussed improvements in the physical environment. There are also aspects of personnel selection and training that are important. Many jobs require teamwork, and if one of the workers does not fit into the team, the whole operation can be affected unfavorably. For example, one company employed teams of three women to operate power mangles for ironing sheets. One of these teams was consistently slower than the others; the women complained of fatigue. The real problem was that one woman did not fit into the group; she simply did not get along with the others. The supervisor transferred her to hand ironing and filled her place on the mangling team with a more compatible woman. The change relieved pressure on all the workers, thus greatly improving the work situation. Friction disappeared at once, and output jumped. The shifted woman had the

Bored people build bad cars. That's why we're doing away with the assembly line.

Working on an assembly line is monotonous. And boring. And after a while, some people begin not to care about their jobs anymore. So the quality of the product often suffers.

That's why, at Saab, we're replacing the assembly line with assembly teams. Groups

of just three or four people who are responsible for a particular assembly process from start to finish.

Each team makes its own decisions about who does what and when. And each team member can even do the entire assembly singlehandedly. The result: people are more involved. They care more. So there's less absenteeism, less turnover. And we have more experienced people on the job.

We're building our new 2-liter engines this way. And the doors to our Saab 99. And we're planning to use this same system to build other parts of our car as well.

It's a slower, more costly system, but we realize that the best machines and materials in the world don't mean a thing, if the person building the car doesn't care.

Saab. It's what a car should be. '

There are more than 300 Saab dealers nationwide. For the name and address of the one nearest you call 800-243-6000 toll free. In Connecticut, call 1-800-882-6500.

Courtesy of Saab-Scania of America and Cox & Co. Advertising Inc.

Many companies today realize that workers who are interested and involved in their work make better products.

aptitude to operate the mangle, but she did not fit in with the other members of the team.

Even when teamwork is not necessary, the presence of congenial people on a job provides a good atmosphere that is conducive to efficient work. The supervisor should be careful to watch his work groups and to note any unfriendliness or complaints about other workers in a group, especially if there are numerous complaints from many in a group about one person. And special care should be taken in observing new employees to see that they are getting along well with their fellow workers.

Many companies are now in the process of developing job enrichment programs (see Chapters 2 and 19). In many cases these programs are designed to change the job situation by providing more interesting tasks for the worker. The managerial system is often restructured so that it is "horizontal" rather than "vertical"; that is, workers participate in decision making and in the management of their own units rather than being told from above what to do. Also, since more complex jobs are often more rewarding, many of the old, simple, boring tasks are being expanded to encompass many duties. A worker in these programs might build a complete unit of equipment rather than just deal with some small part of it.

Many firms and civic service organizations are making use of "training loan and refund" programs. In these programs, an employee takes courses at schools outside of the company to improve his on-the-job skills and thereby increase his productivity. The company may pay all or part of the tuition with the understanding that the employee will complete the course satisfactorily. Such programs are considered part of the company training policy. The satisfactory completion of a course is an indication to the company that the employee will be qualified to perform the required work in his new position.

SUGGESTIONS FOR FURTHER READING

Argyris, Chris, *Management and Organizational Development: The Paths from XA to YB*, New York: McGraw-Hill, 1971.

Finkle, R. B., and W. S. Jones, *Assessing Corporate Talent,* New York: Wiley, 1970.

O'Toole, Richard, *Organization, Management, and Tactics of Social Research,* Cambridge, Mass.: Schenkman, 1971.

Schmidt, Warren H., *Organizational Frontiers and Human Values,* Belmont, Calif.: Wadsworth, 1970.

Shull, F. A., et al., *Organizational Decision Making,* New York: McGraw-Hill, 1970.

Udy, Stanley H., Jr., *Organization of Work: A Comparative Analysis of Production Among Non-Industrial People,* Englewood Cliffs, N.J.: Prentice-Hall, 1970.

TO HELP YOU REMEMBER

1. What are some of the differences between the needs and ambitions of people in earlier times and those of people today?
2. What beliefs are expressed in McGregor's "Theory X" and his "Theory Y"?

3. What are the differences between Herzberg's "hygiene factors" and "motivation factors"?
4. What is meant by a "realistic" goal? Why should a person choose realistic goals to satisfy his personal needs?
5. Briefly describe Helson's "hypothesis of par or tolerance."
6. What benefits can an employee gain from counseling by the company psychologist?
7. Why are job applicants tested? What kinds of tests are used? Are tests reliable?
8. Why do many companies prefer to promote employees from within the organization rather than recruit outsiders?
9. What are some of the things an employee may do to get himself promoted in the company?
10. Why are some courses taken at schools outside the company considered part of the employee's job training?

WORKING WITH PEOPLE, DATA, OR THINGS

Suppose you are self-confident and are looking for an ideal job. You have decided what kind of work you want to do, and you feel that you have the proper skills and ability to be successful.

List some types of companies where you would probably find the type of position that you would like. For each company and job you choose, note some practical considerations that would be involved with this job, such as transportation, special equipment, licenses, and unions.

Choose the firm, from among the ones you have listed, that you think would be the most suitable for your ambition. Describe some of the appealing features of its organization, such as management policies, promotion policies, benefits, and social prestige.

THINGS TO DO

1. Visit several retired workers and ask them to tell you about some of the changes they have seen in their work situations during their years of employment. Be sure especially to ask them about changes in supervision and management.
2. Choose a situation that you have experienced in which there was some difficulty in human relations. Recall what happened and the consequent behavior on the part of those involved. Then analyze the factors in the situation and determine the reasons for the behavior of each person involved.
3. Describe the organization of your school, your community government, or a small business. Do you feel that the pattern of organization most closely follows Theory X or Theory Y of McGregor? Do you find any difficulties in the organization?

PART 2

YOUR PERSONAL
EFFICIENCIES
AND PERFORMANCE

LEARNING AND REMEMBERING MORE

5

What This Chapter Is About

1 WANTING TO LEARN IS BASIC

Max Thorek came from Czechoslovakia to Chicago with a career sparkle in his eyes. His constant companion, a violin, brought him work with a "gypsy" band. To resemble a gypsy, he grew a fierce black mustache, although he was only 18. He did well enough as an imitation gypsy, but he wanted to become a surgeon.

The next spring he tucked the violin under his arm and called on the director of the University of Chicago band. In America, the director told him, violins are not used in bands. But they did need a snare drummer, and he would be paid half the tuition charges.

"Only half tuition? Wouldn't an extra-good drummer really be worth full tuition?"

The band needed a drummer desperately, so the director phoned the University of Chicago president, William Ramey Harper, and won permission to give an exceptional drummer full tuition.

This exceptional drummer hurried to a pawnshop and bought the first snare drum he had ever touched. He settled down in a tenement to learn drumming during the hot summer. Neighbors complained, and he was haled into police court. Judge Sabath let Thorek off when he promised to practice in the cellar.

Then came the first rehearsal of the band that autumn. Thorek now had to prove that he was an exceptional drummer. He drummed in a self-conscious daze until the music for Meyerbeer's *Coronation March* was passed around, a real test for any drummer. The youth lost color as he looked at the mounting series of bravado rolls he would have to play.

After Thorek made one try at the march, the director rushed to the telephone and talked with President Harper. "That new drummer is a wonder," he exulted. "He certainly deserves full tuition."

Thorek had taught himself drumming with a little help from his gypsy friends and was on his way to becoming a great surgeon. In time he learned to operate so skillfully that on one occasion, when his right hand had been injured by the awkward work of another surgeon, he prevented its amputation by operating on himself with his left hand.

Doctor Thorek's progress as a drummer was exceptional because he wanted to learn. He had to master the drum to attend medical school. This wanting to learn is absolutely essential for efficient learning. *Intense effort speeds learning.*

2 LEARNING AND MOTIVATION

Successful learning must be motivated: one must *want* to learn in order to learn, to achieve a goal. Our *primary* goal is what we want to achieve as a life's work, or it may be something more immediate. A primary goal is sometimes called *intrinsic* because it is a basic desire. In achieving a primary goal, we must often strive to satisfy *secondary* goals. As we saw, Dr. Thorek's primary goal was to become a surgeon, but one of his secondary goals was to become a drummer in order to *support* his primary goal. If he had not become a drummer in the university band, he may never have been able to achieve his goal of becoming a surgeon. Becoming a drummer could be called an *extrinsic* need for Dr. Thorek because for him, this achievement was a step toward his primary goal; yet this step was not directly involved in his medical training.

The satisfaction of an intrinsic need can motivate one more strongly than the satisfaction of an extrinsic need. If a person is very determined and ambitious, however, the motivation to achieve a secondary goal may be strong enough to inspire learning as efficient as Dr. Thorek's. On the other hand, a person who is forced to achieve a goal that does not interest him will not be *motivated* and will therefore not make the effort to learn efficiently. For example, a parent may want his son or daughter to become a lawyer even though this may not be the child's ambition. Often, in such a case, the child becomes a mediocre law student.

The goal of every training program is to teach a worker how to perform certain tasks. If the worker lacks motivation, he will not *want* to learn, and his learning will not be efficient. So it is crucial that you choose a career—or any goal, for that matter—that is truly something that you *want to accomplish.*

Industrial training directors have a tough problem making some employees want to learn. Graduates of engineering schools or other special schools sometimes imagine they have already learned everything, and they are often humiliated into wanting to catch on to job details. This apparently cruel treatment of new workers is an effort to shock the self-satisfied into wanting to learn. With this technique, the know-it-alls can expect some jolts.

3 LEARN FROM AN EXPERT

It helps a beginner start right if he has an expert open his bag of tricks. However, many experts are weak in "show-how"; often an expert can do but can't show how. Even if a learner finds an expert who is also a good teacher, it is good for him to spend a lot of time doing rather than just watching, although both are necessary. A new salesman can learn a little by watching a skilled salesman, but he will learn better by trying some selling himself. Watch the expert, but not too long, then *do it yourself.*

The expert trainer follows six steps when helping employees.

1 Tell the "why" first.
2 Have the beginner explain the why.
3 Show how briefly.
4 Let the beginner try it.
5 Encourage the beginner.
6 Motivate the beginner to improve.

But there are also *expert beginners.* They follow these rules when learning new skills:

1 Learn why *before* starting.
2 Watch to see how.
3 Try it to get the "feel-how."
4 Keep trying for accuracy.
5 *Want* to improve.
6 Believe you can improve.

The wise learner sticks to one instructor until he gains some skill. Experts use different methods, and so shifting from one instructor to another causes confusion. The best teacher is the learner's effort to learn and understand why. Tackle new work confidently. It is possible to learn anything until effort has proved otherwise.

 **LEARNING CURVES**

Learning can be measured for progress and end results, and the data gathered can usually be plotted on a graph as a *learning curve.* Since graphic presentations are much easier to read than tabulations and printed numerical material, the learning graph serves as an excellent visual feedback of what is happening in the learning process. If the curve climbs gradually, one can assume that the learning rate is slow; if it climbs sharply, we know that the learning rate is rapid; if it becomes horizontal or flattens out, no learning is taking place. Psychologists refer to long horizontal or flattened curves as "physiological limits" and smaller temporary horizontal lines as "plateaus."

Psychologists are not in agreement about physiological limits. Some feel that physiological limits occur only in motor tasks (typewriting, keypunching, telegraph coding, and so on), for which the limit comes from the nerves and muscles. Other psychologists use the term "physiological limits" to describe the limit of mental capacity (intelligence).

Plateaus are a different matter in that most psychologists agree that they occur in both motor and verbal tasks that are difficult to learn. Such conditions as lack of interest and exhaustion are causes for plateaus. In any event, the complexity of the task involved is part of the reason for plateaus.

Dr. William L. Bryan was the first person to develop learning curves. He used them to measure the progress of students who were learning the telegraph code. His findings, a landmark in the foundations of applied psychology, were published in 1897, nine years after Bryan started the psychological laboratory at Indiana University. (He later became president of the university and held the post for 35 years.) A facsimile of one of the original curves is given here.

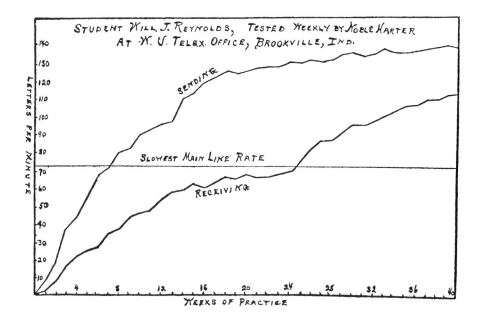

The first learning curve to be published appeared in the *Psychological Review* in 1897.

Dr. Bryan was the first to find that

1 Learning does not progress smoothly. It has ups and downs; there are good days and poor days.
2 Learning is rapid during the first few practice periods, then it slows down as the ultimate skill is approached.
3 There is a plateau in learning, a time when the learner does not seem to improve for a while.

The learning curves of two typewriting students are reproduced here. Study these two curves before continuing this section.

Words per minute

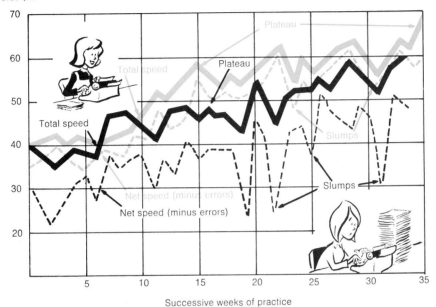

Successive weeks of practice

Key   Average typist
       Superior typist

Courtesy of Packard School

Compare the learning curves of an average typist and a superior typist. Each typist's total speed is represented by a solid line. The dotted lines represent net speed—after errors have been deducted from total speed. The superior typist practiced for accuracy, and there is less difference between her total and net speeds than is shown for the average typist.

5 RAISING A LEARNING PLATEAU

Businesses and individuals run into periods of apparent stagnation— standstill periods when they seem to be getting nowhere rapidly.

When Ignace Paderewski, the renowned pianist, was 25 and already a well-known concert performer, he was on a plateau. He bogged down with his usual practice methods. The practice sheets were thrown out the window, and he started over again, practicing elementary finger exercises and scales. This different kind of practice helped him to correct his errors and enabled him to break through the plateau and emerge with higher skill than before.

It takes more than mere repetition or rote practice to change an amateur into a professional. The professional has not only practiced for accuracy but has also improved his methods in order to rise above his plateaus. Just working on a job in the same old routine way does not result in mastering the job.

When a person is learning to type, for instance, he spells out words letter by letter and finger by finger. This puts a ceiling on speed. The person keeps practicing on this plateau until he begins to type words as a unit, not as single letters. The more frequently used words become typing units: *t-h-e* becomes *the*; *a-n-d* becomes *and*. It is not greater finger speed but larger working units that make it possible for him to get ahead and to leave this first plateau behind.

When a plateau is hit, it pays to analyze the way one is working and figure out improvements. The average typist in our graph, for example, is likely to be held on a plateau by faulty techniques, such as piling letters on top of each other, because she is typing for speed and neglecting to type in rhythm. Maybe it is transposing letters that holds her on a plateau; it may pay her to see if the transpositions are caused by reading too far ahead. When you arrive at a plateau, take stock of your techniques.

A plateau in learning anything usually means that the limit has been reached for the present method of work. It does not help to try to work faster. Look for slight changes in method. Consult an expert or a teacher. Watch others for suggestions. Or improvise some change. One student broke through a typing plateau simply by moving 2 inches farther away from the typewriter. Little things like that blast away a big plateau! To break through a standstill:

Remain confident and encouraged.

Analyze for better methods.

Keep on trying.

Continue practicing to avoid slumping backward from a plateau.

As Paderewski commented, "If I miss one day's practice, I notice it. If I miss two days, the critics notice it. If I miss three days, the public notices it."

Too many learners imagine that they have reached their ceilings. or physiological limits, at the first plateau, and they quit trying too soon. Willis Whitney, the research director who led General Electric Company scientists to many discoveries, often told the scientists, "You get there just about the last thing before giving up."

Keep encouraged. And keep at it. A plateau in progress should be a station where you figure out how to break through.

WHAT IS MEMORY?

Why do some people remember things much better than others do? After considerable study in mathematics, for instance, most people are able to memorize the fact that the number for pi is 3.14. Others have no difficulty in remembering that it is 3.141593. But Frank S. Baldwin, who invented the Monroe calculator and other mathematical machines, memorized the value of pi to 128 decimal places! It was relatively easy for him because he liked working with figures.

Some people remember better because they are interested in the material. Others remember better because of some inborn, but as yet not understood, factors that make it easier for them to retain and recall. And still others remember better than the average person simply because they make an effort to remember. On the average, women are better than men at remembering.

Having a good memory does not mean that you have more brain cells than other people who do not remember as well as you do. Nor does effort to remember seem to increase the number of brain cells; the evidence is overwhelming that brain cells cannot be increased in number. But experiments by Dr. David Krech at the University of California do indicate strongly that proper and stimulating use of the brain increases the size of brain cells and also changes their chemical activities.

There is no nerve or special compartment of the brain that is used exclusively for remembering. *Memory* is merely a term used to label the way facts can be impressed, retained, and later recalled. "Memory" indicates an activity, not a storeroom. Dr. Karl S. Lashley showed that many kinds of nerve and brain cells and most parts of the brain are involved in remembering.

Memory, intelligence, thinking, and other related terms are just convenient for segregating different aspects of mental life for study. Similarly, one talks about the hardness, torque resistance, elasticity, and other properties of a piece of steel.

Your thinking will be sharper if you bear in mind that such terms do not describe concrete objects but powers and properties. Strictly speaking, for instance, we do not have *a* memory; what we have is the *power* of remembering. Don't look for a pigeonhole location for memory in the brain any more than you would look for elasticity in the upper left corner of a steel bar. We can see how remembering works, but we cannot see it.

It is much the same situation with a concept such as the break-even point for costs, sales, and profits. The break-even point is not a piece of machinery, like a duplicating machine; nor is it a definite place, like the top drawer. It is a function—and an important one. Memory, too, is a function. To be precise, we should speak of *memorizing* or *remembering*, not of memory; of *concentrating*, not of concentration; of *acting intelligently,* not of intelligence.

7 LEARNING AND REMEMBERING

It is agreed that learning and remembering are related. We have all taken too many tests during our school years not to be aware that we must establish proof of what we have learned through remembering. The retention of what we have learned is called *memorizing;* however, we don't know much about the actual process of memorizing or remembering.

We do know that learning affects the central nervous system— something happens to it when we learn. Evidently, the greater the amount learned, the greater the intention to learn it, and the complexity of the material learned affects the amount of change in the central nervous system. For example, if we are introduced to someone casually and learn only his first name, we are not likely to retain this name in our memory unless we are impressed with the person and want to see him again. Thus, after a short time the name will fade from our memory. This is short-term memory. Such remembering has a negligible effect on the central nervous system. On the other hand, if we are trying to learn material for a course we have taken in order to pass an examination, remembering will have a deeper effect on the central nervous system.

Some scientists feel that at the time of learning memory is established in the *cerebral cortex* of the brain by means of a filter or scanning process. If the process is successful, we remember what we have learned; if not, we forget it.

Other modern scientists including Dr. D. Ewen Cameron, Allan Memorial Institute, Montreal, and James V. McConnell, University of Michigan, say that chemical changes within the brain cells enable us to remember what we have learned, but the precise nature of these changes is not yet fully understood.

Still other scientists feel that physical changes occur that affect learning and remembering (certain incidents of learning would occur more readily by way of specific nerves).

Memorizing is closely related to learning. The two processes follow many of the same laws. Trying to remember helps us remember, and trying to learn helps us learn. Lack of confidence harms memorizing and also harms learning.

Memorizing helps us to recall past experiences. Learning is broader, dealing with the modification of behavior by use of past experiences. Learning is modification, change. Memorizing or remembering is the impression, retention, and recall of things from the past. Memory is involved in the learning process.

8 REDUCING INTERFERENCES IN REMEMBERING

Avoid trying to remember too many things at the same time. Give things a chance to "soak in."

Retroactive inhibition is when fresh memories affect older ones. Newer memories interfere with slightly older ones before the older ones have jelled. The student who studies business law for an hour and then business organization for the next hour will have his memory for law inhibited by the later material on business organization. If things being remembered are too similar, the processes of remembering them will interfere with each other and get mixed up.

A person who can remember names and faces well may find his memory blurred if he meets too many people at the same time. When getting acquainted with other workers on a new job, don't try to learn everyone's name all at once. Learn the names of a few at a time.

Retroactive inhibition is decreased if the second set of impressions is distinctively different from the first. Thus, you should, when studying, alternate subjects that are different. You might study some business law, then some business math.

Dr. William C. Gorgas, who eradicated yellow fever in Cuba and was chief sanitary officer during the building of the Panama Canal, read three books on three different subjects at once. After studying one subject for an hour, he would turn to another that would not produce interfering memories.

A good way to reduce retroactive inhibition is to alternate intense study with short periods of complete rest or with longer periods of activity in which memorizing is not involved. For example, study for an hour, then write letters for an hour.

A subject studied just before bedtime is usually remembered better than material studied earlier because what follows are some eight hours with no interfering work to erase the new memories.

It is a good idea to memorize in easy stages. Also, keep in mind that you weaken your memory by crowding too many things into it at once. For this reason, cramming for examinations is a most inefficient way to study.

DON'T TRY TO REMEMBER EVERYTHING

Memorizing improves with use, but not with *abuse*. Keep in mind that one can remember better by remembering less. If you have to visit the dentist on the fifteenth, attend a business conference on the seventeenth, and have lunch with a customer on the twenty-first, keep a diary or calendar and make note of these events. Then forget them, but, of course, don't forget to look in your diary or calendar daily if you don't want to miss your appointments. If you have several errands to do during the day, or if you have to buy certain items at the grocery store, list these things on a sheet of paper and refer to your list to see what to get or do next. Cross off the item you have just taken care of.

Use judgment in considering what you want to remember. There's no use remembering a telephone number that you may never call again. Don't try to memorize an entire bus or train schedule; but do try to remember the information that you need to use. There's no point in trying to remember every face you see, but do try to remember customers and associates. It is foolish to try to remember everything in the newspaper, but do remember news of lasting importance or news that

Joan Menschenfreund

One can remember better by attempting to remember less. Keep an appointment book instead of trying to remember all the appointments you make. But don't forget to look at your calendar daily.

has a bearing on your business or profession. Memorize rapidly the things that count, and let the rest become incidental memories.

Intend to remember more than you probably have in the past, but don't clutter up your head trying to remember everything. A flypaper memory to which everything sticks is not efficient in the least — it's a freak of nature.

10 TRY TO REMEMBER MORE

When William Howard Taft was Secretary of War, he cultivated his ability to remember names and faces. On an inspection tour of the Panama Canal, he amazed everyone with his ability to memorize local officials' puzzling names. He remembered the names by repeating them to himself and linking each with some distinctive quality of the person's appearance. He tried to remember, and consequently, he did remember.

When he became President, he neglected to continue this effort to remember names and faces, and so he lost some of his influence over people. Newspaper correspondents, who saw him almost daily, cooled off toward him when he did not remember their names. Taft's memory powers were as good as ever, but he neglected to use them.

George Calvin Carter was Dun & Bradstreet's representative in New Hampshire and Vermont for more than half a century. His memory for confidental details of the businesses in those states gave him the reputation of being the best-informed businessman of that section. His system was simplicity itself and sound psychology.

"I have no special system," he said. "I have just had a good memory and have always made it a point to keep it exercised." Further, he continued, "If something is not worth remembering, I dismiss it immediately. If it is worthwhile, I think about it momentarily in a serious way. My only system is to see that every fact I think may be used again is properly impressed." For one hobby, he remembered the height of every factory smokestack in his states.

When you remember something without trying, it is *incidental memory,* a hit-or-miss variety. People forget most of what they read in newspapers because they read with no special intention of remembering. Likewise, a telephone number that is used only once is quickly forgotten.

Intentional memory is much more serviceable. Simply trying to remember a telephone number or a person's name makes you remember it 50 to 100 percent better. Intending to remember takes only a little longer but makes memories last a great deal longer.

The oft-quoted experiment by James H. Moore illustrates how much it helps if you merely try to remember. His test involved a short story paragraph that had 166 words and contained 67 ideas. Using three groups of about two hundred students, he gave the instructions listed below and then tested subjects to determine how many ideas they recalled.

Instructions Given	Average Number of Ideas Remembered
Count the words	7
Read the paragraph	38
Read the paragraph and remember as much as possible	51

The first step in memorizing more is to try to remember. It also helps to think you can remember, as was proved by Dr. Stanley Moldawsky and Dr. Patricia Moldawsky. See the cartoon below.

How many numbers remembered

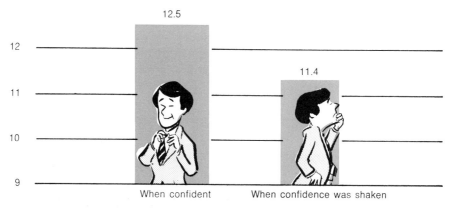

Data from Dr. Stanley Moldawsky and Dr. Patricia Moldawsky

Sixteen persons were the subjects of an experiment to test the relationship of confidence to the ability to memorize long numbers. After being told that there was something peculiar about their memories, the subjects were unable to remember as many numbers.

11 MAKE REMEMBERING PLEASANT

The English philosopher John Locke (1632–1704) pointed out that pleasant experiences tend to be remembered more easily than unpleasant ones. This tells us that *attitude* plays an important role in remembering things. A store manager might well remember a golf date with a friend and tend to forget an appointment with a complaining customer, unless, of course, he had written the date with the customer on his calendar.

Since people tend to forget unpleasant things, it is a good idea to do unpleasant tasks right away, before they slip from your mind. You can look forward to a more enjoyable job later if you get rid of the unpleasant aspects of the job first. Austin Ingleheart, who worked his way up to the position of chairman of General Foods Corporation, once said, "If you break down almost any job, you will find a large percent of it is disagreeable work. I have never had a disagreeable job in my life, but I have had to do a lot of disagreeable things." So we can see that when the boss or a teacher makes work pleasant, we can remember the details more readily. Accordingly, you will remember the names of people you like more easily than the names of those you dislike, so try to like more people, if you want to remember more names.

12 USE IMAGINATION

Russell H. Conwell, who founded Temple University, said that he was a poor student in his early school days. For one reason, he had a sense of humor and was whipped eight times in one day for laughing at the teacher. But a new teacher, Miss Salina Cole, taught the farm boy to improve his ability to memorize by using imagination.

"Look at the word in the book," she told him, "then close your eyes and see it in imagination." The mischievous boy became so adept at this that he could close his eyes and visualize an entire paragraph or page.

"Seeing" things this way is called *eidetic* imagery and gives rise to eidetic memory. Eidetic memory makes it possible for some people to quote many pages verbatim. Such people just "see" the page in their imaginations and read it off. Sir Arthur Conan Doyle had eidetic memory, and it improved as he grew older.

"Hearing" words in imagination also helps. Some people "hear" in imagination more easily than they can "see" in imagination. If you can both "hear" and "see," it helps that much more.

To exercise your memory while you are riding on a bus or train, recall in imagination the people you have met during the day. "See" their faces and "hear" their names. Practice "hearing" their voices so that you will recognize them on the telephone. Since many people have a distinctive footstep, listen and practice "hearing" each kind of step.

For another good exercise, when studying a book or job-instruction sheet, close your eyes for a moment and "see" the items that should be remembered. If you cannot "hear" them, whisper them to yourself.

Even the most vivid memories tend to become blurred and twisted in time.

"It was just after James came to work last summer."

"No, I'm sure it was before then."

So another endless argument starts. It pays to keep a diary or some dated record of events that may have later significance. Many executives dictate memos that summarize every interview and conference, and these memos are filed for possible future use.

Retroactive falsification is unintentional inaccuracy or mixing up in memories. Everyone is a partial liar as a consequence. Memories usually cover the high spots; many details are missing. When trying to recall details, a person is apt to be misled by retroactive falsification.

Numbers are often exaggerated in memory. The salesman "recollects" that the Amazon Corporation bought 200 of his "widgets" five years ago—but the true figure is only 15. These memory distortions are more apt to involve matters in which there is self-interest. Salesmen particularly have to guard against this inclination, lest they earn the

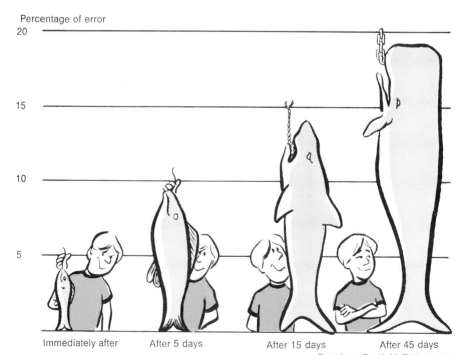

Percentage of error

20

15

10

5

Immediately after   After 5 days   After 15 days   After 45 days

Data from Dr. K. M. Dallenbach

Individuals tested for retroactive falsifications were able to give relatively accurate reports immediately after observing a scene or episode. As time went on, the descriptions became increasingly inaccurate.

reputation of being liars. It is usually safest to deliberately understate what you remember.

The tendency to confuse imagination with memory is called *confabulation*. Many workers confabulate alibis to explain their failure to follow orders.

The gossip, or rumormonger, often confabulates. His overall motive may be spite, or too much curiosity about the personal affairs of others, or feelings of guilt that he wants to shift to others. As the story is passed along the grapevine, retroactive falsification keeps changing it. Details are added to it, numbers are magnified, and soon all resemblance to the original facts is lost. For examples of confabulation, recall rumors you have heard about a company's profits or the number of people laid off, or the story about the unpopular boss's son being thrown in jail, when, in actuality, he only went out of town to visit someone.

Then there are a few people who lack conscience and tell whoppers more easily than honest people tell the truth. In 1834, the German psychiatrist and writer Johann C. A. Heinroth originated the term *pathological liars* to describe such people. They have sick minds, and they can make endless trouble by starting rumors or misleading customers.

The most famous example of a pathological liar was a German cavalry officer, Baron Karl Friedrich Hieronymus von Münchhausen, who retired from the cavalry when he reached 40 and devoted the rest of his life to entertaining his friends with amazing stories told with a straight face. In 1785 some of these were published in a book, and the Baron von Münchhausen type of tall tale became a legend.

Although there are few storytellers having von Münchhausen's talents, it is wise to be on the alert always for both pathological and intentional lying. Many promoters and swindlers, for example, distort their memories so often that they begin to believe their own statements. The pathological liar does not try to tell a consistent story, but the swindler does and carries the blueprints to prove his story. Some high-pressure salesmen incline in this direction; it is wise to weed out these confabulators.

Since normal memories of past experiences usually are lacking in detail, the person who supplies many details may be suspected of some confabulation. When a fisher says the fish weighed four pounds, believe him, but if he adds a number of details that are supposed to convince you that he is not lying—look out!

Avoid the all-too-human tendencies to fill in possible details, magnify numbers, and distort in other ways. Say quickly, "I'm not sure," or "I'll have to hunt it up," or "You're expecting too much of my memory." Don't jump off the deep end and try to pull up something that might be as you remembered it. For example, keep a written record of where you worked, the dates, the pay, the work done, and similar details for use when you apply for a job. Don't get your story mixed up when applying for work. It is better to start a new job with the reputation of having a slow memory than that of having a fast memory for things that are not true.

14 RECALLING AND TYING IN FACTS

Impressing a thing on the mind is only the start of remembering. Being able to recall it when wanted makes the memory cycle complete and useful. The best way to develop recall is to recall—this is the law of use.

Thus, the second time you see Mr. Rivera, mention his name aloud and think of his hobbies, of where he lives, or of interests he expressed when you talked with him before. Every time you see him, mention his name and recall some of the information you know about him. You'll find it easier each succeeding time, and your use of his name will make you more popular with him.

Exercise recall of facts that you have just learned by talking them over with someone. Talk them over with yourself if no one else is interested. Exercise recall on technical points in your work by talking them over with others in the same firm. But avoid such business talk with persons who are not in the same company; you must be careful not to give away company secrets.

Recall can be practiced without talking. Thinking about something —"hearing" and "seeing" in imagination—is almost as good as talking. Many people put their odd moments to work by using them to recall in their imaginations.

Do you recall what you read a few pages back about George Calvin Carter, the Dun & Bradstreet man who remembered the heights of smokestacks? He remembered them by tying them in with the height of Bunker Hill Monument. Every good Yankee knows that this monument is 221 feet high. Mr. Carter made the remembering of chimney heights easy by noting that the left chimney of the Public Service Company generating plant is the same height as the monument; the right chimney, 2 feet higher.

Memory is strengthened by the association of new facts with facts already memorized in ways like that just described. Don't merely repeat the new name or fact, but think how it is related to something you already know. This is using *association*.

You already know Martha Schmidt well. She has a booming voice and is in women's wear. You have just met Louise Schmidt, who has a squeaky voice and is in men's wear. Their names are similar, but the *association of contrasts* helps you remember both more efficiently.

Association of similars makes it easy to recall the outline shape of Italy, the boot. *Association by contiguity* makes it easier to remember things that happened together.

It helps recall if you go back to the original setting or attitude. When you have difficulty recalling someone's name, think back to where you met him; visualize the setting. Don't say to yourself, "Why don't I recall his name?" Instead, ask yourself, "Where did I meet him?" "When did we meet?"

15 PRIME AND WAIT

Did you ever have someone's name on the tip of your tongue, and yet you were unable to recall it? When this happens again, don't try to recall it. Do something else for a few minutes, and the name may pop into your head. The name is there, since you have met this person and learned his name. It only has to be dug out. The initial effort to recall *primes* the mind, but it is the subconscious activities that go to work to pry up a dim memory. *Forcing* yourself to recall almost never helps because it doesn't loosen your memory; it only tightens it.

Students find the *priming method* helpful on examinations. They read over the questions before trying to answer any of them. Then they answer first the ones of which they are most confident. Meanwhile, deeper mental activities in the subconscious mind are taking place; work is being done on the more difficult questions. By the time the easier questions are answered, answers to the more difficult ones will usually begin to come into consciousness. It is often just a question of *waiting* for recall to be loosened up.

This prime-and-wait method is most useful when you are trying to locate a letter that might have been filed under one of several classifications. Instead of tearing the whole file cabinet apart to look for it, think about where it might have been filed, then do some other work for a while. Try to think about the subject of the letter and to whom it was written; perhaps something special happened just before or after you had written the letter. While you are waiting for the recall, do something that does not require much concentration, because concentration is a distraction from your immediate concern for remembering where the letter was filed. About ten minutes later go back to the file cabinet and resume your search. There is a good chance that you will be able to put your hands on the letter the first thing after priming and waiting.

16 HELPING OTHERS REMEMBER

Advertisers hammer their points and trade names into your memory by making the ad interesting and vivid, and by *endlessly* repeating it. Repetition is the key to successful advertising.

Repetition is the standby of conventional teaching—it helps memory. Listen to this imaginary job-training instructor: "This is a *micrometer.* We shall first study the *micrometer.* I am holding a *micrometer* in my hand. The word I am writing on the blackboard is *micrometer.* You will be able to use a *micrometer* to inspect diameters. This *micrometer*

"We were talking about advertising agencies
and the name Geer DuBois came up."

"We were talking about advertising agencies
and the name Geer DuBois came up."

"We were talking about advertising agencies
and the name Geer DuBois came up."

Repetition is a key to successful
advertising.
Courtesy of Geer DuBois Inc.

measures thousandths of an inch." This may sound very elementary and simple, and it may be an exaggeration of what the teacher will actually be saying, but it gives an illustration of one of the primary techniques in teaching. In high school, when you have studied a foreign language or mathematics, you have probably seen how terms and words are repeated again and again. Repetition doesn't have to be dull, and it won't be if you are learning something new when you are repeating something old. This is the secret of good teaching. Learning by *association* and by *rote* are both forms of repetitive learning. In math, a formula may be used to derive another formula; in a language, a phrase may be repeated in several sentences, each providing a new thought or idea.

If you want to remember a name, repeat it to yourself with each fact you know about a person: *"Mr. Smith* has brown hair." *"Mr. Smith* lives in Clifton, New Jersey." *"Mr. Smith* has three children." *"Mr. Smith* is an accountant." Soon you will find that you know the name *Smith* as well as you know your own name. Remember that a customer is always flattered if you can recall his name and use it.

It helps memory to hear a new word *before its meaning is given.* Notice that the imaginary instructor's first statement to his students was, "This is a micrometer." He did not begin by telling them, "We shall now learn how to measure one-thousandth of an inch." He wanted first to impress on them that they were using a new tool, and so he began by calling their attention to it by showing it to them and by using its name. Then he began to show and tell them what it is used for.

The thing you want to remember should be repeated first by name—this is an application of the principle that *the first impressions are the lasting ones.* It is important to realize that when you apply for a new job, it is the first impression you make that will be best remembered by the person who interviews you. It has been demonstrated that the first part of a book is remembered best, the last part next best, and the middle the least.

Emphasis also helps a person to remember. Repetition is one form of emphasis. An instructor may use a pointer or a different-colored piece of chalk to emphasize a point. A textbook may have **boldface** (darker) letters or *italics* to emphasize certain words or phrases, as we can see throughout this book. An idea can be emphasized by *dramatizing* it, drawing it on the blackboard, or changing one's tone of voice when explaining it. A salesman often makes a *demonstration* to get his point across to prospective customers. In doing so he is actually *teaching* them about it, and in all probability, he will use repetition as an additional form of emphasis.

SUGGESTIONS FOR FURTHER READING

Hall, J. F., *The Psychology of Learning,* Philadelphia: Lippincott, 1966.
Lindgren, H. C., D. Byrne, and L. Petrinovich, *Psychology: An Introduction to a Behavioral Science*, 3d ed., New York: Wiley, 1971.

Swift, W. Porter, Ph.D., *General Psychology,* New York: McGraw-Hill, 1969.

TO HELP YOU REMEMBER

1. Define and contrast intrinsic and extrinsic needs.
2. List the six rules for an expert beginner.
3. What is a learning curve?
4. Define and contrast a physiological limit and a learning plateau.
5. What are some similarities between learning and remembering?
6. Define retroactive inhibition. Give an example.
7. Define and contrast incidental memory and intentional memory.
8. How does eidetic imagery give rise to eidetic memory?
9. What are retroactive falsification and confabulation? Why should they be avoided?

WORKING WITH PEOPLE, DATA, OR THINGS

David Appleton is 21 years old and came to work in the purchasing department of the McDow Publishing Company a year ago after quitting the University of Minnesota because he was placed on probation. He was a sophomore pursuing a chemical engineering career. (He had wanted to be an engineer since the ninth grade.) It wasn't that David lacked intelligence; it's just that those two Ds in calculus and trigonometry brought his average down to a 1.75 in his major sequence, and so he lost complete confidence in his ability to achieve his long-range goal of becoming an engineer.

David's been a Level 2 clerk and is in training for a calculation job. He's been in training for six months, twice as long as any other trainee. His supervisor, Don Edwards, knows that he is capable of becoming an accounting clerk, which is a Level 5 job, and eventually a manager, a Level 8 job. He gets along well with the team because he has a nice unassuming manner. Mr. Edwards wants David to up his production rate. His lack of speed has been the primary reason why he hasn't been promoted to a Level 3 position, and Mr. Edwards is concerned. After all, he can't get to 8 (that manager's seat) unless he gets moving.

Mr. Edwards discusses this situation with his manager, Samuel Cross. Mr. Cross suggests that Mr. Edwards talk to David and find out what the problem seems to be. He says, "I don't suppose you can come right out and ask him why it's taking him so long to learn a simple job, but maybe he'll give you a clue to his problem."

Mr. Edwards calls David in to see him for a heart-to-heart talk. It really turns out to be a very perplexing situation because the young man doesn't know why he can't "catch on" and "produce as much as the other guys." When he got up to leave, he said, "I guess I just don't have it, Mr. Edwards; I am really trying, honest, I am."

Directions

Study this case history, and consider the following questions. Be prepared to discuss your analysis in class.

1. What do you see as the real problem?
2. What suggestions would you make to Mr. Edwards regarding the motivation of David Appleton?
3. Do you think that David is really trying or not? Explain.

THINGS TO DO

1. Think back over your own schooling and job training. What made you try harder than usual to learn something. Write a 200-word statement discussing the intrinsic and extrinsic needs that were satisfied. Prepare to report your analysis to the class.
2. Analyze the following learning curves, and interpret their meaning to the class. Are there any learning plateaus or physiological limits?

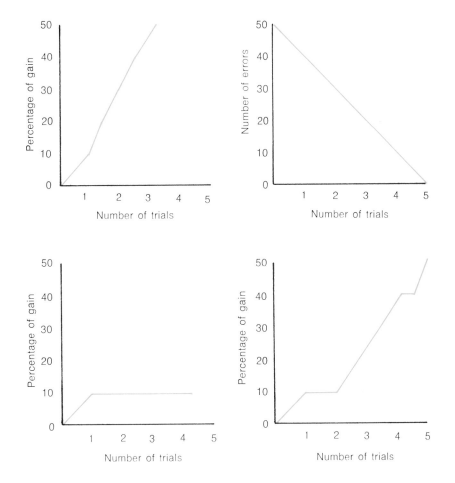

3. Study five advertisements in a business magazine (for example. *Fortune, Business Week, Forbes, Administrative Management, Chemical Engineering*), and report to the class the techniques used to make it easier for readers to remember the product or service being advertised.
4. Interview at least five businessmen who are successful, especially people in sales work, to learn what techniques they use to help them remember names and faces. Record the interviews on tape or in writing, and share them with your class members.
5. Select a simple job (tying a shoe, typing an envelope, making a showcard, planing a board), and teach the job to the class.

SEEING AND READING MORE

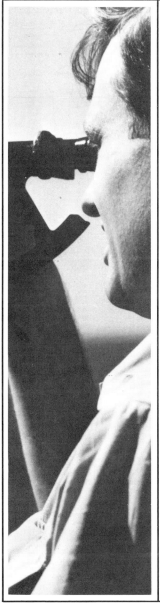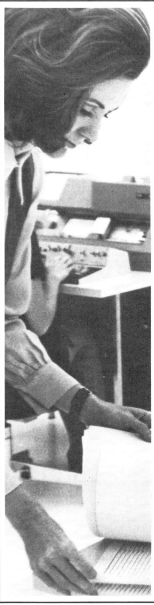

1 HOW DO WE SEE THINGS?

The *senses* are a human being's contacts with his environment. Of the five senses—sight, hearing, smell, taste, and touch—sight is without question man's most cherished sense.

The American Heritage Dictionary describes the human *eye* as a "hollow structure . . . having a lens capable of focusing incident light on an internal photosensitive retina." Notice the similarity between this definition of the eye and the dictionary's definition for the word *camera:* "a lightproof enclosure having an aperture with a shuttered lens through which the image of an object is focused and recorded on a photosensitive film or plate."

The eye "takes pictures" continually when the eyelids are open. The eyelids, of course, correspond to the shutter in a camera. Unlike the camera, however, the eye transmits the picture to the brain through a system of nerves connected to the *retina,* which corresponds to the film or plate in a camera. Light, which appears as a wave, contacts the eye at the *cornea,* which is a tissue that covers the front of the eyeball. From the cornea the light wave passes through the *pupil,* which is the opening in the *iris,* or colored part of the eye. The iris controls the opening of the pupil. The light wave then passes through the lens, where it is focused onto the retina at the rear of the eye. The lens is adjusted for distance or close vision by a set of muscles connected to its sides. These muscles pull the lens flat for distance seeing and relax it so that it thickens for closeup work like reading. The thickened lens is like a magnifying glass.

Many light waves strike the retina at any given moment of seeing. These light waves form an image, or picture, of the thing being seen. This picture is then translated into a "signal" and is sent to the brain via the *optic nerve.* The nerve fibers extending from the left half of each eye go to the left hemisphere of the brain, while the fibers from the right half go to the right hemisphere. In the brain, this complex signal is translated into meaning.

2 VISUAL PERCEPTION AND VISION

Visual perception is *not* the same thing as vision. Vision is mechanical: it is the process of seeing just described in the last section. Visual perception, on the other hand, is the "understanding" of vision; that is, we perceive an object *after* we have seen it, and we perceive it only when we know what it is we are looking at.

In a normal eye, vision is always accurate. This is not the case with perception: we often perceive inaccurately, because the mechanism

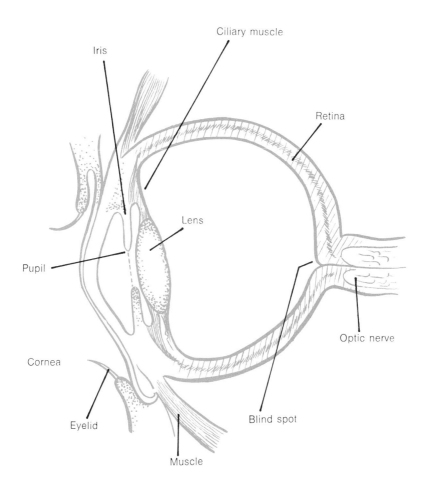

This diagram shows the major parts of the eye. Do you understand the basic function of each part?

of the eye operates with lightning speed, and the mechanism of understanding is much slower. This accounts for "optical illusions" in which the actual image of an object is perceived differently from the way it was seen by the eye. Magicians take advantage of our inability to perceive things accurately; it is this inability which enables them to perform their "tricks." It is our perception of what they do that is actually the trickster.

Dr. Paul D. Leedy gives us the following sentence in his book *Improve Your Reading: A Guide to Greater Speed, Understanding, and Enjoyment.*

FINISHED FILES ARE THE RESULT
OF YEARS OF SCIENTIFIC STUDY
COMBINED WITH THE EXPERIENCE
OF YEARS.

He asks us to count the Fs in this sentence only once. This sentence is designed to test your perception. Most readers find only three of the six Fs. Finding three Fs is poor; four is fair, five is good, and all six is excellent.

Our perception is often influenced by what we think is important. The *of*s in Dr. Leedy's test sentence are not important to most people, so they miss the Fs in them even though their eyes *see* these words. A newborn child sees things mechanically in the same way that older people do, but the child perceives very little because at that age things have little or no meaning. As the child grows older and finds meaning in the things he sees, he will begin to perceive them.

Perception is affected by our culture and environment and by the way we experience them. William Seabrook, in *Magic Island,* his delightful and fascinating book about his experiences in Haiti, relates a story of a missionary who was trying to convert the natives in a certain part of the island to Roman Catholicism. For several years he was entirely unsuccessful. Then one day he had a statue of a certain saint mounted in the front yard of his mission. A few days later natives began to flock to the mission bringing all kinds of gifts in the form of fruit, vegetables, beads, and so on. The priest could not understand this sudden change of interest. He later found out that the statue in the front yard of the mission closely resembled one of the native deities. As a result, the natives thought that the priest had converted to their beliefs. This is an example of visual perception, tied in with cultural values.

Our attitudes, habits, and values affect the way we perceive. For example, when a clothing designer walks into a room, he will immediately look at the people there to see what they are wearing; he may not notice much about how the room is furnished. On the other hand, an antique dealer will immediately look around the room for antique objects and furniture, and he may not notice much about what the people there are wearing.

Perception is of course affected by physical impairment. If we need glasses or a hearing aid and don't wear these aids, we will certainly not be able to take full advantage of these sense organs.

3 VISUAL PERCEPTION, ILLNESS, FATIGUE, AND DRUGS

Illness, fatigue, and drugs all affect our ability to see things clearly and to know what we are seeing. This is clear for the automobile driver who must be alert at all times. He must wear glasses if he needs them, and he must, above all, avoid alcohol and other drugs. He must not drive if he is tired or ill, because these states have an effect similar to that of drugs or alcohol. Both of these states slow down perception so that more things take on the aspect of a magic act, and we see things not as they really are.

Drugs, known as *hallucinogens* (such as LSD and mescaline), cause the users to have vivid pictorial experiences. They see unreal images with exaggerated colors. The following excerpts discuss this mental phenomenon.

> One subjective experience that is frequently reported is a change in visual perception. When the eyes are open, the perception of light and space is affected: colors become more vivid and seem to glow; the space between objects becomes more apparent, as though space itself had become "real," and surface details appear to be more sharply defined. Many people feel a new awareness of the physical beauty of the world, particularly of visual harmonies, colors, the play of light and the exquisiteness of detail.

The article goes on to describe vivid images appearing in the mind when the eyes are closed. It refers to hallucinations ranging from abstract forms to exotic creatures in imaginary time and place situations.

> The "hellish" experiences include an impression of blackness accompanied by feelings of gloom and isolation, a garish modification of the flowing colors observed in the "heavenly" phase, a sense of sickly greens and ugly dark reds. The subject's perception of his own body may become unpleasant: his limbs may seem to be distorted or his flesh to be decaying; in a mirror his face may appear to be a mask, his smile a meaningless grimace. Sometimes all human movements appear to be mere puppetry, or everyone seems to be dead. These experiences can be so disturbing that a residue of fear and depression persists long after the effects of the drug have worn off.[1]

4 EYE TESTS

It is important for everyone to have an eye test at least once a year, even if there is no obvious visual defect. An *oculist* or *ophthalmologist*, a doctor specializing in eye problems, should be consulted for this purpose. If you suspect that you have some problem with your eyes, or if reading gives you a headache, then by all means consult an eye doctor. In fact, certain diseases not actually related to vision can be detected by an eye examination. Eye defects, even slight ones, can reduce your efficiency

1. Frank Barron, Murray E. Jarvik, and Sterling Bunnell, Jr., "The Hallucinogenic Drugs," *Scientific American,* Vol. 210, No. 4, April, 1964, pp. 33-35.

on the job or in school. Many times a child's poor performance at school is the result of poor vision. Once the child's vision is corrected with glasses, his school work may show marked improvement.

Nearsightedness

A person suffering from *myopia,* or nearsightedness, has trouble seeing at a distance. He will not be able to see the 20-20 line on an eye chart; if his case is mild he may be able to see the 20-30 or 20-40 lines. As the case worsens, only the upper lines of the chart will be visible. And in extreme cases none of the lines on the chart will come into view. Myopia usually begins around age 12 and continues to get worse until about age 25. Of course, there are exceptions: some very small children are myopic, and in some cases myopia doesn't begin until the early 20s. The worst cases begin in early childhood.

Myopia seems to be caused by an elongation, or lengthening, of the eyeball. In fact, an ever-so-slight lengthening of the eyeball can cause severe myopia. This lengthening of the eyeball causes images to be focused in front of the retina, not on it. In most cases, corrective lenses can be used to focus the image on the retina. Thus, if he wears glasses, a myopic person can see almost as well as a person with normal vision. He will be able to drive a car and see theatrical performances and movies without any noticeable difficulty. If a person has only a small degree of myopia, say 20-30 vision, the lenses in his eyes will make a partial compensation toward 20-20 vision without the aid of corrective lenses. The lenses used to correct myopia are *concave;* that is, they are thinnest at the middle and widest at the edges.

Farsightedness

Farsightedness, or *hyperopia,* is the opposite of myopia. A mildly hyperopic person may see the 20-15 line on the eye chart with pride, but most hyperopic people have problems seeing *both* far and near. Again, mildly hyperopic eyes will compensate so that reading is possible, but if a hyperopic person reads continually without glasses, he will get headaches. The hyperopic eye is too short; images are focused behind the retina. A *convex* lens, which is thickest at the middle and thinnest at the edges, is used to correct hyperopia by focusing the image on the retina. A convex lens is a magnifying glass. Like a myopic person, a hyperopic person can live a normal life if he is fitted with corrective lenses.

There is a visual defect called *presbyopia* that strikes most people around age 45. The root, *presby,* comes from an ancient Greek word, *presbus,* meaning *old man.* Presbyopia can strike before 45 or a few years later. If a person has had normal vision up to his middle years, presbyopia will appear as a form of farsightedness; that is, the person will begin to have difficulty reading his newspaper or telephone directory at the normal distance of 12 inches. Presbyopia does not affect distance vision, only close vision. A presbyopic person will find that he has to hold his newspaper farther out. Presbyopia is not caused by a deformation of the eyeball, as in the cases of myopia and hyperopia, but by the failure of the lenses in the eyes to focus on close objects. It is actually a muscular disability caused by aging. As in the treatment of hyperopia, a convex lens is used to correct the difficulty, but for presbyopia, the corrective lenses are needed only for reading or doing closeup work. The presbyopic person removes his glasses when he has finished reading, but the hyperopic person does not because his glasses correct his problem of seeing both far and near. When the hyperopic or myopic person reaches middle age, he also gets presbyopia. He finds that with his distance correction, he cannot read, so he has to use another set of glasses or wear bifocals. A middle-aged person with a mild case of myopia may be able to remove his glasses to read.

Astigmatism

When the lenses in the eyes are not spherical or symmetrical, the condition is called *astigmatism.* Thus, if an astigmatic person were to look at the spokes of a wheel, some of the spokes would appear blurred, while others would appear clearly. Accordingly, astigmatism is tested by having the patient look at a chart containing two perpendicular lines. The doctor slowly rotates the chart until one of the lines appears blurred. This will indicate the *axis* where the deformation of the lens occurs. Since the shape of the lens is independent of the length of the eyeball or the operation of the lens muscles, astigmatism may accompany myopia, hyperopia, and presbyopia. It is also possible that only one eye may have astigmatism, myopia, hyperopia, or a combination of defects. Presbyopia, however, usually affects both eyes.

Other Eye Defects

Night blindness, or *nyctalopia,* is the inability to see under conditions of dim lighting, such as at night. It is also called "moon blindness." The opposite of nyctalopia is *hemeralopia,* or day blindness, which is the inability to see clearly in bright light, particularly daylight. Neither nyctalopia nor hemeralopia can be helped by corrective lenses, but sometimes these conditions are improved with vitamin A.

Color blindness affects the ability of the eye to distinguish between certain colors. Dr. John Dalton, the celebrated philosopher, is considered to have "discovered" the visual defect, first in himself and later in others. He wrote about his own color blindness in the *Transactions of the Manchester Society* in 1794. Of the seven colors of the rainbow, he could

The first photograph shows the effects of myopia or nearsightedness, the second shows how objects appear to a farsighted or hyperopic person, and the third shows the blurred zones in the line of vision that are characteristic of astigmatism.

Marsha Cohen

distinguish only yellow, blue, and possibly violet. He saw no difference at all between red and green, so that he "thought the color of a laurel leaf the same as that of a stick of red sealing-wax." The story goes that once, when he was attending a Quaker meeting, he dressed carefully in the customary drab-colored garments worn by the group at that time, but wore a pair of flaming red stockings "to match"! Dalton's report of his case and the cases of 20 other people with the same problem received such recognition that the name "Daltonism" was briefly considered for the defect. There were, however, a number of objections, and the term "color blindness" was adopted.

The most common form of color blindness is called *dichromatism,* which is the inability to differentiate between two colors. Color blindness and night and day blindness affect a person's work more than any of the other visual defects so far mentioned.

Strabismus is a muscular defect of the eyes. One eye cannot focus with the other on an object because of an imbalance of the eye muscles. When the eyes are turned inward toward the nose, the condition is called *cross-eye;* when the eyes turn outward, the condition is called *walleye.* Mild cases are corrected by exercises and corrective lenses, but severe cases usually require surgery. These conditions may affect one eye and not the other, but the effect is the same. Strabismus usually occurs at an early age.

Many firms, to protect themselves under workmen's compensation laws, give routine eye tests to newly hired employees. Other firms use visual examinations to select employees for work that requires close eye work. A few firms give tests every year without charge and furnish glasses at cost to any employee needing them.

Business has a practical interest in helping workers improve their eyesight. Good eyesight is essential for accuracy, production, and safety. It also increases the general well-being of the individual. Poor vision causes tiredness, headaches, twitching eyelids, and, at times, reddening of the whites of the eyes.

5 ARE YOU RIGHT-EYED OR LEFT-EYED?

Most people depend on one eye more than the other: some are right-eyed, others are left-eyed. This condition can be compared to right- or left-handedness, but whether a person is right- or left-handed does not affect the favoring of one eye or the other.

There are tests for determining which eye is favored. For example, simple trial-and-error tests can be made by the individual to decide whether material being copied should be placed on the right or left side of the typewriter for easier seeing.

A better test can be made by looking at an object on the opposite side of a large room through the big end of a short megaphone. (One can be made from a sheet of paper bent into the shape of a cone.) Hold the big end tight to your face so that both eyes are included, and look through the small end at a distant object. Now close your right eye. If the object disappears, you were favoring your right eye. If you can still see it with your right eye closed, you are favoring your left eye. In some cases neither eye is favored.

It has been found that the best angle for copy to be placed on a typist's desk is a tilt of about 40 degrees from the level of the desk. This rule applies no matter which eye is favored. Dr. Vance T. Littlejohn, head of the department of business administration at the Woman's College of the University of North Carolina, discovered that typists felt more fatigue when the copy was flat on the desk and less fatigue when the copy was held at a 40-degree tilt, which is approximately perpendicular to the line of vision.

6 EYE EXERCISES AND HYGIENE

Every half hour or so a person who uses his eyes heavily at work or at school should rest his eyes by looking into the distance or to the other side of the room. Closing the eyes for a few moments is also restful, but don't let your employer get the impression that you are falling asleep on the job!

Alternate your fine and coarse eye work. If work has to be done that is closer than about a foot from your eyes, use a magnifying glass or special glasses.

A good exercise to do after close work is to rotate your eyes. Move them slowly around a large, imaginary circle. Then move them from the lower left to the upper right a few times; then from the lower right to the upper left. Move them along a straight line from left to right a few times. These exercises will help to strengthen your eye muscles.

Excessive use of tobacco is hard on the eyes. Television and movies are about as hard on the eyes as the same amount of time spent doing close reading. Reading on buses and trains is also hard on the eyes because of vibration and bouncing; limit such reading to skimming newspaper headlines. The less motion in the field of vision, the better for the eyes.

People with blue or gray eyes have to be more careful of bright light, especially sunlight, than do those with brown or black eyes. Shaded glasses can be helpful. But direct sunlight is too bright for anyone to read by.

When you get something in your eye, go to the first-aid room or to a physician. Don't put anything into your eyes except a weak solution of boric acid, about ¼ teaspoon to 1 cup of water. The water must be boiled to remove bacteria, germs, and other impurities, and it should be allowed to cool to room temperature before being used.

Scaly eyelids, usually a result of nutritional deficiencies, or a sty, a tiny boil on the eyelid, may be painful or annoying, but these problems are not serious if properly treated. Don't poke with your fingers, but go to the first-aid room or to a physician for treatment.

Inadequate diet may cause temporary discomfort in reading. Usually, in such cases, the eyes need vitamin A. Butter and carrots are a good source of vitamin A. Other fresh vegetables, except potatoes, may contain some vitamin A also.

After high school age is reached, it is wise to have an eye examination at least once a year, whether or not you wear glasses. Change of vision takes place so gradually that you become used to the condition and do not realize that you are using extra effort to see, even to see poorly. Be sure to select a doctor who tests for *convergence,* the coordinated movement of the eyes.

As we turn to our discussion of reading efficiency, keep in mind the importance of the condition of your eyes. Eye difficulty may be one of the reasons for reading difficulty, and unless the eyes are properly cared for, any program for improved reading skills, no matter how intense, is futile.

7 A CASH INVESTMENT IN READING

Morris Fishbein was a brilliant medical student. Speed reading was one of his accomplishments. His colleagues reported that he could read an entire paragraph at one glance and sometimes a page in two glances. When he was a young doctor, the American Medical Association appointed him editor for their weekly journal, a post he held for more than 30 years. To keep himself busy, he started other medical journals. When he retired, the association had to appoint four people to do his work.

Thomas Edison did not have many years of schooling, but his wide reading made him well-educated. His deafness made it easy for him to concentrate on reading. In his laboratory he built up one of the best scientific libraries of his time. He once said:

> When I want to discover something, I begin by reading up everything that has been done along that line in the past—that's what all those books in the library are for. I use these books to prevent waste of time and money, by not doing again the things that have already been done or tried out by others. I generally recommend only those books that are written by men who actually describe things plainly, simply, and by analogy with things everybody knows.

Many people read less than 200 words a minute, while an efficient reader can often cover more than 700 words a minute, and he can glean more from his rapid reading than the slow reader. One of the chief problems in reading is a limited vocabulary: trying to read with a poor vocabulary is like trying to do arithmetic without a good knowledge of the multiplication table. Another contribution to inefficient reading is reading "to kill time." Such reading is not properly directed, and thus sloppy reading habits are acquired. One tends under such conditions to dawdle, and this, in turn, encourages slowness. Many people spend a whole evening reading details in newspapers in an aimless way. This should be avoided. A newspaper or magazine contains the type of material that should be skimmed, unless there is a particular article you want to read in detail.

A well-known ancient Chinese philosopher, Chang Ch'ao, once wrote: "Reading books in one's youth is like peeping at the moon through a crevice. Reading books in middle age is like looking at the moon in one's courtyard. And reading books in old age is like playing the moon on an open terrace. This is because the depth of benefits of reading varies in proportion to the depth of one's own experience."

Efficient reading causes much less eyestrain than inefficient reading. The efficient reader can cover much more material and understand it much better than the inefficient reader. Efficient reading will markedly help to improve the student's grades, and it increases a person's ability to work more efficiently on the job. Many firms have given training courses in reading to their employees. The results of such training have been dramatic.

How can well-educated adults, who have been reading since they were six years old, be retrained to double their reading speed? Haven't their many years of practice made them as perfect as they can be? They have had years of practice, true enough, but it has obviously been the wrong kind of practice. It is that way with many things—the wrong kind of practice only reinforces bad habits.

 ## READ FOR MEANING AND TO GAIN SPEED

The eyes and mind cooperate in reading—the eyes do the seeing, and the mind does the understanding. The aim in reading is to grasp meaning quickly and easily. *Look for the meaning,* not for the spelling. Reading and spelling are two different arts. Here are three lines that can be read with equal ease:

> p r h w
> auto single
> The apple is big and red.

The first line is meaningless. The second line is composed of two unrelated words totaling ten letters. The third line is made up of six related words that make sense, but it is 19 letters long; 19 letters that make sense can be read as easily as 4 that have no meaning. That is one secret of speed reading: *read for meaning.*

Do you realize that you are blind much of the time while reading? Watch your eyes move while you look in a mirror. You cannot see them while they move, for the eyes are as good as blind while in motion. This is why police are trained to read license numbers of moving automobiles with a quick glance, rather than trying to follow the moving license plate. The same principle applies to inspecting products on a moving conveyor or proofreading copy on a moving typewriter carriage.

When you read a line of print, the eye jumps from one place to another along the line. It does not move steadily. It jumps and pauses. It is only during the pauses that the eye sees. During the jumps, while the eye is moving, everything is blurred.

A poor reader pauses much more often than an efficient reader— about twice as many times. The poor reader looks at each letter to catch the word. The efficient reader senses a word from a *quick look at its general form.* You may have noticed a person moving his lips while he is reading "silently." This is one obvious habit that gives away the poor reader. The very poor reader even tries to spell each word by looking at each of its letters one at a time. When you look at a picture, you don't repeat each object in the picture to yourself, but you look at the *whole* picture seemingly at once. When you look at a picture of a man, you don't say, "Now this is his head, that is his nose . . . , his eye . . . , his other eye. . . ." The same rule can be applied to reading. Pretend that a sentence is a picture: look at it and *see* its meaning. The old saying "slow but sure" does not apply to reading. Rapid readers get more sense from their reading. When a slow reader's speed is increased by training, and when he continues to practice, he will learn more from what he is reading.

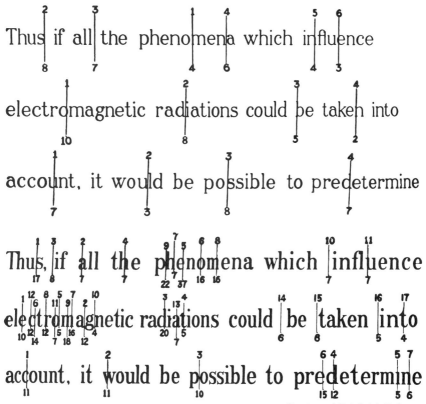

Courtesy of Col. Ralph C. Cooper

These two illustrations show the eye activity of two readers. The vertical lines mark eye pauses; the numerals at the top of the vertical lines show the order in which eye pauses were made; and the bottom numerals show in thirtieths of seconds how long the eye paused. Which reader would you consider the more efficient?

Several types of machines are used to train people to read better. Some of these consist of shutter devices similar to a camera shutter. They flash a phrase or a number on a screen for a fraction of a second. At first, short numbers or single words are used. Then longer numbers and phrases are flashed. The participant is asked to write the word, phrase, or number down as he sees it, and then he is told the correct words or numbers and asked to compare them with what he has written. Thus the participant can measure his improvement. At first he will make many mistakes as the words and size of numbers increase. Also, the speed of the machine is increased.

Another machine holds a page of a book over which a curtain is drawn steadily a line at a time. This forces the reader to move quickly from line to line; the reader must speed up to keep up with the moving curtain.

Reading can be improved without using a mechanical apparatus. After all, the essential apparatus is your own head and eyes. Here are some suggestions for improving your reading now.

Read phrases, not words. Look at more words during each eye pause, and concentrate directly on words, not on letters.

Look at the upper half of a word, not the lower half.

Look at the beginnings of words, not at the endings.

Keep your eyes moving from left to right. Eliminate backward moves. Train yourself to understand the first time you see the words.

Push yourself to catch the meaning. Try to read a line in a newspaper with only two eye pauses. Strive to cover a line in a book in no more than five eye pauses.

Keep your lips and tongue motionless. Control any tendency to spell or pronounce words to yourself. Avoid "inner speech," too — that is, thinking words to yourself. If you read fewer than 350 words a minute, you are probably saying the sounds in some way. Reading seldom becomes silent reading until the rate is 400 words a minute or faster.

Keep alert to catch the meaning faster. Try to read five words faster each succeeding day for a month by catching the meaning of increasingly longer phrases. Look for ideas; don't expect them to hit you on the head. Reading with the radio on slows speed and lowers comprehension: distractions cause bad reading habits.

Keep at it until faster reading is a habit. First try to reach a goal of 400 words a minute; then increase this goal.

10 THERE ARE DIFFERENT TYPES OF READING

A secretary reads the incoming mail for sense, but a stenographer, typist, or proofreader must read for punctuation and spelling, as well as for sense. A student must read a textbook in a way that is different from the way he might read a magazine or novel. Each time we read something, we must consider the purpose of our reading: business reports, newspapers, novels, textbooks, and other reading matter are all read differently because our intention in reading each of these types of material is different. In addition to reading literature, we may be called on to "read" blueprints, schematics of electrical apparatus, charts, and graphs. Whatever we read, we must strive for speed and maximum comprehension. The following rates should be minimum goals for reading development.

	Words per Minute
Study	200
Serious books or textbooks	250
Scholarly journals or business magazines	300
Fiction	400

It is important to choose the right places for reading and the right things to read. Save your eyes: avoid reading on buses and trains. If you must read in these vehicles, don't read anything serious that requires deep thought. Save your time and brains: don't try to read everything. Be selective: read only the newspaper or magazine articles that are of interest. Look at the headlines first to find out what interests you.

11 SKIMMING

Skimming is very fast, but it is not done for accuracy. This is the way to read most newspaper articles. Hit the "high spots" in the headlines. Try to look at the first paragraph of a newspaper article at the first glance. We skim when we are looking for a name in a telephone directory or a stock-market report. With practice you will be able to skim over five or six lines at a glance.

Skimming does not improve your reading speed because skimming is not intended for use in studying or reading serious material. Skimming is like going to a file and looking up a name. If the name you want starts with K, you go directly to the K file. You find the K file by skimming over the other files until you reach it.

Skimming can be helpful as a preliminary to studying. It may be a good idea to skim through a chapter in your textbook to see the headings, key phrases, pictures, and charts. This will give you an idea what is ahead so that you will be in a better position to read carefully the important things. That is the reason for putting the section "What This Chapter Is About" at the beginning of each chapter in this book. You may want to underline the important material with a colored pencil or use a yellow marker on the sentences and phrases that you want to notice when you reread a chapter for more meaning.

12 BUILDING WORD POWER

Many writers prefer to use one long word to convey the meaning of several smaller words. Looking up unfamiliar words in the dictionary slows reading considerably. Thus, the more words you know, the better your reading will be.

Anyone aiming for an executive position especially needs to have a good vocabulary. The executive must often read complicated reports that contain technical words. In many cases, an executive is called upon to translate reports into simpler language for others to read.

On the other hand, sales literature is more appealing to a wider audience if small, simple words are used. Large words often seem pompous to the reader of such material. For example, one paint manufacturer lost sales because his house paint was advertised as being "for exterior use." Many of the readers of the ad apparently didn't know that "exterior" meant "outside." Sales jumped almost immediately after the wording was changed to "for outside use."

John Wanamaker, the founder of a Philadelphia department store, kept a list of new words each day and looked up the meanings every evening. Some evenings, he would continue to read the dictionary as if it were a mystery story. He started this habit when he was ten years old and kept it up for more than sixty years. Some people have to try harder than others to build up a vocabulary. This is due to differences that seem to be largely inborn. Women, as a rule, excel in the ability to learn words.

Make it a habit to look up all new words, words that you are not familiar with, in a dictionary. If you don't have a dictionary immediately available, write the new words down on a piece of paper and save it until you have a chance to look them up. It is easy to develop an interest in words; you might look at the derivation of a new word to see where it comes from. You will see that English is made up of many different languages: Latin, French, German, Dutch, Italian, Celtic, and others. Look for similarities between words, for this will also help you remember them better. Study the way in which a new word is used in the material you are reading, and then try to make up a sentence using the word. If you follow these suggestions, you will find your vocabulary growing, and the more you read, the more words you will learn.

320
Vocabulary score
260

Most influential executives   Least influential executives

Data from Maj. Norman E. Green

Anyone aiming for an executive position should try to develop a good vocabulary. A study of Air Force officers showed a high correlation between their vocabulary scores and their influence on others, as measured by a vote among their colleagues.

13 LEGIBILITY

Legibility means readability; that is, easy to read. In printing, legibility is influenced by the size of the type. Newspaper type is too small for easy reading. The size of type used in advertising booklets and brochures is usually good for comfortable reading.

The length of lines also influences ease of reading. Newspaper line length is easier to read than book line length. A typewritten line across an 8½- by 11-inch letterhead is too long; a sheet 5¼ by 8½ inches, the so-called "half size," allows for a more legible line. Most professional advertisements use short line lengths.

Space between lines makes for better legibility. Lines that are crowded together are difficult to read. A double-spaced letter is more easily read than a single-spaced one. Extra spacing between paragraphs also contributes to reading ease.

There are many different type styles and sizes. Books on printing, which can be found in your local public library, show most of the currently used type styles. The fancier type styles, although more artistic, are more difficult to read than the plain ones. Lower-case letters are easier to read than capitals. This is probably because we are more accustomed to them. Occasionally a fancy type style is used in a trade-mark by an advertiser, but this does not require much reading. It would be risky for an advertiser to use an unusual and unfamiliar type style in the body of an ad that describes a new product in detail.

The color of the paper and the ink used for printing contributes to legibility. Black ink on soft, white paper is good, but there have been experiments using soft shades of off-white paper with a slight green, brown, or gray cast. The starkness of black on white can be tiring to the eyes, but paper with a distinct color is also difficult to read because the color does not contrast with the black ink as much as white does. Glossy paper like that used in most magazines is harder to read because it reflects light like a mirror. Newspapers and telephone directories are particularly difficult to read because of the grade of the paper used and its dark color. Material typed on dark paper can be made more legible by extra space between the lines or by the use of large type. It is always good to use a fresh ribbon and fresh carbon paper.

Legibility was the subject of early psychological experiments. Nevertheless, the findings of this pioneer research are still being applied. Dr. John W. Baird, a psychologist at Clark University, was asked to find a way to save space in printing the New York City telephone directory, as the directory was becoming too thick. Dr. Baird, who had done experiments concerning vision and color blindness, tested the four possible arrangements that are shown in the illustration on page 123. He found that arrangement D had the shortest "look-up time." The D plan was adopted and is still used for practically all big-city telephone books. Dr. Baird's findings were reported in the first issue of the *Journal of Applied Psychology* in March 1917.

The legibility of instrument panels in automobiles and aircraft has become a specialty of *engineering psychology,* which applies psychological methods to the design of machines so that they match human requirements as closely as possible. The armed forces and manufacturers of instrument panels employ professional psychologists for studying the problems of legibility. Some of the findings about how dials and similar displays can be made more legible are summarized in the illustration on page 124.

14 THE LIGHT MUST BE RIGHT

The eyes will adapt themselves to unfavorable conditions and can be used well for a time. Abraham Lincoln studied law by the flickering light from a fireplace, but that was not easy for his eyes. Poor lighting requires more input on the part of the worker. As eye fatigue increases, there is an increase in involuntary blinking. There is also a loss in *visual acuity,* or sharpness of visual perception, when the eyes are used continuously

A. Three-Column Page, Ordinary

Skidmore G W, Res.....63 Bay 20th. Bath Bch 878-J
Skidmore Jas R, Res.....60 Ray. Jamaica 483-W
Skidmore Dr Joel L, Dentist, 707 Church. Rich Hill 498
Skidmore Jos N, Musicn. 562 Central av. Bushwick
Skidmore L R, Res.....573 Clifton pl. Prospect 4514
Skidmore Lewis P, Res..381 Vanderbilt. Prospect 3759-W
Skidmore M G, Res.....73 Clifton pl. Prospect 3774-W
Skidmore Thos, Res.....644 E. 4th. Flatbush 8358
Skidmore Wm S, Res..258 Arlington av. Cypress 1928-J
Skillman Anna L, Res.181 Berkeley pl. Prospect 3825-W

Sleaster Fredk, Res....2047 E 15th. Coney Isl 1795
Slee A M, Grad Nurse..102 Pierrepont. Bedford 4333
Slee Arthur W, MD, Res..97 Halsey. Bedford 7496
Slee Mrs E G, Res.....465 Kosciusko. Bushwick 409-R
Slee John B, Architect....154 Montague. Main 4224
Slee & Bryson, Archts..154 Montague. Main 4224
Sleeper Chas E, Res..815 Sterling pl. Bedford 1088-B
Sleeper T K, Res......135 53d. Boro Park 1088-W
Sleeper Wm H, Plumbg. Heat. 439 Hart. Bushwick 1939-W
  Residence........945 Greene av. Bushwick 1404-J

Slutzky Max, Grocef......1746 Bath av. Bath Bch 317
Slutzky Wm, Dental Lbtry..284 S 9th. Wmsburg 4754
Sluus J H, Res......196 Barclay. Flushing 1330
Smack Mrs A, Res......552 E 5th. Flatbush 3967
Smack Alfred D, Res....586 Quincy. Bushwick 3465-J
Smale M H, LithoTrnsfr Papr. 27 McDug'l. East N Y 1414
Small Bert J, Barber......68 7th av. Prospect 5553
Small C L, Res......Murray. Flushing 7733
Small Chas, Res......1031 Prospect pl. Bedford 2463-R
Small Chas E, Res. 432 74th. Bay Ridge 2629

B. Four-Column Page, Ordinary

Sharon Miss A R, r. 39 Murray. Flushing 2291 R
Slira Alford, Agent, 420 Greenway. South 4381
Skeffington John J, r. 10 Parkside ct. Flatbush 9648
Skehan Chas, r. 177 Jackson. Greenpnt 1667
Skehan Homer I, RI Est, 189 Mutigue Hamilton 2446
Skelbeuger Rev D W, r. Prospect av. RichHill 1101
Skellett Mrs Mary, r. College Pl, LI Flushing 1273W
Skelley Mrs W J, r. 1339 Pacific. Bedford 5373
Skellinger H L, r. 502 Bainbridge. Bushwick 5031W
Skelly Mrs E C, r. 397 I. South 4262W

Slattery Miss Mary K, r. 705 Prsdnt av Bushwick 5320
Slattery P J, r. 115 Crystal. Flatbush 9960
Slattery Peter A, r. 237 Rugby rd. Hamilton 2446
Slattery Thos F, r. 327 Oth. BayRidge 1135
Slattery Wm F, r. East Elmhurst, LI Prospect 1757 J
Slauchter Miss M F, r. 3001 Fulton. Newtown 1482M
Slauchter Wm H, MD, r. 1406 Av H. RichHill 3667 J
Slauson K W, r. 117 Montague. Prospect 4300
Slaven Mrs E, r. 1360 Park pl. Prospect 2734 J
Slavin Electric Co. Seaside Walk. Flatbush 2100

C. Four-Column Page, Indented

Skivsen Miss Anna, r. 154 Prspct av. South 1062 J
Sklar J Mfg Co, Surgl Insts, 133 Flyd Wmsburg 2329
Sklar J, r. 661 Willoughby av. East N Y 3484
Sklar Jos, Cabinet Mkr, 672 Hpkinsn av Sunset 3710
Skarck Albert, Furniture, 39. RichHill 1255W
Sidarz Martin, r. 327 Spruce. Greenpnt 471
Skilool P & Co, Poultry, 228 N 9. Bushwick 3371
Skohlos H, Grocer, 201 Sumner av. Bedford 8310M
Stog Carl G, r. 148 Pacific. Bedford 1529W
Skeglund J V, r. 1341 Bedford av.

D. Four-Column Page, Leaded

Skeetes S H, r. 896 Brooklyn av. Flatbush 8699 J
Skiho Kennels, 341 Montan av. Stagg 4195
Skidmore Abram W, r. 44 Crescent. Far Rock 86
Skidmore C J, r. 95 82. BayRidge 741M
Skidmore Mrs F, r. 22 McDonough. Bedford 4593 R
Skidmore G W, r. 63 Bay 20. Bath Bch 878 J
Skidmore Jas R, r. 60 Ray. Jamaica 483W
Skidmore Dr Joel L, Dntst, 707 Chrch RichHill 498
Skidmore Jos N, Musicn, 562 Central av Bushwick 4514

Slowig Wm, Hotel, Woodside, LI Newtown 269
Sluiter A C, Butcher, 64 Main. Flushing 207
Sluiter A C, r. 188 Madison av. South 2436
Sluter N F, r. 6910. Bedford 4355
Sluter H, r. 980 Lincoln pl. Flatbush 5645
Sluth Martin, r. 577 E 8. Wmsburg 3022
Slutzky Bros, Prod, 228 Selgel. Main 1940
Slutzky Nathan I, MD, r. 344 Jay. Midwood 7031
Slutzker Edward, r. 1025 E 14.
Slutzker Barnett, Staty, Cgrs

Sloan Engineering Co, 246 Hall.. Prospect 4764
  Carwe Dpt, 236 Lafayette av. Prospect 4764
Sloan Franci, H, r. 261 Hancock. Bedford 526
Sloan Frank T, r. 234 E 3...... Flatbush 1443M
Sloan Henry L, 351 Jay..... Main 8185
Sloan Herman J, Meats, 165 Frankin Greenpnt 3059
Sloan Jas, Hay, Feed, 1063 Atlntc av Prospect 79
Sloan Miss Mary E, r. 5623.. South 2552 J
Sloan Robert S, r. Woodmere, LI.. Woodmere 3290
Sloan William C, Elec Cntlr

Slater H, r. 880 Lincoln pl....... Bedford 5816W
Sluth Martin, r. 577 E 8. Flatbush 5419
Slutzky Bros. Prof, 28 Selgel. Wmsburg 894
Sluty Nathai I, MD, r. 344 Jay.. South 1805
Slutzke Edward, r. 1025 E 14.. Prospect 6056W
Slutzker Barnett, Staty, Cgrs Coneyisl 1795
Slutzky I, Cgrs, 531 Flushing av. Main 4333
Slutzky Louis, r. 627 Marcy av. Bedford 7496
   Bushwick 409 R

Smallwood Thos Jr, r. 657 Putn av. Prospect 6636 J
Smart F B, r. 132 Jamaica av. Flushing 633
Smart H C T, r. 398 Lafayette av. Prospect 6994
Smart III T, r. 193 Keap. Wmsburg 4573
Smart Shop, MensFurn, 141 Flthsh av Prospect 6732
Smart T E, Hotel, College Pt, LI. Flushing 1950
Smart W J, r. 21 Decatur. Bedford 3475 R
Smart Wm C, r. 1st. Bayside 2872-W
Smart Wm E Jr, r. Woodhaven, LI. RichHill 2935
Smedley J H, r. Central av. Woodmere 3633W

Smith Dr Alfred E, Dentist, 415 Fltn Main 1081W
Smith Alfred H, MD, r. Springfld, LI Springfld 1881
Smith Allan C, r. 94 2d pl. Hamilton 1145 J
Smith Alvin C, r. 1085 Eastrn pkwy. Main 895
Smith Albnozo, Piano, 25 Flthsh av Bedford 4255
Smith Amelia, r. Highland av. Bayside 2983 R
Smith Amos A, r. 61 Pierrepont. Main 7733
Smith Mrs Andrew A, r. 436 Clusn av Prospect 2048
Smith Anna A, r. Van Sicklen. Coneyisl 2241W
Smith Miss Anna E, r. 413 DeKalb av Prospect 7606 J

Smith Agnes M, r. 18030. South 3756W
Smith Albert A, Electrician, 1426 58 BoroPark 3193W
Smith Albert A, r. 4814. South 322
Smith Albert E, r. 113 St Marks av. Prospect 5880
Smith Albert J, r. 973 E 10. Midwood 4181 J
Smith Albert P, r. 881 New Yorkav. Flatbush 1321W
Smith Dr Alfred E, Dentist, 415 Fltn Main 1081W
Smith Alfred H, MD, r. Springfld, LI Springfld 1831
Smith Allan C, r. 94 2d pl. Hamilton 1145 J

This early psychological test for legibility, designed by John W. Baird and reported in the first issue of the *Journal of Applied Psychology*, March, 1917, resulted in a design plan that is still being used for practically all big-city directories.

Good   Bad

Good   Good

Bad angle   Too high   Too low

Instrument dials should be made to match human requirements as closely as possible. The first row of figures shows that placing a control knob immediately below a dial will associate the two while placing all knobs at the bottom of the panel will allow the operator to adjust them without obscuring the dials with his arm. The next row points out that slight spacing between groups makes it easier to identify a dial. The bottom two rows of figures demonstrate the advantage of positioning instruments so that their faces are either at or a little below eye level and on a vertical surface.

Reproduced with permission from *Ergonomics of Automation* by A. T. Welford, Her Majesty's Stationery Office, London, 1960

for close work. The loss of acuity is most marked under poor lighting conditions, as shown in the table on page 125.

Here are eight conditions for good reading and working light:

1 Try to do your reading in a room with light-colored walls, window shades, and furnishings.
2 Keep windows, lighting fixtures, and walls clean.
3 Use small lights scattered evenly, rather than a few high-powered ones.
4 Eliminate glaring or shiny spots.
5 Have no light bulbs visible to the eye.
6 Allow 2½ watts per square foot for general lighting.

7 Have supplementary local lights for tasks requiring close eye work.

8 When in doubt, turn lights on—save your eyes, rather than the electricity.

A word of warning: avoid the use of direct local light; that is, avoid the situation where there is a bright light near your work, but the rest of the room or area is dim or dark. This type of lighting is undesirable because it causes eyestrain by blocking peripheral, or side, vision.

	Loss of Acuity, in Percent
After 3 hours of reading in:	
Good daylight	6
Totally indirect electric light	9
Semi-indirect electric light	72
Direct (gooseneck) electric light	81

SUGGESTIONS FOR FURTHER READING

Barron, Frank, Murray E. Jarvik, and Sterling Bunnell, Jr., "The Hallucinogenic Drugs," *Scientific American,* April, 1964, pp. 29–37.

Bond, Guy L., and Miles A. Tinker, *Reading Difficulties: Their Diagnosis and Correction,* New York: Appleton-Century-Crofts, 1967.

Chall, Jeanne S., *Learning to Read: The Great Debate,* New York: McGraw-Hill, 1967.

Gregory, R. L., *The Intelligent Eye,* New York: McGraw-Hill, 1970.

Leedy, Paul D., *Read With Speed and Precision,* New York: McGraw-Hill, 1963.

Morgan, C. T., *Physiological Psychology,* 3d ed., New York: McGraw-Hill, 1965.

Wooldridge, D. E., *The Machinery of the Brain,* New York: McGraw-Hill, 1963.

TO HELP YOU REMEMBER

1. Describe the vision process.
2. What is the difference between seeing and perceiving?
3. How does the use of hallucinogens affect visual perception?
4. Describe the most common eye defects and their treatment.

5. What should a person do to keep his eyes in good condition?
6. How do the eyes move during reading?
7. What are eight steps for gaining speed in reading?
8. When should skimming be used?
9. What factors influence legibility?
10. Give eight rules for good lighting.

WORKING WITH PEOPLE, DATA, OR THINGS

1. In his book *Improve Your Reading: A Guide to Greater Speed, Understanding, and Enjoyment,* Dr. Paul D. Leedy proposes certain skill-building techniques, one of which involves developing your visual span by practicing to see certain phrases getting wider and wider as you progress down the page.[2]

    1. Take a 3- by 5-inch card and put a small arrow about midway across the card, with the point of the arrow pointing to the edge of the card as in this illustration:

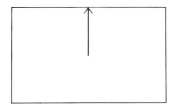

    2. You will find a black guide line running down the middle of [page 127] broken only by phrases of varying lengths. Place the card over the phrases, with the point of the arrow pointing to the black guide line.
    3. Draw the card down the page, so that the first phrase is visible. Be very careful to look only at the *point* of the arrow. Fix your attention on the point, but try to *see* on either side of this point, right *and* left, as far as possible. At first you may be able to see easily the *whole* phrase. If *so,* keep your eyes fixed on the arrow point at the center of the line. Move the card down to the next phrase, and the next, and so on, until you are aware that you are having difficulty seeing the ends of the lines. Try, try to see more. Try to push back the margins of your usable vision. This will widen your eye span. Do not let your eyes shift or steal a sidewise glance. Keep them glued to the center-line point. Work at this for five or ten minutes at a time. In each succeeding practice try to take in the whole phrase more rapidly, until you can see each of them with one quick glance.

2. Paul D. Leedy, *Improve Your Reading: A Guide to Greater Speed, Understanding, and Enjoyment,* McGraw-Hill, New York, 1956, pp. 61-63.

At the extreme right of each phrase you will find a figure. This is the width of the line. The numbers refer to the width in units of type of the phrase. Keep trying until you can see all of the phrases in one fixation. There are two sets of phrases for you to practice on. Alternate your practice. Work on the first group, then on the second. Your one aim in this exercise is to widen your eye span.

an old habit	12
habits to form	14
eyes on the line	16
look at the center	18
do a little each day	20
drill makes the reader	22
see with a wide eye span	24
steady practice helps much	26
try to do this when you read	28
look steadily at the mid-point	30
are you still seeing both edges?	32
if so, your eye span is excellent	34
learn to read	13
read everything	15
you are improving	17
practice this daily	19
stretch your vision	21
work only a few minutes	23
don't let your eyes shift	25
s-t-r-e-t-c-h your eye span	27
see more, and yet still more!	29
this is to help you read better	31
can you possibly see all of this?	33

How well did you do? Each time you work at this exercise, record [on a chart similar to the one] below the maximum span you were able to read. You will want to compare your achievement later with this, your initial attempt.

Date	Duration of Practice (Minutes)	Maximum Span Read
_____	_____	_____
_____	_____	_____
_____	_____	_____
_____	_____	_____

Average: _____   _____

2. This next test, also taken from Dr. Leedy's book, has to do with reading to follow directions (a common practice in business). To find your reading rate for the following directions you must use the following formula:

$$\frac{192 \text{ (total words)} \times 60 \text{ (seconds)}}{\text{reading time (seconds)}} = \text{wpm}$$

How Do I Get to City Hall?

A tourist drove into Centerville and asked a policeman stationed at Center Square how to get to City Hall. The policeman gave him the following directions:

Drive down this street immediately ahead of you. This is Main Street, running south. Proceed five blocks on Main Street, to the intersection of Washington Street. Turn left on Washington Street and proceed east four blocks. At that point you will enter a traffic circle, which has a fountain in the center of it. Drive around the traffic circle, to the right, not quite three-quarters of the distance around the circle from the point at which you entered. A street will emerge from the circle at this point, leaving the circle at an angle to the street on which you entered. This is Conway Street. Proceed along Conway Street two blocks. At this point you will come to a fork. Take the right-hand street at the fork. You are still on Conway Street. Drive two blocks to High Street. Turn right on High Street, one block to the intersection of Federal and High Streets. City Hall is on the northwest corner of Federal and High Streets.

Time: Minutes_____   Reading time in seconds: Seconds_____
Seconds_____   Total words: 192

How efficiently could you follow directions to get to City Hall? Draw a map of the route which the policeman outlined, marking all the points along the way which he mentioned as critical points.[3]

3.   One good reading habit that should help you gain speed in reading is to look only at the beginnings of familiar words instead of at the whole word. Read the following paragraph as fast as possible.

Men have long trave__ the seas without much knowl__ . One of the first to expl__ this fiel__ of scien__ was the great Amer__ , Benj__ Fran__ , who asked sail__ many ques__ and then chart__ their answ__ on a map to fash__ the first cru__ cha__ of the Gul__ Str__ . He char__ the coas__ bay and isl__ and map__ hund__ of strea__ and canals.

Since then, inqui__ have map__ curr__ , reefs, and depths which has led to a maze of oce__ rese__ .

THINGS TO DO

1.   Get your eyes tested, unless you have done so within the past year.
2.   Visit two large companies, and report what the employers in these firms do about eye tests and what measures they take to see that employees correct any problem.
3.   Analyze your work place or your study place for lighting problems and visual distractions. Develop a plan for the elimination or reduction of these problems. Be sure to keep in mind the kinds of reading that you do in the room.
4.   Begin today to keep a list of all new words you encounter during the course of the day, and look up the meanings of the words as soon as possible after seeing them, just as John Wanamaker did for more than sixty years. Record the words and their meanings in a notebook, and add to the list each day.

3.   Ibid., pp. 210 and 214.

LISTENING MORE EFFECTIVELY

7

What This Chapter Is About

1 WHAT IS SOUND?

A drumstick striking a cymbal produces a vibration that our ears distinguish as the *sound* of the cymbal. Sound vibrations move through the air much in the same way that ripples form circles around the point where a stone is dropped into still water. The ripples move outward from that point in ever-widening circles. Thus, we speak of "sound waves." The cause of the sound, in this case the striking of the cymbals, is like the rock entering the water. As soon as the cymbal is struck, invisible sound waves move outward in ever-widening circles that reach the eardrum, a thin tissue inside each ear that vibrates with each sound wave.

A sound wave is composed of a "peak" and a "trough," which can be thought of as the loudest and softest points of the wave, respectively. Scientists who study sound waves call one peak followed by a trough a *cycle,* and they measure sound by counting the number of cycles that occur in one second; thus, a particular sound, such as the one caused by the drumstick and cymbal, can be described in "cycles per second," which is abbreviated *cps.*

The *number of cycles per second,* or the *frequency* of sound vibrations, produces the *pitch.* Pitch is the highness or lowness of sound. The more cycles there are per second—in other words, the higher the frequency—the higher the pitch. We say that the human ear hears sound waves in the range between 20 and 20,000 cycles per second and is most sensitive to frequencies from 2,000 to 4,000 cycles per second.

The loudness of sound is called the *volume*; thus, the volume control on a radio makes the sound louder or softer. It does so by increasing or decreasing the *amplitude,* or height, of each individual sound wave, measured at the midpoint between the peak and trough of the wave.

The loudness of sound is measured in units called *decibels.* For example, a whisper could measure around 20 decibels, while a rock music group with the amplifiers turned up to full volume could measure over 100 decibels.

Regularly spaced waves are said to be *periodic,* and they produce musical *tones.* Noise is produced by *aperiodic* or irregularly produced waves. *Timbre* is a quality of tonal sounds that enables us to distinguish among them. If there were no timbre, we could not distinguish a violin from a flute or recognize the voices of our friends. Timbre is produced by partial waves that accompany the fundamental, pitch, producing waves.

2 HOW WE HEAR SOUND

One of the age-old questions has been: Is there a sound, if there is no one there to hear it? This question can be partly answered by the fact that sound waves do move through the air and displace it; however, without someone there to "receive" these waves as sound, they cannot be described as sound.

The outer ears—the appendages we see attached to both sides of our head—serve a larger purpose than just being supports for eyeglasses or earrings. In fact, they serve as traps for sound. They are like funnels; they guide the sound into the *middle ear* via the *auditory canal*, as shown in the figure on page 132. The middle ear begins at the eardrum. Incoming sound waves cause the eardrum to vibrate. The eardrum, in turn, activates three tiny bones, the *anvil, hammer,* and *stirrup,* so named because of their appearances. The last of these bones, the stirrup, transmits the sound vibrations to the *oval window,* a membrane that transmits these vibrations to the liquid of the inner ear.

There is a passage called the *Eustachian tube* between the middle ear and the throat area. One of its functions is to help balance the air pressure on the inner ear. You may have noticed when ascending in an airplane or in an elevator in a high building that your ears "pop." This discomfort can be alleviated by opening your mouth, chewing gum, or swallowing. These remedies help to equalize the pressure within the Eustachian tube and the pressure in the auditory canal.

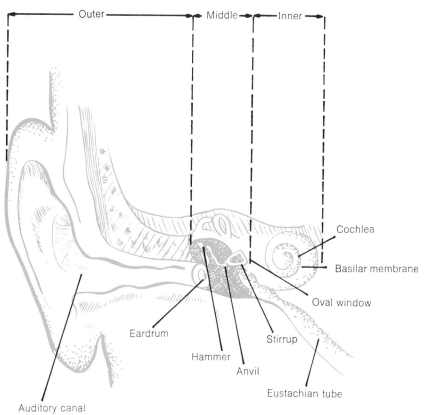

This diagram shows the major parts of the ear. Do you understand the basic functions of each part?

From the oval window, the sound waves are sent into the *cochlea,* or inner ear, which looks like a snail shell and is filled with fluid. Within the cochlea is the *basilar membrane,* which supports the primary receptors of sound, a group of minute hair cells known collectively as the *organ of Corti.* These hairs move with the vibrations of the fluid of the cochlea and activate the nerve cells beneath them. The *auditory nerve* transmits the sound waves in the form of impulses to the brain, just as the optic nerve transmits light waves to the brain.

3 HEARING BY *BONE CONDUCTION*

Dr. Georg von Bekesy, a senior research fellow in *psychophysics* at Harvard University, won the Nobel Prize in medicine in 1961. The field of psychophysics involves the study of the relationship between mental and physical processes. For many years Dr. Bekesy was a research scientist with the Hungarian telephone company, and his work on adapting telephone receivers to the mechanics of the human ear led to a revision of the theory of hearing. Dr. Bekesy wrote:

> Hearing by bone conduction plays an important role in the process of speaking. The vibrations of our vocal cords not only produce sounds which go to our ears via the air but also cause the body to vibrate, and the vibration of the jawbone is transmitted to the ear canal. When you hum with closed lips, the sounds you hear are to a large degree heard by bone conduction.[1]

Dr. Bekesy goes on to say that we hear both by air conduction and bone conduction, and this accounts for the fact that we do not hear ourselves as others hear us—the other person hears us only by air conduction. Dr. Bekesy notes that

> From this point of view we have to admire the astonishing performance of an opera singer. The singer and the audience hear rather different sounds, and it is a miracle to me that they understand each other so well. Perhaps young singers would progress faster if during their training they spent more time studying recordings of their voices.[2]

4 WHAT WE HEAR

As you can see, the structure of the ear is very delicate, and the ear's performance is nothing less than miraculous. We can get a good working picture of the ear by taking an *audiogram,* which is a test that shows how

1. Georg von Bekesy, "The Ear," *Scientific American,* August, 1957, p. 68.
2. Ibid, p. 70.

much pressure is on the eardrum. Amazingly, the audiogram curve is very similar for different members of the same family.

Fortunately, the ear is less sensitive at low frequencies (100 cps), otherwise we would hear disturbing vibrations within our own bodies. In fact, if you block one ear to airborne sound with your finger, you can hear the low tone made by contractions of the muscles in your finger and arm. If our ears were more sensitive, we would be able to hear vibrations in our heads with every step we take. Another amazing ability of the ear is to locate the position of a speaker without seeing him. Also, unlike the eye, the ear can suppress unwanted sounds. Hence, the ear is able to ignore all sounds except the ones purposefully attended to.

5 THE EFFECT OF AGE, NOISE, AND DRUGS ON HEARING

As we grow older our hearing acuity steadily drops. In fact, scientists have proved that the reception of high-frequency sounds by people in their 40s drops 80 cps every 6 months. This is understandable if we consider the fact that membranes and hair cells of the inner ear become less pliable and thus less able to vibrate.

Noises in our daily lives have been blamed for ulcers, high blood pressure, a high divorce rate, the high crime rate, nervous breakdowns, and even insanity. The effect of noise on the hearing organ is, in fact, most serious. Everyone knows that a very loud noise, such as the explosion of a cherry bomb or a firecracker, can cause momentary deafness. However, many people are unaware that repeated exposure to loud noises can cause permanent deafness.

Several studies have proved that frequencies up to 3,000 cps are the most important for understanding speech and that higher frequencies are judged as noise. Yet frequencies higher than 3,000 cps are needed to enjoy music. However, higher frequencies will cause hearing loss with advancing age. Both loudness and high frequency under working conditions sharpen the decline of hearing. Also, it has been shown that the effect of noise on hearing varies considerably from individual to individual.

Many people may not be aware of the fact that hallucinogens, drugs that cause changes in perception, can cause both temporary and permanent damage to hearing. A person under the influence of drugs may "hear" music or conversations that do not exist. Such deceptions are called *auditory hallucinations*. Although, in some instances, the hearing sensations caused by drugs may seem pleasant, like beautiful symphonies, the real danger lies in sensations that are destructive to the auditory nerves, for these can result in permanent deafness. Then, too, there is the danger of long-lasting emotional disturbance resulting from auditory sensations experienced during a "bad trip."

 **DEAFNESS**

At one time ear infections were the major cause of deafness; in fact, they caused death in many cases. Operations to remove the diseased part of the mastoid bone were everyday surgery-room assignments. Fortunately, antibiotics have greatly reduced the problem of infection; most ear infections are now treated and cured before surgery is necessary or before the infection results in hearing loss.

Today, deafness resulting from the destruction of the auditory nerve by exposure to noise, the use of drugs, and so on, is one of the most serious kinds of deafness. There is no cure or remedy for this type of deafness through surgery or by using antibiotics or hearing aids. This kind of impairment is permanent.

Otosclerosis is another kind of deafness, caused by a tumorous bone growth. This disease can usually be treated so that some hearing is restored. The tumor takes the form of a bone that is usually at the side of the skull near the middle ear. If the tumor doesn't affect the stirrup's ability to make its pistonlike movements when transmitting vibrations to the oval window, no harm is done. However, if the bone growth does immobilize the stirrup, it can block the hearing of airborne sound, leaving a person with only bone-conducted hearing. According to Dr. Bekesy:

> A patient who has lost part of his hearing ability because of otosclerosis does not find noise disturbing to his understanding of speech; in fact, noise may even improve his discrimination of speech. There is an old story about a somewhat deaf English earl (in France it is a count) who trained his servant to beat a drum whenever someone else spoke, so that he could understand the speaker better. The noise of the drum made the speaker raise his voice to the earl's hearing range. For the hard-of-hearing earl the noise of the drum was tolerable, but for other listeners it masked what the speaker was saying, so that the earl enjoyed exclusive rights to his conversation.[3]

 LACK OF SYMPATHY FOR THE DEAF

A blind person immediately evokes sympathy; however, for some reason or other, a deaf person rarely commands the same kind of sympathy. In fact, a deaf person often finds that others are annoyed with his disability. And, in many instances, deafness goes unrecognized, and people are quick to judge a person with impaired hearing as being stupid, slow learning, or culturally deprived.

3. Ibid, p. 70.

An English teacher in a ghetto school in California made some interesting observations regarding the problem of confusing a hearing problem with lack of intelligence. In administering a verbal test, she asked her students, "What do you do with a stove?" Obviously, the correct answer is, "You cook with it." However, the students responded with such statements as, "You buy flour and sugar in it," "You buy food in it," and so on. The first reaction to these clearly incorrect statements is a feeling that these children are stupid; however, upon closer analysis, this teacher recognized that the problem was one that concerned hearing. Instead of hearing "What do you do with a stove?" the students actually heard "What do you do with a store?" Fortunately, the teacher recognized the difficulty as being an *aural*, or hearing, problem—a problem of aural discrimination—rather than assuming that the students simply gave unintelligent or unlearned responses. The answers were not incorrect, if what was actually heard is considered.

You can see why the partially or completely deaf person or the person who cannot make aural discriminations sometimes views the outside world as unfriendly and unsympathetic. To protect himself from embarrassment and impatient treatment by others, a person with impaired hearing often tries to hide his problem. This unwillingness to admit his hearing difficulty only brings on more problems.

8 CURES FOR HEARING PROBLEMS

A hearing aid can help in some cases to improve a person's ability to hear airborne sounds. This transistorized instrument amplifies sound and therefore often can compensate for loss of hearing. However, the chief problem of an electronic hearing aid is that there is a limited amount of amplification that the ear can withstand. Too much amplification produces a tickling sensation through the skin tissue of the middle ear. If a person can stand the constant pressure, this sensation can be arrested by using a bone-conduction earphone pressed against the surface of the skull.

Deafness resulting from the tumorous bone growths that prevent the operation of the stirrup may be treated by surgery to loosen the stirrup. A technique was developed in France by which the stirrup is freed by pressing a blunt needle against its right side. Since the surgeon is unable to see the stirrup, the operation is quite risky. For this reason the technique has been opposed in the United States.

Another method to free the stirrup is to drill a small hole in the bony wall of the inner ear. When the hole is covered with a flexible membrane, the movement of the fluid in the oval window can be transmitted to the fluid in the cochlea, thus alleviating the deafness.

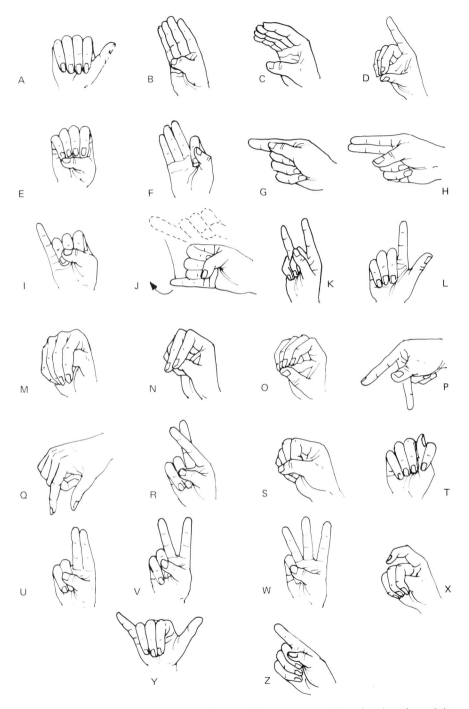

Fingerspelling is sometimes used by those with a permanent hearing impairment to supplement speech and lipreading. Each word is spoken or silently formed on the lips at the same instant it is spelled.

WHAT IS LISTENING?

Listening can be compared with visual perception: it is perceiving or understanding what we hear. Thus listening depends on our ability to hear, just as visual perception depends on our ability to see. So it makes good sense to be aware of our hearing acuteness, as well as of our hearing impairments. A person who is hard of hearing cannot properly hear speech patterns because he cannot hear specific sounds. The ear may not be able to receive certain sound frequencies or volume levels. In such cases, a speaker's message may not be properly interpreted, and so it will not be understood.

Effective listening requires that the hearer receive an airborne, spoken message distinctly so that he will be able to interpret the message exactly as it was intended by the speaker. Understanding a speaker is essential to communication between people.

EFFECTIVE LISTENING IN BUSINESS

Emphasis on good listening is a rather recent development. The first book on this subject was written by Ralph G. Nichols and Leonard A. Stevens; its title is *Are You Listening?* It was published in 1957. These two authors also wrote an article for the *Harvard Business Review* in 1957 entitled "Listening to People." This article has since been reprinted many times and used by many companies in employee-training programs. In particular, the Xerox Corporation used a reprint of this article as an introduction to its Effective Listening program, which is now being used by many firms. The following quote from the *Harvard Business Review* article best illustrates the importance of listening in business.

> Recently the top executives of a major manufacturing plant in the Chicago area were asked to survey the role that listening plays in their work. Later, an executive seminar on listening was held. Here are three typical comments made by participants:
>
> "Frankly, I had never thought of listening as an important subject by itself. But now that I am aware of it, I think that perhaps 80% of my work depends on my listening to someone, or on someone else listening to me."
>
> "I've been thinking back about things that have gone wrong over the past couple of years, and I suddenly realized that many of the troubles have resulted from someone not hearing something, or getting it in a distorted way."
>
> "It's interesting to me that we have considered so many facets of communication in the company, but have inadvertently overlooked listening. I've about decided that it's the most important link in the company's communications, and it's obviously also the weakest one."

The comments of these businessmen reflect the awakening of interest in the skill of listening. The amount of time a worker spends on listening depends on his job requirements.

11 MOST PEOPLE DON'T KNOW HOW TO LISTEN

Sometimes it appears that someone doesn't *remember* something, but the problem could be that he hasn't *listened* to what was told to him. Even with ears that hear well, most people just don't know how to listen. Tests administered to business and professional people at the University of Minnesota showed that immediately after "listening," these people remembered only about half of what they had heard. Other research on listening, carried on at Michigan and Florida State Universities, indicated that after two months, the average listener actually retained only 25 percent of what he had heard.

Listening must be *learned,* and so it requires training. Most of us have had no formal training in listening. We have spent many years learning to read and write, but not to listen.

Dr. Nichols establishes two reasons why students in our schools have not been taught to listen.

1 There has been an overemphasis on the assumption that listening ability and intelligence are highly correlated. Of course, a poor intellect has something to do with difficulty in listening; however, there are also many intelligent people who are very poor listeners. Listening skills must be developed so that we can *understand* and *retain* what we hear.

The ability to listen effectively is a must for any business person.

Bonnie Unsworth

2   We have assumed that by studying reading, we will automatically learn to listen. This is a false assumption, and research has shown that reading and listening skills do not progress at the same rate if only reading is taught.

12   HOW TO IMPROVE YOUR LISTENING

One of the best ways to improve listening is to learn how to concentrate. This is a rather difficult order to fill because we think faster than we talk. The average rate of speaking ranges from 100 to 200 words a minute, but the listener's brain can process words several times as fast. What does the listener do with his idle brain time while he is waiting to hear the spoken words? In many cases, he uses this idle brain time for thinking. Of course, if a listener would use his idle brain time wisely, he would be reviewing the evidence the speaker used to support his point and anticipating what the speaker is going to say next in relation to what he has already said. This is concentration. However, too many listeners use this idle brain time for daydreaming. Drs. Nichols and Stevens illustrate how this precious brain time can be wasted.

> A, the boss, is talking to B, the subordinate, about a new program that the firm is planning to launch. B is a poor listener. In this instance, he tries to listen well, but he has difficulty concentrating on what A has to say.

Too many listeners use idle brain time for daydreaming.

A starts talking and B launches into the listening process, grasping every word and phrase that comes into his ears. But right away B finds that, because of A's slow rate of speech, he has time to think of things other than the spoken line of thought. Subconsciously, B decides to sandwich a few thoughts of his own into the aural ones that are arriving so slowly. So B quickly dashes out onto a mental sidetrack and thinks something like this: "Oh, yes, before I leave I want to tell A about the big success of the meeting I called yesterday." Then B comes back to A's spoken line of thought and listens for a few more words.

There is plenty of time for B to do just what he has done, dash away from what he hears and then return quickly, and he continues taking sidetracks to his own private thoughts. Indeed, he can hardly avoid doing this because over the years the process has become a strong aural habit of his.

But, sooner or later, on one of the mental sidetracks, B is almost sure to stay away too long. When he returns, A is moving along ahead of him. At this point it becomes harder for B to understand A, simply because B has missed part of the oral message. The private mental sidetracks become more inviting than ever, and B slides off onto several of them. Slowly he misses more and more of what A has to say.

When A is through talking, it is safe to say that B will have received and understood less than half of what was spoken to him.[4]

Good listeners engage in some very positive, active listening. They participate mentally in what is being heard, thereby using idle brain time to the best advantage; they try to absorb as much as they can by concentrating. The Xerox Effective Listening program encourages the listener to practice these four mental exercises.

1 Think ahead of the speaker and anticipate the conclusions he will draw.
2 Weigh the authenticity of the facts stated by the speaker.
3 Periodically review and mentally sum up the points the speaker has made.
4 Listen for hidden meanings in nonverbal aspects of speech, such as pitch, and observe facial expressions and physical mannerisms to see if they add any meaning.

A good listener mentally rephrases in his own words the essential ideas of the speaker. This practice forces the listener to grasp ideas, rather than just facts. Facts are useless as isolated bits of information —they must be *related* to form ideas that are meaningful. It is difficult to memorize facts; however, it is possible to memorize ideas, which, in turn, will help you remember the facts.

4. Ralph G. Nichols and Leonard A. Stevens, "Listening to People," *Harvard Business Review,* Sept.-Oct., 1957, pp. 85-92.

Some experts on listening believe that the best way to listen is to think of what a speaker has to say in terms of organization; that is, try to divide what the speaker is saying into parts. The opening remarks of the speaker can be thought of as introductory material that tells us what is about to be said—the actual subject of the talk. Then the speaker presents his *thesis*, or topic. He will state the subject of his talk briefly. This part of the talk is crucial because it is the key to the whole presentation. If it is not completely understood, the listener should tell the speaker that he doesn't understand. This will give the speaker a chance to clarify what he is trying to say, for himself as well as for the listener.

The *body* of the talk will be spent in explaining the thesis. This part of the talk usually includes explanations and examples to support the speaker's thesis. If the listener is to fully understand what the speaker is trying to say, he must listen intently and concentrate on this very important part of the talk. It is during this part of the talk that the speaker may present important data that should be noted by the listener and, if necessary, written down by him. Of course it is up to the speaker to make his talk well organized. The poor speaker will confuse his listener by being inconsistent and presenting unnecessary or extraneous information; he may also provide incorrect "facts."

Finally, the speaker will end up with a *summary* of what he has said. This is the time for the listener to check to see if his listening has been adequate, that is, if he has fully comprehended what the speaker has intended to tell him. This is certainly not the time for distractions.

When you are a listener, put yourself in the speaker's shoes, in a way. You would hope that the listener was trying, at least, to take some interest in what you were saying. To show the speaker your attention, you should refrain from making distracting noises or indulging in other annoying mannerisms. Also, you should refrain from emotional reactions to the speaker or to what he has to say; that is, you should listen to the speaker with an open mind, free from prejudices or convictions. If you allow these elements to come into the picture, you will, instead of listening to the speaker, be planning rebuttals to his "arguments." If necessary, again, make notes, but continue to listen carefully.

Here are some additional suggestions for effective listening.

1 Have your hearing checked regularly, at least once a year.
2 Sit or stand close to the speaker if you have trouble concentrating.
3 Give the speaker complete attention through eye contact, if it is a face-to-face relationship.
4 Don't interrupt the speaker unless it is to let him know that you want something clarified.
5 Avoid doodling or reading when you are trying to listen.
6 Ignore distracting sights and sounds.

Good speakers end their speeches with summaries; good listeners use this time to see if their listening has been adequate.

7   Respond to the speaker by occasionally nodding.
8   If necessary, take notes, but make them brief. Remember that every action you make will tend to distract you from listening and may cause your mind to wander.

13 IT PAYS TO BE A GOOD LISTENER

It has been estimated that a class listening to a teacher, an employee listening to his boss, or an audience listening to a lecturer has serious lapses of attention about every seven minutes. This fact can be a guide to both the listener and the speaker. It is natural to be distracted.

Communication is the key to success in any endeavor involving more than one person. Listening, speaking, and writing are the communication skills. Indeed, the ability to communicate in depth with another person who seeks understanding and friendship is a valuable ability.

The ability to listen effectively is a *must* for any business person. When people in business fail to hear and understand each other accurately, costly errors result. Misinterpreting a spoken order, transposing a customer's telephone number, failing to recognize a customer's irate tone, and failing to remember an important client's name—all because of ineffective listening—have caused businesses to lose many profit dollars. Also, people at work need to know that someone will listen to them. They need to feel that they can talk to their supervisors, their co-workers, and their subordinates about business, as well as about personal problems. Human relations problems are greatly magnified when people don't listen effectively.

SUGGESTIONS FOR FURTHER READING

Burdick, Jeanne, Edith Larson, Grace Mishkin, Roseann Nolan, and Naomi Yocum, *Listen and Think*, Huntington, N.Y.: Educational Developmental Laboratories, Inc., 1969.

Davis, Keith, *Human Relations at Work: The Dynamics of Organizational Behavior*, 4th ed., New York: McGraw-Hill, 1972.

Raygor, Alton L., and David M. Work, *Basic Skills System: System for Study*, New York: McGraw-Hill, 1970.

Vielehr, Alice, *Peace, Happiness, Prosperity for All: A Forum for a Better World,* "Are You Listening?", New York: PHP of America, Inc., February, 1972.

TO HELP YOU REMEMBER

1. What characteristics of sound are described by the terms "pitch," "volume," and "timbre"?
2. Explain how you hear airborne sound.
3. Explain Dr. von Bekesy's hearing theory regarding bone conduction.
4. What effect does age have on hearing?
5. What effect does long-term exposure to loud noise have on hearing?
6. What is the difference between hearing and listening?
7. Why does a listener have idle brain time? How can he spend this time profitably?
8. List five physical ways to improve your listening.
9. Interpret what Polonius, in Shakespeare's *Hamlet*, meant by "Give every man thine ear, but few thy voice."

WORKING WITH PEOPLE, DATA, OR THINGS

Directions

Background information that will help you with this assignment is as follows: Mr. Harry Ford, general manager for the textbook division of a large publishing company, has called a meeting of key people involved in an important new program, an individually prescribed method of teaching elementary shorthand. The deadline for publication of this program was set for December 15, 19—, for a copyright the following year. It is now 10:00 a.m., Monday, October 15, and, of course, the general manager is interested in a status report regarding the production of the program. The following people are representing their departments:

Pete Valdez—marketing department
Carol Salina—promotion department
Frank Monoco—art department
Steve Blake—production department

The marketing staff sends complimentary copies of instructional materials to interested teachers so that they may review the materials and decide whether or not they wish to purchase them.

The promotion department sends promotional pieces (advertising circulars) to prospective buyers (teachers) prior to the new publications.

Listen to the proceedings of this five-member meeting (provided on tape or role-played by other members of the class, depending on your instructor's choice). Each department's representative will give an informal report. If you wish, you may take notes during the meeting. Remember to listen for ideas rather than to irrelevant comments. When the meeting is over, write a 200-word summary on what each of the members reported.

THINGS TO DO

1. Get your ears tested, unless you have done so within this past year.
2. Visit two large companies, and report what the employers in these firms do about ear tests and what measures they take to see that employees correct any problems.
3. Visit the personnel department of two or three large companies, and report what their firms do about in-service training programs for developing listening skills. If the companies don't have such programs, ask how they feel about developing listening skills.
4. Write an evaluation of your classroom or school auditorium as a place for listening. What features are helpful to listeners? What improvements could be made?
5. Listen to a radio or television interview program for a half hour. In a 200- or 300-word essay, summarize the viewpoint of the interviewee.

WRITING
FOR BUSINESS

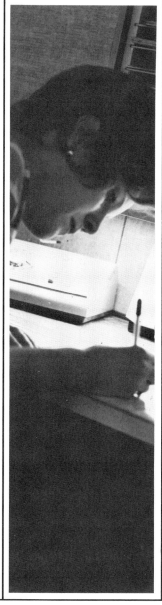

8

What This Chapter Is About

1 COMMUNICATION: THE BACKBONE OF BUSINESS

In an article in *Harvard Today,* industrialist Clarence B. Randall said, "Most management problems require, not knowledge of the nature of matter, but a clear mind, the power of logical analysis, wisdom born of experience, and a talent for communications." One of the most important traits considered by Randall when he was sizing up a prospective employee was the applicant's ability to express himself in both speech and writing. He remarked, "It cannot be repeated too often that the capacity to speak and write the English language clearly is indispensable today for advancement in business."

The ability to speak and write clearly and concisely is especially important for people who work in supervisory positions. Randall suggested that the supervisor "must be able to pass on reliably the instruction which he receives from his superiors" and must also be able to explain the aims and achievements of his company to the public.

Almost every job in business requires some kind of spoken and written communication to others. Often, employees are required to write reports describing various situations that occur during the course of their working hours. Clearly, the ability to write well is an indication that a person can organize his thoughts in a logical way. The chairman of the board of directors of a large New York publishing company once said, "The man who writes well nearly always can think much better than the next man."

2 AVOID BEING POMPOUS, HEDGING, WORDY, AND HYPOCRITICAL

According to author H. George Classen, there are four secret fears that haunt the business writer as he prepares his message. These are:

1 Fear that the reader will think little of him
2 Fear that the reader will hold him responsible
3 Fear that the reader will misconstrue his message
4 Fear that the reader will be offended

The writer tries to present himself as a person who is honest, tasteful, cultured, ethical, influential, dependable, and guiltless. However, the effort to create this good image often leads instead to writing that is, in Classen's words, "pompous, hedging, wordy, and hypocritical." Classen's points are well taken: It makes good business sense to recognize that our fear of having our readers think little of us affects our writing style in that the writing tends to become unclear.

1. H. George Classen, *Better Business English,* Arco, New York, 1966, pp. 14, 15.

The ability to write clearly and concisely is indispensable for communicating technical information.

Al Ruland, City Photographer, Phoenix, Ariz.

The use of extra words to elaborate can lead to *pompousness* in writing, as illustrated in the following sentence:

Your application for employment has been scrutinized through visual observation and it has been recognized as being uniquely rare.

Notice the two unnecessary phrases: "for employment" and "through visual observation." The reader knows that he is applying for employment, and so he doesn't have to be told that he is doing so; the word "scrutinized" implies vision as well as thought, and so "through visual observation" does not have to be stated in the letter. In addition, the word "scrutinized" is pompous and is actually an exaggeration; the word "reviewed" is certainly clearer and more to the point and could not be misunderstood by the reader. The clause "and it has been recognized as being uniquely rare" is meaningless, since it doesn't tell the reader whether his application has made a good or bad impression. If the applicant had served some time in a state prison, this might be unique or rare, but not both, since "unique" means "one of a kind," and "rare" implies "a few of a kind." The sentence might better read: "Your application has been reviewed, and we feel that you are qualified (or unqualified) for this position."

The following sentence in a letter to a debtor shows how the fear of being held responsible leads to *hedging*:

> At this time it is desired to emphasize the gravity of your unpaid balance on this company's books amounting to $898.50; it is hoped that it will be mailed to our office promptly.

Notice the phrases "it is desired to emphasize" and "it is hoped." Impersonal writing that substitutes the vague "it" for "I" lets the writer off of the hook, so to speak. He is not involving himself personally as being the one who is demanding payment; he is simply acting as an agent. By hedging, the writer has not only removed himself from the picture; he has also weakened his appeal by using passive verbs. The straightforward way to write the debtor would be to say, "I am writing to let you know that your account is delinquent in the amount of $898.50; I am therefore urging your prompt payment of this amount." Now, "I" am personally concerned with the debt, and "I" am urging "you" to remit it.

The following sentence is an example of *wordiness:*

> Indeed, Mr. David Browning has done so much more for Consolidated Motors than any other single man in the company has done for the company.

The writer of this sentence seems to have feared having his meaning misconstrued, and so he added extra modifying words and phrases. The words "indeed" and "single" are unnecessary, and the word "company" is mentioned too many times. Thus, the meaning is clouded rather than clarified. This sentence could better have been written as follows: "Mr. David Browning has done more for Consolidated Motors than any other man." There is no need for the writer to feel that a reader won't understand him if he has written his thoughts clearly and concisely.

It is understandable that a writer does not want to offend his reader, but being *hypocritical* is always misleading, and therefore it can never be included among the characteristics of good writing. Consider this example:

> While we are greatly impressed with your long list of accomplishments and expert qualifications, we regret that there is no position in our firm for such an able candidate at this time.

This sentence might encourage the reader to hope that, since he is so marvelous, the company can't do without him for long, and they will try to find some opening where his services can be used. It would be better to way, "We are sorry to inform you that at the present time there is no position in the company for a person with your qualifications," even though this might appear as a rejection. It is unambiguous and lets the reader know clearly that there is no job available.

3 FORMULAS ARE NOT THE KEY TO GOOD WRITING

Most of us have studied letter writing and have had to face special rules, such as "Never begin a sentence with 'I,'" "No sentence should have more than 20 words," "A paragraph should have more than one sentence," or "No two successive sentences should begin with the same word." These rules can be good reminders, but simply following them does not make a writer; they do not help to develop a personal writing style. Unless the writer recognizes why he writes the way he does, realizes the shortcomings of his writing style, and concentrates on developing and improving his own writing, he will never achieve a distinct style of his own. For example, it is very irritating to receive letters that are saturated with "you's" merely because the writer is trying to adopt a "you" formula. True, a correspondence full of "I's" reveals a self-centered attitude, but there is no advantage to replacing "I's" with "You's" unless the writer's attitude changes, too. To communicate effectively, the writer must consider how the reader is likely to receive the message. The writer who can put himself in the reader's position is said to *empathize* or show *empathy*. Consider how the following examples express the same idea.[2]

> I want to get a part-time selling job with your firm so that I may earn money to enroll at the University this fall.

> Will you please consider me for the part-time selling vacancy in your firm. I plan to attend the University this fall and need to earn money to pay for my college expenses.

> Will you please consider my application for the part-time salesman position in your firm. Since I plan to major in marketing and merchandising at the University this fall, you can be sure that I would be an enthusiastic trainee, eager to learn selling.

In the first example, the "I's" bring out the selfish motive; the writer wants, but does not have anything to give. In the second example, although there are fewer "I's," and the "please" has been added, the emphasis is still basically on the writer. The last example is by far the best because it tells the reader the whole story: the writer wants the job, is interested in the work, and is going to the university to study specific courses that will make him valuable to the company. If you were an employer, wouldn't you be most favorably impressed by the writer of the last example?

Letters full of "you's" and "your's" can be patronizing to readers. It is sometimes difficult to distinguish between a patronizing approach

2. Rosemary T. Fruehling and Sharon Bouchard, *Business Correspondence/30*, McGraw-Hill, New York, 1971, p. 25.

and sincerity; the only way to develop the ability to recognize the difference is to cultivate a sensitivity to language, and this comes with experience and lots of writing and rewriting.

4 CREATIVE WRITING REACHES THE READER

A business writer needs creativity to bridge the gap between his own mind and the mind of the reader. Arousing the reader's interest, communicating an idea to him, and stirring the reader's commitment to act on the idea all require imagination. The effective writer relies more on his ability to step outside himself and empathize than he does on his knowledge of literary tricks or stylistic formulas. One author says that successful business writing grows from giving what you have to offer rather than trying to get what you want; such writing results from searching for the best rather than for the most.

To be a successful writer, you must keep in mind your readers' needs and desires. The best way to start is to consider your readers as human beings. For example, if you write to a debtor "You ought to pay your debts," you are not appealing to his human needs; instead, you might write something like this: "Why not pay up your account today so that you can once again enjoy your charge privilege and take advantage of the slashed prices at our May Sale beginning Monday, May 1."

Threats, appeals to higher authority, and similar approaches might move the reader to action, but none of these means inspire the long-term cooperation that can be achieved by a consideration of the reader's human needs and desires.

5 WHAT DO YOU WANT TO SAY?

A successful message is one that gets the point across. The writer must bring his message into focus if he is to gain his reader's attention and hold it. Only an accurately expressed message has a chance of winning the reader's support for the writer's idea. A former Life Saver president, Sidney Edlund, once wrote, "No idea is clear, no goal is clear until you put it in words."

State Your Purpose in Writing

Since clear thinking produces clear writing, the first step is to put your purpose for writing into words. Never start by saying, "I know what I want to say, but I just can't put it on paper." This is a defeatist attitude. If you can't put your main ideas into writing, then you haven't organized them well enough to express them. In this case don't write anything, because it will be disorganized. The following steps should be considered when defining the purpose of your message:

1 State your purpose for writing either orally or in writing.
2 Think about the response you would like your reader to make. Is there something you want to convince him to believe or to do?
3 Consider the subject of the message, and decide which related topics you need to discuss to explain your main subject completely. When you have a letter to answer, a good start is to write in the margins of the letter the topics you want to cover in the answer.
4 Decide on a logical order in which to present your ideas. Write these ideas in order, and number them; then decide which ones are to be omitted.
5 Always plan your message from your reader's point of view as far as it is possible for you to do so.

Keep to a Single Purpose

Try to keep your message as simple as possible. Always remember that your reader is not going to see things exactly the way that you do, even after your have clearly presented your thoughts to him. His emotions, which are unique and unpredictable, will always affect his reasoning.

With this in mind, plan your message in a logical and orderly way so that your reader will understand it and follow the sequence of ideas that are presented. While the reader's emotions cannot be controlled completely by the writer, the writer can appeal to his reader's sense of logic and orderliness.

An expert in creative writing once said, "A reader starts to design his reply as soon as he reads the first sentence of a written communication whether it is a letter he must answer, a report he must evaluate, or an article he will never finish reading." If you want your reader to focus his attention fully on what you have to say in your message, you must stick to a single purpose. Many times a writer will try to include several diverse subjects in one message. This only serves to weaken all the subjects by causing the reader to lose track. If there are several different things you want to say, then the best thing to do is to write several letters, one for each subject.

Organize Your Ideas, and Write Them Down

Ideas or facts supporting your purpose in writing must be stated in a logical manner. For example, suppose a general manager wanted to propose the establishment of a central interoffice mailing service in his company. He would put his proposal down in writing in a report containing the following information: (1) the purpose of the report and (2) the method of achieving his goal, in this case the mailing service. The general manager might begin his report in the following way:

> I suggest that we establish a central interoffice mailing service responsible for (1) picking up and receiving all interoffice mail, (2) inspecting and sorting all interoffice mail, (3) delivering all interoffice mail. . . .

So far we see that the report discusses some of the purposes, but now the method of establishing the department should be discussed in the same orderly, logical way. See if you can write down, as an exercise, some of the ways this interoffice mailing service can be established and operated.

The important thing here is to note that when you try to write down your ideas in a logical order, the ideas will seem to flow in an orderly way. But in writing a report, such as the one shown above, you also have to *sell* your idea to your superiors. The facts alone are not enough. You have to relate the facts to each other to show why the proposed project is essential as well as tell how to set it up.

Make Your Message Complete

As you eliminate the ideas that are not essential to the main purpose of your message, be careful not to leave your reader with insufficient information. The reader can be led off the track in a vain search for an important fact as easily as he can be turned off course by irrelevant statements. For example, the buyer who must interrupt his reading of a sales message to look for the price of the article might easily lose interest in the rest of the message. He may wonder why the writer is hiding this important information, and suspicions about the writer's intention may lead to a result opposite what the writer intended. Many incomplete messages are simply discarded without a response.

 LEARN THE LANGUAGE

Your basic tool for relaying your ideas to others is language. For years, first in elementary school, then in high school, you have been attempting to learn rules of English grammar—how to treat nouns, verbs, prepositions, phrases, clauses, and other constructions. In most cases, these rules have been presented as separate entities without regard to the language as a whole. However, just as preschool children learn the spoken language by listening to words spoken in context and then repeating them to express their own ideas, older children and adults can learn the rules of grammar in the context of developing their skill in written communication.

Grammar should be more than a compilation of rules and parts of speech. In the words of Babson Institute's counsel, Louis Foley, "Real grammar is the life of the language." Without language, communication of ideas would be, for the most part, impossible. We may find the study of grammar boring and dull, but we must always remember that no sentence could be written without it. Thus, grammar should be learned not as an end in itself, but as a means for setting forth our ideas clearly and effectively both in speech and in writing. Indeed, grammar *is* the life of the language.

 MAKE YOUR SENTENCES MOVE YOUR IDEAS

Sentences should move rapidly, smoothly, and simply, and they should be just long enough to express one complete thought. Your words should be precise for clarity. Words that are colorful or vivid will hold the reader's attention because they add interest to your writing. However, too much "color" and joking can cause the reader to be distracted from your purpose.

Get to the Point

The subject-verb-object order is most common in English because it gets to the point. Don't make your reader reread your message to search for the point. Here is an example of a poorly constructed sentence:

> Because our manager has rather absurd ideas regarding minimum performance criteria which must be met by all newly hired employees of at least six months, I find it difficult to remain here as an office worker.

This sentence is not very clear, is it? The pompous and wordy introductory clause hides the main point.

It is usually best to use verbs in the active voice. For example, "John read the book" is preferable to "The book was read by John." The first sentence uses the *active* voice, while the verb in the second sentence is in the *passive* voice. You can see that a sentence like "Mr. Evans needs your report today" moves faster and contains fewer words than "Your report is needed by Mr. Evans today." The passive construction is preferred only when it serves to bring out the important word or idea in a sentence. For example, a store might have a sign reading "Our prices have been greatly reduced—come in and see." This is preferable to "We have greatly reduced our prices—come in and see." This last sentence, although in the active voice, greatly weakens the idea because it emphasizes the subject, "we," when the main idea is reduced prices.

Make Every Word Count

Use your words "economically": don't write anything that is not essential in getting your message across to your reader. Here is a list of some habits that can help a good writer develop a personal style.

1 Avoid using *clichés* (klee SHAY) in place of more original expressions. For example, don't write "Mr. Lopez 'pulled himself up by his bootstraps.'" Instead, explain precisely what Mr. Lopez did to improve his position.

2 Use a current or conversational word in place of an old-fashioned or pompous word and a word of few syllables in place of a longer synonym. Avoid sentences like "John labored with extreme facility" when you can write "John did his work very easily."

3 Avoid making generalizations; your reader may just find an exception. Vague, general terms like "the average American" or "big business" should be used cautiously.

4 Vary your sentence construction to make your writing lively. Occasional questions or exclamations and combinations of simple, compound, and complex sentences provide variety.

The following tables show the words and phrases that should be avoided and those that should be used instead. The first table compares some wordy expressions that are common in business writing to shorter, more precise ways of conveying the same meanings.

Avoid	*Use*
At an early date	Soon (or give exact date)
At that time	Then
At this time, at the present time, at the present writing	Now, at present
Due to the fact that	As, because, since
Enclosed please find	Enclosed is
In the event that	In case, if
Recent date	(Give exact date)
The writer	I, me
Under separate cover	By freight (or whatever means of sending)

Avoid	Use
Up to this writing	Previously
This is to acknowledge	Thank you for
your letter of	your letter of
Your check in the amount of	Your check for
Along the lines of	Like
At all times	Always
By means of	By
In the near future	(State the approximate or exact time)
Inasmuch as	Since

In the following table, the expressions in the left-hand columns are redundant; that is, the meaning of one word in the expression implies the meaning of the other word or words. In the first example, "etc." is the abbreviation of the Latin for "and other things"; the word "and" is already understood in this expression and should not be repeated.

Avoid	Use	Avoid	Use
And etc.	Etc., *or* and so on	Lose out	Lose
Both alike	Alike	May perhaps	May
Check into	Check	Near to	Near
Complete monopoly	Monopoly	New beginner	Beginner
Continue on	Continue	Over with	Over
Cooperate together	Cooperate	Past experience	Experience
Customary practice	Practice	Rarely ever	Rarely
Depreciate in value	Depreciate	Refer back	Refer
During the course of	During	Same identical	Identical
Final completion	Completion	Up above	Above

Use Fewer Nouns, More Verbs

Many writers feel that the nouns convey all the meaning in a sentence, and so, with this rule in mind, they proceed to weigh down their writing with nouns. Whenever possible, let the verb—the action word—carry meaning, too. Look at this sentence:

Departments handling large amounts of interoffice mail shall *make provisions for the use of* an interoffice mailing service.

The phrase in italics can be replaced by the verb "use." See how much simpler and clearer the sentence becomes? The following table shows how one verb can do the job of a long phrase.

Avoid	Use
Give assistance	Help *or* assist
Take corrective action	Correct
Have under consideration	Consider
Be in receipt of	Receive

Keep It Short

It has been suggested that sentences are more readable if they contain no more than 20 words. Certainly, most sentences that appear in business correspondence and advertising material can be confined to this length, but, of course, there are bound to be exceptions. Nevertheless, it is generally agreed that short, straightforward sentences are more readable than long, rambling sentences. A letter that rambles on and on and says nothing annoys the reader. However, cutting a message to the point that it is incomplete or nonspecific is an expensive word-saving tactic. Your best bet for getting your idea from your mind to your reader's is to write clear, concise sentences.

Avoid Trite Expressions

The English language is full of words and expressions that describe things or situations by means of comparisons. Some comparisons are so frequently used that they become clichés. How many times have you

Courtesy of Institute of Outdoor Advertising

The billboard advertiser knows the value of making every word count.

heard "slow as molasses in January," "deader than a doornail," or "white as snow"? How often have you heard people labeled "eager beavers" or "leeches"? These expressions may have seemed very clever when they were first used, but they have become worn out over time.

If you are a novelist or a poet, your ability to replace trite expressions with comparisons of your own may be a valuable talent. If you are writing a business letter or report, however, it is better to keep such comparisons to a minimum. Let your reader know precisely what the subject *is* rather than what it *resembles.*

 # A POSITIVE TONE IS IMPORTANT

It is important to make your messages interesting; they should be persuasive, vivid, and convincing. In a sales letter or ad, you want to *convince* your reader that what you are telling him is true, that your product is worthwhile, or that what you want him to do is best for him. The sales letter and collection letter that follow are examples of appeals to personal interest. This approach gets action.

SALES LETTER

Dear TEEN MAIL Reader:

Are you hip to SUPER, the monthly magazine for the *now* generation? SUPER keeps you tuned in to what's going on—what's really *in*—the latest rock groups, happenings, and styles. If it's in, we put you straight. SUPER really swings!

Now TEEN MAIL readers can subscribe to SUPER at half price. Get 18 big SUPER monthly issues (a full year and a half) for only $3.00. All you have to do is detach this postpaid card and drop it in the mail. We'll bill you later, but you can start enjoying SUPER right away.

Sincerely,

COLLECTION LETTER

Dear Mr. Fowler:

Your account shows an overdue balance of $137.84 for purchases during February and March.

We would like to continue to offer you the privileges of a charge account, but this service depends on the cooperation and prompt payment of our customers.

Please maintain your good credit rating by mailing us your check for $137.84 today. A prepaid, addressed envelope is enclosed for your convenience.

Sincerely,

Notice how these letters are worded. The writer has kept his reader in mind. The first letter, written to teen-agers, addresses the readers in their language and style and makes them feel that the writer is one of them. The second letter, asking for payment of a debt, states the purpose in the first sentence. The writer appeals to the reader's sense of moral obligation by reminding him that the account is a privilege. The advantages of prompt payment are discussed from the reader's viewpoint.

No reader likes to be put into a negative mood. The first letter makes the reader feel young but not immature. The second letter uses positive language to tell how a problem can be remedied. Positive language stresses the light side; it emphasizes what can be done, leaving what cannot be done to implication. Notice how the following negative sentences, revealing an unpleasant tone, can be revised to convey a pleasant and positive attitude.

Negative	Positive
We are sorry that we cannot extend to you more than $500 worth of credit.	You can buy up to $500 worth of merchandise on credit.
We cannot send you the dress unless you indicate your color preference.	You will receive your dress within three days if you indicate your color preference on the enclosed card today.
There are no deliveries on Saturdays.	Deliveries are made Monday through Friday only.
We cannot allow you to return this bathing suit because it has been worn.	To protect our customers, we must refuse to accept returns or exchanges on bathing suits that have been worn.

A POWERFUL TAKEOFF AND A SMOOTH LANDING

The "takeoff" of your message—the first sentence or paragraph—is crucial. It guides the reader into a position of friendliness or hostility. If you are taking off in an airplane and the plane rocks and bumps around, chances are you will feel apprehensive and fearful during the whole trip, but if your takeoff is smooth and even, you will feel a sense of well-being and be confident that the pilot knows his business. Here are some guidelines for your takeoff.

1 Tell what the message is about.
2 Show courtesy and friendliness.
3 Refer to previous correspondence or discussion, if pertinent.
4 Strive for favorable interest or action.

We have already talked about getting the reader's attention by using short, straightforward (subject-verb-object) statements and avoiding long introductory clauses.

The "landing," or last sentence or paragraph, should make it as easy as possible for the reader to take appropriate action and to accept the ideas set forth in the message. For example, if an answer is requested, enclose an addressed and stamped envelope or postcard for the reader's convenience. This will make it *easier* for him to reply. Here are some suggestions for your landing:

1 Leave the reader your friend.
2 If the message is long, summarize it.
3 Emphasize the action you want your reader to follow.

Avoid formal takeoffs like "Referring to your letter of. . . ." This is old-fashioned and dull. Also, avoid landings like "Trusting we shall hear from you soon" or "Thanking you in advance." These are deadly. Here are some more helpful hints.

Rough Landing	Smooth Landing
Looking forward to hearing from you soon, we remain	May we hear from you soon?
Hoping that you will place your order with us soon	An addressed postcard is enclosed for ease in ordering.
Trusting you will give this matter your immediate consideration	Will you please act promptly on this request?

 SOMETIMES, *YES*; SOMETIMES, *NO*

At times you may be called on to straighten things out by letter. Sometimes you will be able to answer with a "yes," while at other times you must say "no." Your job will be all the more difficult if your reader is already hostile. In any case, you must keep your cool and be tactful. Remember that another person's rudeness doesn't make it right for you to be rude in return. As a rule it is a good idea to do the following:

1 Answer promptly—delays can be annoying to people.
2 Always be courteous.
3 Never put the blame on your reader. Avoid such terms as "your complaint," and "your unfortunate experience"; use instead neutral terms like "your letter" or "the incident."
4 Give reasonable explanations. Include only information that is *absolutely necessary*. In a "no" letter, be sure to explain fully your reason for saying no; leave no doubt in your reader's mind.
5 In "yes" letters, don't play a blame game. If you or your company is at fault, apologize briefly. If you are excusing the reader's error, don't play martyr. The main point is that you are granting the reader's request. Indicate precisely how you will go about this and what action, if any, the reader should take.

Here are some ideas that you should consider when you have occasion to write "no" letters:

1 Begin with a neutral or positive statement.
2 Develop your reasons for refusal before actually refusing.
3 Make your refusal clear: don't leave your reader with the idea that there might be a chance later for a "yes."
4 Give your reader an alternative, if possible.
5 End on a pleasant note.

11 APPEARANCE IS ALSO A MUST

Your letter should look good physically if it is to attract favorable attention. It should be typed on a machine with a new ribbon and clean type. An example of a letter that is poor in both appearance and style appears on page 162.

Writers like the one who created this correspondence feel that what they have to offer in their messages is so important that the mechanics of presentation are of no interest. Unfortunately, this is not so. Notice how the sloppy typing and lack of proofreading distract the reader from the real purpose of the communication. Surely, the reader of this letter would not be favorably impressed with the ability of the writer, even though he tells how qualified he is.

Compare the poorly prepared letter with a letter from a person

```
                                        1521 South 5th St.
                                        Logan, PA 19900
                                        Feb. 17, 19--


        Office of the Dean
        Bradford Community College
        Deer Creek, NJ

        Dear Sir,
             I am seeking a teaching position in Mathematics for next term
        (Summer or Fall 19--).

             Until this past Fall I had a teaching assistantship at State Univ.
        I received my Masters degree from State Univ. and passed the qualifying
        exam for phd.   I had to discontinue my pursuit of a doctorate for fi-
        nancial reasons.  I hope to complete my doctorate sometime in the fu-
        ture.

             I am qualified to teach any standard undergraduate course in Math-
        ematics or Mathematical Statistics.

             Presently, I am teaching at the Logan Hospital School, part time.

             If there is a prospectige opening that I mihgt qualify for, please
        contact me as soon as possible.

                                        yours truly,



                                        Stanley Olson
```

Which of the two letters shown here gives you a more favorable impression of its writer?

who is academically less qualified than the first writer and who is applying for a lower-level job. The letter on page 163 is neat in appearance, and there are no errors in spelling and grammar. Notice that the highly trained, well-educated candidate in the first letter *seems* to be less trained and educated than the writer of the second letter, although the facts in the messages indicate otherwise. The physical appearance of the letters has caused this illusion.

```
                              3421 Texas Avenue
                              St. Louis Park, MN 55426
                              March 4, 19--


     Mr. L. B. Golden, Personnel Director
     Office Services Unlimited
     P. O. Box 7007
     Jacksonville, FL 30236

     Dear Mr. Golden:

     Mrs. Rosemary Blackstone, my high school office coordinator, has in-
     formed me of a vacancy in your firm for an administrative assistant.
     Will you please consider me an enthusiastic applicant?

     In June, I will graduate from Normandale Community College, Bloomington,
     MN, where I maintained a B average and an excellent attendance record.
     During my senior year, I was selected from among 100 applicants to be a
     member of the College Administrative Assistant Cooperative Part-Time
     Training Program.  This program allowed me to complete classwork each
     morning and to gain on-the-job experience with a professional adminis-
     trative assistant every afternoon.  It became necessary for me to mature
     quickly in this dual role of student and worker.

     As you will notice on my enclosed résumé, I have participated in extra-
     curricular activities.  Probably the most challenging activity was rais-
     ing $5,000 for our vocational youth organization.  Teamwork and respon-
     sibility are more significant to me because of my club activities.

     On-the-job training for the Liberty Insurance Company allowed me to assist
     the office manager and to understand the scope of his responsibilities.
     Acting as relief receptionist gave me an opportunity to receive and re-
     fer callers and to act as the company's public relations ambassador.

     Will you please allow me a personal interview?  You may reach me by
     letter or call me at (612) 555-1234 any weekday after 4:30 p.m. if you
     wish.

                              Sincerely yours,

                              Pamela J. Eckers

                              Pamela J. Eckers

     Enclosure
```

The following practices will improve the chance of a favorable reception for your business correspondence:

1 Always type your copy.
2 Make your copy neat and free of erasures, fingerprints, dirty letters, strikeovers, carbon and ribbon smudges, and irregular margins. Make sure your typewriter keys are clean.

3   If a letter is short, you can use double spacing; if it is long, use single spacing. Try to confine your material to one sheet, if possible. If this is impossible, then use as few pages as possible.
4   Proofread all copy for errors in spelling and punctuation.

It is customary to include a *résumé* (pron. rezum-ay) with your letter of application. A résumé is simply a data sheet that lists all previous jobs and brief details about your duties at each job; your education, your major field, and possibly supporting courses if they are appropriate; and personal information, including height, weight, health, age, and military service—all of these only if they are pertinent. The résumé usually begins with your name, address, telephone number, and job objective (the kind of job you are looking for). Résumés will be considered in detail in Chapter 15.

SUGGESTIONS FOR FURTHER READING

Fruehling, Rosemary, and Sharon Bouchard, *Business Correspondence/30*, New York: McGraw-Hill, 1971.

Fruehling, Rosemary, and Sharon Bouchard, *The Art of Writing Effective Letters,* New York: McGraw-Hill, 1972.

Gavin, Ruth, and William Sabin, *Reference Manual for Stenographers and Typists,* 4th ed., New York: McGraw-Hill, 1970.

TO HELP YOU REMEMBER

1.   According to Classen, why do people hedge when they write? Why are they pompous?
2.   Do writing formulas work in some instances? What is their limitation?
3.   Explain how changing "I" to "you" can be patronizing to the reader. How can the change be made effectively?
4.   Explain how writing the purpose of your message in a positive statement can crystallize your thinking.
5.   Explain what Louis Foley meant by the statement "Real grammar is the life of the language."
6.   List five suggestions for writing messages that move an idea from the writer's mind to the reader's.
7.   What is a "powerful takeoff" in writing? How can it be achieved?
8.   List five suggestions for making the "no" letter a positive, friendly message.
9.   How can you make your written communication "look good"? Why is the appearance important?

WORKING WITH PEOPLE, DATA, OR THINGS

1. Assume that the following letter has been written to your immediate supervisor and that she has delegated to you the job of answering it. Your teacher will indicate whether the answer should accept or decline the invitation. Use the suggestions listed on page 163–164 to develop an outline of the reply. Then write the reply, based on your outline.

    Dear Ms. Lukas:

    The Virginia Office Education Association Leadership Conference Awards Banquet will take place May 3, 19--, at 7:30 p.m., in the main ballroom of the Seaview Hotel in Norfolk. Will you please accept this invitation to be the guest speaker?

    This banquet is the final event in a three-day conference to be attended by 1,500 office occupations students, their teachers, and representatives from businesses participating in our cooperative program. Awards will be presented by the State Supervisor of Business and Office Occupations to the winners of statewide competitions measuring achievement in office skills.

    Your address should reflect the importance of office skills to new job seekers and should be approximately 30 minutes long.

    Please indicate what the honorarium and travel expenses would be. If possible, please confirm by March 20.

    Sincerely yours,

2. Analyze and revise the following letter.

    Dear Mr. Snyder:

    Mrs. Carson has called to my attention your question regarding the amended fact sheet with respect to the recent increase in benefits for your group.

    The statement "Any claim for benefits under this policy, which had its cause, origin, or beginning prior to the above date will be compensated in accordance with the benefits prior to the amendment date" may be a little confusing; however, I'm glad to clarify it. We administer claims on the basis of hospital confinement. We do not strictly administer on the cause, origin, or beginning basis. Rather, we look at a particular hospital confinement and see when the hospital confinement commenced, not when the condition which precipitated the hospital confinement commenced. If a man who has a chronic condition and if he was not confined, but at work on the effective date of the increase, is confined after that date, even though the condition commenced before the effective date of the increase, he will be paid on the basis of the increased benefit. This is the manner in which our Claims Department administers claims under this statement.

    We're sorry for any unnecessary concern, Mr. Snyder. I hope I have satisfactorily clarified the matter for you, but should there be further questions, just let me know.

    Sincerely yours,

3. Rewrite the following letter to improve the tone by stressing the positive aspects of a negative solution.

> Dear Mrs. Carson:
>
> You must have been disappointed and angry to have the raisins in your cake mix sink to the bottom. We deeply regret this unfortunate occurrence. It is no wonder that you were angry, and we apologize.
>
> The only way raisins will not sink to the bottom in these cakes, however, is if they are chopped very fine. You won't be disappointed or angry any more if you purchase our Streusel Coffee Cake Mix in which the raisins are finely chopped.
>
> Once again, please accept our apologies for this unfortunate occurrence.
>
> Sincerely yours,

THINGS TO DO

1. Visit the personnel department of a large company in the community, and ask to see a copy of the correspondence manual. Report to the class on its contents.
2. Visit the personnel department of a large company in the community, and ask about any in-service training programs for developing and improving employees' written communications. Report your findings to the class.
3. Present to the class a five-minute talk on some aspect of language that is important in good writing. (You could discuss usage, punctuation, parallel construction, and so on.)
4. Collect five business letters, and evaluate them for content, mechanics (grammar, usage, and so on), and visual presentation.

SPEAKING IN BUSINESS

9

WhatThis Chapter Is About

Many centuries ago, Aristotle pointed out the absurdity of mistrusting all speakers merely because they have mastered the skill of speaking smoothly, persuasively, and articulately. He said,

> If it is urged that an abuse of the rhetorical faculty can work great mischief, the same charge can be brought against all good things (save virtue itself) and especially against the most useful things such as strength, health, wealth, and military skills. Rightfully employed, they work the greatest blessings, and wrongly employed, they work the utmost harm.

Obviously, a speaker as eloquent and polished as Aristotle understood some rather basic public speaking theory. He recognized that great oratorical ability could be utilized for both good and harmful purposes. On this basis, a reasonable attitude would be to establish trust on criteria other than speaking style. The real emphasis should be on the message rather than the delivery or performance. A professional speaker may show, by his performance, enthusiasm for or belief in the message, but the message must stand on its own merit. The purpose of speaking, in both face-to-face and platform-to-audience situations, is more than a display of talent. Accordingly, Eugene E. White writes in his book *Practical Public Speaking*:

Thorough research is the speaker's best protection against a "for instance" reaction in the audience.
Courtesy of U.S. Dept. of Labor

Effective speaking is not "a performance" staged to display the ability of the speaker; it is a communicative process designed to stir up desired responses from a particular audience assembled at a specific time and place. To secure these responses, you must develop a keen sense of communication, skill in linking your proposals to the wants and interests of the listeners, proficiency in organizing and developing your ideas in most effective logical and psychological manner, as well as the ability to speak clearly, precisely, and fluently.[1]

The effective speaker avoids flowery language — he gets to the point and concentrates on speaking up and being understood. A good speaker communicates his feelings, attitudes, and ideas to his listeners in a simple, clear, and honest way. He sees that his responsibility is to present his message — not himself — as effectively as he can.

2 WHAT'S THE PURPOSE OF YOUR TALK?

There had better be a purpose for making a presentation; otherwise your audience will be quickly turned off. Richard Borden, in his book *Public Speaking as Listeners Like It*, gives us four audience reactions to a talk: Ho hum! Why bring that up? For instance! and So what? The first, ho hum!, is used to describe audience apathy — who cares? Your opening remarks should be directed toward making your audience *interested* in, or at least curious about, what you are going to say. Then, if your audience thinks, "Why bring that up?" you will not find yourself in hot water. The initial interest you aroused in your listeners must be immediately followed up by pertinent material. This material must contain facts and, if necessary, examples. Don't leave your listeners up in the air; give them a "for instance." Finally, it would be a catastrophe if your audience reaction were, "Why did I come all the way over here to listen to this? I missed a good movie on TV to hear this." You may have had something important and pertinent to say, but you presented it in a way that left your audience with a "so what?" reaction.

One good way to start a talk is to say something to wake your audience out of apathy. You could tell a funny anecdote or something shocking. For example, Henry Ward Beecher, the famous preacher, was to give a talk on the evils of blasphemy. His opening words were, "It's a damned hot day." This surely took his audience by surprise. Then, after he had gained his listeners attention, he paused and then went on to say, "That's what I heard a man say here this afternoon!"

Above all, don't give a bland, mediocre presentation. Such a presentation might be partially effective if it is pertinent, but it will lose

1. Eugene E. White, *Practical Public Speaking*, 2d ed., Macmillan, New York, 1964, p. 6.

your listeners by allowing their minds to wander. Louis Nizer, in his book *Thinking on Your Feet*, points out:

> We have all been oppressed, at one time or the other, by speakers who have nothing to say but who hope to alter the verdict of their mediocrity by endurance. Banality is boring whether it be conveyed in a monotonous drone or in fist-shaking screams. The latter is preferable only because hoarseness sometimes besets the perpetrator.[2]

3 THE AUDIENCE COUNTS

Since a speech is intended primarily to communicate the ideas of the speaker to the listener, the speaker must make his speech listener-oriented; that is, the speaker must consider his audience and let them determine, in a sense, how he will present his spoken communication.

Let us say, for example, that you were giving a talk on improving public transportation in your city or town and that you had to speak before two audiences: first, a parent-teachers association, and second, the city or town council. The members of the parent-teachers association would be interested primarily in the methods of transporting schoolchildren to local schools; the members of the city or town council would be interested primarily in the cost of your proposals. Thus, your speech before the parent-teachers association would emphasize efficient transportation, while your speech before the council would be geared to economic concerns.

Kenneth Burke, in his book *Rhetoric of Motives*, states, "You can persuade a man only insofar as you can talk his language by speech, gesture, tonality, order, image, attitude, idea, identifying your ways with his." The clue here is "talk his language."

Many speakers are, like writers, often too self-centered to be sensitive to their audiences. Ideally, the speaker should *become his audience* and then speak toward himself as his audience. This is explained in an eloquent way by Atticus in Harper Lee's *To Kill a Mockingbird* when he says, "You never really understand a person . . . until you climb into his skin and walk around in it."

To identify the needs and wants of one's audience is no simple task. You may assume that the people who have assembled to be your audience have a common interest that has brought them together for the occasion. However, there are other characteristics that members of your audience might share. Some important factors to consider in speaking to a group are its size and the age, sex, educational background, and economic class of the members, and possibly their ethnic background. If any of these factors are neglected, you might just say

2. Louis Nizer, *Thinking on Your Feet*, Liveright, New York, 1963, p. 20.

something that will unnecessarily offend a large part of your audience. The characteristics to consider when you address an audience of one are much the same as those for a group audience, but they can be more precisely pinpointed.

You can hold your listener's attention and keep his interest by changing your tone of voice, making sudden changes in position, and changing your facial expression. You might also evoke your listener's interest by asking a question so that he can respond and participate in what you have to tell him.

Looking the other person in the face also helps to hold his attention. A salesman looks at his customer's face, not at the merchandise. Experienced speakers find it easier to hold an audience if they look at and talk to first one member of the audience and then to another; this also relaxes the speaker.

4 GATHERING MATERIALS FOR YOUR TALK

Digging for information that will satisfy an audience's demands for a "for instance" is often the most time-consuming and difficult job in speechmaking. The digging process may involve thinking, observing, and communicating with others, or reading, depending on how the speaker intends to establish his "for instance." These activities take time. It isn't always a simple task for the speaker to reflect—to examine his past and present interests, feelings, wants, attitudes, and knowledge in developing cases and recalling personal experiences to support his statement of purpose. Nor is it a simple task to observe the behavior of others or to read and select written materials that will illustrate a point.

Preparation may require some hours of research, but it cannot be avoided. Even if you are an expert in your field, never talk off the top of your head; always make notes on 3- by 5-inch cards that you can refer to as you talk. These cards will serve as a reminder to cover some point, and they will also provide some order in presenting your talk. The more technical your talk is, the more important it is to have it well ordered and complete—as far as possible. In a sense you must become a reporter. Gather the facts, and report your findings to your audience. Part of your research involves, of course, learning something about your audience.

Tell stories and anecdotes to liven up your talk. This story-telling technique is valuable because it gives your audience a sense of reality. If you have heard any of Norman Vincent Peale's talks, you could not escape noticing that they always involve either some story about the speaker's experience or a story relative to the speaker's topic for the discussion.

Another important part of speech preparation is organization. In an organized speech, the ideas are arranged in a logical sequence so that each idea seems to flow from the previous one. The best way to organize a talk is to make an outline. It is obvious that a speech must have an introduction and a conclusion, but what about the "body" of the talk, in which the real presentation is made. This body should be divided into topics. Decide which topic should come first; ask yourself if one idea depends on another idea. If so, put the dependent idea second in your presentation. Of course, if two or more ideas are completely independent of one another, then the order makes no difference.

Keep your speech as short as possible. No one likes to listen to a rambling speaker or to a speaker who continues to talk after he has made his point. A story is told about an automobile salesman who was talking to a customer with animation and gusto. After the customer decided to buy the car and signed the contract, he noticed that the salesman was suddenly very quiet. The customer called this to the attention of the salesman. He asked, "Why are you so quiet now, while before I signed the contract you were so talkative?" The salesman replied, "I talked you into buying this car, and now I don't want to talk you out of it."

An important thing to keep in mind is: if you have nothing to say, don't say it. Louis Nizer tells an interesting story about how Professor Albert Einstein handled an unprepared talk:

> Einstein once astonished a university audience eagerly awaiting a baccalaureate address by rising and saying quite simply, "I did not have the opportunity to prepare a worthwhile thought, so you will please forgive me if I make no speech." He sat down. With due allowance for the brilliance which would have crowned his unborn thoughts, the students could have learned more from this incident. It was a profound demonstration of the relativity between silence and absence of thought.[3]

5 CONCLUSIONS ARE *CONCLUSIVE*

The conclusion of a speech should also have a point to make; it should not just be a summary. In some sense the conclusion should "connect" the audience with your cause. This is the time when the listener knows the subject of your speech and all the topics concerned with that subject. He has an understanding of what you were talking about. But he may also ask himself, "So what? How does this concern me?" Once you have convinced the listener that what you are proposing is good for him, too, you are in a position to urge him to cooperate: to join your association, write to the Mayor, vote for a certain candidate, change a certain condition, and so on. If you can do all this successfully, you are a *dynamic* speaker—a forceful talker.

3. Louis Nizer, p. 30.

6 REHEARSE ALL SPEECHES

Most effective speakers complete their speech outlines at least one day before their speech is to be given. Then they practice "delivering" the speech in private, so that they will not be interrupted. Some speakers prefer to practice reciting their speeches before a mirror so that they can see themselves as their audience sees them; others practice in front of other people to get their reactions directly; some may do both. All these forms of rehearsal help to smooth over the rough edges. Your first speech draft may give a misleading impression to your audience: it may contain a story that will offend some segment of your audience. It is always good to have another person who is familiar with the subject of your presentation look over your speech and listen to the way in which you will deliver it. There are many subtleties that you may have overlooked. A good cook should always have someone else do the tasting. Some speakers even practice their delivery in the actual room where the speech is to be given.

Here are some suggestions that may be helpful when you are rehearsing a speech:

1 Read over your outline silently, and think about what it is saying to you.
2 Read your outline aloud.
3 Give your speech without looking at your outline.
4 Reread your outline silently and aloud.
5 Give your speech again, without looking at your outline.
6 Repeat Steps 4 and 5 until you can deliver the entire speech without hesitation.

Your outline should be used only as a "cue," or "prompter"; it should be glanced at and not studied while you are talking. You should practice this procedure until you can deliver your speech without any hesitation. When you know you can do it, your confidence will cast out any fears you may have.

7 SO YOU'VE GOT THE JITTERS!

Norman Vincent Peale, the renown preacher at New York's Marble Collegiate Church, tells of his problems with stage fright and how they stimulated him into becoming a public speaker.[4]

4. Eugene E. White, p. 10.

I doubt that anyone was ever less likely to become an effective speaker than I. I definitely was not endowed with superior linguistic skill. In fact, as a boy in Ohio, I was exceedingly shy and inarticulate. One of my most important early battles was to acquire adequate poise in ordinary social situations.

Dr. Peale goes on to describe how he felt when he was to make his first public speech:

When I stood up, I became literally stiff with fear. I couldn't get the first words out. In the embarrassed silence, a little girl in the front row giggled and said to her mother, "Gosh, look at his knees shake." That made me so angry that I found my voice and gave a spirited speech.

No one really overcomes some form of self-consciousness or possibly some fright when speaking before an audience in a public place. Dr. Peale admits that even today, he feels a little apprehension before he goes to the pulpit. Nervousness, to a degree, of course, is an asset. It keeps the talker from being dull; it adds a vibrant tone to the voice; it gives the speaker enthusiasm which he can make his audience feel. But, on the other hand, if one is too nervous so that speech becomes impossible, then there is a serious problem. This is no longer "nervousness," but a severe psychological problem that must be dealt with in other ways than making speeches.

The best advice to beginner speechmakers is "tell" your audience what you want to say to them, don't present a "speech." Tell them the way you would tell a friend. You will soon find your words flowing with enthusiasm, because you are interested in what you are saying. And, never talk to an audience about something that doesn't interest you, for your lack of interest will be reflected in your speech, and your audience will become bored.

In his book *Levels of Knowing and Existence*, the late Harry Weinberg, a professor at Temple University, had the following to say about being afraid to speak:

The only things we really fear are our own feelings and sensations. The man who has claustrophobia and the student who fears getting up to speak before a class—what do they fear? Certainly, the man knows there is nothing in close quarters to hurt him, and certainly the student knows no physical harm will come when he speaks. What do they fear? They fear the palpitations, the sweats, the shame—all feelings—that they tell themselves will occur, during the act they are trying to prevent. Literally, it is impossible to fear anything but our own feelings and sensations contrived by our ideas of what will take place.

Obviously, then, "stage fright" is all in the head, and it must be consciously confronted by the person experiencing it. Often we don't respond to stimuli from our environment in logical ways, and so we must check out any present dangers if we are afraid; if there are no actual dangers, then there is no *actual* reason to be afraid. But, then, we may ask, "What makes us afraid, if there is no real, physical danger in our environment?" As Dr. Weinberg so clearly pointed out, what we fear must really be ourselves—our feelings—at the time we are called on to make a talk.

8 LET YOUR BODY COMMUNICATE, TOO

It is now known that people use "body language." The subconscious effect is that the other person can read your hidden attitudes by your bodily movements and positions. For example, a slouching position indicates disinterest; turning aside may mean disagreement or lack of belief in what you are saying; walking toward the speaker shows interest in what he is saying; and so on. Even the way you dress in anticipation of a meeting is a factor of body language. Certain effects of body language have been repeated so often by a person that they can be done consciously to show how the person feels. For example, he may make a fist and hit a table with it to indicate anger or strong disapproval. The concept of body language is becoming more and more important in the field of psychology, and scientists in that field call it *kinetics*. Some common bodily movements made by a speaker are eye contact, hand gestures, facial expressions, and posture.

A theatrical performance always involves the use of body language, but this is learned along with the spoken parts. An actor's entrance onto the stage is often crucial to his total performance because it is his audience's first impression of him, and to repeat an oft-used cliché, "First impressions are the lasting ones."

Sometimes a beginner speaker attempts to force body gestures. This makes him look artificial and detracts from the effectiveness of his talk. If body gestures are to be used intentionally, they should also be practiced before the speech is delivered so that they will appear to be done naturally. If you are relaxed, your body gestures will come naturally anyway, and so, in most cases, it is unnecessary to make special movements. Remember, your speech is not a theatrical performance, but it may contain some elements of one insofar as you are making a public appearance that needs rehearsal. Body language, if planned in advance, should be used to "season" your talk, not to overcome it, and, as a seasoning, it should be used sparingly.

Body language can help your speech, but it can put a damper on it, too. Lack of self-confidence shows up in your body gestures. Nervousness may cause a speaker to stand too erect or hold his hands in an awkward position. If there is a podium, you can always hold on to it; if not, it may be a good idea to walk around a little. This practice may help you relax, and, at the same time, it may arouse interest on the part of your audience. A president of a well-known Southern college used to turn his back on his audience from time to time when delivering a talk. This was extremely effective, because every time he turned to face his audience he immediately drew its attention. This periodic arousal brought the listeners back from their personal distractions.

PERSONALITY IN TALKING

Voice training can help you to speak better. Some voices annoy—they are harsh, too nasal, too loud, too deep, or too high. Other voices naturally calm the listener—they are soft, firm, and assuring, and the tone is right. Strangely enough, many people think that a loud voice

Courtesy of REA Express, Inc.

The effective speaker recognizes the importance of body language. What is this speaker telling us kinetically?

is the most effective kind of voice to have. But it is definitely not. In the old days, before the era of the microphone, loudness may have been an asset, but today, the science of acoustics has eliminated the need for loudness. While a booming voice may be desirable for an auctioneer or a sports reporter, it is certainly to be avoided by a polished speaker who wants to put a point across effectively and convincingly. An effective voice is heard, and not felt.

Sometimes a soft voice is more convincing than a loud one because it makes the listener more attentive so he won't miss anything. This is the "whisper strategy." Skilled salesmen often use this technique; lowering the voice gives the listener a sense of confidentiality. The listener becomes actively involved in "listening." The whisper strategy draws people closer together, while loudness causes them to "draw away."

People who talk professionally — actors, politicians, businessmen, lawyers, and teachers — often seek professional voice training. And wonders can be accomplished if the training is right and the teacher is good. Sarah Bernhardt, one of our most famous actresses, was able to change her thin, high-pitched voice to one with a resonant, deep quality through training. The following "helpful" qualities are desirable in speaking; the "harmful" ones should be avoided.

Helpful	Harmful
Pleasant tone	Annoying tone
Enthusiasm	Spiritless expression
Clear pronunciation	Mumbling
Inflection	Monotone
Confidence	Hesitance
Earnestness	Languidness
Moderate tone	Loudness or too much softness
Rhythm and phrasing	Poor word flow and running words together

Here are some rules that professional voice instructors give to their students.

1   Move the lips to improve enunciation.
2   Talk from the front of the mouth using the tip of the tongue. This relaxes the vocal cords and gives the voice a pleasant quality.
3   Talk from the diaphragm, not from the throat. This gives depth to your voice tone.
4   Practice humming "mmmm-mm-m" and "nnn-nn-n" to develop resonance.

5 Practice saying "yes" with as many meanings as possible. This improves expressiveness. You can make "yes" mean approval, scorn, doubt, irritation, and even "no."

6 Emphasize *key phrases* to gain attention and make instructions clear.

7 Give emphasis occasionally by making the voice softer. This is the whisper strategy.

8 Talk in phrases, with a brief pause after each phrase. Phrasing makes it easier for others to follow your talk, and it helps you to think ahead, too. It also makes it easier for people to take notes.

9 Raise your voice on the last few words of your speech. This has a stirring effect on your audience, whether it numbers one hundred or consists of only one person.

10 Keep cigars, cigarettes, chewing gum, tobacco, pencils, hairpins, and whatnot out of your mouth when you are talking. Things in the mouth are not only unattractive to the audience; they also cause you to mumble, and they force the voice back into the throat where it should not be.

11 Control your tone of voice. Avoid loudness or excessive softness of tone. Remember, a pleasant, clear, enthusiastic voice will serve your purpose best.

 ## SPEECHES OF INTRODUCTION

Businessmen are often called upon to make so-called "after-dinner speeches," which may be either serious or entertaining. These include speeches of introduction, presentation, welcome, and so on. They are often *impromptu*, or unplanned, talks, but sometimes you may know in advance that you will be called upon to make a speech, and therefore you will have a chance to prepare for it. Most books on speech-making contain chapters or sections on impromptu speaking (see the bibliography at the end of this chapter), but we shall be concerned here with the planned speech of introduction, because this is the most popular form of "after-dinner" speech.

A speech of introduction is usually used to introduce the main speaker. If should be brief, and it should contain some biographical information about the next speaker. For example, a speech of introduction might go like this:

Dr. Goldberg received his Ph.D. from the University of Oklahoma. He has been professor of oceanography at the University of Utah for the last 6 years; during this time he has written two books on offshore oil-drilling techniques. He is considered an expert in this area. Tonight, Dr. Goldberg will talk to you on the prospects of offshore oil drilling in the Gulf of Mexico. Dr. Goldberg.

One technique used in introducing a speaker is to tell an anecdote, or story, about the next speaker or about something connected with the next speaker's profession or with the subject of his talk. You can break into an anecdote almost immediately. If you are going to introduce an important person, you can usually skip over biographical details, especially if he is fairly well known, and go right into an anecdote that relates to his profession or something else about him. This technique of telling a pertinent story is exemplified in the following introduction of an ambassador.

> I am sure that most of you are familiar with Ambassador Bruce's accomplishments. But when I was called upon to introduce Mr. Bruce, I was reminded about a story of another ambassador, and that was King Louis XIV of France's ambassador to Spain. Once, this ambassador was returning to the court at Versailles. A few miles before reaching Versailles, his carriage broke down, and the only available transportation was a donkey. So the ambassador rode into the court of Versailles on this donkey, and King Louis happened to be in the garden when the ambassador was approaching. When he saw the ambassador, the King went up to him and said, "Ah, a big jackass on a small jackass." To which the ambassador immediately replied, "One must not forget that I represent Your Majesty." With that, I shall now hand my microphone to Mr. Bruce.

It is a good idea to keep some record of stories that you have heard from time to time, for they may be useful in an after-dinner speech of introduction. While the stories may be amusing or serious, they should, above all, be pertinent. It is a poor idea to start relating achievement after achievement of the next speaker, citing particular years and institutions where he has been employed. This will soon bore the listeners, and you will have done harm to the next talker by providing him an unsympathetic, if not hostile, audience.

11 LEAD A CONFERENCE?

A businessman, especially one who works for a large company, will often find his life at work a continuous succession of meetings and conferences. When these activities involve face-to-face social interaction, they are called *group dynamics*. A lecture presented at a meeting does not qualify as an example of group dynamics because it is not an activity in which several minds react to one another. On the other hand, a conversation among several people is a good example.

The Conference Method

The most widely used of all group dynamics activities is the conference method. Three basic criteria are involved: (1) a group leader to guide the group discussion, (2) an oral exchange of ideas, with each member making his viewpoints known, and (3) a pooling of ideas and viewpoints from the group in order to find effective solutions to problems that are being confronted.

The conference leader is a guide who attempts to (1) help the group members understand their roles and their responsibilities, (2) get the viewpoint of each conferee (rather than always imposing his own), and (3) keep the group on the right track by summarizing frequently.

The conference leader must also exercise leadership qualities. He must: (1) define the conference procedure, (2) extract viewpoints from each member by asking questions, and (3) summarize and close the conference.

Defining the conference procedure follows a brief introduction of those people who don't know one another. Most conference leaders have the foresight to distribute review materials prior to the meeting so that it will be easier and quicker to review the purposes of the meeting at the conference.

After emphasizing the seriousness of the problem and setting the rules for procedures the leader begins with a broad statement about the problem, such as:

> "We've asked you to meet with us this morning to exchange some ideas on how we might solve the problem of the 15-minute coffee break being abused. Some of our people take as long as 30 and 35 minutes each for the morning and afternoon breaks. You recognize, of course, that the 15-minute coffee break is an employee privilege that has proved to be an effective way to maintain high levels of production.

The next thing that the leader does is define the problem in terms of the primary concerns of his group. He might say, "To pinpoint the problem more directly, we would like to discuss why some of our staff feel they are entitled to take more than the 15 minutes given them for their morning and afternoon breaks."

After the leader has narrowed the problem, he presents any facts about the problem, or, more efficiently, he reviews the facts that the conferees already have regarding the problem. For example, "As you can see in the memos that were sent to you for review, we have directed three warnings to every member of the staff, and yet yesterday thirteen people were still abusing the time limit for their coffee breaks."

The next step for the leader is to phrase a group interaction "jumping-off" question that cannot be answered with a "yes" or "no."

The most widely used of all group dynamics activities is the conference method.

Phrasing the question with the word "how" is effective because each participant then has an opportunity to give his viewpoint concerning the problem. The question might be, "Now, then, *how* might we solve our problem of the abuse of the 15-minute coffee break?" A question phrased like this usually triggers spontaneous responses; if it doesn't, the leader will have to call on one of the participants to suggest a solution. Most leaders use a chalkboard, an overhead projector, or a flip chart, and they write down the "jumping-off" question immediately after phrasing it. They then list the viewpoints under the question as each point is made by a conferee. (Even if one of the solutions seems ridiculous, the leader must list it and hope that the participant will withdraw it as soon as he recognizes its absurdity.) For example:

How might we solve the problem of the abuse of the 15-minute coffee break?

1 Discontinue the break.
2 Have employees sign in and sign out.
3 Have coffee and rolls delivered to the work stations.
4 Dock the employee's pay.

Besides listing solutions, the leader has many other responsibilities if the conference is to be successful. He must keep the whole group on the right track and slow them down or speed them up if necessary. He must also try to solve any "people problems" that may arise among his conferees, problems caused by those who like to argue, those who are too shy to respond, individuals who like to dominate the conference, and subgroups who get involved in discussions among themselves rather than with the whole group.

The final responsibility a conference leader has is to summarize the viewpoints made by the group members and close the session.

Brainstorming

Another kind of group dynamics, much less popular than the conference method just described, is called brainstorming. It was first introduced by Alex Osborn of the New York advertising agency Batten, Barton, Durstine and Osborn to encourage creativity.

The primary concern in a brainstorming session is to get a huge number of ideas, even though some may be absurd. In fact, Mr. Osborn believed it was always possible to tame down ridiculous suggestions, and so he actually encouraged the participants to state their wildest thoughts. He did, however, forbid any negative comments.

Besides being asked to suggest new ideas, the participants are also encouraged to "hitchhike" suggestions and combine several ideas to make a better one.

12 THE MAJORITY RULES, BUT THE MINORITY IS HEARD

Large conferences are conducted according to rules so that everyone concerned will have an opportunity to speak. It is usual to conduct such meetings with *Robert's Rules of Order,* a handbook for parliamentary procedure. The rules are extremely formal, but they exist for a good reason—to facilitate the orderly progress of the business at hand and to ensure that the majority rules and the minority is heard. Some more casual forms of meetings invite arguments that only hinder the cooperation of the conferees and postpone the achievement of their goal.

To conduct a meeting efficiently, the presiding officer follows this order of business:

1 Call to order
2 Reading of the minutes of the previous meeting
3 Statement of the *agenda* (the order in which the topics to be discussed will be taken up)

4   Reports of officers and standing committees
5   Reports of special committees
6   Old or unfinished business
7   New business
8   Adjournment

Developing the ability to run meetings smoothly and efficiently can certainly be an asset, and you should take the time to learn about this subject. The difference between a successful meeting and an unsuccessful one often lies with the conference leader or presiding officer.

13 GOAL GRADIENTS AND PUBLIC SPEAKING

Do you gallop through work a little faster just before the quitting bell? Yes? Then your goal gradient is in good shape. The *goal gradient* is the stimulating effect experienced as you near a goal. This stimulating effect makes you work faster and harder in order to finish what you are doing, to complete your goal.

The goal-gradient effect in a talk is the *climax*. When the climax is reached, it is time to stop talking and sit down, like the automobile salesman mentioned in Section 4. You may have heard comments about speakers like this one: "He had me convinced after 15 minutes, but he lost me after that by talking too long." Skilled speakers stop talking while listeners are still intensely interested or after a telling point has been made. To continue after either of those goal gradients is reached is as much of a mistake as a manager's dragging in unfinished work at quitting time. The effective speaker stops before the listener's goal has been passed. He ends early, with a bang. He avoids tapering off to nothingness.

When one is conducting conferences, it is not wise to adjourn them entirely by the clock. A meeting is likely to be more effective if it is adjourned right on the heels of some high spot in the discussion or as soon as a decision has been reached. The decision gives the conference a new *goal*, and dragging in something else to fill in the time is out of step with the effectiveness of reaching the goal.

SUGGESTIONS FOR FURTHER READING

Hasling, John, *The Message, The Speaker, The Audience*, New York: McGraw-Hill, 1971.

Laird, A. Craig, Franklin Knower, and Samuel L. Becker, *General Speech Communication*, 4th ed., New York: McGraw-Hill, 1971.

Robert's Rules of Order, rev. ed., Glenview, Ill.: Scott, Foresman, 1969.
Sager, Arthur W., *Speak Your Way to Success,* New York: McGraw-Hill, 1968.
Smith, Henry Clay, *Sensitivity to People,* New York: McGraw-Hill, 1966.

TO HELP YOUR REMEMBER

1. Why did Aristotle criticize the attitude that you can't trust an effective speaker?
2. What does speaking up and being understood really mean?
3. What are the four attitudes of an apathetic audience described by Borden? How can a speech be organized to change these attitudes?
4. Explain Atticus's statement in *To Kill a Mockingbird*: "You never really understand a person . . . until you climb into his skin and walk around in it."
5. Describe a conclusive ending. Is a logical summary of the ideas presented in the speech a conclusive ending?
6. What are the steps for fixing a speech in your mind?
7. Is stage fright all in the head? What is the object of the fear called "stage fright"?
8. What is body language?
9. What leadership qualities must a conference leader exercise?
10. What is *Robert's Rules of Order?*

WORKING WITH PEOPLE, DATA, OR THINGS

1. With four other members of the class, engage in an informal discussion to demonstrate effective principles of the conference method. Make the discussion one that presents a human relations problem. Your group of five members will be given 15 minutes to carry on the discussion, and the group may choose its own leader. Be sure that you use the chalkboard, a flip chart, or an overhead projector to write the "jumping-off" question and list the conference ideas. (After the conference, you will be asked to submit the problem and ideas to the instructor.)
2. Select a topic, and word a central idea for an informative speech. Using Richard Borden's four audience attitudes as a guide, develop a ten-minute speech to be given to the class. Fix it in your mind, and with or without notes (no manuscript), present it to the class.

THINGS TO DO

1. Collect from four or five businessmen in your community the values of the conference method. Present your findings in a three-minute report to the class.
2. Read a long article (over 2,000 words) in a current magazine relating to business. Present a brief summary and interpretation of the article before the class.
3. Observe two people in a face-to-face communication. Report on what their voices told you about their message, and describe their body language (posture, hand gestures, facial expressions, and so on).
4. Find one or two pages of prose (perhaps a short story) that develop an idea of interest to you. Go over the passage, and underline all sounds clearly and acceptably. Read another similar passage to see if you can articulate all the sounds without studying the words.

ORGANIZING YOUR WORK

10

What This Chapter Is About

Now is the time for us to renew our acquaintance with two unusual men whom we met in Chapter 2. Working separately but in related activities, they brought about some changes that have made modern work life what it is. Frederick W. Taylor came from a well-to-do Philadelphia family, but he did not go directly to college because of eye trouble. Frank B. Gilbreth, who was born in Maine, could not afford to go to college. In any case, both of them were men of action who much preferred working and trying out ideas to studying.

Taylor was one of the first efficiency engineers and the most influential of them all. In place of college, he served an unpaid apprenticeship in a machine shop. Nine years after he completed his apprenticeship, he became chief engineer of the mill in which he had started as a laborer. Meanwhile, by studying at night, he had received a degree in mechanical engineering from Stevens Institute of Technology.

Putting his training to use, he developed the high-speed steam hammer and high-speed steel cutting tools that would work even when red-hot. But the workmen, not the machines, were really the source of inefficiency in industry, he concluded. To improve human efficiency, he originated time study, work planning, and fatigue study. Of the three, his fatigue study is most frequently recalled today. We have already described his study of the men who carried pig iron. As a result, Taylor introduced the rest pause, which became the ubiquitous coffee break.

Frank B. Gilbreth had served his apprenticeship in bricklaying and, by the age of 22, was supervising construction jobs. At 25, he set himself up as a contractor and quickly became well known for "speed construction." He had improved scaffolds and developed new working methods that made it possible to lay a brick with about one-third of the motion and handling that conventional methods required. For fifteen years, using many of Taylor's efficiency ideas plus his own methods of motion elimination, he built skyscrapers all across the country.

At the age of 40, he gave up contracting and devoted the rest of his life to "motion study," which we have mentioned in Chapter 2.

In this chapter we will draw some general suggestions from the great number of reports that have been published in the fields of scientific management and motion economy. Regardless of the kind of work you do, you will find these guides very useful in organizing your work.

2 TIME AND WORK ANALYSIS

Bea Rasmussen, the office manager of a large company, was one of a group of highly skilled secretaries enrolled in a work organization program at a community college. Her first assignment was to explain

Taylor's pre-World War II fatigue study is the subject of this cartoon, which appeared in a university magazine.

Courtesy of *Banter*, Colgate University

{ Terrible Predicament of the Industrial Psychologist Who Lost His Whistle After Blowing for the Rest Period. }

why she thought her work needed to be organized. She explained, "My job is beginning to drive me crazy. I have so many interruptions I can't get anything done. If I don't get a system pretty soon, I'm going to quit." Bea found that her complaint was common among the other students. It is usual for a secretary to be deluged with a flood of details that can easily confuse and confound a worker.

Systematizing any job involves organizing work activities into logical sequences, scheduling work, and following up. Bea began her work organization program by keeping a diary for 2 weeks. Each day she checked off her work activities on a chart. An example of such a chart is the *Time/Work Analysis* sheet shown on page 189.

At the end of 2 weeks, Bea totaled the time segments for each activity, as shown in the *Activity Chart* on page 190. Then she arranged the totals in descending order, as shown on the *Time Breakdown* on page 191.

In analyzing her breakdown, Bea found that she had not had an accurate picture of how she had hitherto spent her time on the job. For one thing, she found that she was spending too much time on the telephone. While she could not control her incoming calls, she could do something about the calls she made: she could group them together and do them all at one time. Bea also saw a mountain of work in her file tray and knew she had not been spending enough time filing. This was

TIME/WORK ANALYSIS*

Date: 6/1/—

Time	Processing Mail	Dictation	Transcription	Straight Typing	Drafting Material	Incoming Calls	Outgoing Calls	Visitors	Boss Conferences	Co-worker Conferences	Filing	Miscellaneous
9:00												✓
9:15		✓										
9:30		✓										
9:45		✓										
10:00	✓											
10:15						✓						
10:30							✓					
10:45									✓			
11:00								✓				
11:15			✓									
11:30							✓					
11:45			✓				✓					
1:00			✓									
1:15			✓									
1:30	✓											
1:45											✓	
2:00		✓										
2:15			✓							✓		
2:30			✓									
2:45					✓							
3:00									✓			
3:15							✓					
3:30				✓								
3:45				✓								
4:00					✓							
4:15				✓								
4:30												✓
Totals	30	75	90	45	15	30	30	15	30	15	15	30

*Ruth I. Anderson, Dorothy E. Lee, Allien A. Russon, Jacquelyn A. Wentzell, and Helen M. S. Horack, *The Administrative Secretary: Resource*, McGraw-Hill, New York, 1970, p. 76.

because she failed to set aside a portion of her daily time for this chore. Bea discovered that she had to organize her day into time segments that would be filled by doing certain kinds of work: filing, typing correspondence, telephoning, opening mail, and so on. Also, she found that

Dates: 6/1/– to 6/12/–

Day and Date	Processing Mail	Dictation	Transcription	Straight Typing	Drafting Material	Incoming Calls	Outgoing Calls	Visitors	Boss Conferences	Co-worker Conferences	Filing	Miscellaneous	Total Hours
M, 6/1	½	1¼	1½	¾	½	¼	½	¼	½	¼	¼	½	7
T, 6/2	½	1	3	¼	¼	¾	¼	–	½	–	½	–	7
W, 6/3	½	1	1½	½	¾	¼	½	–	½	½	½	½	7
T, 6/4	½	1	3	–	½	½	¼	¼	½	½	–	–	7
F, 6/5	½	¾	1½	½	½	½	1	¼	½	½	¼	¼	7
M, 6/8	½	1½	2	½	½	½	¼	¼	½	–	½	–	7
T, 6/9	½	1½	1¼	½	–	½	½	¼	¾	¾	¾	–	7
W, 6/10	½	1½	1¾	–	1	½	½	¼	¾	¼	–	–	7
T, 6/11	½	1¼	2½	–	–	½	½	¼	1	–	¼	¼	7
F, 6/12	½	½	2	1	1	½	½	½	–	¼	¼	–	7
Totals in Hours	5	11¼	20	4	5	4¾	4¾	2¼	5½	3	3	1½	70

*Ruth I. Anderson, Dorothy E. Lee, Allien A. Russon, Jacquelyn A. Wentzell, and Helen M. S. Horack, *The Administrative Secretary: Resource,* McGraw-Hill, New York, 1970, p. 75.

her breaks and lunch hour could be taken at times that would really afford her the best rest before a heavier period of work. She found that the best time to do her filing was during the last 15 minutes before leaving. Her boss left 15 minutes before she did, and so she had a quiet, uninterrupted 15 minutes just for her filing. And, during this time, she found that in addition she was able to code and sort letters to be filed the next day. Bea also decided to make her outgoing calls just after dictation. This was just a beginning, but gradually Bea was able to schedule all her activities to both her own and her boss's satisfaction.

TIME BREAKDOWN

Activities	Hours
Transcription	20
Dictation	11¼
Boss conferences	5½
Drafting material	5
Processing mail	5
Incoming calls	4¾
Outgoing calls	4¾
Straight typing	4
Co-worker conferences	3
Filing	3
Visitors	2¼
Miscellaneous	1½

3 UNSCRAMBLE YOUR WORK

Even after organizing your work, you will very often find that things just don't turn out the way you have planned them. You may have everything set up for your next day's work; then when you come to work in the morning and sit down to start your day, the phone rings at the wrong time, or your supervisor visits you, or you have to attend a special meeting. A hundred things could happen that you hadn't planned on. What you thought was a fine organization plan yesterday evening, before you left for home, today becomes a scramble.

Lena specialized in traffic-rate work. She was clever with figures and skilled with a slide rule. In fact, she was the most efficient clerk that could be found. As word of her abilities spread throughout the company, people began to arrive at her desk at inopportune moments, especially at times when she was deeply involved with her own work.

Soon, Lena was becoming irritable, getting behind in her work, and losing confidence. The office manager noticed this change in Lena and naturally became concerned—perhaps she had troubles at home or was not getting enough sleep. The manager asked the company nurse to have a talk with Lena to try to find out what was wrong.

No, don't visit the psychiatrist! The problem was not emotional instability but *interruptions.* Lena's job had become a scramble.

The office manager assigned a typist to help Lena. Having a job that required less intense concentration, the typist was free to be a "buffer" between Lena and her interruptions, answering all phone calls and interviewing all intruders. If an important problem arose that needed

Lena's attention, the typist would hold it aside until Lena was free. Thus, the unnecessary pressures of a routine day were removed from Lena, and so her job became unscrambled.

The force of an interruption can be reduced if we keep part of our attention on the work we had been doing and part of it on the interruption. For example, if you are interrupted while checking a ledger page, keep a finger at the figure you were checking before you were interrupted. In this way, you can quickly resume your work where you left off, and you can drop a polite hint to the interrupter to be brief. If you have to leave your desk, leave yourself a note to remind you what you were doing before you left your desk. Never rely entirely on your memory.

If you have to interrupt someone, wait, if you can, until the other person is at a break in his work or shows signs of changes in his attention. Don't barge in. Save your questions for an appropriate time: just after coffee break or lunch, for example. Chronic interrupters are pests. Remember that a needless or poorly timed interruption is a crime against personal efficiency. It makes the interrupter as popular as poison ivy. One of the most important jobs of an executive secretary is to "organize" all interruptions for the boss and present them at the right moment. This is an enormous contribution to the executive's efficiency.

When someone interrupts you, try to settle the matter right away. Don't let it hang on and bother you when you are trying to concentrate on your job. Your chain of thought will be continuously interrupted by this distraction. General George C. Marshall, when he was Chief of Staff, avoided having the same interruption a second time by putting a sign on his office door which read: "Once you open this door, *walk in, no matter what is going on inside.*"

Don't interrupt *yourself* by letting your mind wander to other problems. Follow through with the job you are doing at present. If you have to make a call or think of something important relating to another problem, make a note of it on a piece of paper. Treat yourself just as you would when you must interrupt another person—wait for the right time.

Many jobs are a scramble and are done on a catch-as-catch-can basis until they are planned and organized. The private secretary's job is a good example of one that has a tendency to become scrambled because of the huge number of tasks that may be involved. Surveys have shown that secretarial jobs may involve some 871 different duties and that the average secretary has about 132 different tasks. These range from typing letters to seeing that the boss's traffic tickets are paid.

 BACKTRACKING

Making an unnecessary trip is *backtracking*. The usual method for setting a table is a good example of backtracking. First, the tablecloth is spread. Then a trip is made *back* to the kitchen to get the silver. Another trip is made *back* to the kitchen for salt, pepper, and sugar. Still another trip is made *back* for napkins. And so on. Those trips *back* to the kitchen empty-handed are wasteful. The average table can be set with only a couple of trips if things are carried on a tray.

Storing things near to where they will be used is one way to cut down on backtracking. Another way is to plan your work sequence so that one thing leads to the next, and fresh starts are not necessary. A Vermont farmer who customarily walked 3¼ miles a day was able to cut this down to 1¼ miles by carefully planning his work schedule. If your job is to open the mail and distribute it, and if you are also called on to provide office supplies, why not carry the needed supplies along with the mail so that an extra trip or trips needed to bring the supplies can be avoided? Of course, don't overload yourself so that you will drop things. Stooping down to pick things up is also a form of backtracking because *it wastes energy.* You can think of anything that is done unnecessarily as a waste of energy and as backtracking.

A salesman can cut down on backtracking by arranging his calls in a sequence that will use the least amount of time. By efficiently planning his calls, he also saves gasoline, if he has to drive, and shoe leather, if he has to walk. A store salesman can avoid backtracking by making fewer trips to the stockroom. In one chain of retail stores it was found that the average salesman went through 167 operations in selling a pair of shoes. Many of these operations involved backtracking. After taking a customer's foot measurements, the salesman could have brought two or three styles of shoes at one time instead of going back each time the customer was dissatisfied. When he returned to the stockroom, the salesman could have brought back unwanted items. And, to avoid extra trips for each request, he might have tried to find out all the items the customer wanted.

Interruptions cause backtracking, too. Every time you lose your place because of an interruption and have to *find* it again after the intruder leaves, you are backtracking. Always try to complete a task before you talk to the intruder. However, there is one case in which backtracking *appears* to be the more efficient way: this is when signing your name. The best way is to go back and cross the "t's" and dot the "i's" after you have written your name, instead of crossing and dotting in the middle of pen strokes. Actually, this is not really backtracking because it is the most efficient way to write your name. It would be backtracking if you stopped each time you came to an "i" or a "t."

Efficiency experts have found that many jobs are done inefficiently because of backtracking. They have been working out routines for workers to follow to avoid this unnecessary effort. Backtracking is an *interruption* — it in itself is a distraction, and so it cuts down on efficiency. Once again, you don't have to be an efficiency expert to cut down on your backtracking. Just look at your work, and ask yourself, "Is there anything else I can do along with this task to cut down on time consumption?" You may find that this will take a good deal of thought and planning in the beginning, but after a while you will look at this useful effort as a challenge.

5 FINISH YOUR WORK

Finish each task as a unit. Don't leave yourself hanging in midstream, unless, of course, an emergency comes up. A wise boss asks a worker to fit in extra work at a convenient time. Some "unreasonable" actions on the part of workers are due to irritation caused by interruptions in work. One automobile plant had a sit-down strike in the paint department because inspectors interrupted the painters to have them touch up imperfections. This was a twofold blunder: calling attention to mistakes and interrupting work. This problem was easily solved. A touch-up expert was assigned to each inspector. Thus, the regular painters were not taken from their goal-motivated work. The strike had illustrated that a change of work was not helpful.

Herbert Spencer (1820–1903), a noted British philosopher who lived in a world of deep thoughts, avoided time-wasting chatter at his boardinghouse by wearing ear pads at mealtimes so that he could

Careful organization can prevent a great deal of backtracking. Think of ways this person might avoid extra steps on the job.

Courtesy U.S. Postal Service

keep his mind on a thought without interruption. Being a recognized genius, he could get away with such rude behavior. Perhaps you cannot afford bad manners, but you can avoid interrupting others and making them wish they had ear pads.

Part of organizing work is to determine what *can* be done in a specified amount of time. A good supervisor never overloads a worker, but if there is a load of work to be done, the worker should be able to allot a certain amount of time for completing each task. This will give him a feeling of accomplishment, and at the same time he will satisfy the job requirements.

 ## DON'T BE AN ON-THE-JOB HUNTER!

The new salesman looked promising — but his prospects lost interest while he *hunted* for his order blanks. He was a good talker and was able to convince a person to buy his product, but when the golden moment for closing the sale arrived, he couldn't find the order form. This gave the customer time to think, "Do I really want to buy this widget? Maybe I should wait and see. . . . Oh, I've changed my mind; I think I'll wait. I'll drop in another time." Another sale was lost by the "hunter." Save your hunting for the weekends. A word of advice: when you see a fox in the bushes, don't hunt for your bullets.

With this in mind, keep the things you need handy. When a secretary's boss is ready to dictate a letter, this is not the time for the secretary to start looking for a steno pad or pencil. The time it takes to look for supplies that should be at hand may not only lose a customer — and money, as in the case of the salesman who could never find his order forms; it may also cut down on your efficiency as a worker. This is still another form of backtracking.

Employment interviewers sometimes ask applicants for a match or a pencil to see if they know where things are in their pockets or handbags. While this rough-and-ready test doesn't tell too much else about an applicant, it does give the interviewer an idea about a person's efficiency.

Sometimes duplicating a piece of equipment, if it isn't too expensive, saves backtracking time — time taken to hunt for the equipment or to wait for someone to finish using it. For example, every office should have a pencil sharpener. If there is a large amount of duplicating done, it might be a good idea to have more than one copy machine. If a tool is used frequently, it would be good to have several around and handy. "Mary, who's got the staple remover?" "I gave it to Tom." "No, I don't have it; Sheila came in and borrowed it." And so on and on and on!

Back in the early 1930s when things weren't going too well for the young *New Yorker* magazine, Ross was the editor, and one of the writers was Edna Ferber. One afternoon about 3 o'clock, as the story goes, Ross found Ms. Ferber downstairs looking idly at a display in a store window. He said to her in a ruffled tone, "Edna, why aren't you upstairs in the office writing?" She replied succinctly, "Someone was using *the* pencil."

TIRED? OR JUST TIRED OF *THIS*?

It is certainly a very good idea to change tasks about every two hours. After a couple of hours at the same task, a worker can truthfully say, "I'm not tired, but I am tired of *this*!" This is particularly true when work is brought along in a steady flow. Repetitive work results in high mechanical efficiency at first but makes workers inefficient after an hour or so. The endless supply of work, without a break, makes the job seem harder and makes a worker restless. People work best when there is a periodic change every hour or two.

If you can't change your work routine, it is a good rule to try to change some aspect of the work anyway, such as the work tempo. Possibly some other aspect of your work can be varied, such as the order in which it is done. In some factories, where the tempo of work is determined by the speed of a conveyor belt that moves unchangingly, a change of work is provided by allowing workers to swap jobs every couple of hours. For instance, in a laundry a worker might feed the mangle for one hour and then fold laundry for an hour. When it isn't possible to switch jobs, it might be possible to change position; that is, stand up or sit down.

On the other hand, changing tasks too often is also inefficient because this, too, causes a worker to become nervous and uncomfortable. The rate of change depends on the nature of the work and must be determined by experience.

ALTERNATE HARD WITH EASY TASKS

Hard and easy tasks should be alternated. When the task has to be the same all day long, and there are no easy parts to sandwich in, a change of pace will help. Set a fast pace the first hour, then take it easier the next. Always make the first hour a brisk one.

Music is sometimes used for pacing, to alternate brisk and leisurely movements. A half hour of lively tunes is followed by a half hour of silence; then a half hour of waltzes is followed by another period of silence. Continuous music or the same type of music is not so helpful as brief spells that set a change of pace.

The old-time "efficiency engineer" or "systems expert" failed to take into consideration this human need for changing pace. He tried to keep workers at top pace all the time, which cannot be done. Change of pace is supplied in this book by sprinkling easier sections among the more difficult ones.

START WITH THE MOST DIFFICULT

Start with the difficult or disliked task. A homemaker who hates to make beds should do this job first, thereby reducing the feeling of drudgery. Get the difficult part out of the way first so that it is not hanging over your head, haunting you.

There is one exception to this rule. The learner should start with the easier parts of a job for the feeling of confidence it will give him. Tackle the job as it is, of course, but tackle the easier part at the beginning.

PLAN STOPPING PLACES

Work should be planned so that there are definite stopping places at which we can feel that something has been accomplished. Stopping places are needed particularly in routine, repetitive work. The demoralization felt by householders when their belongings are moved pell-mell into a new house is comparable to the feelings of workers when work is piled up in a heap with no stopping place in sight.

Having a big pile of work at one time causes jitters. Workers complain that management has started a speedup when a foreman distributes parts to be assembled by the barrelful. There are fewer complaints and work is actually speeded up when only a basketful of parts is given at a time. People like the security of steady employment, but they cannot do their best work when they have an unending stream of work staring them in the face.

Workers always want to feel they are making headway. The mechanical savings accomplished by the conveyor have been paid for many times over in the cost of labor unrest it sometimes causes. The conveyor and assembly line are here to stay. So is unrest—until conveyor work is organized so that people feel they are making headway. The conveyor has the merit of grouping similar tasks together. Otherwise, it has mostly demerits, though clever management can change some of these into merits.

Organize and plan work so that you think more about what has been accomplished than about what remains to be done. In one sales office, envelopes were being addressed by hand to telephone subscribers across the country. This was unskilled temporary work, and high wages were paid. Yet only a few workers stayed on the job more than two or three days. The boss was a slave driver, they said on quitting. Investigation showed that each worker was given a thick telephone directory and a stack of several thousand envelopes each morning.

To change the system so that it would provide stopping points, the telephone directories were cut apart. Each worker was given one sheet (two pages) at a time. Thus the work was broken into smaller chunks, and each worker had a feeling of headway as each small batch was finished. The workers no longer quit after a couple of days, and the output increased despite the time lost in walking for supplies.

The individual can make better progress if he sets himself definite goals that are close at hand. For example, a person may resolve to improve his vocabulary but never does, because that is a vague goal. But if he makes the goal definite—to learn and to use three new words a day—progress results because he can see results each day. Definite goals encourage "will power."

11 RELAX

No matter how well you have organized your work for the day, your mental attitudes and physical condition can help or hinder your efforts. A tense and nervous person cannot be expected to work at his most efficient level. Try to relax before starting an activity. Take a few moments, close your eyes, and try not to think of anything, or think of something pleasant and diverting like a beautiful garden.

Ruth St. Denis, the famous dancer, was a tense, clumsy girl when she lived on a New Jersey farm; she was anything but poised and graceful. Yet she became a dancer. She made it a habit before each performance to take 30 minutes alone resting and meditating. For her, this was as important as practicing her dance steps.

Paderewski always practiced making his entrance to the stage piano before each recital. He counted the steps he would have to take to the instrument. Twenty minutes before the recital, he locked himself in his dressing room with lights out and relaxed with eyes shut. When it was time for his entrance, he was led to the wings, his eyes still shut. He walked to the piano with his eyes still shut, counting the steps to the piano.

Working at top speed will be self-defeating if it causes a person to be tense or nervous. Unhurried thoroughness makes for greatest speed, accomplishment, and accuracy in the long run. And it does not cause high blood pressure, ulcers, or nervous indigestion. Occasional bursts of speed to break monotony are fine, but even a machine works most efficiently at a steady speed.

Parents are elated when their children first learn to walk. But scientists are of the opinion that most of us never really learn to walk—at least most do not learn the best way to walk.

Walking is really a considerable task for humans. Our bodies are not really designed for an erect posture, and walking puts a strain on both the back and the feet. As you know, we walk on the soles of our feet with heels touching the ground. Therefore, man is a "plantigrade" animal like bears, raccoons, pandas, and kinkajous—they all walk in this fashion.

For best walking, try to walk on the ball of the foot rather than on either the toes or the heels. In this way the weight is distributed over most of the foot. Some people *pound* when they walk; that is because they put too much weight on their heels. Other people *bounce*; they are walking too much on their toes. The ideal way is to *glide*, using the ball of the foot.

The 1-2-3 of footwork in walking is shown in the drawing on page 199. High heels, of course, make the toes do more than their share and make the walk bouncy rather than gliding. High heels make every step like walking upstairs.

Avoid walking in zigzags. This is inefficient, yet most people walk in this way. In the illustration on page 200 the footprints show the proper way to walk.

Climbing calls for changes in walking techniques. For one thing, it consumes several times as much energy as walking on level ground. In climbing stairs, for instance, you should take about half as many steps per minute as you do when walking. Even at that slow pace, you may find yourself out of breath quickly.

For efficient as well as graceful stair climbing, lean forward slightly from the ankle. Put the *entire foot*, not just the ball and toes, on the next step. Put your foot as far back on the step as possible, but not precariously on the front edge. Start up slowly—climbing uses a lot of

Rules for proper walking are to (1) put the heel down first, gently without pounding; (2) roll the foot forward, putting most of the weight on the outside; and (3) push ahead with the toes, gliding, not bouncing.

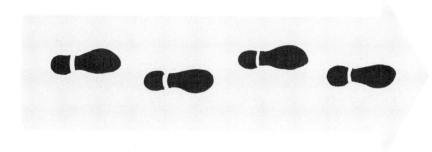

Walking in a straight line, with the feet pointing directly forward, strengthens the arches and provides the best leverage.

energy. By the time you get to the top of the stairs, your heart may be beating twice as rapidly as it was before you started to climb. So take the first steps easily to allow the internal machinery time to shift gears.

13   LIFTING AND CARRYING

One of Frederick Taylor's best-known contributions is what he called the "law of heavy laboring." According to Taylor's law, muscles work efficiently only if workers carry loads only part of the time. For this reason he introduced rest pauses for laborers who were assigned to carry heavy loads. The length of the pause varied depending on the size of the load.

The muscle system has more lifting force when you stand close to the object you want to lift. Don't lean over a chair to try to raise a sticky window; your feet will be too far away from the load. Instead, get up close to the window—down on your knees if necessary—and press tightly to the wall so that your arms are in the position shown at the right in the illustration on page 201. Then you are under the load and can push up rather than pull. In general it is better to push than pull.

The muscle system has more lifting force if you use the bigger muscles in preference to the smaller ones. Lift with your leg muscles, for example, instead of with your arm muscles, and never, never lift with your back muscles.

Using the knees to lift is shown in the second illustration on page 201. The figure on the left is trying to lift in the worst possible way—with the back. Always crouch, if possible; then keep the back stiff and do the lifting by straightening the knees.

When you get up from a chair you are lifting a heavy load—your body. Make the best use of your natural leverage and get up easily and gracefully by (1) pulling one foot so the heel is even with the front edge

Trying to open a sticky window as shown on the left can injure the back. The correct way, shown on the right, is safer and more efficient.

of the seat, (2) pulling the other foot a little farther back, and (3) leaning forward slightly at the same time that you are pushing with both legs. You will not need to push with your arms; if you do, the chair has been poorly designed, since it does not permit you to get your feet under the center of gravity.

Two principles should be observed when carrying loads of any weight. (1) *Get the hands under the load with the palms up.* (2) *Carry the load so that the weight is equally distributed.* In the third illustration

The wrong way of lifting is shown on the left, the correct way on the right.

on page 202, the figure at the left is in the incorrect position; the figure at the right is in the proper position.

It is always wise, at any age, to keep in good physical shape. You can join a gym, or you can run around the block when you get home from work. Then try lifting weights or some other heavy objects carefully to build up your arm and leg strength. Push-ups are good for arm and shoulder muscles; knee bends are good for leg and foot muscles. Bicycle riding is also recommended.

14 VALUE OF SUBGOALS

Many minor goals that can be achieved during the day's activities help personal efficiency. When work is properly organized, there is a spontaneous spurt to finish the forenoon's quota during the half hour before lunch. There is a stronger spurt during the half hour before quitting time in the afternoon. Most production curves show slumps during the closing half hour—indicating that the work has not been properly organized.

This is a continuation of the idea of having many homestretches, but it is worth extra emphasis. Ambitious individuals, driving bosses, and conscientious homemakers make the inefficient blunder of biting off chunks that are too big for a half-day quota. Plan goals so that there

The wrong way of carrying is shown on the left, the correct way on the right.

is a definite stopping place at lunchtime and again at the end of the workday. Better yet, have subgoals you can reach about every hour.

Long automobile trips can be made less fatiguing by planning not just the total mileage for a day, but also numerous subgoals to anticipate. Instead of looking 350 miles ahead, look 35 miles ahead to the next county seat. These subgoals will help you realize your expectations sooner and more often and make the long trip seem easier.

It is astonishing how little things can be goal gradients. In the monotonous job of thinning sugar beets, yellow flags were used to give goal gradients. The flags were stuck in every 100 feet along the rows. Production increased 32 percent. The workers weeded from flag to flag, reaching many subgoals during the day.

Another example is the executive who wanted to cut down on smoking. He limited himself to one cigarette after he had finished the morning's dictation, another after he had checked departmental reports, and more at other natural stopping places in his work. He was astounded how much quicker he finished his detail work and attributed it to less nicotine. While less smoking may have helped, there were also strong goal-gradient effects as each budgeted cigarette served to mark off a subgoal. His day had been organized by budgeting cigarettes so that they gave him several homestretches.

SUGGESTIONS FOR FURTHER READING

Anderson, Ruth I., Dorothy E. Lee, Allien A. Russon, Jacquelyn A. Wentzell, and Helen M. S. Horack, *The Administrative Secretary: Resource*, New York: McGraw-Hill, 1970.

Bittel, Lester R., *What Every Supervisor Should Know*, 3d ed, New York: McGraw-Hill, 1974.

McGregor, Douglas, *The Professional Manager*, New York: McGraw-Hill, 1967.

TO HELP YOU REMEMBER

1. What is a scrambled job, and how can a worker avoid having one?
2. How can a person handle an interruption efficiently?
3. What is backtracking, and how does it lower efficiency?
4. What is an on-the-job hunter, and how can this problem be corrected?
5. Why should tasks or the tempo of work be changed from time to time?
6. What are some good ways to deal with the hard or disliked parts of a job?

7. What can be done to give a person a feeling that he is making headway toward the completion of a job?
8. What are the rules for efficient walking and climbing?

WORKING WITH PEOPLE, DATA, OR THINGS

The Edison Paper Company is a high-quality, long-established firm that has produced paper products for years (bond, envelopes, mimeograph and duplicator paper, stencils, masters, card stock, labels, and so on). Old Mr. Edison recently retired and sold his family business to a couple of young engineers.

One of the first things the new management did was to hire an office manager, David Sommerfield, in an effort to improve the office procedures and cut down office inefficiency.

All the "old heads" around the company were beginning to think that David Sommerfield was an overpaid fraud because for a month he did nothing but observe other people working. Of course, he carried a notebook and a pencil around, but it seemed that he was doing nothing to improve any procedures or cut down office inefficiency; he didn't even act friendly toward the staff.

Finally, one day he called a staff meeting and distributed a stack of forms (what he called time/work analysis forms) to each office worker. The left-hand column of each form had the heading "time" and was broken into 15-minute segments from 8:30 a.m. to 4:30 p.m. (the Edison Paper Company workday).

There were 12 blank spaces for column headings across the top of each form, and the heading "Miscellaneous" was printed over the final column.

Mr. Sommerfield told the staff that he wanted everyone to chart his work activities for a whole month, using one of the forms for each day's activities. He directed them to list each of their major job categories in the blank spaces for column headings. Then, he said, "Date each form, and check the appropriate column for every 15-minute period." He announced their next meeting (in four weeks) and said, "We'll discuss these work diaries then."

On the way out of the meeting, Joe Adams, the accounting department manager, said to one of his department payroll clerks, "What's with this diary kick? They're probably paying the guy fifteen grand, and is this all he can come up with? I would not have believed it if I hadn't heard it with my own ears. Well, I could care less, and if he wants to have us waste time playing this tiddlywinks game that's his business. Old man Edison wouldn't have hired him in the first place. Tell me, will you, how this diary is gonna cut office inefficiency."

Questions

1. Do you agree with Adams that the diary procedure would be too time consuming for its worth?
2. How successful do you think that Sommerfield's procedures improvement program will be?
3. If you were Sommerfield, would you have gone about an improvement program in the same way? If not, how would you have planned an improvement program?
4. What do you recommend should be done at the next meeting.
5. Develop a time/study analysis form, and chart your study time in 15-minute segments. Total the columns for each of your subjects. Then analyze your study time, and try to determine how you can better utilize your time. Finally, reschedule your study time by making an outline of the major blocks of studying to be done. These might be grouped under the headings "routine reviewing" (going over class lecture notes), "regular assignments" (reading and writing), and "studying for special quizzes and exams" (including "pop" quizzes as well as unit tests, midterm exams, and final exams).

THINGS TO DO

1. Talk with some successful executives or their secretaries to find out how they organize their many tasks. Report on how the way they work illustrates some of the principles given in this chapter.
2. Observe the work in a filling station or at a lunch counter, and report how work materials and tools are arranged for efficiency.
3. Talk with a safety director or safety engineer, and report on the safety rules that they recommend following in planning and organizing work.
4. Thomas Jefferson was enthusiastic about having things done as efficiently as possible and has been called the first "efficiency engineer." Find out how he went about improving his efficiency. (You may use library books for your research.)
5. Analyze your own work and study habits, and report on three improvements you should make in organization.
6. Analyze some job you are familiar with, and work out a reorganization plan that provides for cutting down on backtracking, searching time, interruptions, and other inefficiencies.
7. Prepare a short talk on the pros and cons of job simplification and the pros and cons of unscrambling work. Be sure to discuss the difference between the two. You may read articles or books to gather facts to support your talk, or you may discuss these two methods with professional people.

PART 3

JOB
ADJUSTMENT

UNDERSTANDING YOURSELF

11

What This Chapter Is About

Because you are an adult and you have done many things, you probably think that you know yourself pretty well. Don't you? But have you actually taken the time, even as much as a half hour, to think about yourself? Have you ever tried to figure out the things you like best to do, your relationships with different people in your life, your interests and preferences, your prejudices and values? All these are part of your personality. Have you ever thought of relating these considerations to your career goals?

People frequently take it for granted that they understand themselves. Yet they do not evaluate their actions in terms of themselves as individuals, different from all other people. Suppose you had just won $1,000 in a lottery. How would you spend it? Would you buy new clothes, some furniture, a painting, or a motorcycle? Would you give some of the money to a friend who really needs it? By answering these, and questions like them, you will begin to have some idea about what you are like.

Why should you try to understand yourself and the elements that go into making up your personality? By understanding yourself—as completely as possible—you will be in a position to choose the kind of work that you would actually enjoy doing. This is what is known as a career. According to Dr. Herbert N. Greenberg, a clinical psychologist, 80 percent of working Americans fail to achieve successful careers— the type of work that suits their personalities. The symptoms of this failure are frustration; job dissatisfaction; working for money only; the hate-to-wake-up attitude; and eagerness for breaks and quitting time.

A successful career integrates learning and doing and creates a unified, productive environment from the worlds of the home, the community, the school, and the workplace. An understanding of oneself is a first step toward building a career.

You will need to find out what your vocational goals are, because it is likely that you will be spending the next 30 to 40 years working and earning a living. Any activity that is going to occupy that much of a person's lifetime certainly deserves some thought.

After you have determined what vocation you want to pursue, you must then plan to learn about this vocation. Your attention will be turned to *career education,* which will prepare you for the kind of work that you will be doing. In this chapter the word *career* shall be used as a comprehensive term to include what is commonly referred to as job, work, vocation, occupation, or profession.

Many people don't think of pursuing a career. They live routine lives and work to earn money for some immediate objective, such as buying a car, a house, clothes, or food. Of course, a person can live through his entire life relying on odd jobs, and perhaps he will be able to buy some of the things he needs with the money he earns, but this life style will usually lead to feelings of insecurity and dissatisfaction.

2 APPROACHES TO UNDERSTANDING YOURSELF

Perhaps you consider yourself just an average person. Especially when you are a young grade school pupil, your life may seem quite similar to that of your classmates, but already there are distinct differences in intelligence, athletic ability, family life, hobbies, and a host of other aspects of your personal world that make you unique. This uniqueness may seem to make it difficult to choose a career. If you are unlike anyone else, how can you find a job tailored to your personality?

The answer is, of course, that it is unrealistic to seek a career designed just for you. However, it is possible to assess your personality and to match your talents, interests, and aptitudes to the job opportunities that are available. Many psychological tests have been developed that allow you to compare yourself to the average person sharing your interests and abilities. The more you learn about yourself, the better you will be able to decide what career is likely to bring you success and personal satisfaction.

The U.S. Employment Service, a department of the Department of Labor, has compiled the *Dictionary of Occupational Titles,* a comprehensive listing and description of the various types of jobs available in this country. This two-volume work is intended primarily for placement counselors, but its wealth of information is useful to anyone interested in choosing a career. For each occupation listed in the *DOT* (as the dictionary is commonly called), there are six worker trait components, or factors that are necessary for acceptable performance on the job. The worker trait components are as follows:

1 Training time (general educational development, specific vocational preparation)
2 Aptitudes
3 Interests
4 Temperament
5 Physical demands
6 Working conditions

In the following sections, ways in which you can develop understanding of yourself will be discussed. Each worker trait component will be defined and discussed, and both informal and formal methods of self-evaluation will be presented. After evaluating each component in terms of yourself, you will be in a good position to select a career that will be suitable for you and meaningful to your life style.

3 TRAINING TIME

Although some jobs are easy to learn, even the simplest ones require some training. At the very least, the worker must be made aware of his duties, and in a more complex situation, the experience of years of work and study may be part of the necessary training. Training for a career begins with general educational development.

General Educational Development

Through formal and informal education, a child learns to reason and follow instructions and acquires such tools as language and mathematical skills. This general education is not taught with a specific career in mind, but it is a vital part of the worker's training. Can you imagine, for example, a pharmacist who couldn't read? The six-year-old studying his primer may not know that some day he will use his reading skill to interpret prescriptions and identify medicines by their labels, but it is easy to see the importance of this general skill to the specific career situation. Even workers whose jobs involve mostly physical activity need some level of general education. A truck driver who could not read a road sign or gasoline gauge would be as unable to perform his job as an illiterate pharmacist.

You can get a rough idea of your own general educational development by rating yourself on the scales on pages 211 to 213. (In the following sections you will have a chance to rate yourself on other worker trait components.) Remember that these scales are only rough indicators. They tell *how you perceive* the quality of your performance. If you are very conceited, on the one hand, or very modest, on the other, your attitude will influence the way you rate yourself. When you are in the process of applying for a job or planning a career, more objective tests may be used to evaluate your abilities. For example, an employer may request a transcript of your school record or may administer a test. However, you can use your self-evaluation in deciding on a career. You can look up in the *DOT* the occupations that interest you and compare the score you have given yourself to the requirements of the jobs.

As a first test of general educational development, rate yourself on the level of your reasoning ability. You will note that the abilities progress from understanding concrete, specific ideas to complex, abstract reasoning. Rate yourself on a scale of 1 to 6 according to the number of your highest level of skill. For example, if you are capable of learning the principles of a system, such as bookkeeping or electrical wiring, and then applying those principles to a practical problem, you can reason at level 4. If you can achieve level 4 but cannot use logic or scientific thinking to define a problem, as described for level 5, then your score would be 4.

REASONING ABILITY

1 Can you apply common-sense understanding to carry out simple, routine, one- or two-step instructions and deal with routine situations?

2 Can you apply common-sense understanding to carry out written or oral instructions involving many simple details? Can you deal with slight variations in a standard procedure?

3 Can you apply common-sense understanding to carry out written or oral instructions or follow diagrams? Can you deal with situations that vary considerably from your routine?

4 Can you learn a system and use it to solve practical problems? Can you deal with many variables in a situation where only limited standardization exists?

5 Can you use principles of logical or scientific thinking to define problems, collect data, establish facts, and draw valid conclusions?

6 Can you apply principles of logical or scientific thinking to a wide range of intellectual and practical problems? Can you learn symbolic languages such as formulas or musical notes? Can you reason about abstract ideas?

In the study of yourself in the area of mathematical development, a similar procedure may be followed. Evaluate yourself on a scale of 1 to 5.

MATHEMATICAL DEVELOPMENT

1 Can you perform simple addition and subtraction? Can you read, count, and record figures?

2 Can you add, subtract, multiply, and divide whole numbers using rules of arithmetic?

3 Can you use arithmetic for problems involving fractions, decimals, and percentages?

4 Can you follow ordinary arithmetic, algebraic, and geometric procedures in standard applications?

5 Can you apply knowledge of advanced math and statistics, such as calculus, factor analysis, and probability? Can you work with theoretical ideas and develop original applications of math?

In the area of communication or language development, you can evaluate your level of comprehension and expression in the English language. You will observe that your rating on this aspect of your general education is important in determining your advancement in a career.

As you answer the following questions, assume that you are trained to do the work described. For example, in answering Question 3, do not discredit yourself if you have not been *trained* to read blueprints. Ask yourself, "Do I understand English well enough to *learn* this skill?"

LANGUAGE DEVELOPMENT

1 Can you learn your job duties from oral or written instructions? Can you write such identifying information as names and

addresses of customers on orders, or product descriptions on tags or tickets? Can you prepare an oral or written request for supplies?

2 Can you file, post, and mail business forms? Can you copy data from one form onto another and type final copy from a rough draft? Could you conduct simple interviews for a survey (such as a census) or guided tours of points of interest to the public?

3 Can you perform the duties of an executive secretary, such as transcribing dictation, handling mail, and making appointments? Can you perform the duties of an employment agency counselor, such as interviewing potential employees and contacting employers? Can you interpret technical information in such sources as manuals or blueprints?

4 Can you write or edit technical or legal articles and documents? Can you give a lecture on an academic subject? Can you perform the duties of a social worker, such as counseling clients about vocational rehabilitation, marriage, or mental hygiene? Can you evaluate technical engineering data?

The normal method of evaluating your general educational development is to interpret the scores made on standardized tests. These scores will enable a potential employer to compare you with other applicants for a position. If you know your score and your rank compared to the scores and ranks of others who have taken the same tests, you will know what problems in these areas—reasoning, mathematics, and language—you face in competition with others seeking similar careers.

Specific Vocational Preparation

Whatever career you choose, your employer will be interested in your *specific vocational preparation*. This is the part of your education that is concerned with training you for a particular career. Vocational courses in school, training in the military, special courses, and the pursuit of a hobby are all sources of specific vocational preparation that are available to you even before you begin your first job.

While you are working, further vocational preparation is available in the form of apprenticeships, in-plant classroom training, supervision and instruction on the job by an experienced worker, and experience in the lower-level jobs in your chosen career. Specific vocational preparation should not be confused with the orientation programs that some employers offer to introduce newcomers to company rules and customs.

4 YOUR APTITUDES

Training is obviously essential to a successful career; without it, no worker would know how to perform even the simpler tasks involved in his job. Equally important are your *aptitudes*, the special capabilities and natural talents that enable you to learn from your training and to perform the jobs you have learned.

When a person has a very strong aptitude, it is usually easy to notice, and if the person is given appropriate training, it is possible for him to develop a real talent for performing a particular task or activity. For example, the Australian tennis champion, Evonne Goolagong, played with sticks as a young child and used them to bat small objects. As she grew older, intensive coaching enabled her to turn this natural ability into a successful occupation. Of course, relatively few people have the aptitude to become champions at tennis, or, for that matter, in any activity. It is the exceptional aptitude, combined with training, that creates the stars in any field. If your aptitude is of a lower level than Evonne Goolagong's, it is not likely that you will become a world champion, but with training and practice you may have enough skill to become a champion in your own neighborhood.

Intensive coaching enabled the Australian tennis champion Evonne Goolagong to turn a natural ability into a successful career.

United Press International Photo

Any job or other activity requires certain levels of particular aptitudes for the individual to perform adequately. The *Dictionary of Occupational Titles* lists eleven basic aptitudes that are required to a greater or lesser degree for various occupations. As you consider each aptitude, you can rate yourself on a scale of 1 to 5, with 1 indicating the top level of the population and 5 the lowest level. You can then compare your aptitude levels to the requirements of careers that you are considering for yourself.

Intelligence is the aptitude for general learning. People who can understand instructions and basic principles and who can reason and make judgments are considered intelligent. They generally do well in school.

Closely related to general intelligence is *verbal aptitude*, the ability to understand the meanings of words and to use words effectively. Verbal aptitude involves the abilities to understand sentences and paragraphs and present information or ideas. Because so much of our thinking and communication is expressed in words, it is easy to confuse verbal aptitude with general intelligence, and so we must be careful not to underestimate intelligent people who do not have a way with words.

A third aptitude that is associated with academic success is *numerical aptitude*. However, it is easier to identify activities involving numbers than it is to distinguish verbal activities from activities requiring general intelligence. Numerical aptitude means being able to add, subtract, multiply, and divide with speed and accuracy. A study was made of recent high school graduates who had taken a test for numerical aptitude. It was shown that their scores could be used to predict their grades in accounting and other school subjects involving numbers.

The last aptitude that is specifically related to the ability to do well in school is aptitude in *spatial relations*. This is an ability to comprehend forms in space and understand relationships of plane and solid forms. Students who do well in the field of industrial arts score high when taking an aptitude test measuring understanding of spatial relations. They can visualize objects or forms of two or three dimensions and can think in terms of geometric forms. You can rate yourself on a scale of 1 to 5, with 1 being the highest rating of how well you think when you leave the two-dimensional field.

The first four aptitudes are closely related to each other and to many of the courses taken in school. A review of the discussion concerning general educational development will help you understand the relationships between the aptitudes presented and education.

Now let us examine other aptitudes you may have that lead to very important careers but are not so closely tied to schoolwork. These aptitudes are form perception, clerical perception, motor coordination, finger dexterity, manual dexterity, and eye-hand-foot coordination.

Form perception is an ability to notice important details in objects or in pictorial or graphic material and to make visual comparisons, discriminate, and see small differences in shapes and shadings of figures and widths and lengths of lines. This aptitude is very important in areas such as graphic arts. A vice president of an engraving company stated that if an applicant for a position in the art department had this aptitude, he could be taught what was required on the job very quickly. If he didn't have this aptitude, there would be no point in employing him.

Clerical perception has the same relationship to words and numbers that form perception has to pictures and graphs. Clerical aptitude is an ability to perceive pertinent details in verbal or tabular material. A high level of this aptitude is essential in business and office occupations. The owner of a printing plant said that he was amazed by the problems he had with people who tried to read proof when they did not have a clerical aptitude. In the office they could not file documents. He also found that this aptitude was necessary for typesetters. When one considers that approximately 15 percent of the working population of this country is engaged in business and office occupations, the importance of this aptitude becomes obvious.

Motor coordination, finger dexterity, manual dexterity, and eye-hand-foot coordination will be presented together because they are closely related physical abilities of the individual. Successful telephone linemen and splicers have the aptitude of motor coordination. *Motor coordination* is the ability to coordinate eyes and hands or fingers accurately in making exact movements quickly. *Finger dexterity* is the ability to move the fingers skillfully and manipulate small objects rapidly and accurately. Observe that your jewelry repairman has this aptitude; so do the thousands who work on assembly lines producing such things as TV sets and instrument panels. *Manual dexterity* is the ability to move the hands easily and skillfully. An example of workers having this aptitude is the people who cut meat in packing plants. Their hands move so skillfully and quickly that one can hardly follow the movements as the workers trim the meat from the bone. In many manufacturing jobs, this aptitude is necessary. *Eye-hand-foot coordination* is the ability to move the hands and feet in response to what one sees. An example of an activity for which this aptitude is important is playing an organ. The organist must coordinate the visual stimuli of the written music with the hand and foot movements. Rate yourself 1 to 5 on these aptitudes, with 5 being the highest score.

The last aptitude to be mentioned is *color discrimination.* This is the ability to recognize similarities or differences in colors, identify a particular color, and match or contrast colors. A foreman for a telephone switchboard installation crew said that motor coordination, accuracy, and color discrimination were essential skills for his workmen. He could not use people who could not discriminate colors because the wires are wrapped in different colors that serve as codes. Each colored wire has a particular use or position. You can easily rate yourself on this aptitude.

All careers employing the working people of this country require one or more of the aptitudes that have been discussed. But more than aptitude is needed for a successful career. You may have a strong aptitude for clerical work but not want a job that would lead to a career in

Finger dexterity is an important aptitude for one who plans to do watch repair work.

Courtesy of the District of Columbia Public Schools

business. A counselor observed that there are many young workers entering the counseling office who have aptitudes for specific jobs in careers but who do not want to develop these aptitudes. Their reasons will be discussed in the following sections.

5 YOUR INTERESTS

You hear people say, "I didn't do well in that course (or in that work) because I wasn't interested." They imply that the activity was not satisfying to them, and they found it difficult to put forth the necessary effort to perform at least on an average level. Other people look upon interest as motivation. It was found by one consulting psychologist that if a person had an interest in a specific career area, he would persist in pursuing his goal in spite of doing poor work. On the other hand, if he had no interest in a specific career area and then did not achieve satisfactory rewards, he would drop that career goal and seek something else.

Interest may be defined as a preference for certain types of activities. Super and Crites[1] discuss four types of interests and say that they vary according to the method of assessment. *Expressed interests* are specific interests that are made known by a person; they are preferences. *Manifest interests* are expressed through participation in activities. *Inventoried interests* are another person's estimates of one's interests based on responses to a large number of questions concerning likes and dislikes. *Tested interests* are manifest interests, but under controlled situations, not life situations.

It might be of help to do an informal rating of your interests using the suggestion given in the *Dictionary of Occupational Titles.* Five pairs of interest factors are provided; a positive preference for one factor of a pair implies rejection of the other factor of that pair. Which of the following situations do you prefer?

1. Donald E. Super and John O. Crites, *Appraising Vocational Fitness,* Harper and Brothers, New York, 1962, pp. 378–380.

Activities dealing with things and objects.	*or*	Activities concerned with people and the communication of ideas.
Activities involving business contact with people.	*or*	Activities of a scientific and technical nature.
Activities of a routine, concrete, organized nature.	*or*	Activities of an abstract and creative nature.
Working for people for their presumed good, as in the social welfare sense, or dealing with people and language in social situations.	*or*	Activities that are nonsocial in nature and are carried on in relation to processes, machines, and techniques.
Activities resulting in prestige or the esteem of others.	*or*	Activities resulting in tangible, productive satisfaction.

These pairs indicate the main kinds of occupational interests. They will help you to determine whether you prefer working with people or with things, or in concrete situations or with abstract ideas.

Dr. Greenberg, whose study was mentioned in Section 1, placed part of the blame for widespread job dissatisfaction on the lack of exposure of people to different interests. Another consulting psychologist, in discussing characteristics of successful career salesmen, makes the statement, "I have never seen a person succeed as a career salesman who did not have the interest in activities which interest salesmen, but I have seen many who had the interest, as measured by the inventories, fail." Therefore, while interest is a necessary ingredient in a satisfying career, it is only part of the formula.

There are many standardized tests for determining interests. They are useful because, as Super mentions, inventoried interests help to reveal the role of interests in vocational adjustment. They definitely point the way to career selection. Among the most widely used tests are the *Kuder Preference Record* and the *Strong Vocational Interest Blank.* Your counselor can advise you in selecting an inventory that will help you choose a career.

 YOUR TEMPERAMENT

There are many definitions of "temperament." A practical assessment is provided by the *DOT*'s list of occupational situations to which a worker must adjust. As you read the following list and determine which situations you consider most suitable to your way of working, you will gain a clearer idea of your *temperament* or the emotional response you are likely to make to your environment.

1   Situations involving a variety of duties often characterized by frequent change.
2   Situations involving repetitive or short-cycle operations carried out according to set procedures or sequences.
3   Situations involving doing things only under specific instruction, allowing little or no room for independent action or judgment in working out job problems.
4   Situations involving the direction, control, and planning of an entire activity or the activities of others.
5   Situations involving the necessity of dealing with people in actual job duties beyond giving and receiving instructions.
6   Situations involving working alone and apart in physical isolation from others, although the activity may be integrated with that of others.
7   Situations involving influencing people in their opinions, attitudes, or judgments about ideas or things.
8   Situations involving performing adequately under stress when confronted with the critical or unexpected or when taking risks.
9   Situations involving the evaluation (arriving at generalizations, judgments, or decisions) of information against sensory or judgmental criteria.
0   Situations involving the evaluation (arriving at generalizations, judgments, or decisions) of information against measurable or verifiable criteria.
X   Situations involving the interpretation of feelings, ideas, or facts in terms of personal viewpoint.
Y   Situations involving the precise attainment of set limits, tolerances, or standards.

In order to understand your temperament better, for the purpose of selecting a career that will provide a suitable environment, you may record the numbers or letters of the situations you consider suitable to your temperament and compare your picture of yourself to the temperaments required for various occupations listed in the *DOT*.

There are many inventories used by career counselors to help you predict how you and your temperament will fit into a particular career. These inventories enable you to describe yourself and reveal behavioral characteristics as you perceive yourself. Widely used inventories are *The Guilford-Zimmerman Temperament Survey*, the *Minnesota Multiphasic Personality Inventory*, and the *California Psychological Inventory*.

Your self-description may be what you wish you were or what you are in most situations. You can do two things that will enable you to be more objective in this important area and that will help you understand yourself. You can ask others how they see you in the various areas measured. Secondly, you can look at your "track" record—what you have done in the various encounters with others. Look at your school record. Look at your community record. If you are not pleased with what you have done or not done, you can change your behavior to help achieve your career goals. Your awareness of your temperament is very important. As a consulting psychologist observed, "Of all the measurements used to predict success in careers, if I could use only one instrument, it would be an instrument to determine temperament."

A personnel manager expressed the same viewpoint when he said, "I have seen persons who had everything it takes—aptitudes, interests—fail because of temperament. Eighty percent of the people who fail in jobs do so because they can't adjust to situations and to other people and not because they lack ability or aptitude or knowledge." When one knows his temperament, he can do one of two things: he can accept it and seek a career that supports it, or he can take steps to change it and meet the demands of a career for which he has the aptitudes, interests, and training to enter.

 ## YOUR PHYSICAL TRAITS

Even if a job is primarily sedentary—that is, if it can be performed with the worker in a seated position—there will be some physical requirements. The *Dictionary of Occupational Titles* lists six sets of physical activities that different jobs require in varying degrees. The extent to which you are capable of performing these activities will determine whether you can undertake a particular career. For example, you may not have the physical strength required for the longshore worker's lifting activities, but you may be strong enough for the lifting activities demanded of a mail carrier or a florist. For any given career, you must be able to meet all the minimum levels of physical demands. The factors listed in the *DOT* are as follows:

1 Lifting, carrying, pushing, and pulling
2 Climbing and balancing
3 Stooping, kneeling, crouching, and crawling
4 Reaching, handling, fingering, and feeling
5 Talking and hearing
6 Seeing

You can evaluate yourself against these factors and determine for yourself your weaknesses and what you will have to do if you are to meet the minimum demands for the entry-level jobs in your chosen career. One additional physical requirement is size. For example, some police work requires that you be at least a certain minimum height. An evaluation of physical requirements can be made very easily, and in some cases deficiencies can be corrected.

8 WORKING CONDITIONS

Working conditions are the physical surroundings or the environment in which one works on a specific job. This worker trait component may be overemphasized if one is considering a career objective. In order to achieve long-range career objectives you may have to endure some displeasing conditions temporarily in order to reach your goals.

Working conditions may be closely linked with the physical demands of a job, but these conditions are also related to other components discussed. For instance, you might respond favorably to outside work and have the physical capacity to climb and the aptitude to work with your hands. If so, you would look with favor on a career as a repair lineman for a utility company.

One question that applies to every job is whether it is to be performed inside or outside, or whether indoor and outdoor activities are almost evenly divided. Temperature is a factor that must be considered. Outside jobs, especially, may expose the worker to extreme heat or cold and to sudden temperature change, but there are also inside occupations that involve extremes of temperature. For example, a butcher may work in a refrigerated room, and a steelworker may be exposed to the heat of a furnace. Working near wetness or in a humid atmosphere is also associated with climate (including artificially controlled inside climates).

Some jobs involve unpleasant conditions that the worker must be prepared to endure if he is committed to his career. One problem is noise or vibration. Where industrial machinery is used, for example, intermittent or constant noise may be a distraction or even a danger to hearing. Exposure to vibration over a long period may also affect the worker's health. Some occupations, such as coal mining, are dangerous to the respiratory system over time. These are the jobs that expose the worker to fumes, odors, and toxic particles and that are performed in places where there is poor ventilation. Finally, there are jobs that are considered hazardous because they expose the individual to the risk of bodily injury. For example, a window washer might never have an accident and might retire in excellent physical condition, but while he is working, he is more likely to have a dangerous fall than the people looking out the window.

9 EVALUATION BY OTHERS

How much do you value the thinking of your friends? Do you feel that they really know and understand you? How much do you trust their advice about your career goals and the traits necessary to achieve these goals? If you value your friends' opinions, have them give you their

Consider working conditions when you are choosing a career. Some jobs may expose you to extreme noise vibration and sudden changes in temperature.

Courtesy of Columbia Gas Distribution Cos.

evaluations of your general educational development, your aptitudes, your interests, your temperament, your physical traits, and your reaction to working conditions. If there is general agreement among your peers that your own evaluation is accurate, then you are supported and should have confidence in your future actions. If there is disagreement, take another look at yourself. Consider the possibility that those who disagree with you may have a point. Ask them how they arrived at their opinions. If there is not a clear and obvious direction in your career choice, you may want to take standardized tests and seek help from vocational counselors.

Older people who have observed you for a number of years can also assist you in evaluating the worker trait components. Your parents may evaluate you, or a teacher in whom you have confidence can give an opinion of your strengths and suggest areas that need improvement. Any adult who has had experience in the world of work and is interested in you can be of help. If you can develop the insight to see yourself as others see you, your chances of making a wise career choice are improved.

SUGGESTIONS FOR FURTHER READING

Neff, Walter S., *Work and Human Behavior,* New York: Aldine, 1968.
Nosow, Sigmund, and William H. Form, *Man, Work, and Society,* New York: Basic Books, 1962.
Russell, Ivan L., *Motivation,* Dubuque, Iowa: Wm. C. Brown Company, 1971.
Super, Donald E., and John O. Crites, *Appraising Vocational Fitness,* New York: Harper and Brothers, 1962.

U.S. Department of Labor, *Dictionary of Occupational Titles,* Washington, D.C.: Government Printing Office, 1965.

Zytowski, Donald G., *Vocational Behavior,* New York: Holt, 1968.

TO HELP YOU REMEMBER

1. Why is self-understanding important in choosing a job?
2. Why is your school record an important source of information to consider when you are choosing a career?
3. List five places that provide specific vocational preparation.
4. What is the relationship of interest to success in a career?
5. What is the difference between interest and temperament?
6. What are the six sets of physical traits listed in the *Dictionary of Occupational Titles*?
7. What variations in climate can occur in an indoor environment?
8. What is the value of consulting adult acquaintances when you are choosing a career?

WORKING WITH PEOPLE, DATA, OR THINGS

Three examples of people who went to an occupational counselor are given below.

Case 1: A former major league pitcher walked into a counselor's office. He said that he wanted to take up insurance sales work. He took several tests, and they indicated that as he saw himself he did not take criticism and was not an aggressive person; he was also not interested in activities that successful insurance agents found satisfying.

Case 2: A young woman walked into the counselor's office at the request of school officials. She was failing courses in the language development area (English courses). Some aptitude tests were administered, and the counselor discussed with her the kind of work she liked. She said that she wanted to work with her hands, had no objections to the physical demands of a job, and came to school for one thing, to become a potter.

Case 3: A forty-year-old man was a failure as a salesman for a flour mill. He was sent to a counselor, who, after discussing the man's problems with him, suggested that he take a temperament inventory, an interest inventory, and a values test. The man had finished high school, was married, and had two children who were in high school. His self-evaluations indicated that while he was interested in people, it was as a helper or social service person, not in a business way. Also, his temperament test indicated that he liked routines in which there were few confrontations and almost no call for aggressiveness.

Directions

Based on what you have learned in this chapter about worker traits, what advice would you give each person if you were counseling him about his career?

THINGS TO DO

1. Visit a factory or other large business in your community to find out what programs are provided for the specific vocational preparation of the employees. Report your findings to the class.
2. Ask your school counselor to give you one of the inventories mentioned in this chapter. Then work with the counselor in interpreting the results.
3. Obtain a copy of the two-volume *Dictionary of Occupational Titles*, and study how to use it until you can match your personality traits with at least three different careers or occupations.
4. Draw a picture of yourself (regardless of your artistic ability) as you imagine yourself ten years from now. Draw yourself in a job situation, in a house, or with people. Be sure to show how you will be dressed and what you will be doing. If you want to, you can cut pictures or other material from magazines and make a collage of what you will look like.

DISCOVERING YOUR VALUES

12

What This Chapter Is About

1 WHAT IS A VALUE?

You may visit a friend and see an attractive ornament in his home, and you may ask him what its value is, or worth. He may reply that it is worth so many dollars, or he may tell you that he doesn't know its worth in dollars, but that it has sentimental value, which cannot be measured in terms of money. It is the second kind of value we want to discuss in this chapter. We can say that a *value* is the personal worth that someone puts on an object or an idea because that object or idea is of particular importance to him.

A person may value his freedom, love, respect, independence, wealth, or skill. Since every individual has many values, we speak of "a set of values." A set of values is an underlying system of beliefs about what is important in life to a person. Something that one person considers a value might not be a value for another person. For example, one person may value work because it is fulfilling, while another person may consider work a drudgery to be endured only because it provides money to buy valued material objects.

A good test to use to determine if you have a value is to notice how strongly you react to something. For example, how would you react to these social issues: honest government, environmental protection, social justice, human rights, or public education? If you have a pet peeve or a strong conviction on any of these matters, then you can say these are your values. Because values are important to a person, they produce emotions and influence behavior. If you value your work in school or on the job, praise from your teacher or employer will make you feel good. This "feeling good" is an emotion, and it shows that your work is one of your values. In fact, praise often spurs a person to do better work, and, as this happens, the work value will become higher on his list of values.

Often we can see our values influencing us when we are in contact with other people. Just as our values tell us how we should feel and act, they guide our reactions to the behavior of others. We all tend to judge other people's actions by our own standards—our values. If you have heard someone bemoaning the fact that a marriage is breaking up, then you can bet that marriage is a value for that person. The importance of this value to the person can be determined by how emotional he becomes while he is telling you about the problem and by how much time he devotes to thinking and talking about it.

Think about yourself. Are most of your friends pretty much the way you think they should be? If so, then you have chosen friends who have value systems similar to your own. As we will discuss in a later section, we seldom get along with people whose value systems are very much different from our own. And in our society we can see many conflicts between opposing sets of values: mental and physical, liberal and conservative, religious and atheistic. The point is that to work better with others, we must watch their behavior for clues to their values. We should learn to spot those people with whom we can get along easily and also those with differing value systems with whom it will be more difficult and require more effort to feel comfortable.

One simple way of looking at different kinds of value systems is to characterize them as thing-oriented, idea-oriented, or people-oriented. If you meet a person who loves to construct furniture, machinery, or other material objects, it is a safe bet that his value system is thing-oriented. If someone loves to think or imagine, that person's value system is idea-oriented. Someone who really likes working in a group has a value system that is people-oriented. Everyone has values involving all three categories, but usually one of the three—things, ideas, or people—is at the core of an individual's value system. Where do your values fit in? What do you suppose you would have to do to get along or work with a person who has a value system that is oriented differently from your own?

Considering that values largely direct or produce our actions, our emotions, and the ways we choose friends, make decisions, solve problems, and work, we can easily understand why values are a very powerful governing force in our lives.

2 WHAT ARE YOUR VALUES?

Finding out what your values are is a way in which you can get to know yourself better. What, then, are your values? Think about the following questions. If you react strongly to any of them, see if you can tell what value is involved. How would you feel if

You were hired for a good job, one you wanted very much?

You were unjustly accused of cheating on an exam?

Someone told you that he loved you?

Someone called you an insulting name?

Your feelings, or emotions, about each of these questions will be strong or weak, depending on the values you place on each of the conditions. In answer to the first question, would you say, "I really feel great about getting this new job; I was really hoping against hope that I would land it—I was even scared to think about the possibility." Or would you say, "Even though I did apply for that job, I was hoping that they wouldn't hire me — it's really too much responsibility for me, and I didn't want to hassle it, but I guess I'll take it because I need the money."

Just as our emotions show us our values, so do our actions. For example, what would you do if you

Saw a person being attacked by a mugger on a dark street? Suppose the victim was your neighbor.

Saw thieves stripping a car in the street? Suppose it was yours.

Saw vandals painting obscenities on a church wall? Suppose you belonged to the congregation.

Saw an injured dog? Suppose it was your neighbor's pet.

Knew a person had been fired from a job because of racist or sexist prejudice? Suppose that person was a close friend of yours.

We learn to analyze problems, like these, that face us. Accordingly, we try to think of alternative actions that we might take, choose one of these alternatives, and act upon it. Our values will determine which of the alternatives we will take. The stronger we feel about a particular problem, especially a pressing one, the quicker will be our response. For instance, if you were confronted with the first situation given above, and the person was a stranger, you would probably call a policeman. The values you would be acting on would include a sense of justice and respect for other people. But if you knew the neighbor personally and were therefore closer to the problem, you might try to hit the mugger or otherwise drive him off without waiting for a policeman. The values you would be upholding would be the same, but your emotional and behavioral responses would be stronger.

The strength of our responses to problems is one determining factor in how well we do in school, in love, in business, and in all other activities. (Of course, aptitude is also critical.) If we feel strongly that each student or worker should be given the freedom to do what he can do best, then we would get upset if someone made us sit and do nothing but tighten nuts on machines passing down an assembly line. If we believed that health was important and that good health came from being outdoors in the sunshine and fresh air, it would be foolish to take a job in a coal mine or factory. On the other hand, if a person felt that security and regularity were very important, he might find satisfaction in tightening nuts or in working in a factory. Think about yourself. Where do you like to work? What do you like to do when you work? Whom do you like to be with when you work or study? It all depends on what *you* value!

3 HOW DO WE LEARN VALUES?

How do we acquire our values—those attitudes that make us act and feel as we do? Where do our values come from? There are at least three sources.

When we are very young, we tend, under normal circumstances, to revere our parents as if they were gods. To us, they are big, strong, and able to do almost everything. They bring us nice things and give us love, but they also yell at us and punish us when we do something that they think is wrong. Therefore, we try to be like them as we are growing up. Little boys often try to act like their "daddies," and little girls imitate their "mommies." Almost every child has at one time or another tried on his parents' shoes, literally to be in the shoes of adults, who are large, strong, independent, and capable. Under normal circumstances, what child wouldn't want to be in his parents' shoes? Thus, the first source of values is our parents. What our parents tell us to do is right, and what they forbid is wrong—that's all there is to it for a very young child. And so we grow up in an environment of right and wrong that has been set up for us. Mother may say, "Now, you should be nice to other children and let them play with your toys." Or she may say, "Be careful with your toys; they're expensive, and the other kids might break them." In this way you begin to learn values.

We learn from our parents about money. There is a story about a wealthy man and his son. The father was once told by a friend, "I can't understand it, you are so wealthy and such a skinflint, yet your son is such a spendthrift." The old man replied, "My father was poor, and my son's father is rich." At some point along the line, the son began to have another idea of how to value money—to use it because it's there, not to save it because it's there. Here we see a conflict in values.

Conflict is necessary, and it makes life interesting, too. Finding out that your parents can be wrong is often a painful experience, but it is an enlightening one also. You hurt, but you learn. As your environment is enlarged, you begin to learn from authorities and other sources besides your parents—teachers, older friends, relatives, newspapers, the TV, and so on. These become your second source of values, and when you detect disagreement among them, you begin to realize that you must not always take what someone has to say for granted, even though you may respect that person.

Somewhere between the ages of 12 and 18, we get the idea that our parents are pretty stupid. They seem different from our friends. Many young people, especially today, have acquired values that are considerably different, even radically different, from those of their parents. When parents try to correct their teen-ager's behavior, at least to what

United Press International Photo

Our first source of values is our family. When we are young our parents seem able to do almost anything and we want to be like them when we grow up.

they think should be correct, the trouble begins; arguments and strife ensue. Scarcely a day goes by without some disagreement. Many parents feel that they are the bosses just because they hold the purse strings. If a son or daughter does not obey, they will, appropriately or not, withhold the child's allowance. Even the word *allowance* implies parental control.

Many parents, and young people, too, don't stop to realize that everyone is an individual with his own set of values and that no two people really think exactly alike.

Carl Jung, one of the early psychoanalysts and disciples of Sigmund Freud, called the process of acquiring a personal set of values *individuation*; it is a process by which one becomes an individual. All people at some time or other must examine their values, and this process of examination should continue throughout a person's life. Every so often people should reassess their values to see if they are useful in terms of what they are doing with their lives and in terms of what other people around them are doing. The process of finding one's values and disagreeing with the values of others, even those who are close friends or relatives, is part of maturing—growing up. A mature person has an open mind; he recognizes that what he believes is important. But at the same time he is willing to hear other points of view, and above all, he respects other people's ideas even if he disagrees with them.

Today many people, especially older people, are taking a new look at their values; some of the traditions they have cherished for years are being re-evaluated. And it is the young people, this time, who have something to teach the older people. This definitely was not always the case. Many parents are beginning to ask themselves, "Were the 'good old days' so good after all?" The father who worked at a job he disliked in order to preserve his valued sense of security can learn a new value from the more adventurous son or daughter who is willing to take a temporary job because it offers the value of work satisfaction.

When a person has sorted out the basic values he has learned from parents and other authorities, he can then learn other values from actual experiences, the third source of values. This process of learning from experience goes on throughout life, but it becomes particularly useful when a person has achieved *autonomy*—when he has become a separate individual, free of the overpowering effects of other people's value systems. Autonomy means that we can react to a situation in a way we feel is right. For example, suppose you go mountain climbing. The climber tied to the rope with you falls. You save his life. From that actual experience, what might you learn about the value of life? No one could have *taught* or even showed you that value.

One of the most difficult things to do is to establish for ourselves a consistent set of values. The conflict between two values often produces inconsistency. For example, at some times a person will say he believes in not drinking alcoholic beverages, but at other times, because he values social acceptance, he will take a drink. This is an inconsistency, and if a person lets inconsistency become a habit, he becomes a hypocrite. Hypocrites are people who do not act on the values they claim to hold. Another example of inconsistency would be a person ranking the value of freedom high but ranking equality low. One could say that that person values his own freedom but not freedom for others. Or, if a person ranked the value of affection high but ranked respect low, he could have a selfish need to get affection without giving it to anyone else.

We often do things that we feel deep down we shouldn't be doing. If we go against a value, we will feel bad. If, for instance, we place a high value on honesty and then do something not quite aboveboard, we are immediately affected—we point a guilty finger at ourselves and say, "Shame on you." Inconsistencies in our values will only make us unhappy; they will make us feel guilty. Therefore, most people try to do what their values tell them to. People who usually live up to their values tend to be happy, satisfied people. They have consistent value systems. The most effective way we learn values when we are grown is by experiencing things and evaluating, or judging, how we behaved during the experiences.

If we feel we behaved badly in a situation, we try to correct the behavior. If the situation does not matter, we usually will not try to change the value involved. For example, if a person failed a test and felt that he should have been able to pass it, he would try to change his behavior and pass the next test. His value would be success in school, or the value of a high grade, and he would try to change his behavior to satisfy that value. But if a person felt that tests were not important, he would not try to change his behavior in order to pass the next test. What we do in life is largely determined by our experiences and by how we feel about them in terms of values. It is important that the choice of marriage, careers, living places, life styles, and friends and other vital decisions be made on the basis of their agreement with our values.

Sometimes it is not possible to satisfy one's values. Many compromises are necessary in our complex society. When you put a great many people together in a city or school or business, not everyone can do what satisfies his values. It is not always possible, for example, to uphold the value of total individual freedom. Because compromise is sometimes necessary, and because it is not possible always to do what we want, it is important for each person to understand his own priorities. For example, there are some values each person would die for. Those values are of high priority for each person. But there are other values that are not so important; those values we would compromise. Satisfied people are people who do not compromise their most important values but are willing to compromise their less important values.

From the process of living we learn values, and they come to us in various strengths. How do we come to understand our values well enough to shape our lives around them? How do we come to know which values are very important and which are minor, or even subject to change, so that we can compromise some and vigorously uphold others? This process of learning more clearly about our values is called values clarification.

4 CLARIFYING VALUES

Values are not something like a shirt that we put on and take off. They are not things, like a car or typewriter. Values are like living, organic creatures that are born, that grow, and that sometimes die. Each person's value system is constantly growing, changing, and expanding as the person has new experiences and meets new people. Each person finds new exceptions to old rules and learns that old behaviors do not always fit new situations. And each person finds that some things never change, some needs never go away, and some truths can never be attacked.

Our minor values are always changing. The less important values change more often and more readily than the important ones, which are convictions.

If we are not under the influence of some authority, we will freely choose one solution to a problem. The fact that we freely choose one solution, as opposed to any others, shows us that there is something important about that solution. If we can name the factor that is important about a solution, we would name a value. One point of distinction needs to be made: there are some cases that really do not have more than one solution. We all have to eat, and therefore eating is not a value. But a person could choose a certain type of diet. For example, if a person chose a vegetarian diet, it would indicate that there was something important about that particular way of meeting the need to eat. The choice of a particular diet would indicate a certain value—in the case of a vegetarian diet, the value of a total respect for living animals.

But what about people who make a choice only for a few seconds, or days, or weeks? If a person makes a decision to do something important but soon forgets about it, his action shows he really did not have a value. This tells us that one way to judge a value and to tell if we have a value is to determine how seriously we feel about a decision. If we choose freely but impulsively, we probably will not show that we have a value. If, however, a person seriously thinks about the consequences of a decision and goes ahead and makes it, it is a sure sign that a value has been followed.

The next aspect of clarifying a value is determining the way we feel about it. If we are satisfied or content with a value, we know we have

Bruce Anspach/EPA Newsphoto

What are the values reflected by this person's choice of diet?

made it our own. We defend it, we respect it, and we encourage other people to share it.

The last part of the clarification process concerns action. If we really believe in something, we will act on it with determination. We will make decisions and carry out solutions that reflect our values. In that way we publicly uphold a value. We show other people that we believe in it by what we do.

It would be interesting to look back on your life and try to think of your earliest values and follow them up through grammar school, high school, and college to the present. Can you remember any important changes you have had in your thinking that have affected your values? If you have been aware of your values and how they have changed since early childhood, you are well on the way to self-understanding.

If a person is not certain about his values, he will make poor choices, or he will let others do the thinking for him. He will be easily influenced. He will take a job simply because a friend told him about the job or casually recommended it; he will get married because his parents want him to or because his best friend got married; he will stand by and allow an injustice to occur without trying to do something about it. Many of us are confused about our values. It is difficult to distinguish between a change in values and a situation in which we have simply not lived up to a value. The distinction is often revealed by our reaction to our behavior. Here are some questions you can ask yourself in assessing your values:

1   Should I make this choice?
2   Am I serious about this choice?
3   Will this choice satisfy me and make me proud to tell others about it?
4   Will I consistently take action to carry out this choice?

If the answer to these questions is "yes," then we can attach a value to the choice. We will have a clear idea of what we intend to do and be successful at it, whether it be choosing a career, getting married, continuing our education, raising children, or following a certain life style.

5 LIVING WITH YOUR VALUES

There is an old saying that "after you have made your bed, you must lie in it." Once you have decided on a set of values, and these values have determined your choices, you are committed to carry out these choices. Values are useless unless people live by them. As we have seen, values can be thought of in terms of *decisions, commitments*, and *implemen-tation*. The last of these terms, *implementation*, is the part that we live with because implementation means carrying out, or making the effort to satisfy a value.

Most problems that arise in a person's life can be helped, if not solved, by his values. But a problem is difficult to solve if there is more than one solution, and if each solution is supported by a value that does not conflict with the values that support the other solutions. However, this rarely happens. Usually one of the values used for solving the problem will be more important than any of the others, and this value will be the determining factor. Many solutions may be right, but one is *more* right than the others.

Of the three phases, decision, commitment, and implementation, decision is often the most difficult, because it is the initial phase of a problem with which you are immediately confronted. For example, you think you want to be a lawyer. How can you decide? As a lawyer you can be guaranteed a good starting salary, at least these days. But, while money is important in our society, is it your most important value? Maybe your desire to see justice done is higher on your value scale than making a lot of money. Or perhaps you are interested in some aspect of law, such as corporate law or constitutional law. Then, again, you may want to become a politician, and you may feel that as a lawyer you will have more opportunities to pursue this course. Another reason for becoming a lawyer might be that your family wants you to because your father or mother was a lawyer. Perhaps being a lawyer means acquiring social prestige in your community, and your family is willing, if not anxious, to give you financial support for this goal. But if this is the only reason for becoming a lawyer, it is not a very strong one, and you can be reasonably assured that you will be only moderately success-ful at best. If your family is pressing you and offering you financial aid in some pursuit, then you are involved only *passively* in that pursuit. If you can't find any other reason for following this course, then most certainly it should be abandoned. You can see that making a decision, the initial phase, may require considerable effort.

Once you have made a decision, you should then pursue the course. This is the commitment phase. It is not as difficult as decision making. This phase is actually almost implied with the decision. You could say that commitment means that you are on the right track; but you still have to go along that track to your goal.

Implementation may often be more difficult than making a deci-sion. This is the phase in which your decision is to be carried out. You may want very much to be a lawyer, but you will need seven years of higher education. Even if you have finished college already, you will have to face three years of law school, and then you must work for an agency or law firm for a number of years to be trained. Some law schools are better or more prestigious than others, and some law firms are also more prestigious than others. Some of the so-called better law firms first select fledgling lawyers from prominent or wealthy families who are good customers, then next from among those who have graduated from the top law schools. Today, law schools are crowded, hard to get into, and expensive. Applicants are selected on the basis of academic records in college and stiff intelligence and aptitude tests. After you have chosen your school and are accepted, you have to study law. To be a successful lawyer takes time-consuming effort. And to be good requires careful training, most of which is done by you. Your goal is certainly realizable, but commitment and a thorough plan for implementation are essential.

Most musicians agree that if you want to be a violinist or a pianist and play the violin or piano well enough to perform the most difficult pieces, you have to begin studying at about five or six years of age. But if you have ten fingers and are healthy and reasonably musical, you should be able to learn to perform well on these instruments at older ages. You may not be a genius or a *virtuoso,* but you can achieve your goal—if you really want to. Emanuel Feuermann, the world-famous cellist, began to study his instrument in adolescence, after being told that this was too ripe an age to start aiming for outstanding performing ability.

Of course, there are certain things that are impossible to do. Your failure, if your ambition was to become the King of England, would be shattering, and there are very few openings for the Presidency of the United States. But, barring a few occupations or vocations, most goals can be achieved if there is genuine commitment and well-planned implementation.

 THE CONFLICT OF VALUES

Because values are important and arouse many emotions in each of us, conflicts are likely to arise when two or more people get together, unless the people have complementary value systems.

How many times have you been in a situation that made you uncomfortable? Where were you, and who was with you? Would you say that your values were the same as the values of those you were with? What about the times you have been in situations in which you *were* comfortable? Were your values in agreement with the values of the other people in those situations?

With whom do you find a value conflict? Your parents? Your teachers? Your employer? Acquaintances? When you have identified those who have a value system that conflicts with your own, the important question is, How do you deal with them? How can each person handle the battle between value systems?

As a woman, what would you do if an employer or teacher told you to start wearing longer, "more decent" dresses? As a man, what would you do if an employer, parent, or teacher told you to cut your hair? Obviously, you would be in a battle of values. But how would you handle the situation? What emotions would be aroused and expressed? What action would you take?

The action you would take would depend on the strength of the values you hold and on how you weigh the consequences of each possible action. If there was a possibility of being fired or expelled from school for taking one form of action, most people would reject that action. If you could make a point once and uphold your values without too much opposition, you would probably be able to make the same point again. In real life, we often do only those things that do not get us into a lot of trouble. There are some notable exceptions to this, of course. People sometimes believe so strongly in a value, whether society agrees or not, that they do get into "trouble" and sometimes welcome confrontation. If everyone did only those things that didn't get them into a lot of "trouble," there would have been no Christian faith, no American revolution, no peace marches, and so on.

In values conflicts the rule is to find out how far you can push your values and how much you can allow other people to push their values. If you always let other people push their values on you, you are probably indecisive, passive, or generally thought to be "weak." If you always pushed your own values on other people, you would generally be thought to be selfish, domineering, pushy, or egotistic.

In finding a balance between pushing your values and letting other people push theirs, we all make compromises. We all find ways of accommodating the opinions and beliefs of other people, and we seek ways of having them accept our views and opinions. Compromise, however, means that neither side "wins"; both, in a sense, lose, because each is giving up something to the other, but so also does each side win something. The important thing is to learn or decide when you can afford to give up and compromise and when you cannot.

Sometimes it is vital to compromise. If you are a group member and the group has a task to do, it would be foolish of you to insist that only your values be respected. You would be interfering with the rights of the other group members to uphold their own values. But, on the other hand, if the group you are with decides to do something that is obviously harmful to yourself or others, it would be foolish of you to ignore your own values and go along with the group. What would you do, for example, if you were with a group of friends who decided to steal a car? Would you join them and participate in the theft? Or would you take action on your values of justice and respect for the rights of others?

The battle of values does not have to be a disaster. Through intelligent restraint and compromise, many conflicts can be eliminated. For example, sometimes the value of peace and harmony is more important than the value being defended, and we would do better to allow the opposing value to prevail. At other times, though, each person must defend a value, regardless of the unpleasantness of the consequences. Learning to make the decisions about how to react to a conflict in values is a large part of becoming a satisfied, successful individual.

We have touched on some of the results of value conflicts between children and parents, but since values are largely learned from our parents, major conflicts are more often the products of different circumstances—economic class, race, ethnic background, religion, or life style.

Economic Class and Values

Your economic class will determine in large part many of your values. According to many middle-class workers, the rich live in luxury without making a physical contribution to society by actually working, and the poor have to be supported on social welfare by the "hard workers." Although some rich people work, it seems to the middle class that they really don't have to do so, and some poor people who work are considered a threat to job security in middle-class terms. Although the "work ethic" is valued, there is disagreement on how far it should be applied. Thus there is a conflict of values even though there is mobility in our class system; that is, people can move from class to class.

Race and Ethnic Group and Values

Race is another story. It has been used in the past and even in present times as an excuse to keep people poor. This situation is changing, although slowly. Unlike mobility in the class system, there is no mobility with regard to race: a black man can't become white, and a white man can't become black, brown, yellow, or red. Each racial group wants to look after its own interests, but when this self-interest becomes the value of racial supremacy, serious conflicts, counterproductive to the *human* race, develop. Immigrants from foreign countries and their offspring who maintain the traditions of their homelands are called *ethnics*. Many ethnics are looked down upon by the natives, and so they are forced to seek values that come to their defense. To this end, ethnics sometimes try to gain control of certain occupations, local political parties, or religious groups. This immediately creates a conflict. More ethnic mixing has been taking place lately in this country as different ethnic groups learn that they share common values.

Religion and Values

Religious conflicts have often been the result of ethnic differences. Two ethnic groups in one country or neighboring lands may choose different religious sects more for purposes of national identification than for moral or ethical beliefs. The attempts of religious sects to impose their beliefs on one another by force has been a major source of conflict throughout human history. The great misfortune is that the conflict is not one of moral beliefs but of power-seeking groups of people.

Life Style and Values

Life style has become, of late, an important source for conflicting values. Many people are beginning to examine the traditional institutions in terms of their usefulness. For example, people ask themselves, "Shall I share my family in communal living with other families, or should I maintain a nuclear family life style?" There is an assortment of possibilities among life styles, and you will ultimately choose a life style in accordance with your values.

The life style you choose reflects your values. Some people choose to work and live together in a communal living arrangement.

Bruce Anspach/EPA Newsphoto

Values and Cooperation

No matter which values you use and prefer or consider more important, you will encounter other people with opposing values. This is unavoidable. Therefore, you should try to develop tolerance, which is the capacity to listen to another person's point of view and to try to understand his values just as you would hope that he would try to understand yours.

The same values that separate people can also bind them together. Thus, people of the same class, race, ethnic background, religion, or life style have something in common. We can see that values help us to communicate with other people and bring them together in a common bond. Groups of people should modify their values in such a way as to help one group without putting down or excluding other groups. After all, we are all members of the human race first. Therefore, what benefits humans in general should be highest on our list of values. The other values should be secondary.

VALUES AND YOUR FUTURE

As we have mentioned, values play an important role in your choice of friends and career. There are hundreds and thousands of careers from which you can choose. How do you make a selection? One factor in choosing a career is your value system.

As we have said, we each have differently oriented value systems. Some individuals like to work with things, while others prefer working with ideas or people. Also, some people place a high value on such considerations as being outdoors, working under close supervision, obtaining high status or high pay, or using skills to the best advantage. We have discussed clarifying value systems; when people come to clarify their value systems they are better able to define the kind of career that will be in agreement with their strongly held values. Of course, choosing a career also depends on such considerations as ability, interests, and aptitudes, and they too are related to values.

Look at your own activities. What do you really enjoy doing? What would you do regularly if you had the chance? Your answers will indicate both your interests and your values. Now, what are you good at doing? What abilities do you have? Your abilities also will indicate some of your values, such as pride in workmanship, communicating with people, or helping people.

In summary, then, every person should have a clear understanding of how complex he really is. Values, abilities, interests, commitments, decisions, and actions all go into making us what we are and what we will become.

SUGGESTIONS FOR FURTHER READING

Beamer, Charles, *You! Crisis Resolution Games, and Commitment Games*, Austin, Texas: Miller Productions, Inc., 1972, 1973.

Pfeiffer, William J., and John E. Jones, *A Handbook of Structured Experiences for Human Relations Training,* Iowa City, Iowa: University Associates Press, 1972.

Simon, Sidney B., Leland W. Howe, and Howard Kirschenbaum, *Values Clarification: A Handbook of Practical Strategies for Teachers and Students,* New York: Hart Publishing Company, 1972.

TO HELP YOU REMEMBER

1. What does a person's behavior reveal about his values?
2. How does a person's value system affect his relationship with other people?
3. What is the main source of a child's value system?
4. What forces influence a growing person to alter his value system?
5. What is individuation?
6. What four questions can you ask yourself to determine whether a decision you have made is based on a strong value?
7. Give an original example of the implementation of a decision.
8. On what basis can a person decide whether to compromise a value?
9. List four aspects of a person's position in society that are likely to influence his values.

WORKING WITH PEOPLE, DATA, OR THINGS

In a small printing plant, the main accounts are local industrial advertisers, for whom the plant prints catalogs and brochures. Because the volume of work is heavy and schedules are tight, the manager expects each worker in the plant to put in at least 15 hours a week in overtime. Overtime pay is time-and-a-half for the first five hours and double thereafter. One of the workers feels needed at home and places a strong value on family activities. The worker confronts the manager with a request to be excused from overtime work.

Directions

Let two members of the class role-play the situation. The entire class should participate in a discussion considering the following questions:

1. What values did the manager express? What were the worker's values?
2. How strongly did each hold his values? Do you feel they were justified?
3. Did the worker and the manager reach a successful compromise? Could you improve on their solution?

THINGS TO DO

1. Interview several adults whom you respect. Ask them to list at least ten strongly held values. Be a listener, and do not try to influence your interviewees. Discuss one of your lists in class, indicating which values you share and which you do not. Be prepared to explain your reaction to the list.
2. Study and report to the class the values promoted in one of the following: a radio or television commercial, a newspaper editorial, a televised athletic event, a speech by a politician (either printed or broadcast), a movie. How does the message encourage the audience to adopt the values that are presented?
3. Develop a chart similar to the one below, and keep a record for a week of values on which you have acted.

Example

Value	Decision	Commitment	Implementation
Independence	To buy a car	To earn money to pay for the car.	Visit school employment office; post a notice in the student union offering to type papers.

13

What This Chapter Is About

"That young Thomas boy is clever with tools. We need an extra mechanic, so I'll hire him to help us make clocks." It was as easy as that for Eli Terry to find "who could do what" in the old days when businesses were small and the owner knew almost everybody in the neighborhood. The employer knew which young men had a natural bent for work with tools and which for work with books or figures—and also those bent on loafing or starting arguments with other workers.

Nowadays, however, workers to be selected usually are strangers, and only limited time is available for sizing up a job applicant. This quick sizing up of a stranger's fitness for a specific job can be more accurate if one knows some of the assets and liabilities of human capacities and skills.

Some people are called "quick as a cat," others "as slow as molasses in January." Sometimes a supervisor says, "John is ten times the worker that Fred is." Such figures of speech make individual differences seem greater than they are.

The first person to make satisfactory comparisons showing how great individual differences are was Dr. David Wechsler, who was a professor of psychology at New York University's College of Medicine. He found that in comparing bodily characteristics such as height, the measurements of the tallest and shortest persons on the street differ by a ratio of about 1.25 to 1. (This does not include circus giants or dwarfs.) People's bodily measurements seldom differ by more than 25 percent. This is not a great difference, although it can be important when the best height for a typist's chair or an assembler's bench is being determined.

Individual differences in muscular control are greater than differences in bodily measurements. The fastest person moves at about twice the speed of the slowest, and the difference is similar between the speediest and slowest typists applying for their first jobs. In many factory production departments, the best worker turns out twice the work of some others, even when there is a piece-rate plan of payment.

The differences are still greater when mental factors enter into performance. People vary by a ratio of 2.5 to 1, for instance, in their ability to remember numbers.

In intelligence, or general mental horsepower, people vary by a ratio of about 3 to 1. That is approximately the ratio in brain power between the brightest executive in the firm and the dullest worker on the simplest job.

When it comes to learning difficult material, such as advanced accounting, the best and poorest students differ by a ratio of a little more than 3 to 1.

John, therefore, cannot be ten times better than Fred, although Fred may take three times longer to learn the job or may turn out only one-third as much work as John. But that is enough difference to change a profit into a loss.

2 THE NORMAL DISTRIBUTION OF ABILITIES

Can people be separated into "fast" and "slow" groups? While some people move with twice the speed of others, most people are neither fast nor slow, but in between. The chart "Reaction Time of 1,000 Machinists," prepared by Dr. André Fessard, shows measurements for French machinists. Some took only 125/1,000 second to move when they were given the signal, and others took 245/1,000 second. But notice from the chart that half of these machinists, the large in-between group, took only from 165/1,000 to 185/1,000 of a second.

The average person is in this big in-between group. The percentages taper rapidly from this average group toward each extreme in speed. This tapering off, which leaves only a few people at each extreme, takes place when any quality is being charted, whether it be height,

Data from Dr. André Fessard

An experiment testing the reaction times of a thousand experienced machinists resulted in a normal distribution. Most of the subjects reacted with a speed midway between the slowest and fastest. Approaching these extremes, there were fewer and fewer subjects.

intelligence, cooperativeness, neatness, or musical ability. When a random sample of people is charted on any ability, the curve is bell-shaped, indicating a normal distribution of abilities.

This normal distribution makes it impossible to separate people into clear-cut types or classes. It would be necessary, for instance, to measure some 3,500 machinists to locate 100 whose reaction times were as fast as 135/1,000 second. While the goal is to employ the most capable workers, a compromise has to be made with the normal distribution. To find many from an extreme end of the distribution is like looking for a needle in a haystack.

When the same opportunities are offered to fast and slow workers, the differences among people are not eliminated by practice or training. Practice sometimes increases the differences. The person who was speedy at the start is apt to improve more than the one who was slow at the start. The new worker who is best on the job the first day is likely to be best after a year, unless he becomes self-satisfied and lets himself slump. Practice helps people improve but does not shift the normal distribution greatly.

The illustration on page 247, "Individual Differences in the Ability to Read Business Material," shows that training and experience do not eliminate the normal distribution. This type of reading ability profits more from training than did the simple reaction times of the French mechanics. Beginning students, for instance, do not average as well as professional accountants. This is partly because some beginners have a low aptitude for understanding such terms as "inventory reserves," "depreciation allowances," and "funded debt." Another reason is that beginners, even

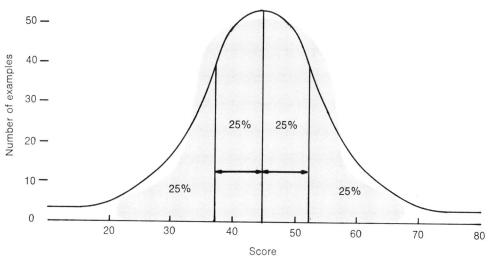

The normal distribution curve for the measurement of any quality is bell-shaped. In a perfect bell-shaped curve, half the number of examples fall in the middle range, one quarter are in the low extreme, and one quarter are in the high extreme.

those who have the potential to become professional accountants, are not yet familiar with business vocabularies and business thinking.

But there is still a normal distribution among the professional accountants of long experience. They average higher than the beginners in ability, of course; but even experience and the elimination of the less capable have not altered the normal distribution much. There is still a "normalish" distribution curve for professional accountants; it is merely shifted toward the higher end of the scale.

3 EXPERTS ARE MUCH LIKE OTHER PEOPLE

Do experts have abilities that others lack? No. As we would suspect from the normal distribution curve, the expert merely has more of the aptitude than most other people. Even the idiot has some intelligence,

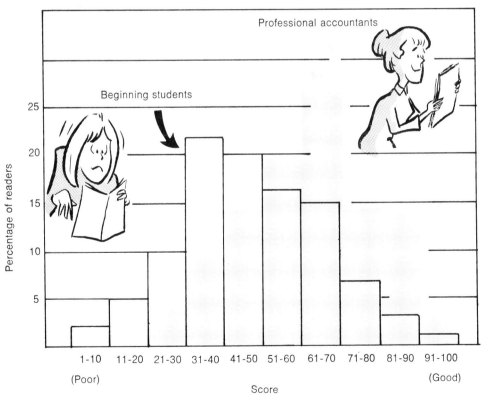

The distribution of ability to read business material follows normal curves in this comparison of 275 professional accountants and 5,328 beginning students in accounting. Although the average score for the professionals is higher than that for students, the curves do overlap.

and your senator may have three times as much. *We are all alike in the kinds of abilities we have, but we differ in the amounts of each ability.* You have some musical memory, although it may be small; Toscanini could remember the score of an entire opera. To find the right worker for a job, we do not ask, "Does he have the ability?" but "How much of the needed ability does he have?"

Are experts likely to be shortchanged in other abilities? Experts are no more shortchanged than the rest of us who are not unusually skilled or talented. It is not true that if a person is outstanding in one ability he must be weak in some other to "make up" for it. The person who is superior in one ability is likely to be superior in related abilities, and his chances of superiority in unrelated activities are average. Consider the variety of fields in which Benjamin Franklin and Thomas Jefferson were successful and the variety of abilities each man had. On the other hand, Abraham Lincoln made an equally significant contribution to the history of our government, but he was not the scientist Franklin was, nor did he have Jefferson's talents in architecture.

Each person has strong and weak abilities. Geniuses are no more an exception to this rule than the feebleminded. These little variations are of importance, however, in the specialized occupations in modern industry. The person with high dexterity for handling a screwdriver on an assembly operation, for instance, may be low in dexterity in using tweezers when he is transferred to a related operation. These ups and downs in what would appear to be closely related abilities account for the failure of some employees when they are transferred from one job to another.

To learn how a new worker's various skills or aptitudes rank, some companies put new employees in a pool where they are tried out first on one kind of work and then on another. Very shortly, the company has a good basis for making a practical decision as to what kind of work best suits a worker. Of course, many workers do the same thing themselves in times when jobs are plentiful by trying one job and then another until they find the jobs and the bosses they like best.

4 JOB ANALYSIS AND SPECIFICATION

Ralph is employed as a machinist; all he does is grind rough edges from iron castings. Edgar is also employed as a machinist, but he uses a complicated machine to make parts according to blueprint specifications. Ralph and Edgar have the same job title, but very different abilities are needed for the two jobs. When one is hiring a person or taking a job, it is more important to know the exact nature of the work than the title given the job.

A *job analysis* is a study of each operation involved in a certain job. It includes information about the essential abilities, experience, and training needed to do the job. A *job specification* is a listing of characteristics needed on a job and can be made after the job analysis is completed, using the job analysis as a guide. The table "Worker Characteristics Required" lists 47 characteristics that the United States Employment Service considers when it is making a job specification. Many state and company offices follow this list of characteristics. These characteristics are based more on common sense than on profound psychology, and they are very helpful for sizing up a person for a definite job. (You will find more detailed analyses of primary human abilities in *Sizing Up People* by Donald A. and Eleanor C. Laird, published by McGraw-Hill Book Company in 1951.)

WORKER CHARACTERISTICS REQUIRED

Job Title_____

Indicate: *H* for high ability needed   *L* for low ability needed
           A for average ability needed   *O* when not needed for this job

1. Work rapidly for long periods	26. Arithmetic computation
2. Strength of hands	27. Intelligence
3. Strength of arms	28. Adaptability
4. Strength of back	29. Ability to make decisions
5. Strength of legs	30. Ability to plan
6. Dexterity of fingers	31. Initiative
7. Dexterity of hands and arms	32. Understanding mechanical devices
8. Dexterity of foot and leg	
9. Eye-hand coordination	33. Attention to many items
10. Foot-hand-eye coordination	34. Oral expression
11. Coordination of both hands	35. Skill in written expression
12. Estimate size of objects	36. Tact in dealing with people
13. Estimate quantity of objects	37. Memory of names and persons
14. Perceive form of objects	38. Personal appearance
15. Estimate speed of moving objects	39. Concentration amidst distractions
16. Keenness of vision	40. Emotional stability
17. Keenness of hearing	41. Work under hazardous conditions
18. Sense of smell	
19. Sense of taste	42. Estimate quality of objects
20. Touch discrimination	43. Unpleasant physical conditions
21. Muscular discrimination	44. Color discrimination
22. Memory for details (things)	45. Ability to meet and deal with people
23. Memory for abstract ideas	
24. Memory for oral directions	46. Height
25. Memory for written directions	47. Weight

5 PRIMARY OFFICE FUNCTIONS

There are several ways of determining the qualifications needed for a job. One way is to make an analysis of people who have been successful at the job. In analyzing successful secretaries, Dr. W. W. Charters and Dr. I. B. Whitley found that the following traits were mentioned most often by the executives with whom the secretaries worked:

PERCENTAGES OF EXECUTIVES MENTIONING DESIRABLE QUALITIES FOR SECRETARIES

Quality	Percent	Quality	Percent
Accuracy	86	Initiative	71
Responsibility	82	Tact	68
Dependability	75	Pleasantness	64
Intelligence	75	Appearance	64
Courtesy	71		

Another approach may be taken—a consideration of the specific requirements of the job. Some 139 different clerical operations take place in offices. An analysis of 192 different office jobs by Dr. Albert B. Chalupsky revealed that these operations may be grouped into only a few major categories, aside from shorthand and typing:

Office Operations
Keeping inventory and stockkeeping
Supervising
Computation and bookkeeping
Communication and public relations

These, plus typing and shorthand, may be considered the *primary office functions* (POF).

Numerous subsidiary functions are involved in each POF. Details or functions are listed according to the frequency with which they occur:

Keeping Inventory	
Issuing parts and supplies	Folding, dusting, and delivering
Keeping records	Locating positions of supplies
Filling in forms	Estimating needs and costs
Counting objects and supplies	Allocating costs

	Supervising
Assigning duties	Approving requests
Reviewing activities	Transferring records
Instructing	Organizing records
Checking for accuracy	

	Computation
Making detailed reports and records	Transferring records
	Operating keyboard
Using calculating machine	Organizing (compiling) data
Using adding machine	Filing and locating
Balancing accounts	Allocating costs
Posting	
Handling checks and money orders	

	Communication, Public Relations
Receiving customers	Organizing layout of letters
Handling complaints or overdue accounts	Paying out or receiving money
	Giving information
Composing letters	

In the evening the office worker's diary entry is likely to include most of these functions, plus a few others that do not commonly occur.

 ## RIGHT PERSON—RIGHT JOB

Psychological analysis helps to find the right person for the job, as can be seen by studying the profile of Samuel Q. He had been in personnel work and was doing well enough, but he did not enjoy the clerical and computing details of that job and was not able to use his strong sales drive.

Samuel Q. resigned his personnel job to become a life insurance salesman and "went like a house afire" in his new occupation. His insurance earnings, entirely on a commission basis, are five times his salary in personnel. Equally important, he enjoys his new work and is much happier. Though the personnel work did give him the satisfaction of doing a worthwhile social service, so does selling insurance.

Study the characteristics charted in the "Profile of Samiel Q." to become familiar with some of the human qualities that vocational psychologists must know about to place the right person in the right job. The profile is the result of self-evaluation by Samuel Q. on interest and temperament psychological assessment measures.

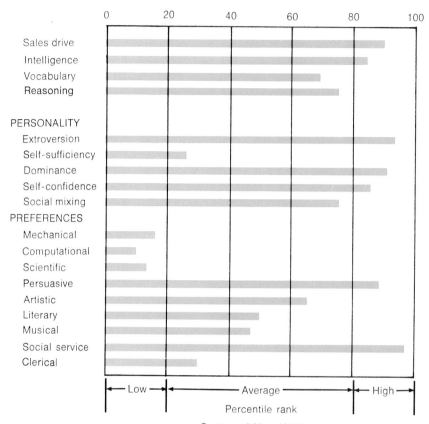

Profile of Samuel Q. A successful life insurance salesman had been doing moderately well as a personnel man. The graph shows the percent of people he exceeded in each characteristic—his percentile rank. This is the term most frequently used to indicate a person's standing in a group.

7 PRIMARY VOCATIONAL INTERESTS

Primary vocational interests (PVI) have also recently been studied. The summaries of primary vocational interests shown on pages 253 and 254 are based on work by Dr. Joy P. Guilford and colleagues at the University of Southern California.

Some of the ingredients that enter into these primary interests are given beneath each interest heading, along with an illustrative question. A "yes" answer to a question indicated a leaning toward the interest. The first ingredient listed contributes a little more to the primary interest than the second ingredient, and so on down the list of ingredients. The questions are not a test, but they are added to help make the meanings of the ingredients clear.

PRIMARY VOCATIONAL INTERESTS

Mechanical

Manipulating	"Would you like to run a turret lathe?"
Constructing	"Would you like to cut and glue things together?"
Precision	"Do you like to make exact measurements?"
Cleanliness	"Would you like a job where your hands get dirty?"

Scientific

Investigating	"Would you like to help a scientist do research?"
Theorizing	"Would you like to figure how the moon causes tides?"
Mathematical	"Would you like to study how electronic computing machines work?"
Logical	"Do you like to look for errors in reasoning?"

Social Welfare (Seeing the needs of others and wanting to help them)

Welfare of others	"Would you like to work with a group to help the unemployed?"
Communicating	"Would you like to write a booklet explaining traffic laws?"
Personal service	"Would you like to serve as personal secretary or aide?"
Civic-minded	"Would you like to work with a group to get out the vote?"

Aesthetic Expression (Participating, not as a spectator)

Music	"Do you like to play some instrument or sing?"
Literature	"Would you like to write a short story?"
Drama	"Would you enjoy taking part in a play?"
Graphic arts	"Do you like to plan a furniture arrangement?"

PRIMARY VOCATIONAL INTERESTS
Continued

Clerical

Computing	"Would you like to figure out a payroll?"
Clerical	"Would you like to look for letters in a file cabinet?"
Mathematical	"Do you like to study algebra and geometry?"
Administrating	"Would you like to supervise a branch office?"

Business (Working in a commercial atmosphere with others)

Administrating	"Would you enjoy managing a business office?"
Selling	"Would you like to work as a salesman on a commission basis?"
Contacting	"Would you like to contact firms to start a trade association?"
Communicating	"Would you like to write a letter to a newspaper explaining the trade association?"

 PRIMARY PERSONAL INTERESTS

The *primary personal interests* (PPI), in contrast to the PVI, are concerned more with activities that are personally satisfying to the individual himself. They supplement the PVI by showing what the person is likely to want from the job in order to be happy in it.

The vocational and personal interests are interrelated in actual life, and employers should give more attention to workers' personal interests than they usually do. For example, an applicant may have high business interest (PVI), but he may also have a high interest in outdoor work (PPI) and would presumably be more satisfied in a business job that was outdoors—possibly work with a contractor—than he would be in one that kept him cooped up indoors.

PRIMARY PERSONAL INTERESTS

Wanting Adventure

Exploring	"Would you like to explore a cave?"
Risk taking	"Would you like to drive in an automobile race?"
Outdoor life	"Would you like a job that is mostly outdoors?"
Nature	"Would you like to be in a forest of giant trees?"

PRIMARY PERSONAL INTERESTS
Continued

Aesthetic Appreciation (Being a spectator, not creating)

Literature	"Would you like to browse in a library?"
Graphic arts	"Would you like to make a collection of drawings?"
Drama	"Would you like to watch a dramatic group rehearse?"
Music	"Would you like to attend a series of symphony concerts?"

Conforming (Having an ethical emphasis)

Conscience	"Would you feel uneasy about getting a raise you did not merit?"
Custom	"Do you believe in the saying, 'When in Rome do as the Romans do'?"
Competing	"Do you work best where competition is keenest?"
Discipline	"Do you think stricter parents would lessen juvenile crime?"

Wanting Diversion (Escaping from routine)

Playfulness	"Do you like to play with pets?"
Romanticism	"Do you like to read about movie stars?"
Athletics	"Do you enjoy active sports and exercise?"
Problem solving	"Do you like to work crossword puzzles?"

Wishful Thinking (Substituting satisfactions and indirect outlets)

Comical situations	"Do you like to watch circus clowns?"
Daydreaming	"Do you like to think how it would feel to be a hero?"
Indirect hostility	"Do you enjoy hearing the boss berate a person you dislike?"
Amusement flight	"Do you want more time for fun and amusement?"

Wanting Attention

Recognition	"Would you like to have a business named after you?"
Social status	"Do you like to be seen talking to important persons?"
Exhibitionism	"Do you like to do unusual things so people notice you?"
Assurance	"Are you uneasy if you don't know how you stand with others?"

PRIMARY PERSONAL INTERESTS
Continued

Resisting Restrictions (Wanting freedom in personal work and habits)

Individualism	"Are there too many straitlaced people who spoil your fun?"
Unsystematic	"Do you dislike following a fixed schedule?"
Disorderly	"Do you feel that some people are just too orderly?"
Independence	"Do you want to work for yourself rather than for somebody else?"

Outdoor Working

Agriculture	"Would you like to tend a vegetable garden?"
Open spaces	"Do you think a forest ranger has an interesting life?"
Constructing	"Do you like to build things?"
Manipulating	"Would you enjoy painting garden furniture?"

Physical Push

Stamina	"Can you work long hours without feeling tired?"
Self-reliance	"Do you make weighty personal decisions without asking for help?"
Aspiration	"Do you expect to earn more than most people your age by 10 years from now?"
Persistence	"Can you plug at a job even when the end is not in sight?"

Aggression (Expressing hostility)

Direct	"Do you let a person know you dislike it when he edges ahead of you in a line?"
Coercive	"Do you like to make others correct their mistakes?"
Indirect	"Do you like to see the villain made a fool of and punished?"

The Following PPI Are Not as General as the Ones Previously Listed
Realistic Thinking (Dealing with intangibles and concepts)

Mathematical	"Do you like to work complicated mathematical problems?"
Logical	"Do you like to figure out things by rules of logic?"
Organizing	"Do you like to plan things for the sake of efficiency?"
Problem solving	"Do you like to plan strategy for a game or business deal?"

PRIMARY PERSONAL INTERESTS
Continued

Cultural Interest (Being a broadly informed citizen)

Civics	"Would you like to be in a group to improve the parks?"
Communicating	"Would you like to write letters telling about a charity?"
Literature	"Do you like to read best-selling books?"
Social science	"Do you like to read about the causes of poverty?"

Orderliness

Surroundings	"Would it embarrass you to be seen with your workplace cluttered?"
Personal	"Do you keep everything in its place?"
Seriousness	"Do you think too many people waste time joking at work?"
Cleanliness	"Do you dislike work that involves grease, dirt, or paint?"

Sociability

Making friends	"Do you enjoy being friends with all kinds of people?"
Initiative	"Do you often get up a party without waiting for someone else to?"
Affection	"Are close friendships extremely important to you?"
Personal service	"Do you like to help a person find where to buy some article he wants?"

Physical Fitness

Activity	"Do you like physical exercise?"
Dominance	"Would you like to tell people what to do in an emergency?"
Healing	"Would you like to try to cure mentally disturbed people?"
Recognition	"Would you like to be recognized as an expert in something?"

Precision

Exactness	"Would you like to inspect jewels for small defects?"
Science	"Would you like to work with scientific instruments?"

Precision (Continued)

Detail	"Would you like to adjust the alignment of a typewriter?"
Computing	"Do you enjoy adding up a long column of figures?"

Wanting Variety

Adventure	"Do you want to change your place of living frequently?"
Travel	"Would you like to travel to have some new experiences?"
Personal service	"Would you like to be a companion to some old person?"
Risk taking	"Do you like thrilling, dangerous activity?"

Wanting Sympathetic Environment

Assurance	"Do you want others to know how hard you are trying?"
Approval	"Are you bothered when others do not encourage you?"
Comfort	"Do you dislike being in the rain?"
Controlling others	"Do you like to persuade others to agree with you on how a job should be done?"

Ambition (Wanting social and professional advancement)

Aspiration level	"Do you expect to be better off than most people your age 10 years from now?"
Responsibility	"Do you like to make plans for others?"
Recognition	"Do you want others to realize you are successful?"
Social status	"Do you like to belong to groups of higher-status people?"

Social Initiative (Being competitive, but socially minded)

Initiating	"Do you like to lead groups of people?"
Competing	"Do you like to surpass others?"
Gregariousness	"Would you like to be a member of many clubs?"
Tempo	"Do you usually get where you are going in a hurry, even when there is plenty of time?"

These primary vocational and personal interests are undoubtedly of basic importance in matching jobs and people. When the interests match what the job needs, the person is probably motivated to work with a will. In addition, the person whose job uses all his predominant interests gets much more satisfaction from his work. These PVI and PPI merit reviewing, and your review will be more interesting and practical if you make a note of the name of someone you know who you think is especially involved in each interest. Is his work such that he can use that interest in it?

People whose jobs use all their predominant interests get more satisfaction from their work. A career in professional plant care and maintenance could be the answer for a person with a vocational interest in business and a personal interest in plants.

Courtesy of Foliage Plant Systems, Inc., Clifton, N.J.

USING YOUR UNFULFILLED INTERESTS

It is relatively easy to find a job for which one or two of a person's interests may qualify him. But it is more difficult to find a job that provides opportunities for the person to follow all his strong interests. There might be a job calling for only five primary interests, for example, but the young person on the job has a dozen interests he is eager to exercise. Subtract five from twelve and you see that seven interests are not satisfied by his workday activities.

Modern business and factory methods tend to limit the chances for following one's full range of strong interests. Most work is now done indoors, giving one fewer chances to follow an interest in outdoor activity. Mass production by assembly-line workers of goods designed by someone else has cut down the opportunities for aesthetic expression in the work itself. Simplifying jobs and reducing them to routine procedures means that many workers are unable to follow some of their strong PPI in their work.

When too many interests are not satisfied, people have feelings of frustration and dissatisfaction. Some people shift from one job to another, hoping to find one where the "leftover" interests will be used. These people may not be consciously aware of what makes them restless, but the frustrated interests are often a factor.

Dr. Jean Spencer Felton, in the publication *Man, Medicine, and Work,*[1] provides an explanation:

> New stresses have appeared in the transition from mechanized industrial society to automated mass society. Increasing fragmentation of all work processes now is characteristic not only of the factory, but also of the large white collar organizations, and of the formerly exempt spheres of agriculture, mining, forestry and fishing. Work, itself, in consequence, has lost much of its meaning for the worker, but not solely because of his loss of identification with a completed product. The tool itself was originally an extension of the craftsman's arm. Later, the machine was simply a larger, more powerful extension of his body. With the advent of automation, man is transformed finally from tool-user to machine-watcher. His separation from the act of creation is complete, as is his sense of involvement in what is created. His response is often a retreat from meaningless work into an obsession with equally unsatisfying recreation.
>
> Industry's attempts to re-enlist the worker's commitment to his job have ranged from the stopwatch school of industrial psychology to more sophisticated wage-incentive and profit-sharing plans, counseling, and coffee-breaks. Too often, however, these activities have consisted of efforts to oil the organizational system much as delicate machinery is oiled. They have failed to be convincing because they have ignored the underlying problem—that personal effort is valued less than "teamwork," and that the organization takes priority over individual skills and honest human relationships. Inevitably, the worker regards his efforts as trivial.
>
> Plant safety was not achieved by adjusting people to lead poisoning. Neither will mental health in industry be accomplished by attempting to adjust workers to stresses which they clearly regard as intolerable. The worker will be restored to himself and to his work exactly as he was finally protected from toxic exposures: by determining his needs and adjusting the work environment accordingly . . . whether through job rotation, through including him in the making of decisions which affect him, or through other means. This process itself is merely an extension of the historic philosophy of occupational medicine, ". . . the promotion of optimal health, productivity, and social adjustment."

1. Dr. Jean Spencer Felton, *Man, Medicine, and Work*, U.S. Department of Health, Education and Welfare Bulletin No. 1044, Washington, D.C., 1964.

Sometimes the job shifter is lucky and finds a job that matches his interests better. As a rule, more of one's interests are satisfied when a job requires a degree of skill or offers variety and the possibility of promotion. Just switching jobs is not as effective as preparing for a job that can tap more interests.

After-hours outlets for the leftover interests are extremely useful. Some firms have hobby and activity clubs that provide outlets for interests that may be stifled on the job. Most communities also have many activities that allow people to exercise the PPI that are not used in daily work. It is probably good mental hygiene for a person to take part in such activities to round out his work and increase his satisfaction with life.

The work of a prime minister, for instance, calls for a variety of interests, but it does not provide an opportunity for aesthetic expression. Therefore, Winston Churchill took up oil painting as a hobby.

A self-employed pharmacist uses a variety of interests in his profession, but his interest in outdoor work is unsatisfied. He organizes a local fish and game club. Others whose PPI for outdoor work is unfulfilled take up hiking, go on camping trips, or become "sundowners" as they putter around their homes and land on the fringe of the city.

The owner of a small office-supply business found that his strong social-welfare interests were "left over." He became active in a local social-service organization. Now he is so wrapped up in the welfare work that his wife has agreed to run the office-supply business.

Courtesy of Kraft Foods

An after-hours outlet for an unfulfilled interest is good mental hygiene.

A bookkeeper had a strong interest in craft activities that she could not satisfy by working on ledgers. She found that she could satisfy this interest and other leftover interests by helping out in Girl Scout activities.

A young clerk in an attorney's office had a strong leftover interest in sociability because the other staff members were older than him. After several months of increasing frustration, he accidentally ran across a hobby group that gave him an outlet for sociability as well as cultural interest.

Under modern business conditions, most workers of all levels need some off-the-job activities to take care of unfulfilled interests. Suitable after-hours outlets can be very helpful in rounding out life and easing adjustment to the job.

SUGGESTIONS FOR FURTHER READING

Borow, Henry, *Man in a World of Work,* Boston: Houghton Mifflin, 1964.

Hoyt, Kenneth B., et al., *Career Education,* Salt Lake City, Utah: Olympus Publishing Co., 1972.

Isaacson, Lee E., *Career Information in Counseling and Teaching,* Boston: Allyn and Bacon, 1971.

Roth, Robert M., et al., *The Psychology of Vocational Development,* Boston: Allyn and Bacon, 1970.

U.S. Department of Labor, *Occupational Outlook Handbook,* 1974-75 Edition, U.S. Government Printing Office, 1974.

TO HELP YOU REMEMBER

1. How great are the differences between people in various types of abilities?
2. What is normal distribution? What is a bell-shaped curve?
3. How do experts compare with average people in their range of abilities?
4. What is the difference between a job analysis and a job specification?
5. What is meant by POF? How is information about the POF of a job used?
6. What does a profile of ability show?
7. What is meant by PVI and PPI?
8. According to Dr. Felton, what problems has automation brought to the work environment?
9. What is the problem of unfulfilled interests, and how can it be relieved?

WORKING WITH PEOPLE, DATA, OR THINGS

The personnel department of a large pharmaceutical laboratory is developing guidelines for the staff of interviewers. Look over the lists of PVI and PPI, and prepare a list of questions to be used in the initial screening of applicants. The questions should help to determine whether the applicant's interests are appropriate for each of the following jobs:

receptionist

secretary

laboratory technician

copywriter for advertising in professional journals

THINGS TO DO

1. Read a biography of a famous person whose work interests you. Make a list of the person's outstanding abilities. Place a check beside the items that are related to his or her main occupation. What conclusions do you draw about the range of this person's abilities?
2. Using the list "Worker Characteristics Required" (see page 249), evaluate a job that you are familiar with or interested in. Indicate whether high, average, or low ability is required for each characteristic.
3. Interview someone who has been working at a particular occupation for several years. What PVI and PPI does his job fulfill?
4. What are some of your interests that are not fulfilled at school or work at present? How do your spare-time activities use these interests, and what additional activities should you investigate?
5. Interview a representative from the personnel department of a large business to learn whether the company offers programs to help employees fulfill their leftover interests. Report your findings to the class.

DECISION MAKING AND YOUR CAREER

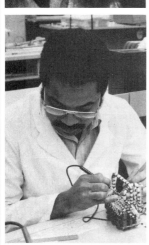

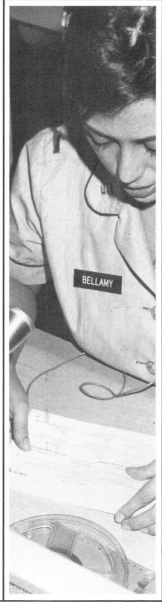

14

WhatThis Chapter Is About

1 WHAT IS A DECISION?

One dictionary defines *decision* as "the act of making up one's mind." Before action can be taken, a decision must be made. If you were in a room with four exits, you would have five choices, or possibilities, for action: you could remain in the room, or you could leave it by any one of the four exits. But, before you took advantage of one of these alternatives, you would first have to decide which one it would be.

From the time you wake up in the morning to the time you fall asleep at night, you are continually making decisions. Some of them are so minor that you are hardly aware of making them. When the alarm clock rings in the morning, you make your first decision of the day: whether or not to get out of bed. And your last decision of the day is made when you hop into bed in the evening.

We are most aware of decision making when we are confronted by important choices, such as which courses to pursue in high school, whether or not to go to college, whether or not to get married, or which career to follow.

We have learned in Chapter 12 that our decisions are based on our values. If one value is more important to us than another one, it will determine which decision we will make on a particular question at a particular time. Even though an individual says he wishes he could decide differently in a situation of freedom, what he actually does indicates what he values most highly. For example, suppose a person said he really would like to buy a brand-new car. But suppose that he received a large sum of money and was told to do anything with it he wanted. If he put the money into savings instead of buying a car, it would indicate that, no matter what he said, he values security above the status associated with having a new car.

We can learn how to evaluate all the possibilities that go into making decisions that are important in our lives, especially how to choose the right career. When decisions have such a far-reaching effect, it is necessary to spend additional time and effort engaging in a thoughtful and logical decision-making process. In making decisions about career choices, the process must be conscious and carried out with the awareness of as many facts and variables as it is possible to obtain. Individuals are rarely sure enough of their decisions to feel completely secure, but one can make decisions with a greater probability of success if as much knowledge is gathered as possible.

At one time or another we have all heard someone say, "If I had the chance to do that all over again, I would do it differently." But the chances are that that person would act exactly the same way because of his values and circumstances at the time of his decision. Looking back at that decision from a vantage point in the future, the person might have knowledge that could not have been available at the time the decision was made.

Decision making is complex and often frightening because it involves many factors over which we have little or no control—the place where we are living; our finances; our health; the attitudes of our family, friends, teachers, and business associates; as well as our own personality makeup, which figures importantly in all our decision making. Even factors that may seem unimportant, such as the weather or the amount of adrenalin in our blood, influence important decisions. Nevertheless, most of the difficulties that affect our decision making can be offset if we clearly understand what we are doing and the reasons for it. That is why it is important to learn *how* to make decisions.

2 IMPROVING YOUR DECISION MAKING

The primary requisite for effective decision making is the ability to judge and evaluate all the elements involved with a particular decision. Each element must be carefully weighed. For example, if you are offered a job in a distant state, there are many factors of varying importance to consider, such as

The salary.

The opportunity for advancement.

Your social life. Will you want to leave old friends and make new ones?

The type of work involved. Will it be fulfilling?

The company, its products, and its size.

The type of city or town where the company is located.

Availability of transportation.

The quality of schools (if you have children).

Availability of houses or apartments.

Availability of social activities.

Climate.

Each one of these factors may be subdivided. For example, the last item, climate, includes a consideration of humidity and temperature range, which may have a direct bearing on your health and physical disposition and those of your family. Then, too, what about the alternative of not taking this job. Are there other job offers? These considerations all have to be analyzed and evaluated.

Because decision making is so complex and often frightening, it is wise to use a systematic model. There is currently a debate going on about whether man can learn how to make decisions. Some psychologists and behavior analysts say that some people can make decisions and some cannot, but others believe that anyone can learn how to control his own life by learning how to make effective decisions. For people who find it hard to make a decision, learning a decision-making process often makes the task easier. Once the process is learned well enough to become a part of the person ("internalized"), it is very easy to make decisions, even important ones.

Unfortunately, however, many people avoid decisions throughout their lives. Those people are controlled by others. For example, a person who refuses to make a decision about a career may have the choice made for him by his parents or circumstances. He may be lucky or unlucky in the choice, and if he is unlucky he will never find satisfaction in the choice. Only by exercising every ounce of decision-making capability we possess can we lead truly productive and satisfying lives.

A DECISION-MAKING MODEL

Learning to make decisions is really a question of *how* to make decisions rather than *what* to decide. Each step of the decision-making process must be considered carefully by the individual making a choice, and he must decide on the basis of his values, circumstances, and available information. The steps in the decision-making process are as follows:

1 Recognize that a choice exists.
2 Generate alternatives.
3 Evaluate the consequences of each alternative.
4 Choose an alternative.
5 Take action.
6 Review the plan.

By understanding these steps, an individual can apply them to problems that will face him in the future.

Recognize That a Choice Exists

Before any decision can be made, an individual has to realize that a choice does exist and that there are alternative solutions to the problem that is facing him. Once a person believes that a decision must be or can be made, there are several considerations. First of all, the problem to be solved must be defined as clearly as possible. The more clearly the problem is defined, the easier it will be to solve. One must be careful to define the real problem and not symptoms of the problem. For example, a machinist was considering leaving a job because his work was not noticed by the supervisor. He thought that was his problem. With the help of the company counselor, he learned that he was expecting immediate rewards rather than striving for longer-range goals. Gradually, with help, he learned how to postpone gratification—to wait for a raise and a promotion instead of rushing through his tasks in a useless search for those rewards.

Once the problem is defined, the individual must make an accurate assessment of himself, or others involved in the matter, and of the social and economic factors that affect the problem. One must also be able to discriminate between his own actions and the actions of other people. A person faced with a decision might ask himself these questions: What do I want to do? Will society and my economic situation allow me to do what I decide? Am I acting on my own values, or am I going along with someone else's decision?

Each individual must realize that the decision he will make is his own and that he must accept the consequences of that decision. All decisions, of course, involve some uncontrollable factors, but each decision is the responsibility of the one who makes it, and he must be prepared to act on the results.

Generate Alternatives

A common fault in decision making is that one often considers too few alternatives. There is often a feeling that only a few alternatives exist. Sometimes it seems that no choice is possible and that one must simply accept the situation as it is. The problem usually is that the individual just does not know how to gather information about the alternatives that are available to him.

Few people are really adept at seeking information. This skill, too, must be learned. For example, an individual making a career decision must identify all the kinds of educational and career information he needs. He must learn sources of job information, such as counselors, employment agencies, and want ads, and he must investigate leads from these sources. Each individual must also gather as much information about himself as he can. In Chapter 11, we discussed some tools that are useful for this purpose.

The information that is gathered should enable the person to list the several alternatives that are open to him, estimate the possibility of success of each one, and determine the possible satisfaction each alternative will bring in terms of personal values, interests, abilities, aptitudes, and experiences.

Courtesy Brook Street Bureau of Mayfair, Ltd.

An individual making a career decision must learn sources of job information and investigate leads from these sources.

Information about available alternatives and their possible success and rewards is very important to the decision-making process, but often the most carefully gathered data is not used to its best advantage. Some people are unable or unwilling to use the available information. This reluctance may be due to a distorted perception of the situation or a refusal to acknowledge facts that contradict one's wishes. Often it is an attempt to avoid the responsibility of making a decision and living with the consequences. Refusing to make decisions, however, is really a decision in itself—a decision to drift along and not take control of one's own career choices and the direction of one's own life. The freer a person can become to accept and use the information he gathers about available alternatives, the more freedom he will have in his career choice.

Evaluate the Consequences of Each Alternative

An evaluation of the consequences of each alternative requires the use of every bit of evidence one has gathered about a problem and about the different ways of solving it. One must also understand his own values and goals, the effect they will have on the choice of a particular alternative, and how they will relate to the possible outcomes and satisfaction to be obtained from each alternative. The competent decision maker will use facts to predict the outcome and estimate the probability of success of each of the alternatives.

A person must use the data he has obtained to help himself look at the probable consequences of each alternative. Each alternative has the potential to offer the individual good or bad results, both immediately and in the future. Essentially, this step of the decision-making process involves looking very closely at the relationship between what one does and what effect that action will have on a career choice. One might say to oneself such things as, "If I decide not to go to college my parents will be disappointed." Their disappointment would be a consequence of the decision not to go to college. The next question is, "Is that consequence acceptable to me, or must I find another alternative?" Another example would be a worker who might say, "If I take this specialized training in computer programming, my chances of going into a higher-paying job are good, but it may mean moving to another city." The next question here might be, "What are the chances of these things happening?"—and so on.

Objective data (statistics and other straight factual information) is necessary and helpful in evaluating the consequences of each available alternative, but the emotional parts of a decision must also be taken into careful consideration. Educational and career decisions require a particularly high level of personal involvement; when we make decisions about education and careers, we get all caught up in our personal values and feelings about ourselves. One cannot, and should not, eliminate the emotional and subjective part of decision making; one should be aware of the influence it has. For example, Anne had a strong mathematical ability, and training and job opportunities in accounting were available to her. These objective facts all suggested that she consider an accounting career. Her subjective reaction, however, was unfavorable. She just wasn't interested. What did interest her was playing the piano. Objective information showed that she also had an aptitude for this career, and even though there were fewer job opportunities, she decided that the emotional satisfaction success would bring was worth the risks involved.

Choose an Alternative

Choosing an alternative involves the final processing of all the information an individual has gathered about himself and his alternatives. Keep in mind that some information is more important and therefore should be given more weight than other information. Each person must decide which of the solutions relating to his career choice is best for *him*; that solution will be a little different from anyone else's. Each person might ask, "What plan best fits all the information I have gathered and evaluated?"

A wise plan is the one best suited to satisfy the individual's own desires and achieve his goals under the presently anticipated circumstances; it is flexible enough to allow the individual to take advantage of any new opportunities or changing conditions that may develop. There may be only one best decision for the present, but it is a good idea to establish a hierarchy of plans so that if the first alternative does not work out as anticipated, others will be available. For example, a young high school graduate was faced with the problem of what to do next. The top-ranked decision he made was to try to get into a premedical program in college. The next decision, the one that ranked second, was to obtain training to be a medical technologist. As it happened, he was not accepted into any premedical program, and so he used his next best alternative: he was trained in medical technology. With this training, he became better qualified for more advanced study in medicine, and when he applied again to a premedical program, he was accepted. In fact, when he entered medical school he did very well because of his other training. Since he had planned for several different alternatives, he was able to make the most of his career. He became a successful doctor.

Because each person wants to increase the probability that what he wants to happen *will* happen, he must determine the best way to exercise whatever control he does have in a situation to bring about the desired results. By developing skill in exerting control through a series of actions, one continues to increase the probability of successful outcomes for himself and becomes an increasingly more effective decision maker.

A good check on the soundness of your decision and your established hierarchy, or ranking, of plans is to determine whether or not your plans consistently follow from the definition of your problem and the information you have gathered and considered. You might even write your definition of the problem on a piece of paper in one column, the different solutions you have considered in a middle column, and the plan you have decided upon in a third column. Either think to yourself, "Does this make sense?," or show your work to someone you respect and trust. Ask that person the same question. If your plan appears, in all respects, to be a good solution to the problem, good! If not, rethink and revise your plans to make them consistent with the career problem you have defined, with the information you have learned, and with the values you believe are most important.

Take Action

Once a person had selected for himself the best available alternative, the next step is to act. After a career decision has been made, the individual must seek the appropriate training (through formal education or on the job), plan his time for study to acquire the necessary skills, test the decision he has made by these actions, and then evaluate the consequences. If the consequences are good, the individual is ready to plan the next step or goal. If the consequences are bad, the individual must reconsider and must implement his second alternative and compensate for lack of success with his first decision. Making decisions is a process that is never completed; it continues all through life. One should learn the process and become increasingly efficient in its use.

Review the Plan

The goal one has chosen should be the best one possible at the time it is planned. As one gathers additional experience, it should be reviewed in light of the accumulated experience and knowledge. Whether one finds that his decision and plan are satisfactory or whether he feels he should alter the plan or shift to an alternate plan, he should act without letting the original decision lead him into or keep him in an unhappy career experience. In general, however, if an individual was thorough and careful in the first five steps of decision making, any modifications will be minor ones. Any plan should be reviewed periodically and updated to suit the needs of the individual.

There is considerable comfort for an individual in having a plan for his educational and vocational future. What is most important, by following a process of decision making, one will have good plans and good reasons for pursuing these plans, and the probability for success in a career will be good.

 PERSONALITY AND CAREER CHOICE

Our relationships with others, our ethics and religious beliefs, and the importance in our lives of material goods usually form "anchor points" to which we tie our other values; in other words, they are our basic values. In particular, they underlie our career decisions. It is, of course, important to remember that as we grow older and our environment changes, our personalities will also change in accordance with our changing perception and understanding of our environment. This is a continuing process, and it is the sign of a *maturing* person.

But there is still that "basic anchor point," the self, the I, the me, which is now called by custom the *ego*. It is the core around which our personality is molded, so to speak, and it never completely changes. It is the root of all our tendencies; it even supersedes the requirements of all needs. In effect, it is the "superneed" because without it, we would not have a sense of our individuality; we would have no identity.

Clearly, our changing values, as we mature, are continuously affecting our relationships with others and our interests. This cannot be helped or overcome, and it affects our careers. We may spend a great deal of time and money on one career, and later we may find that we are losing interest in it. But in most cases in which people have lost interest in the careers that they have chosen, the decision to choose the career did not have a strong foundation. Therefore, it is crucial that we know ourselves as well as possible.

A change of career should be a modification rather than an abrupt change. An example of an abrupt change might be a lawyer becoming a bartender. But if a lawyer becomes a law librarian, for instance, the law would be a common ingredient to both professions. This change would be *evolution*; that is, the person would have started out with a certain career in mind but would later change his vocational direction within the same general field. Another example would be a pharmacy student deciding to become a doctor or nurse. The interest, in either of these choices, would be medical. Hence, the basic medical interest would *evolve* into a mature choice of career, even though it might not be the career of the student's original choosing. But if a person trained for a career in medicine decides later to become an accountant, even though he might get an accounting position in a hospital or dispensary, this would be considered an abrupt change in careers. An evolutionary change indicates that a person is maturing and working things out. He has basic skills and interests, but he may not at first choose a career that best uses his skills. An abrupt change doesn't take previous training and skills into account; it involves a total disregard of past work and an entirely new field that requires different skills and additional training. Therefore, it should be avoided, if at all possible.

5 SOCIAL SYSTEMS AND CAREER DECISIONS

There are elements beyond the individual's control that exert an influence on his vocational decision making. An example is the society into which he was born or in which he was brought up. Parents almost always want their children to pursue a particular career. They may consider the child's abilities or the prestige within the community of certain careers, but whatever the basis is for their choice, they usually have some opinions on what is best for their children. At one time sons or daughters would force themselves to follow the dictates of their parents. Unless the child had an especially strong career goal, he would submit to family pressures and even succeed to some degree in the line of work that he was guided into. It is good for parents to want their children to live the best possible lives, but the question is, "What is best?"

Changes in vocational direction should be made within the same vocational field. What are some possibilities for evolutionary changes of career for someone trained in chemistry?

Courtesy of NCR Co.

In our society, as well as in other "developed" societies, the goal has often been "gold." Young people go into medical careers as doctors not because they want to *cure* but because they want to *earn*. Later, often when it is too late, they find that they hate this profession. They have social and financial commitments that make a change unadvisable. One important rule to remember: Never pursue a career unless you really want to do the work involved or find at least some major aspect of that kind of work self-fulfilling.

Women and blacks especially have suffered the brunt of social pressures. Many middle-aged women today were brought up in a society that told them, "A woman's place is in the home"; "Women shouldn't go to college or take up vocations—no man wants to marry a woman who is smarter than he is." Around the turn of the century, one young woman was told to quit taking violin lessons, in spite of her talent, because the violin "would make her chin flat," and she would be unattractive to men. Once a bright black eighth-grader was advised not to take college preparatory subjects in high school because, as his adviser put it, "You can never expect to become anything more than a waiter." He ignored this advice and went on to become the founder of a multimillion-dollar record company.

This story illustrates the fact that social discrimination has often been the guide for career selection. For example, women were "guided" into the nursing professions and discouraged from going to medical schools to become doctors. Blacks have been traditionally "guided" into blue-collar jobs, but many blue-collar craft associations, unions, and guilds have discriminated against blacks in their memberships. Thus, most jobs open to blacks were unskilled. Discrimination on the basis of religion and national origin has been less apparent in the United States in recent years, but it was quite commonly practiced in the nineteenth century, especially against Irish, Jewish, and Italian immigrants in the East and Asian immigrants in the West. Yet we are still trained to think of certain careers as belonging to particular groups of people. Consider, for example, these modern stereotypes of male and female roles. The secretary is almost always "she," unless a particular secretary is pointed out as being a man; similarly, a nurse is always "she." A maid is always "she"; in fact, "maid" really means "young woman." On the other hand, a "boss" is always "he"; virtually all professionals—doctors, lawyers, architects, accountants, professors, engineers, and so on—are usually referred to as "he." There is an apt story that illustrates this point. A man and his son were in an automobile accident. The father was killed immediately, but the son, critically injured, was taken to a nearby hospital for emergency surgery. The doctor, entering the operating room, took a look at the boy and said, "I cannot operate on him, he is my son." In answer to the question "Who is the doctor?" which follows this story, most of the replies go something like this: "Did you say the father was really killed?" "The father wasn't really killed." "The father came back to life." "The father was really a ghost." "I give up, who is *he*?" A surprised or sheepish look usually follows when the answer is given: "The doctor is the mother." So we see how ingrained are our attitudes toward who does certain jobs. In spite of the fact that women have been doctors for a long time, we still think of doctors as *men*, unless otherwise specified. "Dr. Wallace won't be on the floor this afternoon, *she* was called to the emergency room."

There are national laws against discrimination based on race, religion, sex, and national origin. Some states also have similar laws. But, what about the physically handicapped? While it is true that they are often limited by a physical disability, such as blindness, deafness, amputation, or inability to walk, there are still many jobs that these people could do in spite of their particular handicap, and they can perform these jobs as well as "normal" people can. They may be discriminated against because of a company's fear of legal liabilities in case of an accident, or because of a deformity that is unattractive. The handicapped person who is discouraged from making certain career choices because of social pressures suffers more handicaps than his physical disability.

Education is also part of the social system that molds our ways of thinking and helps to determine a person's choice of a career. Two decades ago, a student went to college to widen his horizons and become cultured. He studied foreign languages, art, philosophy, literature, music, mathematics, and history. Then when he left school he found that many jobs for which he was totally untrained were open to him. Department stores, for instance, used to grab college graduates and put them into their "executive training" programs. Jobs would start at a whopping $65 per week.

Courtesy of Chase Manhattan Bank

In spite of the fact that women have been in the law profession for some time, lawyers are still often thought of as men.

Today, however, companies don't like to train untrained workers except for certain types of jobs, usually those for which training is not available elsewhere. But in most cases, before you are trained on the job you have to be trained at school. A job in a department store may require a major in marketing and retailing; a career job in a bank or stock brokerage house may favor those pretrained in money and banking in college or business school. This emphasis on academic training for a vocation is becoming more and more widespread.

Thus, choosing an education has become a major decision in career planning. Also, an education means that there are more options in career choice. To say that education is the agent of occupational mobility means that it is hard either to change jobs or move upward within one job without education. Usually, though by no means always, the more education one has, the farther one can go in a career.

 ## INDUSTRIAL ORGANIZATION AND CAREER CHOICE

The organizational structure of businesses and industries affects career choice and behavior. Every business, especially a large firm, has established rules and conditions that may create certain problems of adjustment for its workers. Each worker is required to modify his behavior so that he will be able to fit into the organization. Some of the problems he will encounter are as follows: (1) dealing with authority, (2) satisfying security needs in the face of competition and business politics, (3) adjusting to routine work and hours, and (4) resolving personal conflict between creativity and conformity.

When you begin a new job you must do things the way your employer wants you to do them: he is the *authority*. But at the same time, if this authority presents a conflict in values, you will not be a cooperative worker. Thus, one consideration in a career decision is the work environment. Of course, you might have chosen the right career but the wrong job within it. For example, you might want to be a teacher, but you may find yourself working in a school with an unsympathetic administration. In this case you must either change jobs or try as best as you can to "get along."

Every job involves a certain amount of competition. This can bother the person who is seeking job security, but it can stimulate others to improve their performance and can make for extra interest. The amount of security you need and the competition involved with a job must fit into your value structure. Sales jobs are often competitive because the salesman can be measured by the amount of sales he makes. If you shun competition, you might prefer a job that is less competitive than sales work.

Do you like to work during the day? at night? Today there are job openings for different shifts during the day and at night. In many cases, depending on your choice of career or job, you will be able to choose your own hours. Some jobs call for changing shifts. Mail carriers and department store personnel often are subjected to changes in shifts. In a department store, one day you may work from 9:00 a.m. to 5:00 p.m., another day from 1:00 p.m. to 9:00 p.m. A bartender may work from 11:00 a.m. to 8:00 p.m. or from 8:00 p.m. to 4:00 a.m. Hospital workers also have many shifts available. One hospital worker, a specialist in respiration, worked from noon on Friday to midnight the following Sunday, covering a period of 40 hours. He ate and slept at the hospital and worked long shifts of 16 hours at a clip, but he had four days off—Monday, Tuesday, Wednesday, and Thursday.

If you like to be left on your own, you won't want a job that needs a lot of supervision. In this respect, being a salesman would be ideal because you can usually make your own hours in this type of job. There are restrictions, however, such as having to be on hand when your potential customers are available. For instance, if you are selling life insurance, you will have to work evenings—visiting clients when they are home in the evening, usually after dinner; if you sell to retail stores, you will have to be available when the store owners or managers are free to talk to you. But most people must conform to a set of working hours that doesn't change, usually during the day from 9:00 a.m. to 5:00 p.m.

Ed Lada

A life insurance sales representative will often visit clients when they are home in the evening. Before deciding on this career, one must be prepared to adjust to such a schedule.

Creative jobs involve special skills, and they are the least "organized." Unless you are working for yourself, you will probably have to conform to some company rules, but you will still be able to express yourself creatively. Some creative jobs are in the fields of writing, interior decoration, carpentry, hair styling, and clothing design. Creativity can be exercised in an office, where a worker may devise efficient methods of performing his duties. However, these variations in procedure may have to be adapted to the rules and customs of the particular firm. Some people prefer to go into their own businesses, while others feel they can do best under conditions in which company discipline sets the hours for work and the duties to be performed. Your own preference is one of the many factors you must consider in deciding on a career.

SUGGESTIONS FOR FURTHER READING

Centers, R., and D. E. Bugental, "Intrinsic and Extrinsic Job Motivation Among Different Segments of the Working Population," *Journal of Applied Psychology*, Vol. 50, pp. 193–197, 1966.

Gross, E., "The Worker and Society," in H. Borow (ed.), *Man in a World of Work,* Boston: Houghton Mifflin, 1964.

_____"A Sociological Approach to the Analysis of Preparation for Work Life," *Personnel and Guidance Journal*, Vol. 45, pp. 416–423, 1967.

Herver, V. H., "Vocational Interests of College Freshmen and Their Social Origins," *Journal of Applied Psychology*, Vol. 49, pp. 407–411, 1965.

Lauman, E. O., and L. Gutman, "The Relative Associational Contiguity of Occupations in an Urban Setting," *American Sociological Review*, Vol. 31, pp. 169–178, 1966.

Liberty, P. G., E. Burnstein, and R. W. Moulton, "Concerns with Mastery and Occupational Attraction," *Journal of Personality*, Vol. 34, pp. 105–117, 1966.

Reisman, D., *The Lonely Crowd*, New Haven, Conn.: Yale, 1957.

Vroom, V. H., *Work and Motivation*, New York: Wiley, 1964.

Whyte, W. F., *The Organization Man*, New York: Simon & Schuster, 1956.

TO HELP YOU REMEMBER

1. What is a decision?
2. Why is decision making an important process to learn?
3. What are the six steps involved in decision making?
4. How do values and information affect a decision?
5. What is meant by "evolution" of a career choice?
6. What influence might parents have on a person's career choice?
7. What pressures does ethnic, racial, or sexual discrimination place on a person choosing a career?
8. List three jobs that have traditionally been considered appropriate for women and three that have been considered inappropriate.
9. How does the organizational structure of business affect career choice?

WORKING WITH PEOPLE, DATA, OR THINGS

Here are descriptions of four people who are facing career decisions.

Terry: Terry's parents live on a small farm in a rural part of the state. Terry is bright and does well in mathematics, science, and vocational agriculture. But Terry would like to become a lawyer. His parents also want him to become a lawyer and are willing to help him pay for going to law school. Terry's school counselor has tested Terry and told him that he does not have enough verbal ability to be a successful lawyer. If *you* were Terry, what decision would you make about your career and education?

Cassandra: Cassandra comes from a family of six children. Her father left home when she was ten, and she has helped take care of the other children since then. Now she is eighteen; she has just graduated from high school and would like to become a doctor. Her mother and grandmother, however, feel that she should stay at home with her brothers and sisters until she gets married. They feel that it would be too much of a strain for the family to pay for medical training. Cassandra's counselor told her that she has the ability to become a doctor or anything else she wants, and she has the personality traits of patience and kindness. If *you* were Cassandra, what decision would you make about education and a career?

Raymond: Raymond's father is a senior vice president of a bank. Both of Raymond's parents graduated from well-known universities, and his mother has a master's degree. Raymond has always had an interest in building things and is so good that he built a summer cabin all by himself. His parents expect him to become an architect. To do that he would have to go to a four-year university. Raymond's high school grades are good, and he has the ability and aptitude to become an architect. But he has saved over two thousand dollars and would like to use the money to buy a motorcycle and tour the country for at least a year. Then, he wants to get a job as a carpenter's apprentice. After that, he says he might go to college and he might not. He and his parents have had several bitter fights about the subject. If *you* were Raymond, what decision would you make about your education and career choice?

Roslyn: Roslyn is twenty-three years old. She has a good-paying job as a secretary for a publishing company. She also has a baccalaureate degree in elementary education and a teaching certificate. Roslyn was unable to find a job teaching school in the town where she chose to live. She is unhappy in her present work, despite the pay, and would like to take another job, but she is afraid to make the move. If *you* were Roslyn, what would you decide to do?

Directions

1. Considering all the factors discussed in this chapter, make a decision for each of the above people.
2. Form small groups of three to six members each, and share your decisions about each person. Discuss the differences, and see if your group can arrive at a consensus about what would be the best course of action in each case.

THINGS TO DO

1. Define a problem you are facing right now with regard to either a career choice or an educational choice. Write the definition of the problem in a column to the left side of a piece of paper. In the middle column list all the alternative ways of solving the problem. You may have to do research to find all the solutions. Next, consider the consequences of each alternative. For each alternative, put a minus sign by the negative consequences and a plus sign by the positive consequences. Pick one of the alternatives. In a column to the right side of the paper, describe a plan you intend to follow to put your decision into effect. When you finish, form small groups of from three to six members each, and share your plans. Criticize *constructively* any flaws or gaps you see in your fellow group members' plans.

2. Prepare a brief report telling about one decision you have already made. Explain how you went about making the decision and what the outcome or result of the decision was, and describe one decision you will make in the future as a result of your previous decision.

COPING WITH JOB APPLICATIONS AND INTERVIEWS

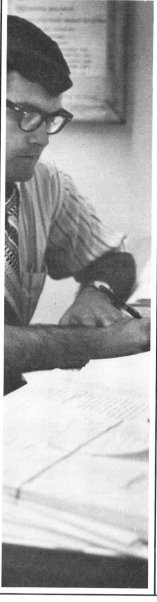

15

What This Chapter Is About

1 THE MOST VALUABLE RESOURCE—YOU

This country is blessed with many natural resources—timber, oil, gold, iron, coal, and uranium, to name a few. But its most valuable resource is its people—its human resources. And the most valuable part of that resource is *talent*. Each person has a potential within him, and when that potential is released, talent is put to use in the form of creative energy.

Most people release their creative energy on the job; at least they should, because they spend the greatest part of their valuable time at work. An employer uses the creative energy of his workers to improve his business—the services and products he has to offer. No building would have been built, no machine invented or manufactured, and no product sold without the full use of human talent.

Everyone has some talent to offer; you don't need to be a genius. But the best job for an individual is the one that enables him to make the fullest possible use of his talents. Thus, the job a person seeks should be the one that he can do the *best*.

Whenever anyone applies for a job, he is actually selling a prospective employer his talents. He is, in effect, a *product* himself. The task of the applicant is to present what he has to sell in the best possible way to the best possible buyer. You can look at job hunting as a sort of campaign. There are various ways to prepare yourself and the materials you need for this campaign. One of the most important materials you will need is your *résumé*, which is a data sheet giving all the information about yourself that a prospective employer will want to know in order to hire you for the job he has to fill.

2 YOUR BEST SALES TOOL—THE RÉSUMÉ

The information you include in your résumé is crucial to your getting any job. Many companies have application forms that are similar to résumés, but it is still best for you to have your own résumé. The chief purpose of a résumé is to give an employer a sort of profile of yourself by listing past jobs, education, and any personal information related to the particular job you want.

Your résumé should be typewritten on an 8½ by 11 sheet of white paper *without lines*. Be sure to clean the type on your typewriter so that it will print clearly and neatly. Neatness and organization are extremely important when you make up a résumé. A résumé that is smudgy and hard to read or not well-organized will turn off an employer.

Begin your résumé by giving your name, address, and telephone number. It is a good idea to place your name at the top center or on the left-hand side *alone*. Your name should be placed at least 1 inch from the top of the sheet to leave a sufficient margin. If possible, your name should stand alone, not immediately followed by your address, so that your résumé can be spotted quickly among others. If you place your name at the top center, you can skip a few spaces, at least two, and put your address at the center or either side. Be sure to leave a ·margin of an inch or so on both sides of the sheet. Always include your ZIP code after the state. Use abbreviations sparingly: St. (Street), Av. or Ave. (Avenue), Rd. (Road), Pl. (Place), Bl. or Blvd. (Boulevard). Numerals can be used for numbered streets—1st St., 2d St., 3d St., 4th St.—but the numbers can also be spelled out—First St., Second St., Third St., Fourth St. Sometimes this is better, especially if there are other abbreviations in the address. Don't abbreviate the name of your city, town, or village, but you should abbreviate the name of your state with the two-letter abbreviations used by the U.S. Postal Service. Immediately beneath your address place your telephone number, including your area code.

A useful element on your résumé is your career or job objective. The employer should know exactly what type of job or career you are looking for. This entry can be omitted if your résumé is very long, or if you are applying for a specific opening.

If you mail a résumé to a prospective employer, it should be accompanied by a brief letter explaining your purpose, including your intended choice of work. Even though the job objective listing on your résumé might repeat this information, it is a useful entry because your papers may be separated. If the entry is included, it is customary to type the heading, or title, using all capital letters, followed by the job description in upper- and lower-case letters.

The next heading on the résumé is BUSINESS EXPERIENCE or PROFESSIONAL EXPERIENCE. Under this heading you list your *last job first*, then your next-to-last job, and so on. If you held a job for two years or more, it is not necessary to include names of the months in the dates. Thus, you would write, for example, 1970–1972. If you held a job for less than a year, write, for example, June 1975–September 1975. The dates are important because they tell an employer how much experience you have had. For each job, write the name and address of the company you worked for. The telephone number may or may not be included. Your immediate supervisor can be excluded, but you can use his or her name as a reference at the end of your résumé—with permission, of course. Then under the name and address of the company, give a brief description of your job duties (no more than five sentences in the usual case).

You may list your jobs in an order that is different from the one suggested above. For instance, you may group similar jobs, especially if there is a certain type of job you prefer. Suppose, for example, you are interested in being an advertising copywriter and you have had two copywriting jobs, but in between them you had two sales jobs. You can group the copywriting jobs under the heading POSITIONS AS COPYWRITER and the other jobs under the heading OTHER POSITIONS HELD. This arrangement has two advantages. (1) It puts your copywriting experiences together so that an employer can see all the related jobs you have held in this area. (2) It places emphasis on your copywriting experience, when the jobs related to this type of work appear first on your résumé. It is not a good idea to leave out jobs you have had, because then time periods that have been unaccounted for will appear. This might give an employer the idea that you were unemployed because you were ill or were not a steady worker. A résumé indicating time that has not been accounted for looks funny; an employer may think that you are trying to hide something. If for a few weeks, or even a few months, you had a job that did not pertain to your vocational goal, that job can be omitted on your résumé. Also, if you have had summer jobs while you were in school, weigh the value of including them on your résumé. No prospective employer wants to read unnecessary information about employment that does not pertain to the job he is offering. On the other hand, in the case of young workers applying for their first entry-level jobs, the list of temporary positions reveals a general positive attitude toward the world of work.

The next heading is EDUCATION. Under this heading give the *last* school you attended first. List only high schools, colleges, and business or technical schools. For each school, give the type of graduation award you received, such as the type of degree, certificate, or diploma. You can state your major subject and minor subject, if any, only if they *pertain* to the type of position for which you are applying. The date of graduation is optional. Also list any relevant courses you have taken in addition to those in schools.

Another useful heading on the résumé can be PROFESSIONAL AND BUSINESS ASSOCIATIONS. Under this heading, first list the association you belong or belonged to that best represents your interest (not the last one you joined); then list the second most important association, and so on. You can include extracurricular activities at school. After the name of the association you can state any office you held in that association, and also the term of office.

It is not necessary to list personal information, unless, of course, it pertains to the work you are going to do. It is against the law for employers to request information about age, sex, religious preference, ethnic background, or political beliefs. It is acceptable, but not necessary, to indicate your marital or military status. A photograph, once considered a useful addition to the résumé, is no longer advised because it is a nonverbal way of communicating some of this personal information.

Your résumé should usually fit on one sheet of paper, unless you are applying for a very high-level job and you are required to submit a detailed biographical report. For this reason it is not advisable to add any unnecessary material to your résumé. And most employers are definitely not interested in personal problems, if they don't affect your work.

The last item should be REFERENCES. Try to find out the address *and* telephone number of each of your references. This gives the company the option of calling or writing. A reference may be a teacher or other adviser in school, a previous supervisor, a friend, or an acquaintance, such as your doctor, dentist, banker, or landlord. References from people you have not worked with are called "character references." In general, business references are preferable because they know more about your work habits and abilities than character references. Do not ask relatives to serve as references. The employer will wonder whether people who have a personal interest in your welfare can also evaluate your qualifications objectively. If you wish, you can use the sentence "References will be supplied upon request." This eliminates the necessity of listing names, addresses, and telephone numbers. Of course, you should be prepared to supply a list of people who have agreed to recommend you.

If you are mailing out a few résumés, these can be typed very neatly. But if there are quite a few companies you wish to contact, it is a good idea to have your résumés printed by an offset printer. The charges are nominal, and printing will save you a great deal of trouble and effort, especially if you are not an efficient typist. If you are applying for your first or second job and your résumé seems scanty, you can double-space the information to make it fill the page. Otherwise, single spacing is used, except between entries and headings, where double or triple spaces can be used. There is a variety of styles for résumés. The above ideas are merely suggestions, but the important thing is to include *all necessary material* and present it in a way that is clear and easy for the reader to follow.

Never include in your résumé your salaries in past jobs or the salary you want for your prospective job. This will be discussed in the interview. Listing a particular salary will affect your chances for bargaining later. *Always leave this question open.*

Also, never indicate on your résumé why you left your last job. Clearly, you won't be tempted to tell a prospective employer that you were "fired for incompetence." There are various reasons why you may have been "laid off": work slowdown, job discontinued, business dissolved, cutback for economic reasons, and so on. Most employers will not hold these problems against you. And, if you quit, it could have been because of dissatisfaction, minor health problems, or other acceptable reasons. This matter, if it comes up, and it may well come up, can be discussed at the time of the interview.

Again, it must be emphasized that neatness, correct spelling and grammar, and good organization are the keystones for any résumé. Remember, too, that a prospective employer gets his first impression

```
                          Norma Ramirez

                          987 Oak Street
                        Winford, MA  00999
                          (617) 555-6768


    JOB OBJECTIVE

    Executive Secretary


    BUSINESS EXPERIENCE

    June 19-- - present:  Secretary, Advertising Department, Fine's Department
         Store, 1900 Center Avenue, Winford, MA 00998.  Answering interoffice
         and outside correspondence, typing, filing, operating office machinery.

    June - September, 19-- and 19--:  Clerk-typist, Department of Motor Vehicles,
         4210 Main Street, Winford, MA 00998.  Summer job; typing and filing re-
         cords.

    September - June, 19-- and 19--:  Student assistant in Admissions Office,
         John Quincy Adams Junior College, Pine Manor Road, Warrington, MA
         00980. Part-time job during school year; typing and filing correspon-
         dence, conducting campus tours for prospective students.


    EDUCATION

    John Quincy Adams Junior College, Warrington, MA, AA degree, June, 19--,
         Secretarial Sciences Major.  Courses in business psychology, busi-
         ness communication, shorthand (120 wpm), typing (70 wpm), filing,
         business machines.

    Winford High School, Winford, MA, graduated June, 19--.


    PERSONAL INTERESTS AND ACTIVITIES

    Extracurricular activities in college:  Assistant business manager of
         Patriot, yearbook; captain of women's hockey team; member of Ski Club.

    Extracurricular activities in high school:  Advertising manager of Winford
         High Reporter, newspaper; member of intermural girls' hockey team.

    Hobbies and other activities:  Volunteer work reading to geriatric patients,
         Warren County Medical Center; skiing; folk dancing; pottery.


    REFERENCES

    References will be furnished upon request.
```

It is important that a résumé be neat and complete.

of you from your résumé. After he has seen your résumé, he will decide whether it is worthwhile for you to come in for an interview. A well-written résumé tells him something about you before he has even judged your job experience: that you are a well-organized, neat, clear thinker. A résumé prepared with care tells him how determined and sincere you are in your ambitions and goals.

One of the tricks to success in finding a good job is to be at the right place at the right time. This should not be left to chance: it should be deliberate and planned. Although getting a break also helps, especially if you are trying to enter a field that is overcrowded and highly competitive, the person who makes his own "breaks" is more likely to achieve his career goals than the person who relies on luck or chance.

The aim of this chapter is to help you find a job without the help of friends and family, although their help can be useful. There are three other ways to approach job hunting: (1) Look through the want ads in your local newspapers. (2) Check out employment agencies. (3) Get a directory listing the companies in the field that you would like.

Want Ads

Most of the major newspapers in the larger cities, and even in smaller communities, carry want ad sections entitled "Classified" or "Help Wanted." The ads are placed in the newspaper by a company that is looking for a certain type of worker. Employment agencies also place similar ads. You yourself can place an ad, but the cost will restrict you to a few lines. Listings of people like you who are looking for jobs are usually entitled "Situations Wanted." Placing such an ad can be a very effective way to seek employment.

A typical "Help Wanted" ad looks like this:

```
         PROGRAMMER
          ASSISTANT
            8AM-4PM

  We seek an individual with a minimum
  of 1 year experience in RPG language,
  Tape/Disk Systems.

  We offer an EXCELLENT salary and
  comprehensive benefits within a sophis-
  ticated environment geared to further-
  ing professional development.

     Apply Personnel, 9 AM-3 PM
       55 Water Street, NYC
       North Building-3rd Floor

          CHEMICAL
            BANK
   is an equal opportunity employer
```

Here is a typical "Situations Wanted" ad:

```
  ACCT, Recent degree, mature man,
  Salary secondary to obtaining experience
              G68  TIMES
```

The Help Wanted ads are usually listed in alphabetical order by kind of job. Thus, ads for accountants will be in the As, ads for book-keepers in the Bs, ads for copywriters in the Cs, and so on. The ad just gives enough information to let you know what type of person is wanted for the job and what the qualifications are. It is no longer legal to make restrictions as to age or to specify "male" or "female," but a job might require you to be free to travel, have a car, or be a college graduate in a certain field of study. Some jobs specify the amount of experience required in months or years.

Want ads may request that you send résumés to certain box numbers or that you call a certain telephone number. They may specify that you write, not appear in person. This means exactly what it says, even though an address may also be given. It is bad taste to barge in. If you send a brief letter along with your résumé, you will get a reply very soon in most cases, but if you don't hear from an employer within two weeks, you can assume that the position has already been filled.

Many Help Wanted ads are "blind"; that is, they do not indicate the advertiser's name. Blind ads are often used by large companies to help direct responses to the department that is interested in hiring. It may seem awkward to write to an anonymous employer. Unlike the situation described in Chapter 8, in which the applicant was writing to a known employer who had been suggested by the school office co-ordinator, answering a blind ad means writing to a stranger. Therefore, the covering letter should be more reserved. When you reply to an ad by letter, it is a good idea to cut the ad out of the newspaper and paste or tape it to the top of your letter. Your letter should be short, simple, and courteous, like the following example.

Gentlemen:

This is in response to your ad for a cost accountant in last Sunday's *World Herald*. As you can see from the enclosed résumé, I have had several years' experience in this field.

I hope that you will find my qualifications satisfactory and that you will contact me to set an appointment for an interview at your convenience.

Sincerely yours,

Avoid closings like "Hoping to hear from you in the near future," or "Thanking you in advance for your consideration." Such expressions are meaningless and cause extra work for the reader, especially if he has to read a large number of replies to a newspaper ad. Most of the information should be contained in your résumé. Salary is rarely discussed in a "first letter," even though it may be specified in the ad. Sometimes ads specify that the applicant indicate his salary requirement, but a direct answer should be avoided. If this is not possible, then indicate about what *annual* salary you are looking for.

In a Situations Wanted ad, you have to give information to a prospective employer. It should be about five lines at most. Notice in the Situations Wanted ad on page 288 that most of the normal punctuation has been omitted, yet it is still clear. Punctuation may take up too much space, and since you are usually charged by the line, the cost of your ad is raised if the copy runs over even a little on a new line. The first thing you should state in the ad is the type of work desired; then indicate your areas of competence, and finally the way to contact you. The style in these kinds of ads is "telegraphic"; that is, the ads are like telegrams. Unnecessary words and punctuation are omitted; just the barest message tells the reader what is being offered.

Employment Agencies

The purpose of the employment agency is to be a "broker" between the prospective employer and the employee. The people who work at employment agencies are usually trained in personnel work, which is finding employees for companies. But instead of working for a company, they work for an agency. The agency "screens" the applicants for a client company so that people who are not qualified for a job won't apply to a company. Thus, in a sense, the employment agency "weeds out" people for a company. This can be a great help for a large company, although many large companies have their own personnel departments. However, these departments are often involved in many personnel activities other than hiring. For example, they may be involved in health insurance benefits, payroll, and employee relations in general.

A privately owned employment agency is paid for its services. In many states the fee is set by law, and in most cases it is paid by the client company. The agency requires a résumé, and, in addition, there is usually an application or form, to be filled out by the job seeker. Larger companies also have an application, which we shall discuss later. The agency submits your résumé and application to the company seeking personnel with your talents.

All states have state-run employment services to help job seekers find work. These agencies charge no fees to either the company or the potential employee. Besides just acting as a broker, state agencies provide other services, such as employment or career counseling and aptitude testing. The process at a state agency is slower and usually more careful than that of a private agency because the personnel counselors are paid straight salaries and don't depend on commissions for each placement as in a private agency.

A different kind of employment agency is a college "Placement Office." Since the placement office charges no fee, the application process may also be slow. Again, you will be required to fill out a form, and a résumé will be helpful here. Also, in recent years, colleges and universities have made arrangements whereby many large companies send personnel people to recruit employees directly from school. Usually one or two days during the year are set aside when these company job recruiters arrive and set up booths. They will consult with students and provide applications that can be filled in and immediately returned to the recruiters. This recruitment service is open to all graduates and, in most cases, to students who have taken a series of courses but have not graduated. The company recruiters will take the applications from the students so they can be reviewed by their companies. Later, the selected students will be contacted for further interviewing and eventual hiring.

Company Directories and Trade Journals

Many companies and businesses that have similar products or services have formed associations. These associations publish directories listing the member companies; the directories are available in many public libraries. One such directory is the *Literary Market Place*, published by R. R. Bowker Co. of New York and London. This yearly directory lists most of the publishers in the United States and Canada, magazines, newspapers, radio and television stations, and data processing services, among other items. In the back of this directory is a useful section entitled "Reference Books of the Trade." Listed in this section are other directories, yearbooks, and bulletins of book-related companies. For example, the *Encyclopedia of Associations* is one such entry. It is described as follows:

> A guide to the national organizations of the U.S.: agricultural, avocational, business, cultural, educational, fraternal, Greek letter, labor, medical, nationality & ethnic, professional, public affairs, scientific, technical, social welfare & veterans. 6th revised edition.

The *Literary Market Place* and similar listings and directories give the names, addresses, telephone numbers, names of executives, and divisions for many organizations and businesses, as well as a brief description of the products or services offered. You can look up a company you are interested in working for, find the name of the manager of a certain department, and write to him directly. He will usually write to you to let you know whether he is interested in hiring you. If he is interested, he will tell you how to apply to his company, and he will probably set up an interview for you. You may not hear from a company for quite a while, sometimes as long as a year, so don't get discouraged if you don't receive a reply from a company right away. It takes time for an opening to occur, and then various people have to be consulted about considering your application—that is, your résumé and the accompanying letter.

Many organizations also publish journals and magazines to keep people in the fields they represent up to date on the various happenings in their industry. If you are interested in going into a specialized type of work, by all means secure a journal that publishes articles related to your field.

One example is *Stores*, the monthly magazine of the National Retail Merchants Association, Inc. In addition to news articles about retailing, there is a classified ads section that lists job openings, businesses for sale, and situations wanted. Other magazines are not published by trade organizations but are directed to readers interested in specific industries or groups of related industries. For people interested in toy and hobby merchandising, Geyer-McAllister Publications offers the magazine *Playthings*. These magazines also have classified ads.

4 COMPANY JOB APPLICATIONS

Even after you have submitted a résumé and a covering letter, many of the larger companies will require you to fill out an application. This application will include much of the material already on your résumé, but you will have to fill it out anyway. The purpose of the application is to provide additional information that may not be on a résumé, and it usually contains a place for the person who interviews you to make notes. Also, many applicants don't have résumés, and so the application must provide job information about these people also.

When you fill out a company application, you should be as brief as possible—you should not duplicate exactly the style on your résumé. Also, you should, if possible, answer *every* question; if you don't, it will look as though you are careless or want to conceal something.

Some questions that will appear on a company application are not answered on the average résumé. Such questions may be: "Are you willing to travel?" "Do you own an automobile?" "Can you drive an automobile?" "What is your draft status?" "Why did you leave your last job?" Additional information, such as salary requirement, previous salary, physical characteristics, outstanding debts, status of your health, and so on, may be called for.

The company application will give you an opportunity to provide references. List the name, position, address, and telephone number for each reference, even if this information is given on your résumé. Although a reference check is usually made only after the field of candidates has been narrowed to a few, you will want the employer to have your list of references handy, in case you are one of the applicants being seriously considered.

Unfortunately, some company applications were made up many years ago and have not been changed, and so many unnecessary or unlawful questions may be asked with regard to sex, age (or date of birth), religious affiliation, or race. If you don't want to answer these, you can put a line through them; the reason will be understood.

One item that is almost always required, even if a space for it doesn't appear on an old application, is your social security number. If you don't have this number memorized, you should carry your social security card. It is very important for an employer to have this number.

Again, neatness counts when filling out a company application. *Print* everything except your signature. *Always use a pen,* never a pencil. And if you have an opportunity to fill out the application at home—if you are requested to take it home or if it has been mailed to you—by all means *use a typewriter,* wherever possible. When you have completed the application, look it over carefully to make sure *everything* is filled in correctly. Some applications are confusing as to which line is to be used for what. Be sure that *every question is answered.*

5 PSYCHOLOGICAL AND APTITUDE TESTS

In about half the larger firms, applicants are given a series of psychological and aptitude tests to determine their percentile standings with regard to qualities that personnel research has shown are needed for certain jobs. These may be called "personnel tests," "placement tests," "classification tests," or "occupational tests." The tests often make it possible for the applicant to be placed in the right job.

But test results are seldom the sole reason why an applicant is hired or passed over. The interviewer may decide that there is something undesirable about an applicant and reject him, despite a favorable showing on the tests. Therefore, the interview is a critical part of the employment process, even when placement tests are used.

6 THE INTERVIEW—DOS AND DON'TS

When you are asked to make an appointment for an interview—with the person who will actually hire you—you have passed the acid test: your résumé and application have told the company that you are satisfactory, if not well-qualified, for the position you are trying to get. The interview will be the last "hurdle" you will have to get over before you are hired. Thus, the interview is crucial because it will tell your future employer many things about your personality that can't be seen from your résumé or application. You could say that the interview is a "live personality test." It is a waste of time for you and the company, and also a waste of money for the company, if you do not work out in the job you are hired

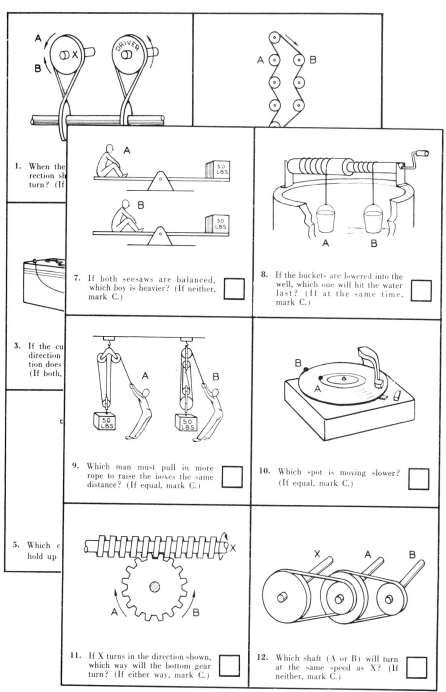

A
B
X
DRIVER

A B

1. When the
rection sh
turn? (If

A
50 LBS.
B
50 LBS.

7. If both seesaws are balanced, which boy is heavier? (If neither, mark C.)

8. If the buckets are lowered into the well, which one will hit the water last? (If at the same time, mark C.)

A B

3. If the cu
direction
tion does
(If both,

A
50 LBS.
B
50 LBS.

B
A

9. Which man must pull in more rope to raise the boxes the same distance? (If equal, mark C.)

10. Which spot is moving slower? (If equal, mark C.)

5. Which c
hold up

X

A B

X A B

11. If X turns in the direction shown, which way will the bottom gear turn? (If either way, mark C.)

12. Which shaft (A or B) will turn at the same speed as X? (If neither, mark C.)

STOP. GO BACK AND CHECK YOUR WORK.

Aptitude tests often make it possible for an applicant to be placed in the right job. These are items from a test to measure mechanical aptitude.

for. This is why most companies use extreme care to find out as much as possible about an applicant before hiring him.

Every applicant wants to make a good impression on the interviewer. It is equally important for the applicant to give a *true* impression so that he will be placed where he has a fair chance to succeed. A falsely favorable impression may merely mean eventual failure and rapid dismissal. For self-confidence and later success, it is sometimes better for an applicant to be turned down than to get a job in which he cannot succeed. Applicants should, therefore, keep their sights set reasonably at the outset and give honest impressions.

Often, however, applicants show up poorly when being interviewed. Eagerness to win the job, uncertainty about their real abilities, and the newness of the interview situation combine to make applicants tongue-tied, fidgety, and forgetful; thus, they are likely to make weak impressions.

Demonstrate in everything connected with the interview that you know how to make profitable use of time. If you have an appointment, be right on time, neither late nor early. Carry a book, newspaper, or magazine with you so that you will be able to make good use of the waiting time before the interview begins.

Let the interviewer make the first moves. Business favors employees who have initiative, but it is wary of those who are too aggressive. Take your tip from the interviewer. Let him be the one who first offers to shake hands. Then wait for him to start the conversation.

Don't sit down immediately when you enter the interviewer's office; wait for an invitation. And when you do sit, don't slump carelessly into the chair. Sit up straight and be alert; show that you are ready to listen to the interviewer.

Don't smoke or chew gum. If the interviewer offers you a cigarette, you can accept with thanks. If you don't like his brand, you can tell him that you don't smoke, but not that you prefer another brand—this is always unflattering.

Make the interviewer feel important. This is a basic principle in all human relations. It is usually neglected when applying for work, since the applicant is striving hard to give a good impression of himself. If the interviewer gets off on a "talkathon," listen to him patiently, even if you are bored with his reminiscences or "sermon."

Learn your interviewer's name from the secretary or from the nameplate on the desk or door. If this is not possible, ask the interviewer what it is. Always address him or her as "Mr.," "Ms.," "Miss," or "Mrs." *Never use first names,* unless the interviewer specifically makes this request.

Always carry an extra copy of your résumé with you so that you will be able to give accurate information about your work history if you are asked about it. Be fully familiar with the information on your résumé before you arrive at the interview. Refer to the résumé only when absolutely necessary.

You may be asked about your hobbies and about the clubs to which you belong. This information sometimes gives some insight into your abilities. For instance, if you are applying for a job as an electronics technician, and the interviewer learns that you are a "radio ham," he knows that you have more than minimum knowledge of your field.

Don't brag or bluff during the interview; let your record speak for itself. Many applicants try to "impress" the interviewer. This is a waste of time and effort because, in most cases, a clever interviewer will catch on to it.

Don't argue with the interviewer or say anything disparaging about a previous employer. The interviewer may even try to trick you into an argument by taking sides with your previous employer, but remember that "boosters" are more likely to be hired than "knockers."

Make a good personal appearance. Dress in clean, pressed clothing, and be sure your shoes are clean and polished. A neat and tidy appearance is always a good starter. Your appearance is the interviewer's first impression of you, and if this first impression is bad, the interviewer will be looking for other bad characteristics rather than the good ones. This dress rule applies even if you are applying for a factory job, or for a job as a waiter or garage attendant.

Be in good physical condition for the interview. If you are sick or not feeling well on the day you are supposed to appear, it is better to telephone the company, tell the truth, and make another appointment rather than appear looking ill and listless. Be sure you get enough sleep the night before the interview; this will help give you a "fresh" appearance and enable you to show enthusiasm.

Be relaxed, yet alert. Relaxing is easier if you hold something familiar in your hand, such as the book or magazine you were reading while you were waiting to be called into the interviewer's office.

7 HOW TO GET MORE BENEFITS

Bargain *discreetly* with the interviewer. After your appearance, manner, and previous record have made a favorable impression, the question of salary and other details must come up.

The beginning salary is not too important for the first job. The pay you do not get at the start will be made up later as you make good. A beginner can seldom be demanding about salary.

If you are applying for a job with a small company, you will be able to do more bargaining than with a large company, where the pay scales are usually fixed and yearly salary increases established in advance. Other benefits in large companies, such as vacation, sick leave, and health insurance, are also fixed. But in a small firm you may be able to get an extra week's vacation in place of a higher salary, for instance. In smaller firms, there is more leeway for bargaining. But be careful not to overstep yourself if you really want the job.

Try to get an idea of the salary from the interviewer. Avoid volunteering such information. If he asks pointblank what salary you want, answer obliquely by turning the question back to him. Ask him, "What do you usually pay for this kind of job?" or "What figure would you suggest?" Use strategy to lead the interviewer to mention a figure first, but he will seldom mention first the highest salary the company will be willing to pay for the job you want. Aim high, but don't let the interviewer's first offer disappoint you to the point of rejection. Keep the door open; tell him you want time to think it over, or something to that effect. This will let him know, too, that you are not overjoyed with his offer. Even if you have had better offers from other companies, don't raffle yourself off to the highest bidder. There are other things to consider before accepting a job, such as the working conditions, hours, vacations, health insurance, and other *benefits* that might not be the best in the company that has made the highest salary offer. If you have to work longer hours for higher pay, it might not be worth it. Of course, the job duties are the prime concern.

You will also do a little interviewing yourself, usually toward the end of the conversation. The interviewer may ask you if there is anything else you would like to know. You will want to know where the job leads. That is, can you advance to higher positions or positions with more responsibilities, or is the first job just a dead end? What about salary increases? Other questions may come to your mind. You may want to plan what to ask before you arrive at the interview. This is always a good idea, because then you will know in your own mind exactly what you want.

End the interview on a favorable note, even if you have not accepted the job. Don't hang around; stand up, thank the interviewer, extend your hand, and leave. A cheerful, confident departure that shows initiative has caused many interviewers to retain more favorable impressions than if the interview ended on a sour note.

SUGGESTIONS FOR FURTHER READING

Biegeleisen, Jacob Israel, *Job Résumés: How to Write Them, How to Present Them,* New York: Grosset & Dunlap, 1969.

Hoppock, Robert, *Occupational Information,* 3d ed., New York: McGraw-Hill, 1967.

Rood, Allan, *Realizing Your Executive Potential,* New York: McGraw-Hill, 1965.

Winter, Elmer, *Women at Work: Every Woman's Guide to Successful Employment,* New York: Simon & Schuster, 1967.

TO HELP YOU REMEMBER

1. In what way are you a "resource" for an employer?
2. What categories of information are usually on a résumé?
3. What does the physical appearance of a résumé tell about the applicant?
4. What information should *not* be included on a résumé?
5. What are three major sources of information about job openings?
6. What information does a want ad usually give?
7. What is a "blind" want ad? How should it be answered?
8. Of what importance are references? Whom should a job applicant ask to serve as references?
9. List eight kinds of information from among the many kinds required on applications.
10. List four "tips" that will help make an interview successful.

WORKING WITH PEOPLE, DATA, OR THINGS

The questions listed below are frequently asked during interviews.
1. In what type of position are you most interested?
2. What are your future vocational plans?
3. Why did you choose your particular field of work?
4. What qualifications do you have that make you feel that you will be successful in your field?
5. Why do you think you would like this particular type of job?
6. What are the disadvantages of your chosen field?
7. What courses in school did you like best? Least? Why?
8. Have you ever changed your major field of interest while in school? Why?
9. If you were starting college all over again, what courses would you take?
10. Do you feel you have done the best scholastic work of which you are capable?
11. How do you spend your spare time? What are your hobbies?
12. Do you think that your extracurricular activities were worth the time you devoted to them? Why?
13. What have you learned from some of the jobs you have held?
14. Have you ever had any difficulty getting along with fellow students and faculty?
15. Do you prefer working with others or by yourself?
16. What kind of a boss do you prefer?
17. How did previous employers treat you?
18. Do you like routine work?
19. Do you enjoy attention?
20. What have you done that shows initiative and willingness to work?

21. What percentage of your college expenses did you earn? How?
22. How did you spend your vacations while in school?
23. Are you looking for a permanent or temporary job?
24. What job in our company would you choose if you were entirely free to do so?
25. What do you know about our company?
26. Why do you think you might like to work for our company?
27. Would you prefer a large or a small company? Why?
28. What are your ideas of salary?
29. Are you primarily interested in making money, or do you consider the interest value of the job to be as important as income?
30. How much money do you hope to earn at age thirty? thirty-five?
31. Are you willing to go where a company sends you?

Directions

Students should divide into pairs. One member of each pair should interview the other, using the questions (or as many as can be covered in the time allowed by your teacher) as a framework for the interview. If you are the interviewer, do not simply fire the questions at the applicant. Instead, conduct the interview as a conversation, the way it would be in reality. Familiarize yourself with the questions before the interview. You need not ask the questions in the order presented.

Each interviewer can fill out an evaluation form similar to the one on pages 299 and 300. The information should be shared with the whole class, but it should be shared without specific reference to personalities. Just evaluate the interview itself, as a single incident.

INTERVIEW EVALUATION REPORT

(Fill out immediately after each interview, and return to Employment Supervisor with application.)

Name of Candidate _____

Character Appraisal

	Excellent	Good	Acceptable	Poor
General First Impression				
Personal Appearance				
Initiative in Conversation				
Ability to Express Himself				
Potentialities				
Final Impression				

(Check appropriate characteristics.)

Personality		Poise and Manner	Maturity
_____Dominant	_____Quiet	_____Alert	_____Unusual
_____Strong	_____Affable	_____Overbearing	_____Advanced
_____Average	_____Friendly	_____Confident	_____Normal
_____Passive	_____Breezy	_____Average	_____Insufficient
_____Timid	_____Naive	_____Nervous	
		_____Awkward	

Vocational Appraisal

Amount of experience　Sufficient for supervisory position_____
　　　　　　　　　　　Sufficient for intermediate level　_____
　　　　　　　　　　　Sufficient for entry level　　　　　_____

Educational background　Extensive training　　　　　_____
　　　　　　　　　　　　Average training　　　　　　　_____
　　　　　　　　　　　　Would need training program_____

Other qualifications_____

Positions for which candidate is qualified_____

Additional Comments_____

_____　　　　　_____
　　　　Interviewer　　　　　　　　　　　　Date

THINGS TO DO

1. Go to at least one business or company, and ask for a copy of the job application form. When all the class members have brought their copies to class, the forms should be compared in groups of from six to ten members each.
2. Ask a professional interviewer or personnel officer to come to your class and tell about what he or she looks for on an application or résumé or during an interview. If no one can be found who is willing to speak to your group, have one class member interview an interviewer.
3. Ask an employee of a private employment agency to come to your class and talk about the services the agency offers.
4. Using the sources of job information described earlier in this chapter, spend two days finding out about as many jobs as you can. Keep a list of the jobs, and compare the entries you make with those of other class members.
5. Write a résumé for yourself. Then have at least three friends or adults comment on it. Share your résumé and the comments with the class.

ADJUSTING TO A NEW JOB

16

What This Chapter Is About

1 SURVIVING THE FIRST DAY

For some people the first day on a new job can be almost horrifying. Most people have a feeling of "numb anxiety" that begins when they enter the premises of their new job, and this feeling will continue until it is time to go home. As a new employee of one day, you will doubtless ask yourself, "How will I do? Will they like me? Suppose I can't do this job?" Questions like these reveal a basic human fear, the *fear of change*. It is quite natural for us to be uncomfortable when faced with this, or any other, new situation: we have to meet new people and remember their names; we will have new rules to learn; and there will be new problems to face.

Floundering around on your first job as you try to "find yourself" is more or less expected. Yet it is both undesirable and unnecessary. You can make a deliberate effort to find out about what you will be doing from your fellow workers, and they will be all too glad to help you. Your presence will give them an excuse to break their routines. But don't be overzealous and annoy others, especially if they seem preoccupied with other problems.

If this is your first job, you will be entering into a new and strange environment. Your co-workers will not be "playmates" as they were at school or college. Some areas of your new life at work will be freer, and others will be more restricted. Many old habits will have to be changed, since there is interdependence in the new world of work. You will, for the first time, be "earning a living." Your job is a necessity, and it must be taken seriously.

It will take time to grow used to your new environment on the job. There is always some training period, which may be formal or informal depending on how complicated your work will be. Some companies have actual classes that new employees must attend for several weeks, while for other jobs all that is necessary is a period of a few weeks to find out where supplies and equipment are located and who does what in the department or area.

On page 303 there are some ways in which your life will change from the time when you attend school to the time when you take your first job.

The most lonesome time of life may be the first few days on a job. In fact, many workers who have been on the job for some time still do not feel totally at home in their groups. If that is their feeling, imagine how much greater is the loneliness of the newcomer! Some companies recognize the newcomer's problems and train their supervisors to give special attention to new workers, encourage them, help them get acquainted with others, and break the ice generally.

At School	At Work
Moving among friends	Moving among strangers
Most associates your age	Most associates older
Groups based on friendship	Groups based on duties
Intermittent work	Steady work
Daily changes in routine	Same routine
Short hours	Longer hours
Frequent and longer vacations	Fewer and shorter vacations
Frequent tests and grades to let you know how you are doing	Little knowledge of how you are doing
Promotions each term	Promotions rarely
Usually a lot of homework	Homework rare
Regulated length of time spent in one grade	Indefinite length of time spent on one work routine

Established workers seldom go out of their way to extend a welcome to the newcomer. They tend to be clannish, and in companies where morale is poor, they may even go out of their way to make a new person miserable. Some firms try to overcome this tendency on the part of older workers by asking a popular worker to act as a sponsor, or as a "big brother" or "big sister," show the new person the ropes, and help him get acquainted. The new employee can also do much to ease his own path and minimize the strain on his self-esteem during the first few weeks. Here are some guidelines:

Be friendly, but not aggressively so.

Get acquainted with a few more people each day, but keep out of cliques.

Ask older workers for advice, but don't try to show them up.

Be on guard for practical jokes, and laugh along if you're caught.

Expect it to be a slow process to come to know your fellow workers and be accepted by them.

New workers are often inclined either to try to prove themselves the first day or try to hide. An important thing to learn before that first day is when to talk and when to listen. You can learn much more, in any situation, by listening and asking discreet or pointed questions than you can by talking a lot or trying to show how much or how well you can do. People in a work situation are generally pleased if someone asks them about their jobs. Experienced workers will almost always take time out to explain their job to a newcomer, and the newcomer can learn more by talking with the old hands than he can by reading any book of rules.

Data from Dr. Daniel Katz and Dr. Robert L. Kahn

52% Felt thoroughly included

12% Felt excluded

7% ?

29% Felt included in most ways

Even among long-established work groups, such as the one represented here, many workers are lonesome because they do not feel accepted by the rest of the group.

There may be many frustrations that first day on the job. The new worker may feel useless—a fifth wheel dragging everyone down. Or he may feel that his talents, tested and proved in school, are going to waste. But each new worker must come to realize that as he learns about the job and about his employer, his apprehensions will soon disappear.

2 LEARNING TO FEEL AT HOME

Learning to feel at home on the job does not mean learning where you can prop your feet up on a desk. It means learning the nitty-gritty details of getting along with the people on the job and with the work.

After moving into a new house, you will need about 6 weeks before you grow used to it and begin to feel at home. It takes that long for the average person to change his previous notions of home. A few people cannot change their ideas, and so they never feel at home.

Adjustment has to be made on any new job. Just as in changing his home, the average person can expect about 6 weeks to pass before he begins to feel at home on the new job. It will take longer if a person has been with another company for many years. Expect the new job to seem strange the first few days, but also notice that it continues to seem more "natural" every day.

Many well-qualified people "stub their toes" and fail to make progress on the job because they neglect to learn the ins and outs and the ups and downs of the organization. You must learn the way around an organization just as you would around the building. Some rules and regulations, for instance, are unwritten customs. These can be followed without any loss of individuality.

People in some organizations use first names readily; in other organizations, last names are used with the appropriate title. Keep your eyes and ears open, and do as others do in such matters. These customs may seem minor, but if you overlook them, others will say, "So-and-so does not seem to fit into our organization," or, "He is a good enough worker but does not seem to be our type." It takes more than job skill to fit into an organization. So learn your way around, first thing.

Every company of any size has factions. A few small firms are riddled by factions scheming against each other. In studies of mental health in industry, Dr. Robert L. Kahn made a nationwide survey of personal stress arising from such internal conflicts. About half of the employees and executives interviewed were "caught in the middle" between conflicting factions. In most instances, a member of a faction held a position in the company above the person being interviewed.

Study your boss just as he or she is studying you. Learn the soft spots—they may be fishing, grandchildren, travel experiences, or what-not. Your boss probably has hard spots, too, such as being pernickety about accuracy, promptness, personal appearance, and working right up until the bell rings. The boss is a big part of any job and the one you must depend on for promotion. So learn to know your boss, and act accordingly.

Fellow workers also have tender spots. Watch for them so that you will be able to get along well with your colleagues. You cannot change them, but you can humor them. Differences in personality and people make work interesting; neglecting to observe individual differences can be the start of a dead-end job. Judgment about people and situations is of great importance in business, and tests have been designed for use in rating employees on this critical quality. The items shown here were taken from the *Business Judgment Test*.[1]

1. Used with permission. The *Business Judgment Test* is published by Martin M. Bruce, New Rochelle, N.Y.

If my supervisor criticized my work, I would

_____ compare my record with co-workers for him.

_____ explain the reason for poor performance to him.

_____ ask him why he selected me for criticism.

_____ ask him for suggestions about how to improve.

If I were addressing a group at a luncheon and a parade went by which disturbed us, I would

_____ ask the group to adjourn until the parade was over.

_____ request the group to disregard the noise from the street.

_____ walk to the window to watch the procession.

_____ ask the group what they would like to do.

If I was doing a much better job than the other people in my department, I would

_____ ask for a transfer to a better job.

_____ request a raise in salary.

_____ slow down a little so as not to stand out.

_____ continue as though there were no difference.

A new vocabulary has to be learned on each job. Companies develop their own "lingo." What one firm calls a "yellow second sheet" another calls "railroad paper." One firm calls it "onionskin," another, "flimsies." Sometimes company words and phrases develop. In one company an office supervisor was perpetually battling with typists who made strikeovers. In this firm strikeovers were called "Miss Crocketts," after the supervisor.

On the more formal side, there are many details you will need to know to fit into an organization. For example:

Whom should you notify by telephone when you are unable to go to work?

When you change your address, whom should you notify?

If there is a company newspaper, where should you send a news item?

Where can you cash a check in the building?

Can you borrow money from the company?

How do you request new equipment or arrange for repairs?

Where should you report in case of an accident?

Can you use the company telephone for personal calls?

Can you buy at a discount through the company?

Who grants wage increases? What standards do they use?

How can you get insurance through the firm?

Can you receive medical advice?

Can some officer give you legal advice?

How can you use the company library?

Where do you report that an article has been lost or found?

Whom should you tell if you figure out a better way of doing a job?

Whom should you inform if you lose your paycheck?

What should you do if you see indications of dishonesty?

How should you go about trying to get a job for a friend?

Who can help you on a tax problem? Who can explain company benefits and paycheck deductions?

How could you arrange to take an advanced course?

How do you arrange for friends to visit the company?

Learning such ins and outs about a company is almost like getting acquainted with a foreign country. Get well acquainted with the corner of the business world in which you work, and don't expect it to be just like other corners.

Unfortunately, many workers have to learn those vital things on their own. In Dr. Kahn's survey, two out of every five said that the company had failed to give them information about the unwritten customs and how the workers were expected to perform and behave.

Some of the unwritten customs of a place of business can be found in any social situation. Status, politics, and gossip are three areas of relationships between people that frequently are surrounded by unwritten customs. A new worker who unintentionally violates one of

Percentage of workers   60

40

Not given information by company

Given information by company

Data from Dr. Robert L. Kahn

One survey of an office group showed that 60 percent of the workers were informed by the company about unwritten customs and expected behavior, but 40 percent had to find out this information on their own.

the unwritten rules may become the target of gossip, particularly if he breaks one of the unwritten rules involving status.

Every worker in a business has certain privileges: a bigger desk than other workers, a telephone on his desk, a private secretary, or a window with an outside view, for example. Strange, quirky things are connected with status, and a worker who has his status challenged, even unintentionally, by a newcomer reacts with hostility. For example, a writer was hired by an educational consulting firm. He happened to get an office that had a large desk in it. He did not know that the supply clerk had simply forgotten to put a small desk in the office. The writer became the subject of snide remarks and office gossip when the older hands thought a newcomer was being given greater status than they had, all because his desk was as large as the boss's desk and bigger than theirs.

Politics seems to permeate almost every business. Office politics generally has to do with who is winning the battle to get ahead; it often consists of speculation about who is in line for a promotion or raise, who may get fired, and the methods that different workers are using to get ahead. As in any other social situation, workers criticize each other's performance and behavior.

Office gossip is similar to office politics, but gossip deals more with personal matters—who bought a new wig, who is dating whom, who is playing sick to miss work, and who is stealing office supplies, for example. Personal grudges are usually at work in gossip, and frequently the grudges have a basis in some form of jealousy. Gossip has destroyed the careers and damaged the lives of many people, but it has never been shown to do anyone any good. And because of its bad nature, one can infer the nature of people who practice it.

There are a few basic rules about how to deal with status, politics, and gossip:

1   Mind your own business; doing your own job as well as you can will require all your energy.
2   If someone asks your personal opinion of another worker, do not say anything negative or personal. You can bet that if you talk about other workers, pretty soon they will be talking about you—so don't get the whole thing started.
3   Learn through observation and listening what the unwritten customs are in your place of work. By learning these unstated rules you can avoid breaking them or getting tangled up in the human relations problems that can result.

3 LEARNING THE JOB

For the first few days or weeks a new worker is on a job, his main task will be to learn his job well. Only then can he contribute anything of value to himself or his employer and fellow workers.

To help new workers learn their jobs, many employers provide training. Formal training usually consists of classes or study materials for new workers. Classes are provided when there are many people who will perform the same kind of work, such as salesmen or management trainees. These classes will be similar to college courses, but they are usually much shorter, and there are no tests. There may be homework assignments, however, as in regular school classes. As was pointed out in Chapter 14, many companies now require that workers get most of their training in a technical or business school or college before taking a job. This has always been true for stenographers and typists.

Management trainees are usually college graduates who have majored in the particular type of discipline that will make them suitable for a company. However, there is still a good deal of informal company training necessary to provide them with a working knowledge of the particular operations followed by the company. In order to understand these operations fully, then, the trainees are required, in most cases, to

Courtesy of Webster Division, McGraw-Hill Book Co.
Many employers provide formal classroom training to help new workers learn their jobs.

work for a month or so in each of several departments. In a retail department store, for example, the trainees spend time behind counters, in the credit department, in the buying department, and in the stock department. This diverse work experience gives the trainees a familiarity with store operations that will help them when they assume their management roles.

The most frustrating kind of initiation is to be put on the job immediately and wished good luck. Not knowing how to do the work and not having anyone assigned to train you presents the problem of learning to do the job by yourself. If this happens, find someone to whom you are responsible who can provide feedback on your performance. In many jobs, each worker has considerable freedom to exercise his decision-making capabilities and define the duties for himself. In such a situation, each worker must first establish the boundaries of what he can do and then establish his own goals within those boundaries.

The key to being a successful trainee is your attitude. If you can cultivate the attitude that you can learn and get along with co-workers, you will have a higher potential for success. Here are some things to keep in mind.

1 Pay attention to your fellow workers; always be pleasant and cooperative.
2 Take some initiative in the beginning, but not so much that you will appear to be an upstart. Gradually learn the best way to present more of your own ideas as time goes on.
3 Don't be too critical, especially as a beginner; after all, the company is still in business, so it must be doing something right.
4 Learn how to "train yourself" through observation and listening. And don't be afraid to ask questions.
5 Don't be an "expert" too soon, especially if the person charged with training you has been with the company for many years. Accordingly, don't blame yourself for not always making good judgments. Remember that you are a beginner, and for this reason you are not accustomed to thinking along certain lines.
6 Encourage yourself; look for the good things you are doing. Self-encouragement put Benjamin Franklin on good terms with good fortune. And learn to encourage others when it is your turn to do the training. Other people need to have their pride fed, too.

Personal goals have a lot to do with the training of a new worker. If the worker has only short-term or immediate goals for a job—he is doing it only for money—then he is likely to learn only enough to do his job well enough not to get fired. But if a person has long-range goals for his job—if the job is part of the career development pattern he has decided upon—then he is more likely to learn everything he can about the work. He may talk with older employees, read company literature, work in the company library, spend outside time learning how to do his job better, and so on. For the career person, training is a continuous process, not an event that occurs only at the time the job is begun.

4 MAKING NEEDED ADJUSTMENTS

In many situations, there are conditions outside of your personality that can produce trouble. There are things about every job that are frustrating or annoying. If the new worker is aware of these things and their potential for causing trouble, he will be able to adjust to his job with a minimum of friction. Here are some tension-causing situations that you are likely to encounter.

When you are promoted, of course you will be glad, but there will be jealousy among your competitors. And you may feel apprehensive about fulfilling the responsibilities of the new job.

You may be given new equipment. Everyone in a company can't have new equipment to use, and so this will cause envy.

You may be asked to help out with a job that you *feel* is beneath your level.

You may have your hours shifted, especially if you work in a large company or factory, and this may seem a kind of demotion.

You may *feel* that your boss or supervisor is watching you too closely—that he or she is breathing down your neck.

You may be removed to another location, away from people you have come to regard as friends—people with whom you may take breaks and lunch. This may *seem* to be a reprimand.

The method by which you are paid may be changed—for instance, from a weekly to an hourly rate. You may *feel* that this change will cause you to lose prestige, even though you may be actually earning more take-home money.

It may please you to have a telephone on your desk, but it may make others feel that you are preferred; also, if your telephone is removed, you may look at this as a demotion in some sense.

If your supervisor seems too friendly, your fellow workers may think that you are a "company man," looking for preferential treatment.

Besides these problems, there may be others of a more personal nature. You may feel that your talents are not being fully utilized. Your job might have unclear standards, and you may have poor instruction with little praise or information about how you are doing. You may also feel that you are making slow progress or none at all and that your job has failed to live up to your expectations of it.

The final area of adjustment centers around the relationship between the boss and his workers. Usually, workers must either accept their bosses as they are or look for other work when conflicts arise. Sometimes a worker can find another position with the same company. This may be possible if he is valuable, that is, if he has talents that are useful for the company.

When an individual goes to work, especially for the first time, his attitude toward the boss is a mixture of respect, fear, and wanting to be liked. When young people are hostile toward their families, they often feel some hostility toward the boss, regardless of how considerate he or she is. It is common for inexperienced workers to feel nervous when they talk with their boss. The intensity of this nervousness will vary from individual to individual. It is a good idea for a worker to respect his boss's authority, but not be frightened by it.

It seems that the people whom you work with will be like your family in some sense. Your co-workers will be like brothers and sisters, your bosses like parents. This association between the "job family" and the home family is very normal, since we tend to compare strangers to those we know the best—our family and friends.

5 ADJUSTING YOUR PERSONALITY TO THE JOB

As we have seen, there are many external factors in a job—especially a new one—that may be frustrating, but one of the chief difficulties for anyone is adjusting personality to suit a new life style. While the people with whom you work may seem to be like members of a family, they are actually not like your family, and therefore they will not be as tolerant. For example, one can have a relative who is loved even though he is argumentative, but there are few companies that will be tolerant of the person who constantly argues, unless he is the owner.

Learning to adjust our personalities to the job situation is something that we all have to do. Some people are more flexible in their attitudes than others. It is always helpful if a person has a chance to work when he is in high school or college—at seasonal summer and Christmas jobs as well as part-time jobs. These jobs give a young person a sense of how to work on a team so that later, when he has to work full time, he will have a good idea of what is required of him and will be better prepared to meet the requirements.

We have to learn to curb our impulses and cultivate the art of making decisions. We also have to learn to accept a situation for what it is. Certain aspects of a job won't change overnight—there will be many annoyances, and we will have to be able to cope with them in a way that will be useful to ourselves and to the company.

A *mature* person knows his shortcomings regarding his personality, and he is able to look at his situation from the other person's point of view as well as from his own.

Most job situations are inflexible; that is, a job has certain duties for a worker to perform in a routine way. The word *routine* itself implies inflexibility. Many workers with very different personalities may have filled a certain job in a company. They have to adjust to the job; the job cannot adjust to them. If a worker cannot adjust to a particular job, he must either find another position with the company or seek a new job with a different company. A worker may be able to negotiate for certain changes in his routine, once he has established himself in a job as a good worker. Of course, requests for changes must be reasonable and must be made at the right time.

The key to success at any job is *compromise*. Even though compromise may be a violation of our sense of values, it may be necessary for attaining one's goals later.

Job stresses frequently produce changes in people's personalities or bring out negative aspects of personality that they or others had not noticed before. Owen D. Young, the farm boy who became chairman of the General Electric Company, once said, "The man who can put himself in the place of the other man, who can understand the workings of other minds, need never worry about what the future has in store for him." An Indian saying about the same ability is: "Let a man walk a mile in my moccasins before he tells me how to walk better."

One way to reduce personality clashes is to develop the habits of listening, cooperating, assisting, accommodating, and understanding. Try to put yourself into the other person's situation and understand his job problems from his point of view. This may give you some insight into what he is going through so that you will be in a better position to understand his problems.

The larger corporations provide special training for executives and supervisors to help them understand the personalities of the workers under them so that they can head off personality conflicts. In a smaller company, the boss or owner-operator is on top of the situation, and so he is in a better position to note any trouble, but at the same time there is no formal training program for him to attend. Often he has to figure out what to do on the spur of the moment. Sometimes he is successful, and sometimes he is faced with crises.

Some personality traits are obviously undesirable in the work situation. They form the basis of the following list of characteristics that both the newcomer and the old-timer should strive to avoid.[2]

Engaging in idle gossip	Coaxing others
Petty lying	Continually criticizing
Cheating in games	High-pressure selling
Crowding to the front of lines	Putting on airs
	Bragging about oneself
Coughing in others' faces	Slapping others on the back
Sniffling	Being too inquisitive

2. This list is taken from studies by Dr. Hulsey Cason.

Cracking chewing gum	Not curbing sexy talk
Spitting in public	Acting disrespectfully toward older people
Not preventing body odor or bad breath	
	Having a bossy manner
Losing one's temper	Using endearing names for casual acquaintances
Habitually arguing	
Looking glum	Having a gushing manner
	Cutting up to get attention
Monopolizing conversations	Trying to be funny
	Overusing slang
Giving unasked-for advice	Speaking in baby talk
Hurrying others	Talking too loudly in public

Life and business are filled with frustrations. Being thwarted in many things we should like to do or be or have is inevitable. Thus, people who adapt their desires gracefully to what is possible, rather than grumbling or fighting over what cannot be changed, are least frustrated and have the least nervous tension.

Dr. Daniel N. Wiener has found that frustrations are not so serious when they are recognized. He compared successful and unsuccessful salesmen as one instance. Both groups of salesmen had about the same frustrations. But the difference was this: the successful salesmen recognized their emotional problems; the unsuccessful salesmen did not admit the existence of theirs. The successful salesmen, knowing and admitting their emotional problems, were able to adjust themselves to frustrating circumstances, and so nervous tension did not develop.

Most frustrating problems can be solved easily. It is lucky that this is so, for life is crammed with frustrations. Frustrations caused by the everyday environment are easier to eliminate than those carried inside the mind. Frustrations carried inside may take the form of hostility, suspiciousness, overweening ambition, or a striving for perfection, and they are much harder to eliminate than frustrations caused by the outside world—frustrations that may be caused by the antagonism of the gossip, the bully, and the domineering boss, for example.

Frustration builds on itself. When we frustrate others by attacking them, they are likely to frustrate us in return. Push them, and they push back—as in family scraps and arguments between management and labor. The nagging boss is gossiped about, and his workers are inclined to be revengeful.

People who are too strict with themselves expect too much from life, or their ambitions are too high. They create more frustrations for themselves daily and are their own worst enemies.

William James, who became the first professor of psychology at Harvard, started out to be a naturalist and tested his interest in the field by going on an exploratory trip to Brazil with Louis Agassiz. The hardships of the journey into primitive country cured him of the wish to be a naturalist. At 22, James wrote in his diary:

> I am now convinced that my forte is not to go on exploring expeditions. . . . I am convinced now that I am cut out for a spectator rather than an active life. I became convinced some time ago that I was one of the very lightest of the featherweights. Now, why not be reconciled with my deficiencies? By accepting them, your actions cease to be at cross-purposes with your faculties and you are much nearer peace of mind.

People who have good personality balance take life as it is. They may be regretful at times, but they adjust their aims and desires to reality without bitterness. On the other hand, some people are motivated by their frustrations. They have poor personality health. They fight back at frustrating circumstances and neglect to enjoy the good parts of their lives.

To save yourself the frustration jobs bring, and to help adjust your personality to a job, consider these suggestions:

1 Learn to relax at your work.
2 Do your job tasks in the order of their importance.
3 When you are presented with a problem, solve it then and there, if you have all the facts you need.
4 Put enthusiasm into your work; only you can raise a dull job above a dismal level or keep a bright job shining!

SOLVING JOB-RELATED PROBLEMS—GRIPES, GRIEVANCES, AND FEAR

No matter how well a worker is adjusted to his job, problems will arise. There will be job-related problems and problems that are not job-related but that affect a job. A dissatisfied supervisor, a faulty machine in need of repair, or a need for additional supplies are examples of job-related problems. Personal problems, too, affect one's job.

The wrong ways to solve problems are through backbiting, gossip, sabotage, stealing, absenteeism, slacking off on the job, and silence. When workers are angered about a problem with their job, they frequently use one of the wrong ways to solve the problem. The best way to solve a problem is to realize that a reasonable solution must exist. Many gripes and grievances that a good worker has are justified. But when a problem occurs, he must know the person to whom he can take it. Then together they must try to seek a solution, perhaps by some form of compromise or accommodation.

Some companies hire professional counselors to listen to the complaints of both employees and customers. Their function is essentially to listen. First they listen, and then they ask the complainer to repeat his complaint. The second telling will be much calmer than the first. And, often, something else will be included the second time around. One thing that the counselor tries to do is to bring out the positive things in the complaint, but of course, if the complaint is well-founded, its true nature is not hidden or obscured.

Workers can report accurately on poor ventilation, slow promotion, or a grouchy foreman and make other similar complaints. But there

Percentage whose supervisors listened

High-morale workers   Low-morale workers

Data from Survey Research Center, Univ. of Michigan

A study in a utility firm showed that workers who knew that their supervisors would listen to grievances had higher morale than workers who felt that their supervisors did not listen.

are many irritations they cannot explain because people have motives and mental mechanisms of which they are not aware. They may be dimly aware of some feelings but hesitate to talk about them. Such feelings, concealed beneath the surface, may mean more in terms of human relations than the peeves of which they are clearly aware. These beneath-the-surface feelings are concerned with desires, motives, impulses, and ambitions.

Some job-related problems can be prevented before they arise. These problems are usually associated with fear, and fear is one of the most injurious feelings that inflict workers. Fear of the boss has already been mentioned, but fear of failure is stronger. And there are other fears: fear of rejection by co-workers, fear of disapproval by one's supervisor or superior, fear of losing one's job and of the loss of security that would result, and sometimes even fear of success.

Eliminating fear is perhaps the most crucial personality adjustment workers must learn to make. The company cannot usually help workers lose their fears, except by listening and counseling or by giving training and encouragement. The key to preventing fear lies in each individual; it is up to each person to face his fears squarely, fight them, and go on to more important tasks.

To fight fear on a job, a worker must first know *his* job well. Confidence dispels fear. Confidence comes from a belief in one's competence and ability to take correct actions. The knowledge that one can do a job well allows little room for fear to creep in.

Facing fear may be more difficult than learning a job. Overcoming fear of the boss, for example, may require that a worker deliberately force himself to talk with the boss. With certain kinds of bosses, the fear may be openly discussed. But in any case, the person who is afraid must take definite steps to meet his fear head on. Fear has a habit of chasing you until you turn around; then it becomes only a shadow.

The last way of fighting fear is to simply mind your own business. Don't speculate about what may or could happen to you on a job. Deal with the here and now, not the if and might. Fantasies about what might or could or should have been lead to disillusionment and frustration.

 MAKING PROGRESS—GETTING PROMOTIONS

Achievement is a value our society ranks very high, and many workers are achievement-oriented. They want to progress on the job, do well, and be promoted. It should be understood that there are different kinds of achievement and progress. For the compositor who has just received an award for 50 years of continuous employment, achievement is a long career of service. For another man, rising from middle management to president would mean achievement. Progress might be interpreted as learning more and more techniques of painting or as earning 10 percent more salary each year.

How does one know if progress is being made? That depends on the goals each worker sets for himself. If a worker has the goal of making money, how his supervisor feels about him as a prospect for a raise is very important. For the worker who has a goal of steady employment, progress is measured by how much tenure he is given or how long his contract is written for.

Co-workers can give feedback on how they think a person is progressing; production standards or quotas can give an idea of how a person is progressing; and workers may be evaluated formally by means of checklists of behavior or performance and by tests of different kinds.

Jobs usually follow a pattern similar to this: a worker is hired; he is trained; he goes through a trial period of from 6 months to a year; and finally he and his work are evaluated prior to his being considered for a raise or promotion.

Each worker must decide if one of his goals is to get a promotion or raise. If it is, there are certain things he must do. If simply doing a good job is the worker's goal, then he can be less concerned with the things that groom one for a promotion or raise.

If a person's goal is to be promoted or receive a raise in salary, he must first balance hope and expectations with reality. He may hope for a big raise at a certain time, but the company may simply not have enough money for a raise at that time. Another worker may expect to be promoted when there is no open position for him to be promoted into.

One way of putting oneself in a position to be promoted or receive a raise in salary is to never stop learning. As discussed earlier, training for a person who is career directed never stops; it is a continuous process of development. The person who seriously wants to achieve in a job must make learning a priority. This person must talk with advisers and other people who can teach him their special knowledge; he must read books and journals that provide additional information about his job; and he must acquire additional training or degrees.

Learning becomes an acute problem with every promotion. You may be a "bigger shot" after promotion, but you are a beginner on a new job at the same time. If extra learning has not prepared you for the new job in advance, you must scurry around to make good. James B. Conant, for instance, had devoted his life to chemistry, but at the age of 40, he was unexpectedly elected president of Harvard. Thereupon, he quit reading his beloved chemical journals and studied the history of universities in order to learn his new job. His promotion came unexpectedly, and he had to bone up after advancement. Usually, it is the other way: those who have boned up win advancement.

Off the job, too, associate a bit with people from whom you can learn something worth knowing for your professional progress.

Although routine jobs have been simplified, the higher positions have become more complicated. Competition makes the higher positions today more demanding; so do government regulations and organized labor. The widened responsibilities that come with an increase in firm size require special preparation; old-fashioned business sense and the diligent work of yesterday are no longer enough. More self-development is necessary to move up.

This has resulted in a paradox: Today, there is a smaller proportion of openings for executive work, yet firms are hard pressed to find people who are qualified. That is why firms are scrambling to hire people who have broad training for business and why leading companies are setting up facilities for training their promising junior executives.

The paradox is highlighted in Dr. Mabel Newcomer's book *The Big Business Executive.*[3]   Dr. Newcomer found that in 1900 some 19 percent of the top executives owed their positions largely to having invested their own money in their firms. A half-century later, only 7 percent of the top executives owed their high positions to personal investments. From 1900 to 1950, the percentage of people who worked their way up to the top spots increased—from 18 percent in 1900 to 51 percent in 1950.

Since everyone is different, the type of preparation a worker makes for advancement on the job depends on the kind of person he is. Still, in general it can be said that the person who makes advances is:

1 Hardworking (Work is done correctly, and often more than just what is necessary is done.)
2 Loyal to employer and fellow workers (Gossip and belittling others are avoided.)
3 Cooperative (Employers and co-workers are supported, and praise is given.)
4 Enthusiastic (Interest in work is shown.)
5 Competent (A job is done well because it is thoroughly understood.)
6 Capable (Leadership is shown in making sound decisions.)

These standards may seem old-fashioned, but they are still the criteria by which a worker is judged. By following these simple rules, one can make progress and achieve goals—and derive much satisfaction in the process.

---

3. Mabel Newcomer, *The Big Business Executive,* Columbia University Press, New York, 1955.

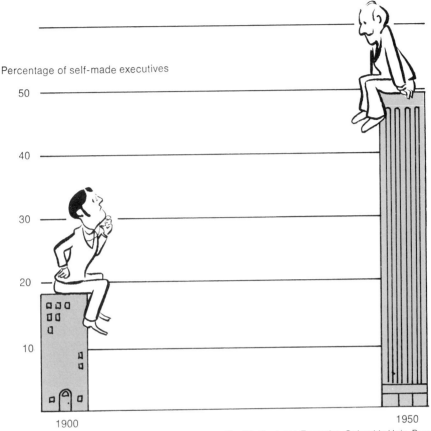

Percentage of self-made executives

50

40

30

20

10

1900   1950

Data from Dr. Mabel Newcomer, *The Big Business Executive*, Columbia Univ. Press

Increasing percentages of executives have been working their way up to their positions. In 1900, only 18 percent of the executives had worked their way through the ranks. By 1950, the figure had jumped to 51 percent.

SUGGESTION FOR FURTHER READING

Calvert, Robert, Jr., and J. E. Steele, *Planning Your Career,* New York: McGraw-Hill, 1963.

TO HELP YOU REMEMBER

1. List five differences between the school and job environments.
2. List three guidelines for easing the first few weeks on a new job.
3. List at least seven of the formal rules or procedures a new worker should learn about his place of employment.

4. How can a worker deal with office politics, gossip, or status?
5. What types of activities might be included in the informal training of a new employee?
6. Compare the relationship between a young worker and his boss with the relationship between the worker and a parent.
7. What are some of the causes of frustration at work, and how can they be handled?
8. Describe the right way to handle job-related problems.
9. How can a worker determine whether he is making progress on the job?

WORKING WITH PEOPLE, DATA, OR THINGS

The following cases involve workers who have problems adjusting to new jobs.

Case 1: When Sandy got her new job, she was scared to death. The first day at work, a few girls in the work processing center spoke to her, but most said nothing. Her supervisor also seemed very unfriendly and did not explain nearly enough about what Sandy was expected to do. Sandy went to work typing letters and memos, filing the carbon copies, and distributing the originals to other secretaries. After two weeks on the job, Sandy was completely lost. She felt that she had no friends at work, that she did not understand her job, that she did not know if she was doing her work correctly, and that she did not know what to do about her problems. What five suggestions could you give Sandy?

Case 2: Carlos had graduated from a university with a degree in business administration 6 months before he was hired by the branch office of Variety Foods Corporation in a nearby city. His job was to monitor the inventory level in one section of the plant. Carlos sat all day each day, reading reports gathered by supervisors and recording the data in different log books. The only interesting part about his job was giving the data to the computer programmer and watching the data processing going on. Carlos believed that his talents were being completely wasted by the company, even though he had only been with it for a few months. Twice a week he was required to sit in on all morning meetings, and several times he had almost voiced his criticisms of the way the company was using him. What five suggestions could you give Carlos?

Case 3: Linda recently finished her residency and is now a full-fledged pediatrician. She has a new job in a large clinic. The head of staff introduced Linda to the other doctors at a staff meeting, but he has given her no specific instructions as to what her duties will be. Give three suggestions for helping Linda solve her problem.

Case 4: Marvin has been a sales clerk for an auto parts distributor for two years. He participated in the company's initial week-long training program. He has been sick 11 days in 2 years and has been absent 6 days for personal reasons. Marvin feels that he should be given a raise, since he has not had one in 2 years; he also feels that he should be promoted to a more responsible job. He is a good worker, as evidenced by his supervisor's written reports. Give five suggestions for how Marvin might proceed to handle his problems.

Options

1. Write out the suggestions you would give each person.
2. Form groups of from three to six members each, and develop one list of suggestions for each worker in the cases. The lists of suggestions should be developed by consensus: each member can add a suggestion or more, but all the group members must agree on which are included.

THINGS TO DO

1. Go into the business community and interview one employer or owner of a business that has more than three or four workers. Ask which qualities in workers the employer likes and which qualities he does not like. Also ask what would make him fire a worker and what would make him give a raise or promotion to a worker. Report your interview results to your class.
2. Interview one adult worker (a parent or friend). Ask these questions: What adjustments did you have to make when you began working? What was the most difficult adjustment to make? What frustrations do you experience on your job? How did you handle each problem? Share your interview results with your class.
3. Call or visit at least one company, possibly one you might seek a job in some day, and learn (1) what training it offers new employees, (2) what work rules it expects its employees to follow, and (3) what its policies are with regard to promotions, raises, and company benefits. Share your findings with your class.
4. Obtain a copy of an employees' manual from a company in the community. Be prepared to report to the class the company's policies regarding absences, lateness, hiring, firing, promotion, and raises. Discuss in class whether you consider the policies fair and whether you would like to work under such conditions.

PART 4

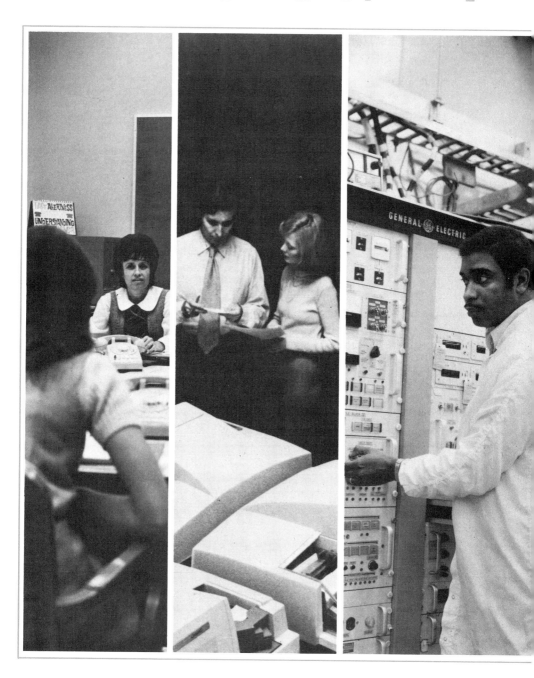

HUMAN RELATIONS

COMMUNICATION IS BASIC

17

WhatThis Chapter Is About

1 OUR WORLD OF WORDS

The rapid proliferation of new ideas, particularly in our technological progress, has brought, and is continuously bringing out, new words to describe things we had not known in the past. Some of these new words, like *satellite*, are actually old words with new meanings. (Originally, *satellite* referred to moons, planets, or other heavenly bodies orbiting around larger heavenly bodies.) Other words, such as *nylon* and *Dacron,* are coined trade names and are not related to any existing words.

When something new is invented, it has to be written about to be described to people who are unable to see it. Sometimes the old languages are not adequate to describe the operations of these inventions, and so the inventors or manufacturers must make up new words to facilitate description.

We have been talking about people communicating with each other using words, but now we have another form of communication — communication between people and machines called computers. New languages are being invented to make this type of communication possible. Perhaps you have heard of some of these languages: ALGOL, FORTRAN, BASIC, and ENGLISH (not to be confused with the spoken language, English). Naturally, these computer languages, which consist mainly of abbreviations of English words and symbols, are not spoken.

In our technological society, we will need to have more effective words at our command. And this may actually mean saying and writing less, but talking and writing more efficiently.

2 COMMUNICATION AND WORDS

The writer S. I. Hayakawa said, "The meanings of words are *not* in the words, they are in *us*." Words, of course, are the necessary ingredients of verbal communication. Words can make us feel good or miserable; they can make us lose our tempers or keep our cool; they can persuade us to take action or convince us not to move. However, it is the *meaning* and *understanding* behind words that are the essence of communication. How the receiver interprets the words is the real test of the message. And that interpretation is based on more than the dictionary definitions of the words. Two basic forms of communication — verbal and nonverbal — work together to convey the message from the sender to the receiver.

Verbal communication occurs in speaking and writing. The choice of words is extremely important in conveying a precise meaning. For example, a description of an apple as "a crisp, golden delicious apple" is likely to cause a reaction totally different from the reaction to the words "a hard, yellow delicious apple," even though the same apple is the subject of both messages. The sign language used by the deaf, called *dactylology*, is really a form of verbal communication because in this system of communication, hand and finger positions are used to spell or signify words visually.

There are other physical gestures, however, that are *nonverbal* forms of communication. Facial expressions showing joy, sadness, or anger, and body expressions indicating tiredness, intensity, and enthusiasm do not relate to specific words but to ideas that would require many words to be expressed verbally. The meanings of physical actions and mannerisms are much more general than those of words. This is what makes nonverbal communication distinctive. And nonverbal communication is extremely important in human relations, perhaps as important as direct verbal communication.

Courtesy of Metropolitan Life

Feelings are often most effectively communicated nonverbally.

3 A TWO-WAY CONNECTION

The effectiveness of communication, whether it be verbal or nonverbal, rests on the exchange of ideas between *two* people. This means that although you may be communicating between yourself and more than just one other person, you are still communicating with each person separately. For example, if you are talking with three friends, trying to explain a plan to them, you are explaining it to friend number 1 *and* friend number 2 *and* friend number 3—even though it seems to you that you are talking to all three friends at the same time.

Not only must a message be effectively conveyed; it must also be effectively understood by its receiver. Thus, the message is transmitted, or sent, and received. This is what is meant by a "two-way connection." The sender of a message is successful only if his message is understood by the receiver. A man crying desperately for help in the middle of a desert where there is no one around to hear or understand his pleas can hardly be considered an effective communicator, no matter how well he expresses himself. No matter how well a speech is delivered, if the audience doesn't respond to it, there is little or no communication.

 ## THE COMMUNICATION PROCESS

In his book *Human Relations at Work: The Dynamics of Organizational Behavior,* Dr. Keith Davis gives six steps in the sequence of communication.[1] These steps are as follows:

1 Ideation
2 Encoding
3 Transmission
4 Transfer of initiative (to the receiver)
5 Decoding
6 Response (of the receiver)

Ideation, according to Dr. Davis, is creating an idea or choosing a fact to communicate. The sender must have something meaningful to say to the receiver. Therefore, the sender must think before he speaks.

Encoding is the translation of the idea or thought to be communicated into *symbols* that will make the sender's idea receivable to an audience. Symbols stand for things; the symbols may be words (sounds that represent things), hand signals, or other signs. Encoding also involves the selection of media that will attract the attention of the receiver. An idea such as the promotion of a pharmaceutical product will be encoded in one way to reach doctors in a professional journal and in a different way to reach the general public by television.

Transmission refers to the means by which the encoded communication is to be made, the channel through which the message must pass from the sender to the receiver. The channel should be as free as possible of all interference. One form of transmission is the face-to-face

1. Keith Davis, *Human Behavior at Work: Human Relations and Organizational Behavior,* McGraw-Hill, New York, 1972, pp. 386–387.

interview in which the encoded thoughts of the interviewer are passed to the listener (receiver) by words through the air. The interviewer attempts to select for his channel a time and place that will be free of distractions and interruptions. Another example of transmission is sending a message by radio transmitter; the message, in the form of electromagnetic waves, travels through the air to the radio receiver.

Transfer of initiative is also called *reception*. This means that the receiver is able to receive the message. In other words, the channel is open. If a message has been transmitted verbally to the receiver, this means that the receiver is "listening attentively" to the message.

Decoding is done by the receiver. The message that has been transmitted to the receiver is translated *by him into meaning*. If the form of the message is verbal, in spoken or written words or symbols, it must be made meaningful to the receiver. This is where *understanding* comes into the picture. The closer the receiver's interpretation of the meaning is to the meaning intended by the sender, the more successful the communication is. Even a simple statement of fact is subject to some variety of interpretation. Since the meaning of a message rests with the communicators rather than with the words or nonverbal symbols, the receiver will consider the message in the particular context in which it is sent. He may consider the intent of the sender and think, for example, "He's just saying that to distract me from the real point of our discussion" or "He's trying to show that he agrees with me."

> The encoding-decoding sequence is somewhat like the activity involved when a famous British castle was moved to the United States. The castle could not be moved in one piece; consequently, it had to be disassembled stone by stone, with each stone marked as to its proper location. This was similar to a sender who has an idea and encodes (dismantles) it into a series of words, each marked by location and other means to guide the receiver. In order to move it (transmit it), he had to take it apart by putting it into words. The reassembly of the castle stone by stone in the United States was similar to a receiver who takes words received and mentally reassembles them back into whole ideas."[2]

The *response* is the action taken by the person or persons receiving the message. In some sense, the response or action by the receiver should provide feedback to the sender so that he will know that his message has been received and understood. This, then, completes the process of two-way communication. The response may also be the beginning of a new communication sequence. In responding, the receiver may send out a new message that encodes and transmits his own idea. The original sender, now in the role of receiver, takes the initiative and decodes the new message. His response may begin a third sequence, and the process can continue as long as both parties are willing.

2. Ibid., p. 387.

Ideation	Encoding	Transmitting
Receiving	Decoding	Action

Communications of all sorts—spoken and written verbal messages and nonverbal communication—can be broken down into these six steps.

5 THREE-DIRECTIONAL FORMAL COMMUNICATION

Since communicating involves a two-way, not a one-way, connection, obviously it is impossible for the sender alone to complete the communication process. In business, it is especially important that the process be two-way. For example, a superior may talk *downward* to his employees, but until the employees have responded to their employer's message, the work of the company cannot be accomplished. An *upward* communication process is needed to complete the connection.

Also, because staff and interdepartmental interaction is so important if a business is to function smoothly, communications will flow horizontally, or sideways, as well.

Downward Communication

A supervisor should never talk *down* to his employees in the sense of being scornful or condescending; however, there are certain things that he talks *about* to workers in lower-level positions.

First, the boss may give job assignments either orally or in writing. Oral job instructions should include *who* should do the job, *what* should be done, *why* it should be done, *when* it should be done, and *where* it should be done.

Supervisors have come to the conclusion that job instructions should be written if there are more than five job directions. Written directions should also answer the who, what, why, when, and where questions.

Both oral and written job instructions should phrase the directions by *asking for* rather than *ordering* cooperation. (Remember that basic human behavior is naturally hostile if feelings of being "somebody" are challenged.)

The supervisor quickly learns which employees require more detailed instructions and which employees require a brief outline of directions. The supervisor who uses a vocabulary appropriate for the occasion stands the best chance of making the two-way connection with the employee.

Second, the employer or supervisor talks to his employees about things the employees want to know, such as work methods, shop rules, pay practices, employee benefits, appraisals, and advancement practices. The supervisor who talks about company news matters when the information is *new* or current has a better downward communication flow. It does not take the work force long to lose respect for the supervisor who makes stale confirmations of "old news."

Upward Communication

There is much communication in business that flows upward from the employee to the employer and supervisor in the operations of a company. If a company doesn't encourage this upward flow of information, severe problems may result.

There are certain subjects that an employee of a business will want to talk about with his or her supervisor or employer.

First, the employee will want to discuss various matters for which he or she is responsible, such as performance standards, delay in accomplishing what was expected, quality of production, input and output, and so on. Such information given honestly and sincerely prevents many problems of misunderstanding.

Second the employee may want to talk to the boss about complaints, criticisms, disagreements, and other matters that are controversial. This kind of information may place a supervisor in a position of intelligently solving problems before they multiply.

Percent whose supervisors told them what the company was doing

High-morale workers   Low-morale workers

Data from Survey Research Center, Univ. of Michigan

Effective downward communication plays an important part in worker morale. A study of utility workers showed that almost half of the high-morale workers had been given "inside" information on what the company was doing whereas fewer of the low-morale workers were "in" on company secrets. Wage scales and working conditions were the same for both groups.

Third, without taking the role of the stool pigeon, the employee often loyally informs the boss of how the workers feel about things in general (information, of course, that was not gained in confidence).

Finally, the employee may want to talk to the boss about personal problems that have an effect on job performance.

The importance of upward communication is illustrated by a study made by a large Minneapolis–St. Paul, Minnesota, firm. A list of ten items was presented to 3,000 employees and to their supervisors. The employees were asked to arrange the items in order of importance. The supervisors were asked what order they thought employees would choose.

The employees ranked the ten items listed on the questionnaire in the following order:

1   Full appreciation of work done
2   Feeling of being in on things
3   Help on personal problems
4   Job security
5   High wages
6   Interesting work
7   Promotion in the company
8   Personal loyalty of supervisor
9   Good working conditions
10   Tactful disciplining

The supervisors of the employees, however, ranked the ten items quite differently, according to what they *thought* was most important to least important to their employees. This is the order chosen by the supervisors:

1 High wages
2 Job security
3 Promotion in the company
4 Good working conditions
5 Interesting work
6 Personal loyalty of supervisor
7 Tactful disciplining
8 Full appreciation of work done
9 Help on personal problems
10 Feeling of being in on things

Notice that the three items considered most important by the employees were what the supervisors thought were least important to employees. Such misinformation can easily occur when the channels for upward communication are blocked.

Horizontal Communication

The team effort necessary in running a business results in horizontal communication. Co-workers use *horizontal communication* when seeking and giving advice on both business and personal problems, when training replacements, when meeting at small conferences or company social gatherings, and so on.

Many employees cannot function at top efficiency unless they have a good communication flow with their co-workers. Maslow's hierarchy of needs, discussed in Chapter 3, refers to the horizontal communication needs as social needs—the feeling of belonging, of being one of the "gang," and of being accepted by the group. Obviously, none of these needs can be satisfied unless healthy horizontal communication is possible.

INFORMAL COMMUNICATION— THE "GRAPEVINE"

You have probably heard someone say, "I heard it through the 'grapevine.'" The grapevine is usually a form of oral communication that is informal; you could call it a system by which rumors are spread. The term *grapevine* goes back to the Civil War, when intelligence telegraph wires were strung from tree to tree and thus resembled a grapevine. The messages transmitted by these lines were often garbled and unclear.

Hence, the grapevine has come to be regarded as a transmitter of unclear messages of uncertain origin.

However, the use of the grapevine in communicating is not necessarily bad. Actually, it is a natural, normal interaction that is indestructible. Any organization can be assured that bringing people into contact with one another will encourage them to be active on the grapevine. Since managers are stuck with the "grapevine" and recognize that it is influential, both positively and negatively, they should learn its characteristics and try to listen to it and influence it.

Speed and the Grapevine

The most important characteristic of the grapevine is that it has the speed of lightning and is faster than any of the formal communication processes. Because the grapevine is not subject to the constraints of formal communication within the organization, it can also spread information that

The Bettman Archive

The term "grapevine" goes back to the Civil War when intelligence telegraph wires were strung from trees and poles and thus resembled a grapevine.

is intended to be kept secret. One slip on the part of an executive speaking casually to a clerk is all that is needed to leak the news. Then, almost instantly, everyone seems to know. The problem with information spread by the grapevine is that there is no way to check such information for accuracy. Sometimes it is worth even a long wait for the official announcement of important news just to be certain that you are getting all of the facts straight.

Rumor and the Grapevine

Whenever information is transmitted without the support of proof, it is said to be a *rumor*. Rumor is the untrue communication of the grapevine. The grapevine does not always carry rumor; however, rumor is the grapevine's worst feature. There are two characteristics of rumor, as indicated in the research of Gordon W. Allport and Leo Postman.[3] First, rumor has to be information that is of great interest; second, rumor has to be ambiguous (understandable in more than one way). Therefore, when the rumor is transmitted from one person to another, it becomes even less reliable because each person chooses details in the rumor to fit his own circumstances.

The best way to deal with a rumor is to get to the cause. Most rumors start because people are uninformed; people start rumors to meet a situation with more understanding. A rumor can make them feel more secure because it fills an information gap and accounts for the unknown. One of the best ways to combat rumor is to prevent rumors from starting by opening all means of formal communication channels — downward, upward, and horizontal — and by keeping people informed about things that are happening in the company.

After a rumor has started, however, the best way to squelch it is to present the true facts in any way possible. One young manager, faced with the problem of firing an elderly worker who was no longer productive on his job and who had been warned several times, anticipated that some of the other elderly employees would incorrectly interpret his reason for releasing the man and consequently begin a grapevine rumor. To cope with the situation, he brought the elderly gentleman into his office at closing time on Monday (while the other workers were leaving for the day), informed him of his release, and, of course, reviewed with him the reason for termination. The next morning at 9 a.m. the manager called a staff meeting for key members of the staff and informed them of the action taken and the reasons for taking the action. The manager's face-to-face factual session was instrumental in preventing a rumor that management was going to fire all the older workers and replace them with younger personnel.

3. Gordon W. Allport and Leo Postman, *The Psychology of Rumor,* Holt, New York, 1947, pp. 33–34.

7 COMMUNICATION AND HUMAN RELATIONS

If people are to get along with one another, there must be good communication between them. In this area freedom of communication is essential, for if workers are uptight, they won't feel free to communicate with each other or with their supervisor. And we can see that freedom of communication is a must if a company is to operate at maximum efficiency. Dr. F. Kenneth Berrien, a Rutgers University psychologist, prepared a survey to determine workers' attitudes in experiments for the Office of Naval Research. Listed below are two groups of questions asked that were concerned with freedom of communication.

FREEDOM TO COMMUNICATE WITHIN THE WORK GROUP

If you need advice about your job, how often do you ask someone in the group you work with?

How free do you feel to talk about things within your own work group?

If you have some personal problem, how often do you talk it over with someone in your own work group?

FREEDOM TO COMMUNICATE BETWEEN THE
WORK GROUP AND EXTERNAL SOURCES

Does your supervisor ask your opinion when a problem comes up that involves your work?

How frequently does your supervisor hold group meetings with you and other employees doing the kind of work you do?

If you have a suggestion for improving the job in some way, how easy is it for you to get your ideas across to the supervisor?

Do you feel that you can influence the decisions of your supervisor regarding things about which you are concerned?

Do you feel that you are told all you need to know in order to do your job to the best advantage?

How free do you feel about taking complaints to your supervisor?

8 COMMUNICATION BY MANAGEMENT

Dr. Keith Davis tells us that good managers achieve successful results in their organizations through communication. His concept of a typical "bottleneck" condition that exists between management and workers is illustrated in the figure on page 338.

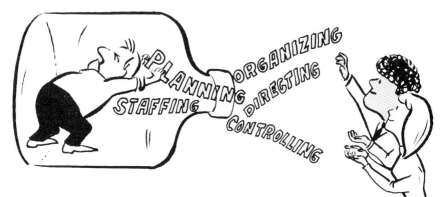

Based on Keith Davis, *Human Behavior at Work: Human Relations and Organizational Behavior,* 4th ed., p. 380

Managers carry out their responsiblities through the work of the people they supervise. Therefore managers' activities must pass through the bottleneck of communication.

Results of Effective Downward Communication

One of management's greatest challenges in leadership is in the area of communication. Managers must pass information to workers, often through supervisory personnel, and that information must be clear and understandable. In effect, the information must be *usable* by the working staff to which it is directed. Clearly, results depend on the workers' understanding and on their being able to apply directions sent down to them from management in vertical communication.

In business, results are strategic; in the long run they are really more important than what is being done. Dwight D. Eisenhower once described leadership as "getting people to do what you want them to do, when you want them to do it because they want to do it." His definition of leadership could also answer the question "Why communicate?" Communicate to get the right things done, to get results. Effective communication makes it easier to get the action desired. And effective communication is a crucial aspect of effective leadership.

There are some people who believe that the best way to get something done is to "order" that it be done. In some instances this kind of communicating may work; however, most people naturally resist such action-getting tactics because they feel thwarted. One of the basic principles of human relations is that people want to feel important. In other words, they want to feel like "somebody." People naturally resist imposed change because their personal ego, their pride of achievement, or their feeling of being somebody is challenged. It's much more comfortable and satisfying to do things the old way; people feel more secure simply because it's "old hat."

Modern thinking regards action-getting downward communication as persuading people to do things. Persuading or motivating others to do things involves giving as well as receiving understanding. The person who sends a message must make his message understandable; in fact, it is his responsibility to prevent misunderstanding. Realizing that the receiver has innate feelings of hostility to change, the sender needs to communicate through persuasion—winning commitment from the receiver.

Roadblocks to Communication

What happens when communication between management and workers is blocked? A breakdown in vertical communication can cause misunderstanding that results in insecurity, hostility, conflict, and lack of motivation on the part of the workers. In the long run breakdown in vertical communication will, without question, adversely affect productivity, which depends on cooperation between workers and management. Three important barriers to vertical communication are physical, personal, and language barriers.

Physical barriers are probably the least complicated to cope with because they are easily discovered, and the only decision to be made with regard to them concerns their removal. Some physical hindrances are distance, noise, poor hearing, inefficient messengers, and inefficient interoffice mailing systems. Most of these difficulties can be corrected. For example, if a manager tries to pass his ideas on to his work group over the roar of noisy machinery, he is in danger of not being heard or, equally serious, of being only partially heard. (The din could cause a "filter" through which only some of the manager's ideas pass.) If the manager can turn off the machines (and this is probably not always feasible) or talk to his group in an adjoining quiet room, he can remove the physical barrier, in this case noise, and eliminate the communication roadblock.

Personal barriers are more complicated than physical ones, but they are not insurmountable. They hinge on psychological feelings and social attitudes. Thus, they involve a person's emotions, values, and judgments, which may conflict with those of another person. When someone says, "That's *his* side of the story," the implication is that *he* (the other person) has colored or distorted the facts and thus made them different from the way the speaker sees them. This type of barrier can be eliminated or partially eliminated through understanding. Sometimes a mediator may be necessary to help two parties understand each other's positions in a dispute. People, by nature, do not like to change their minds; no one wants to be wrong. A person who is forced to change his mind may put up defenses because he feels that being wrong and found out will give him a sense of inadequacy, which we all try to avoid. Of course, the easiest solution is to admit one's error, to have the attitude that no one is perfect. We all make mistakes.

Language barriers naturally occur in verbal communication. The difficulty here lies in something being said or written by one person and misunderstood by another person. In this case the receiver of the message has not received the message intended by the sender; there is misunderstanding, not disagreement. Such cases can easily be remedied if the sender of the message clearly explains his meaning to the receiver.

SUGGESTIONS FOR FURTHER READING

Allport, Gordon W., and Leo Postman, *The Psychology of Rumor,* New York: Holt, 1947.

Bittel, Lester R., *What Every Supervisor Should Know,* 2d ed., New York: McGraw-Hill, 1968.

Davis, Keith, *Human Relations at Work: The Dynamics of Organizational Behavior,* New York: McGraw-Hill, 1972.

Fleishman, Alfred, *Sense and Nonsense: A Study in Human Communication,* San Francisco: International Society for General Semantics, 1971.

Hasling, John, *The Message, the Speaker, the Audience,* New York: McGraw-Hill, 1971.

Hayakawa, S. I., *Language in Thought and Action,* New York: Harcourt Brace Jovanovich, 1949.

TO HELP YOU REMEMBER

1. What do we mean when we say that "communication is a two-way connection"?
2. Describe the six steps in the communication sequence.
3. What are the three directions in the formal communication processes?
4. Is every story a grapevine rumor? Why or why not?
5. Why is communication basic in business?
6. Explain Davis's theory of how management passes through the bottleneck of communication.
7. Why do people naturally resist those who "order" change in behavior?
8. Name and explain the three major roadblocks to communication.

WORKING WITH PEOPLE, DATA, OR THINGS

Sally is one of several clerical and secretarial employees in a large department, supervised by Mrs. Jimmenez. Sally is intelligent, attractive, and highly motivated and does an outstanding job in terms of the amount of work she can turn out. She is probably the best producer of all the workers in the department. However, she happens to be the kind of person who remains aloof and ignores others. She makes no effort to assist the others and tends to rub them the wrong way. She has a superior attitude that causes resentment and makes the others feel uncomfortable.

Although Sally produces at a high level personally, her poor relationship with the other workers actually reduces the total productivity of the work group. She is a good employee when viewed alone; she is a very poor employee when viewed as a member of the group.

Since it is the company policy to promote from within, Mrs. Jimmenez accepts a promotion into another department and is replaced by one of Sally's co-workers. Sally is very disturbed; she feels that she should have received the promotion because of her exceptional ability. She decides to discuss the matter with the personnel director to determine why she was not selected for promotion.

In the interview, the personnel director outlines Sally's human-relations difficulties with her co-workers and points out that being a manager requires an understanding of human relations and an ability to communicate with other employees. It was management's feeling that Sally would have too many personality conflicts and that her promotion would impede team effort and productivity.

Questions to Consider

1. Was management correct in bypassing Sally because of her difficulties even though she was the most skilled worker? Discuss.
2. If you were the personnel director, how would you handle Sally's case at this point?
3. If you were Sally's close friend, how could you help her?

THINGS TO DO

1. Write to one or two personnel directors of large companies in your community, and request any case problems relating to communication problems. Present them to the class.
2. Prepare a 3-minute talk to be given to the class explaining a new idea regarding student freedom. Remember that the communication process involves a two-way connection and that audience understanding is part of your responsibility as a speaker.
3. Listen to a speaker on television or radio communicating an idea. Write a criticism of his ability to convey understanding, and give your interpretation of his idea. Include a discussion of any words he used that have several meanings.
4. Be prepared to discuss in class the adage "one picture is worth a thousand words."
5. The following statement appeared in "The Number One Problem," *Personnel Journal,* April, 1966, p. 237. "A manager's number one problem today can be summed up in one word: Communication." Be prepared to support or oppose this statement in class.

HUMAN RELATIONS ARE EVERYBODY'S BUSINESS

18

What This Chapter Is About

An account of the experiences of Reuben, a farmer's son, will be a good start toward proving that some of the features of modern business life are quite different from those of life at home or school.

Reuben did not like the way his father bossed him on the farm or the way his mother tried to keep track of his spare-time pleasures. So, shortly after his eighteenth birthday, he left home to go to work in a small city.

There he earned more money each week than his father had given him each month. No early rising to do morning chores, and on Sunday he could sleep all morning. It was good to feel independent. The second week he made a down payment on a stereo system. But the landlady objected when he played it mornings on awakening.

That prompted him to move to another rooming house, closer to work. The new landlady scolded when he forgot to leave his mud-covered rubbers on the porch. The supervisor was beginning to annoy him, too.

Reuben thought things over, and after studying the want ads in the Sunday paper, he went to the big city to work. His new foreman supervised 130 men and was too busy to find fault with the new worker. The men on each side of him ate their lunches together and ignored him. He stood in line to punch the time clock, to board the bus, to buy a movie ticket, to eat from the lunch wagon, and to use the crowded laundry in his neighborhood.

It was a lonesome life, with nothing to anchor to. He saw thousands of faces, but few familiar ones. He talked with few people, and when he did, his voice was sharp, and he often said the wrong things.

This new independence, about which he had dreamed, was not such a tasty dish. His personal morale began to decline. The thought of going back to the farm occurred to him, but he quickly put it out of mind — he was not going to complicate life any more than necessary.

Poor distraught Reuben failed to realize that his life, like everyone else's, was bound to be complicated by people. He could not get away from them by running from the farm to the small city or from the small city to the big one, for each of us is in partnership with hundreds of others. Our culture is built upon an interdependence of people, and the degree of interdependence has been growing steadily over the years. Some of Reuben's primary interests were frustrated.

For centuries, people worked mostly outdoors, with no bosses but themselves. Their work was coarse and did not require accurate use of muscles or fine work with the eyes. The work was either solitary or with the immediate family. Now all that has changed. There has been a slow revolution that requires us to use effort to adapt ourselves to changed conditions. Chief among these changed conditions is the association and interdependence of large groups of people—the lonely crowd.

Knowledge about human relations and the problems of human relations is vital to the individual today. Many people are bogged down in their human relations without being aware of it.

Although today job ability counts—perhaps more than it used to in some jobs—one must be able to get along with people on all kinds of jobs in order to get ahead. Corporations must now consider human relations in most of their activities. Accordingly, in 1950 the Harvard Graduate School of Business established a professorship in human relations, which was named after a long-time dean, Wallace B. Donham. The first person to hold this professorship was Fritz J. Roethlisberger, who started out as a chemical engineer but became famous for his studies of cliques and social factors in industry.

2 HUMAN RELATIONS—A PERSONAL MATTER

"Human relations" is simply relations between people. Whenever two or more persons are together or work together, problems in human relations may arise.

Since businesses emphasize human relations, some people have inferred that human relations concern corporations only. Yet every individual—hermits excepted—is surrounded by a sea of human-relations problems. Many of life's difficulties are caused by individuals who botch their human relations.

Contacts with others may be brief, but they may be momentous. A surgeon noticed, for instance, that his office patients seemed to be surly and critical. He blamed their bad humor on the humid weather—until he overheard his new typist-receptionist give patients curt orders rather than friendly greetings.

Brief contacts with strangers over the telephone also may either build or wreck human relations. When the first telephone exchange was installed in Boston, men were hired as operators. But the men had a tendency to talk back to impatient customers, and so they were replaced by tactful and patient women. Now, as the telephone company combats the human-relations problems of sexual discrimination in employment, men are once more joining the ranks of telephone operators and are learning the courtesy of which they were once considered incapable.

If you had some bad luck, would your associates feel sorry for you, or would they say (behind your back, of course) that it served you right? If you were in a jam, would friends try to help you out of it? Do co-workers volunteer to help you when extra work has to be turned out or something breaks down? When someone is hostile toward you, do others rally to your defense?

With good human relations, you are more likely to receive priceless help from others. Sometimes you get help because you have given help to others. This is the principle of reciprocal behavior, which we will come to in a later section of this chapter.

Percentage not promoted

Personality and character

Lack of skill

Data from a study by H. C. Hunt

Although job ability is very important, one must be able to get along with people in order to get ahead. A study of the reasons workers were not promoted revealed that only 10 percent were passed over because of skill deficiencies. Almost 80 percent were held back for reasons of personality and character.

3 HUMAN RELATIONS BEGIN AT HOME

The individual's approaches to human relations begin in the family. Sometimes family relationships are rough. Unappreciative parents can strain children's home relationships to the breaking point. That was why Dorothea L. Dix, the prison reformer, ran away from home to live with her more appreciative grandmother.

A nagging wife made home relations so uncomfortable for John Fitch, steamboat inventor, that he left home and family.

School brings problems in human relations, too. Some solve the problems of getting along with cranky teachers by quitting school.

Others solve the human-relations problems in school by learning how to get on the good side of a cranky teacher.

There is another strain on human relations when you begin your first job. The boss may be crankier than any teacher. Matthew Vassar, founder of Vassar College, walked out—his solution for a clash of temperament between him and his first boss, a tailor. Later, Vassar took stock of himself and changed his philosophy from running away to "My motto is progress."

There is often an impulse to walk out or talk back when relations with others become unpleasant. That is sometimes the only solution that occurs to a young person. (And many older people can think of nothing more constructive.) This accounts for some of the high turnover in jobs. One large electrical corporation, for instance, found that employees who had left school because they had trouble getting along with teachers seldom stayed on the job for more than two months. Apparently, these people had the habit of walking out rather than trying to get along. This firm no longer hires applicants who left school because of difficulty with a teacher. After all, it takes two people to make a difficulty.

Evasion, or walking out, seldom solves a problem. And it may start the habit of evading rather than solving.

4 PERSON-CENTERED ATTITUDES ARE NEEDED

"That turret lathe sounds a bit sick. Get the master mechanic right away. That machine cost too much to let it break down. I'll be back in half an hour to see how she's going," said a factory superintendent.

Late that afternoon, while this same superintendent was studying some specifications, he was interrupted by Gertrude, a typist, who stood in his office doorway. Her left hand was covered with a blood-stained handkerchief. She had nicked a finger on the paper cutter.

"Don't stand there acting like a baby," he barked. "You know where the first-aid room is. Don't be so clumsy next time. Accidents cost money."

That was all the attention he gave Gertrude, but he dropped other work several times to check the condition of that precious lathe. He was machine-centered. He babied the machine but left the injured typist to her own fate.

People who are centered on machines, profits, or themselves are likely to have difficulties in human relations. Every individual is the center of his own universe, and an individual's likes, interests, and aspirations have to be considered by others. Each of us is part of the workaday world.

There is a prevalent belief that people in some occupations are inclined to be less person-centered than others. Accountants, engineers, research and laboratory workers, and people working in the financial field may be less person-centered than people in other fields; that is, their interests are often directed toward things rather than people.

It is difficult for many to believe that the worker-centered boss gets more output in the long run than the production-centered boss, but research has shown this to be true.

THE PRINCIPLE OF RECIPROCAL BEHAVIOR

The golden rule expresses the principle of reciprocal behavior. Aristotle taught a version of that rule—"We should behave to people as we would wish people to behave to us." Reciprocal behavior is an ageless principle.

You get back what you hand out—sometimes with interest added. That is the principle. If you smile, the other person will probably smile too. If you complain, he is likely to do the same. If you ignore him, he will ignore you.

YOU-POINT—A KEY APPROACH

Listen in on conversations, and you will be amazed to hear how often the word "I" is used. It is the most frequently used word in the language. But for good human relations, "you" should be used more often.

It is not as easy to quit using "I" and substitute "you" as you might think. You almost have to turn your thinking upside down to get the habit of making the other person a center.

The executive who says, "I want these letters done by three o'clock" is taking the wrong point of view. His secretary would like the job better if he used the "you-point" and asked, "You can probably have these done by three o'clock, can't you?" It is still an order from the boss, but what a difference it makes in the attitude of the person who is given the order!

In everyday requests, this you-point should be cultivated. "I want to borrow your book" should become "Will you lend me your book?"

When you say the word "you," put a little vocal emphasis on it. Make the "you" a bit louder and sweeter than other words. "*I'm* glad to see you" should be transformed to "It's good to see *you!*"

There is much more to the you-point than just using the word. When buying gifts, for example, we usually buy for the other person something we want ourselves. But the tactful person buys something he knows the other person wants. There was a standing joke in one small company because the owner always gave a chess set to each employee on his fifth anniversary with the company. The owner was wild about chess and imagined the employees were, too. He lacked a you-point, for chess was the last thing that interested any of them.

The importance of the reader-centered message has already been discussed in Chapter 8. You remember that the reader-centered message involves much more than merely changing "I" and "we" to "you" and "your."

7 FROM FAMILY SUFFICIENCY TO MODERN BUSINESS

The you-point, reciprocal behavior, and person-centered attitudes are more needed now than in the past because working conditions have changed greatly. You will be better able to get along with others if you understand how these changes have affected human relations.

At the time of the Declaration of Independence, the interdependence of individuals did not extend much beyond their immediate families. The family was the unit of industry—and there were big families, with seven to ten children.

Most of the food, clothing, and soap—even the furniture—was made by the members of the family. They were kept as busy as a hive of bees and were very dependent on each other. When the family needed something, a member of the family made it, or the family did without. There was little ready cash, and there were no installment plans. The family entertained itself at home. So many things had to be made and done at home that the children were trained to work early in life. Every member of the family had useful work to do and felt needed.

A few individuals who had particular abilities specialized and did work that others found difficult. Many family names originated from a special ability of an ancestor. Such vocational names include Baker, Butcher, Carpenter, Carver, Clark (clerk), Cooper, Mason, Shoemaker, Smith, and Taylor.

Eli Terry was one individual who had a special ability. He was a "born mechanic." When he was twenty—while Washington was still President—Terry made his first wooden clock, works and all. It is still keeping good time! Terry moved to Plymouth, Connecticut, when he was 21, and during the winter he worked beside the fire making clocks. When the roads dried out in late spring, he loaded the clocks he had made that winter onto a cart and peddled them up and down the countryside. He had to be a good trader as well as a good mechanic, for often there was no money for a clock, and so he took hams or homespun woolens in exchange. The reputation of his Yankee clocks spread.

By the time Thomas Jefferson was inaugurated, selling the clocks was so easy that Terry, then twenty-eight, hired two helpers. One of them was a fourteen-year-old boy, Seth Thomas, who became a skilled cabinetmaker. He built sturdy cases of cherry, maple, and pine for the tall grandfather clocks.

With this expansion, Terry lost some of his independence. He and his helpers worked together in the shed in Plymouth Hollow from sunup to sundown. The hours did not seem long, since they were working together as friends and neighbors. They still had the family spirit, though they had now formed an industrial group.

Young Seth Thomas was a go-getter as well as a craftsman. When he was twenty-four, Thomas bought out his boss and put more push into the business. He built a small factory on the western part of the Hollow and soon hired twenty men to work with him. They were not enough, so he increased production by hiring families around the Hollow to make parts in their homes.

These workers were paid once a year. Payday consisted of settling the employee's charge account at the store Thomas operated. Today this practice seems strange, but it was not until 1812, when a New Haven carriage maker named James Brewster instituted weekly paychecks, that the modern method of compensating employees was practiced.

Human-relations problems pyramided as the country and businesses grew. The Seth Thomas story is used here because it concerns one of the oldest widely known firms that was founded early in the history of the nation's business and is still doing business at the old location.

Courtesy of Seth Thomas Division, General Time Corp., Thomaston, Conn.
This photograph shows two workers from the Tower Clock Department of the Seth Thomas factory.

For miles around Plymouth Hollow, families punched out, polished, and fitted parts for Thomas clocks right in their own kitchens. The shed grew into a factory building, and power was drawn from the Naugatuck River. This factory was a group of separate shops. The head of each shop was a contractor who had been given a contract to make certain parts. The contractors dickered with employees over wages and such, which relieved Seth Thomas of some details, but the dickering also produced some ill feeling and discrimination.

Any problem that Thomas might have had as a fourteen-year-old lad in getting along with his boss and one fellow worker had multiplied. He now had a factory full of workers and a valley full of families to give him problems in human relations. He could no longer work side by side with his employees. Many were strangers to him, though they knew him by sight, and all respected him. But those contractors who ran some of the departments—they were the villains in the valley.

And today, with over 200 million people in the United States, sheer size has multiplied our human-relations problems far beyond anything Thomas could have imagined in his day.

Working conditions and hours are vastly better than in the "good old days." Workers do not have to wait a year for their pay and then take it out in trade at a company store. They are not chiseled by a department contractor. They have their own athletic teams, magazines, and parties. Employees get hot meals in the cafeteria and have pension and sick-benefit arrangements, two weeks' vacation with pay, bowling alleys, and attractive meeting places for recreational activities.

Each morning, employees come from 5, 10, or 20 miles away to file past the time clock. In the afternoon, they scatter to their widely separated homes. It used to be just Plymouth Hollow folks. Now they come from surrounding towns and counties. It is no longer neighbor working beside neighbor.

That is the situation now across the country in most factories and offices. Many employees are practically strangers to one another and have scarcely a speaking acquaintance with the boss. Human-relations problems of individuals and of businesses are more complicated.

CONGESTION, SPECIALIZATION, AND MOBILITY

The shift from family industry to factory industry is more recent than you may have realized. There has not been time to make full adjustments to the changes. Present-day business and industry are only a generation or two old.

When Seth Thomas went into business for himself, there were no cigarettes, no baseball, no steel, no vertical files or carbon paper, no interchangeable parts. Adhesive postage stamps were yet to be invented—in England in 1839. The first in the United States were used on July 1, 1847, in New York City. The speediest transportation was on the Erie Canal—1½ miles per hour at 1.5 cents per mile.

Health conditions were poor; the death rate was high. Plumbing, pasteurizing, screens, and sewers were almost unknown. Vaccination for smallpox had been developed by Edward Jenner in 1790, but people did not believe in it and apparently preferred to die early or be disfigured by the pox as their fathers were. Back in Seth Thomas's day, the life expectancy at birth was only thirty-five years. Today it is seventy years and poses other problems.

In 1830, Oliver Newberry, the "Steamboat King of the Great Lakes," carried his business papers around in his stovepipe hat. And the Bank of England was the first building in the world to put "In" and "Out" signs on its doors that year—at the suggestion of Samuel B. Howlett, a military engineer who had been annoyed by the confusion caused by traffic moving in and out of the Bank's new building. In the United States that year, only 73 miles of railroad tracks had been laid, but the country's canals totaled 1,277 miles. There were more than 8,000 chair factories in the United States, most of them employing only one or two workers in addition to the proprietor. Graham bread and graham crackers were introduced by Sylvester Graham, a doctor and food faddist. There was no business school until Peter Duff started his in Pittsburgh in 1840.

Ready-made "store suits" did not appear until after the Civil War. Contractors who had made uniforms for soldiers during the war converted their businesses to civilian ready-made suits. These store suits usually were better tailored than homemade ones, so the needle trades zoomed ahead. Thus, more people joined the ranks of employees and added the job of getting along with fellow workers and bosses to the job of getting along with members of their families.

The railroad and the telegraph, giving mobility and means of communication, expanded at about the same time that the suit industry did. They widened horizons and, at the same time, increased interdependence. But it was the automobile and the telephone, around the turn of the century, that brought the biggest changes. More folks became footloose. Contacts were widened. People became less permanent residents. You could pick and choose where to work.

We're on the move! In a typical year about 30 million Americans move. People move from job to job; the average person stays only 3½ years with one company.

This mobility broke up family solidarity, as the more ambitious or more disgruntled broke away from the family hearth to try their wings elsewhere. Families themselves became mobile, moving from city to city, as employment opportunities shifted. Today, families are so much on the move that few families in most suburbs have been there as long as five or six years.

Electric motors and safety devices made the modern elevator possible; the elevator, in turn, made high buildings practicable. Story was piled on top of story, until office buildings and factories now often contain small cities of workers. City congestion came—and came to stay.

As cities grew larger, workers grew smaller, figuratively speaking. The individual all-around workman has become well-nigh extinct. His place has been taken by *integrated groups of specialized workers* who can turn out more and better work at lower cost. Mass production has been a great cost reducer, but it has increased the problems of human relations. The individual works more and more at less and less, and some individuals are so specialized that they work at practically nothing. That is an economic gain, but it has been bought at the price of increased strains on human nature. Frank W. Pierce, a mechanical engineer who changed to personnel work and became president and director of Standard Oil Company of New Jersey, said:

> We are apt to overlook the reward which lies in the deep personal satisfaction from doing something worthwhile. The worker who merely solders two radio connections hour after hour does not gain that personal satisfaction of creating—but the high school boy who builds a crude radio set that actually works has a great thrill from his accomplishment.

Henry Ford II observed:

> Mass production did not invent the human equation, but did alter it in a number of important respects which we have been slow to take into account. Under mass production large numbers of people flocked to the assembly line, each to perform a highly specialized duty. Mass production produced great concentrations of people. And it produced the difficult problem of specialization, where the individual loses sight of the social usefulness of what he does.

That all-too-human desire to be noticed as an individual is also cramped by congestion and specialization. Individual recognition is difficult when there are several hundred others working in the same plant or building. As a result, many workers feel like forgotten men who are lost in a sea of strange faces—lonely in the crowd.

Back in Seth Thomas's time, families averaged seven to ten children. From infancy, each individual had practice in getting along with a group. Give and take and the inevitable compromises of human relations were learned early. Today, when the working world calls for unlimited give and take, families have an average of only two or three children. As a result, the first experience of some individuals in making the compromises of personal desires that are necessary in human relations comes only after they leave home to make their way in the world. They have to learn rather late in life that the world requires partnership and teamwork, not the play of personal whims.

All these changes have made human relations the central problem for most people today. The changes have given some a feeling of futility that is a symptom of poor personal morale.

 ## PEOPLE WHO ARE HARD TO GET ALONG WITH

"Each good American company should be a kind of experiment to find how people work best together," says Edwin H. Land, who is best known for inventing the Polaroid camera and related devices.

Human relations are a stumbling block for those who have not cultivated the knack of getting along with others and for people who live or work with individuals who are hard to get along with.

Reuben was an example of the first group. He did not cultivate the knack; instead, he evaded the issue by moving away from his human-relations problems—like the boy who quits school because he doesn't like his teacher.

Examples of the second group are the employee who likes the job but does not like the boss and the employee who likes the pay but does not like the people with whom he has to work.

It is necessary early in life to realize that about one person in ten will be difficult to get along with all the time and that others will be difficult perhaps one-tenth of the time. These touchy, cantankerous, troublesome people cannot be changed as easily as a troublesome machine can be adjusted. "Telling them off" does not help in the least. You simply have to learn to get along with them like the mountaineer with the erratic clock; when the hands showed 6:30 and the clock struck 4:00, it was 10:00.

It is easier to get along with these cantankerous people if you try to figure why they are that way. Look upon them as people who have interesting differences, not as personal enemies.

Some people think the fault is theirs when they cross paths with hard-to-get-along-with people, but do not let them undermine your own self-confidence. They do not dislike you—they dislike themselves most of all. Although employment interviewers try not to hire bothersome types, you will still find plenty of "pests" in your working environment.

In sales work, particularly, it is necessary to take people as they are. The salesperson must be pleasant, cooperative, and helpful to all. He may not want some of his customers as neighbors, but he handles all kinds so that they will remain customers.

In sales work particularly, it is necessary to take people as they are. The salesperson must be pleasant, cooperative, and helpful to all.

Courtesy of The Singer Co.

It takes all kinds of people to make the world. You will always be running into rude, fault-finding, bossy, critical, suspicious, moody, outspoken, buck-passing, belittling, deceitful, jealous people and others who are a pain in the neck. If such a person really becomes a stumbling block in your working environment, talk it over with your boss or with someone in the personnel department.

LEVELS OF HUMAN RELATIONS

A human-relations problem may be largely *individual*, such as getting along with a crotchety neighbor or domineering co-worker.

It is often a problem of one group getting along with a different group, such as members of one church getting along with members of another church or diesinkers getting along with the time-study men. These are *group relations*.

The problems may be still wider, as when people of different races have to live in the same community and work together. These are problems in *race relations*.

When the relations between nations are involved, they are *international relations*.

Poor human relations may result in family spats and lawsuits to break wills or in neighborhood feuds. They range from these to religious quarrels, labor strife, race riots, and wars. Defective relations are the starting point for all these catastrophes.

The preamble to the constitution of the United Nations Economic, Scientific, and Cultural Organization, known more familiarly as UNESCO, tells us that "since wars begin in the minds of men, it is in the minds of men that the defense of peace must be constructed."

11 MORALE

The person with high morale believes in himself, in his future, and in others. He thinks his work is worth doing and that he is doing a good job at it. *Morale* in the individual is his zest for living and working — or lack of it. High morale helps a person to take minor irritations in stride, to work under pressure when necessary without blowing up, and to get along with people who want to take more than they give. High morale makes a person unbeatable.

Good personal morale is evidence that the person has adjusted his whims and aspirations to life as it must be lived. He is in harmony with the world around him, and there is harmony in his own little world. He has found how to have happiness and remembers the happiness rather than the barren moments. He has found off-the-job outlets for his leftover primary interests.

There appears to be a cycle through which a worker's morale swings during his working life. Dr. Nancy C. Morse has found a fall, then a rise, of workers' satisfaction, as reported for office clerks. The working conditions and treatment were the same for all these white-collar people in the home office. But the workers went through what can be called an "occupational morale cycle."

The new employee tended to have high morale about the new life and opportunity. But after a year this honeymoon bliss was over. After two years the work was becoming humdrum, and enthusiasm was at the low point. Some of this declining morale may be due to a wish to get married after the second year of employment, but the new workers do not yet feel financially able to take the step. We have seen earlier that the average person changes jobs about every 3½ years — when the cycle for occupational morale hits bottom.

Things seem to pick up after five years on the job. Although it is the same old routine, and the pay is not much different, things seem rosier. After five or more years the worker has probably shifted some of his aspirations and come to adjust realistically to the situation as it has to be. He decides to put up with what has to be put up with. He has found how to be accepted by the others in the work group and how to get along with the few "characters" who would otherwise be irritating. And he has some pride in his job accomplishments as well as after-hours hobbies to exercise leftover interests.

A person's morale is a rough index of how well he has solved his human-relations problems. Good morale came easier in the day of the three-person village firm. Today, it has to be worked for. That is why modern business has made an important niche for experts who are trained in psychological methods to ease the strains on human relations. In the next few chapters, we'll see how they do it.

SUGGESTIONS FOR FURTHER READING

Davis, Keith, and Robert L. Blomstrom, *Business, Society, and Environ-
    ment: Social Power and Social Response*, 2d ed., New York:
    McGraw-Hill, 1971.
Litterer, Joseph A., *The Analysis of Organization*, New York: Wiley, 1965.
Walton, Richard E., and Robert B. McKersie, *A Behavioral Theory of
    Labor Negotiations: Analysis of a Social Interaction System*, New
    York: McGraw-Hill, 1965.
Wrench, David F., *Readings in Psychology: Foundation and Application*,
    New York: McGraw-Hill, 1971.

TO HELP YOU REMEMBER

1. How can conflicts resulting from interdependence best be re-
    solved?
2. How does this book define human relations?
3. In what places, in addition to business, are there human-relations
    problems?
4. Differentiate between person-centered and production-centered
    attitudes. Which are usually most successful?
5. Tell how the principle of reciprocal behavior works.
6. Give some examples of the "you-point." What is the "you-point"?
7. How does the Seth Thomas story illustrate the changes that have
    taken place in American industry?
8. How do congestion, specialization, and mobility affect human rela-
    tions?
9. How can one best get along with cantankerous people?
10. Define morale.

WORKING WITH PEOPLE, DATA, OR THINGS

Read and analyze the following case. Answer the questions, and be prepared for class discussion.

Betty Andrews has been a mail clerk with a company for two
years and performs satisfactory work. Several months ago she pur-
chased for herself a stereo and a quantity of the latest hit records. Soon
after that she developed the habit of humming and whistling while working. Betty was no artist—her sounds were not very pleasing—but she
derived much satisfaction from her habit, and so she hummed and
whistled throughout the day.

Fellow workers in the mail room who worked near Betty made
no complaints, but her supervisor, Mary Jo Tancabel, was annoyed
and disturbed by her habit. At first, she thought Betty would "stop the
music" when the newness of the stereo wore off. Unfortunately, the
practice persisted; in fact, it became worse.

Finally, Miss Tancabel spoke privately to Betty and requested that she stop her humming and whistling during working hours, as the habit was disturbing and distracting. Betty seemed to take the criticism very well and was quiet for several days. But then she started again.

After a couple of hours of humming and whistling, Miss Tancabel walked up to Betty and, in front of the entire mail-room staff, shouted, "Stop that darn humming and whistling. Do you hear me? Stop it!" After a moment or two, an embarrassed Betty stated softly, "Nobody else complained except you. None of the other workers cares if I'm happy and show it. All of us do our work. Your problem is that you don't like me, and you're just like most supervisors; you can't adjust to the fact that people are different. But, do *we* have to adjust to supervisor's differences and habits? You bet we do." Miss Tancabel told Betty to keep quiet and to get to work. Betty did as she was told.

Questions

1. Is there a problem here? Discuss.
2. What do you believe would have happened if Miss Tancabel had not said anything to Betty?
3. What should Betty do now? What should Miss Tancabel do now? Justify your views.

THINGS TO DO

1. Develop a script for role-playing the following situation: It's a week before Christmas, and the company gives you, the chief clerk, a 5-pound box of candy but doesn't give anything to the other employees in your department.
2. Look for local evidences of congestion, mobility, and job specialization. Analyze ways in which these affect human relations.
3. Make a survey of the frequency with which people use "I" and "you." If possible, look at some actual business letters. Also, go to some public place and record the "I's" and "you's" used in conversation; write the words in two separate columns on a file card held inconspicuously in your hand. What do your tallies indicate?
4. Think of some traffic officer, bus driver, receptionist, or other person who seems to get along very well with strangers. What is there about the person and the person's job that may explain his or her ability? Can you compose a list of at least six rules to guide others?
5. Develop a role-playing situation for a human-relations problem in which you have found yourself either at home, in school, or at work. Try not to color the situation with any of your own opinions, emotions, or prejudices. (This may be difficult for you to do.) In other words, try to tell it the way it really was.

MOTIVATION AND THE WILL TO WORK

19

What This Chapter Is About

1 MAKING JOBS MORE DESIRABLE

Do workers restrict their output because they are lazy? Do they work only because they have to make a living? Are they more interested in making a lot of money than in doing their jobs well?

We can get some understanding of these questions if we look at a firm in Michigan that was having janitor trouble. The janitors had become surly, careless, complaining. Those who did not quit were knee-deep in complaints. The brush handles were too long or too short; the waste cans were too heavy; nothing was right. Such a flood of trivial complaints means that something is wrong in human relations. Human problems that the complainers themselves do not understand are often the cause of such petty gripes.

Analysis of the janitor trouble by Dr. Irwin A. Berg showed that the company was neglecting some important human considerations. Janitorial work was considered a simpleton's job. Employees looked down on the janitors, gave them ridiculous nicknames, and occasionally made their work seem especially dirty by outbursts of perverted humor.

The situation became so ugly that it was discussed at an executive conference, and action was planned to alter the human relations that caused the trouble. A campaign was mapped to show the janitors and other employees that the janitors' work was worthwhile and to build respect for the janitors as individuals.

Positive aspects of janitors' work were emphasized in talks with supervisors and in company magazine articles. Everyone was reminded that janitors prevented slips and falls, improved health conditions, and protected company equipment. Janitors had to be trustworthy, since they had access to desks and offices containing valuables and secret documents. Examples were cited to show that janitoring was big business — an automobile firm's need for 5,000 janitors, 750 janitors employed at Rockefeller Center, and so on.

As evidence of a janitor's importance, the job title was changed to "custodian," and the janitors were given coats bearing that word.

These tactics changed employee attitudes. The new title and uniform were evidences of importance and helped to bring about the changed attitudes. The custodians became proud of their new status, and their self-respect returned. Complaints melted away, and morale rose as the work was upgraded in public esteem. *Upgrading is more than promoting a worker; it includes making the job more desirable in terms of social approval.*

Many vexing human-relations problems can be relieved equally easily. Whenever there are evidences of strained relations, an analysis should be made to find out what human needs are being thwarted. People are not disagreeable because they prefer to be, but because they are frustrated. Discover what the frustrations are, and correct the conditions that cause them. Better yet, *anticipate possible frustrations, and keep them from developing.*

Frustrations are seldom due to hunger or physical discomforts. Also, shorter working hours or more pay would not have improved the janitors' morale. Like all humans, they wanted things that are more desired than money—things that money cannot buy. They were being deprived of a basic human need, the need to feel that one's work is worthwhile and respected.

2 HUMAN NEEDS AND MOTIVES

As we discussed in Chapter 3, the desire to satisfy personal needs stimulates effort; therefore, it may be wise to review briefly the discussion of human needs. According to Abraham H. Maslow, these needs are (1) basic physiological needs, (2) safety needs, (3) affection needs, (4) esteem needs, and (5) self-realization needs.

We can divide this set of five needs into two general categories: the needs necessary for maintaining and perpetuating life, and the social and psychological needs. The first of Maslow's five needs is in the first category, and the rest are in the second category. The safety needs, number 2 on Maslow's list, are on the borderline; they include needs for physical shelter and bodily protection and comfort as well as a psychological need to feel secure and unthreatened.

The social and psychological needs are needs of the mind: they build up our morale. Thus, they give us security, love, and friendship, respect for ourselves from ourselves and others, and a sense of fulfillment that gives *meaning* to our lives. These needs provide problems for employers because they are very complex and vary from person to person. We can see that the biological needs are much easier to identify and to satisfy than the social and psychological needs.

Since the biological needs are essential to our physical well-being, they come first on Maslow's list. For this reason, they are our *primary* needs, while our social and psychological needs are *secondary* needs. We are most concerned with secondary needs in this chapter.

Secondary needs develop a variety of motives in different people. Sometimes these motives are interacting; therefore, it becomes quite difficult for employers to detect just what the motives are. Also adding to their complexity is the fact that the same motive can cause different behavior at different times, and sometimes the same behavior can be the result of different motives. For example, the same behavior, tardiness, could be the result of lack of respect for the supervisor, lack of interest in the job, or the lack of self-respect.

Dr. Keith Davis characterizes secondary needs as follows:[1]

1   They are strongly conditioned by experience.
2   They vary in type and intensity among people.
3   They change within any individual.
4   They work in groups, rather than alone.
5   They are often hidden from conscious recognition.
6   They are nebulous feelings instead of tangible physical needs.
7   They influence behavior. It is said that we are logical only to the extent our feelings let us be.

3 OUR STRONGEST NEEDS

Dr. Edward L. Thorndike, the second psychologist to be president of the American Association for the Advancement of Science, conducted studies of needs in this country based on how people spend their money; he assumed that how they spend money reflects what they want the most. For example, one young woman saved her money, stinting herself on food, in order to buy a mink coat.

Biological needs came out at the top of his list. The figures showed that 56 percent of the money people spent had gone for satisfying their hunger for food. Another 15 percent went for fancy purchases, such as seasonings that made the food a source of greater pleasure to the senses of taste and smell. Around 10 percent of their expenditures were for companionship, and only 3 percent for social approval (that mink coat).

Doctor Maslow approached the question of strength by observing that some motives take priority over others—you forget your hunger if a fire breaks out while you are eating a beefsteak—and in the order presented in his list. Go without food for a few days, and your motivation to be social or feel respected will be overwhelmed by an animal-like and selfish struggle for food—as happened in concentration camps.

The want to be social takes precedence over the want to feel respected. Workers stall on the job and lower their self-respect in order to satisfy the want to be accepted as one of the crowd, which has higher priority in the system of human motivation.

The want to feel respected takes priority over the want to do work one likes, as shown by the many who do work that only half interests them in order to be in jobs that have prestige in the community. Related to this is the fact that placing workers on jobs that fit them best may not count so much in the long run as handling them so that their feelings of personal worth are enhanced.

1. Keith Davis, *Human Behavior at Work: Human Relations and Organizational Behavior*, 4th ed., McGraw-Hill, New York, 1972, p. 45.

A very practical implication of this order of priorities is that people are likely to be motivated most strongly by what they do not have. If you have lots of self-esteem, for instance, you are not given an incentive if a salesman directs his appeal to self-esteem. That may be why people with self-esteem are not stampeded into buying cars of the latest model. But if a person's self-esteem is threatened in some way, he is strongly motivated to save it.

4 CATTELL'S PROPENSITIES

Dr. Raymond B. Cattell of the University of Illinois proposed a grouping of motives based upon experimental and mental-test data. The following account of his findings is quoted from *How to Get Along With Automation.*[2]

> The catalog of human propensities we will give is adapted from his book, *Personality and Motivation Structure and Measurement.*
>
> We catalog these propensities in the order in which we can be most certain they exist, not according to their priority over one another. Seeking companionship, at the top of the list, is much more firmly established as a propensity than is seeking comfort—yet think of all the effort moderns make to secure comfort and convenience. Perhaps moderns give more attention to their comfort than to being pleasant companions because it is easier to buy comfort. More on such aspects shortly.
>
> In studying this condensed catalog of propensities (and we recommend it be studied carefully), think about the possible survival value to early mankind each might have had. Seeking companionship, for example, was probably essential to individual survival during the few hundred generations when people lived as hunters with only sticks and stones to catch animals. Bands of hunters could be more successful and safer than lone hunters.
>
> Some scientists think this propensity for companionship explains why modern teen-agers go around in gangs, but with nothing to hunt but strangers whom they attack. Although the survival value of some of our propensities may no longer be needed in an automated world, we come into it equipped with them, and we might as well learn to get along with them.
>
> Think also about how some of these propensities could have helped mankind advance from a primitive to a civilized state. Seeking information, for instance, could lead men to discover how to grow foods, make weapons and tools from metals, and centuries later harness electricity and then atomic energy.

2. Donald A. Laird and Eleanor C. Laird, *How to Get Along With Automation,* McGraw-Hill, New York, 1964, pp. 330–333.

Courtesy of Walker Color Candids

Marriage is often motivated by the general propensity to seek companionship. This propensity may date back to the days when partnership was essential to individual survival.

SOME GENERAL HUMAN PROPENSITIES

Propensity	Activities It Could Motivate
Seeking companionship, wanting to be with people, especially those one feels at ease with	Going where the crowds are Wanting congenial fellow workers "Lonesome pay" for isolated jobs Marriage and home life Telephone talks with friends Teen-age gangs; adult clubs, lodges Avoiding people of other races or beliefs [in favor of people more like oneself] Solitary confinement as punishment
Protectiveness, wanting to protect one's children, the helpless	Coddling children, pampering pets Societies for prevention of cruelty Aiding the sick, poor, charities Providing opportunities for children

SOME GENERAL HUMAN PROPENSITIES (continued)

Propensity	Activities It Could Motivate
	Hostility toward big country that attacks weaker country Do-gooding for employees
Seeking information, wanting to explore and satisfy one's curiosity	Finding out how things work Wanting to know what is going on in neighborhood, firm, world Visiting new places. Watching construction work Magazines, newspapers, newscasts Gossip columns Higher education, study, research
Escaping danger, wanting to be secure	Taking pills, vitamins, etc. Buying insurance of various sorts Seeking job security Locking the house Avoiding crowded traffic Wanting strong national defense Wanting better police, fire protection Working to prevent wars
Seeking self-assertion, wanting to be master of one's own fate, and to stand out among people	Planning one's own work; being one's own boss Striving to "come up" in the world Inclination to correct others, to argue Trying to look fashionable, attractive Looking for more money, more personal power Seeking acquaintance, autographs of famous people Rivalry for promotions Daringness and showing-off; high spending Browbeating spouse, employees, others

SOME GENERAL HUMAN PROPENSITIES (continued)

Propensity	Activities It Could Motivate
Seeking comfort, wanting to have creature comforts and sensory pleasures	Pleasing sounds, sights; music at work
	Tasty food, flavors, sauces and spices
	Soft chairs, beds; easy-riding automobiles
	Heating and air conditioning
	Demands for better working conditions
	Wanting more pay to buy more comforts

Three other propensities were suggested by Dr. Cattell's research, but these were not as clearly proved as the six just listed:

Seeking help when in trouble, distress, or pain
Seeking sleep or rest
Wanting to make things; craftsmanship for the fun of it

Still other propensities may be uncovered as additional tests are devised to get at them, but we can only guess what they might be.

5 MOTIVATION IS LIKE A TREE

The relationships between urges, needs, and wants can be brought out by visualizing them as making up what might be called a "tree of motivation." The soil that gives the roots nourishment may be compared with the deep urges. Depending on the soil, the roots may take up more love than hostility. Or the roots may be feeding in a balanced soil—neither acidic nor alkaline—in which love and hostility are in equilibrium. Continued frustrations may upset the acid balance in this soil, and the result could be peculiarities in motivation and behavior.

The biological needs may be compared with the roots, which start the energy-giving substances up the trunk of the tree. The contributions from the roots are blended to produce a balanced sap, as a rule. As energy-giving materials get above ground, they branch off to the limbs.

There are also the whims of climate to consider (and perhaps a few injurious insects); these may frustrate this flow and affect the branches and their fruit.

The climate comes from other people—it is the human climate of the home or workplace. (The insects, too, are likely to be people.) If the climate does not give the top branches enough sunlight, the tree becomes half dead or dies from the top down. You have heard of people who seemed only half alive on the job; the bodies were there, but the spirit was missing.

6 DOES CULTURE CHANGE?

Anthropologists who have studied mankind claim that people today have the same nerves, glands, and brains that their remote ancestors had some 50,000 years ago. Scientists can find no evidence to indicate that the bodily machinery has changed physically in ways that might produce changes in behavior or human nature. There is no doubt that we are just like people who lived 50,000 years ago as far as reflexes, digestion, thyroids, and the like are concerned.

But purposeful human conduct involves emotional and intellectual elements. The conditions under which people grow up and live alter the things that are "natural" for them to do. Every society or community or company has taboos, or prohibitions, that are imposed on the conduct of its members. Millions will not eat meat, for instance, because their religion does not permit them to.

Other taboos, or social pressures, mold what we call "human nature." Taboos kept women out of office work until 1862, when a central New York State banker, General Francis E. Spinner, was United States Treasurer. His office staff trimmed paper money by hand. About twenty men were employed in this work, but there was a manpower shortage during the Civil War. General Spinner obtained Lincoln's permission to hire Jennie Douglas to cut paper money. She became the first woman office employee in the government. In October of the same year, seven other women went to work cutting and counting money. The taboo was disappearing because of the crisis.

It was not until 1868 that the federal government employed a woman stenographer. She was Katharine Hayes Chapin Barrows, aged 21 at the time. The taboo was broken to give her employment because her husband happened to be personal secretary to William H. Seward, the Secretary of State. (Later she took her degree in medicine and, with her husband, was for many years a leader in prison reform.)

Taboos make people of one generation seem far different from those of another; but, in fact, the differences are due to changing taboos and customs. Underneath the skin, they are as people have always been. In daily life we see and deal largely with conduct or behavior that has been modified; it may be very different from what is under the skin.

The Victorian period provides many examples. For instance, the idea of women working in the same offices as men was horrifying, but it was right and proper for women to flock to witness public hangings. About half of the 20,000 people outside the Stafford jail on June 14, 1856, were women; they were there to watch William Palmer, a young physician, be hanged for administering strychnine to patients so that he could collect their insurance.

Victorian mothers wanted their little boys to be soldiers. Foremen, in the nineteenth century, enforced orders by knocking their men down, and promotion to foreman was sometimes determined by an all-around fight. The man who lasted longest became boss. Combat was in the atmosphere; boxing matches were fought bare-knuckled, with no blows barred. The mentally disturbed were chained and beaten. People were jailed for debts and hanged for stealing horses.

The Bettman Archive

It was not until the late nineteenth century that the taboo preventing women from working in the same offices as men began to be lifted.

7 PEOPLE ARE NOT MACHINES

Many incentive systems fail to produce results because they look on human nature as a machine. Drop the coin in the right slot, and out comes the wanted response. We may be that mechanical at the reflex level, but not in our complicated daily lives.

We have attitudes and resistances between a stimulus and our response to it. No use giving an automobile more gas when its brakes are set. The miser has his brakes set one way; the spendthrift has his brakes set another way. Social pressure set the brakes one way during Victorian days and today sets them in another way. The brakes in Louisiana are not set the same as the brakes in Maine. Coffee does not "taste right" in Louisiana unless it contains a large amount of chicory seasoning; in Maine people imagine chicory gives coffee a "bad taste." This difference is due to tradition, not to climate.

The technique of dealing with employees as machines includes giving a pep talk, a prize, a bonus, a vacation with pay, or a threat of discharge. But the brakes should be taken off first. The boss may need to be changed, or goal gradients set.

A group of young women in an embroidery factory provides an interesting illustration. The workers had been paid on an hourly basis. The manager concluded they would be stimulated to be more efficient if they were paid instead on a piece-rate basis.

Their production at hourly rates had been 96 dozen a day. Under the new piece rate, it promptly fell to 75 dozen a day.

Apparently, the opportunity to earn more money was not the right coin in the slot to motivate the women. Christopher A. Lee reported in the magazine *Human Factor* that second thought uncovered the fallacy in the piece-rate scheme in this situation.

The women all lived with their parents, and each turned her pay over to the head of the house. Had they been living in their own apartments, the situation would have been different.

So the plan was changed to motivate the women with something they wanted and could use themselves. The women were told that when they finished the day's quota their job was over for that day and they could do what they liked from then on. By the second day, the supervisor was astonished to find that the workers had finished 100 dozen by 2:30 and were ready to leave for the day.

People respond to a total situation. Double pay for those janitors (Section 1) would not have changed the critical factors in the total situation. Fifty or more methods of "incentive" payments have been tried and have failed in many firms because the total situation did not match the motives of the workers.

This is shown by the fact that there are a few records of businesses where noble experiments—religious participation, employee participation in management, or extreme profit sharing—have produced amazing results. Usually, these methods succeed only in the organization initiating them and fail when other firms try them. The method produced exceptional results for the originator because it was part of the total situation created by a colorful leader. The owner thought his "system of incentivation" did the trick. But it was the *general atmosphere* his personality spread through the business that produced the results. When he died or retired, the wonderful system usually failed to work anymore.

Sometimes, if the coin in the slot works, it works too well, though only briefly. Dr. G. H. R. von Koenigswald tells an entertaining story in this connection about his discovery of the bones of prehistoric man in Java. When he observed that the native diggers were nearing a pit containing priceless ancient bones, he offered them 10 cents for each piece of bone they could find. "The result was terrible," he said. "I had underestimated the business ability of my collectors. Behind my back they broke the larger bones into pieces to increase the number of sales." That explains why the skull of the first *Pithecanthropus erectus* to be discovered was obtained in 30 fragments; it took months to piece them together. "Beating the rate" is also done with great cleverness in most factories which still try that method as a basis for motivating the workers.

Before a decision is made to adopt some incentive, the situation needs to be analyzed; then changes can be made that will preserve the good attributes of human nature while rejecting the bad ones. This involves *depth psychology* — looking beneath the surface of a person to see what actually lies behind complaints or to see what may cause stresses and frustrations.

8 WE ARE ALWAYS MOTIVATED

Sometimes we hear someone say, "George would be a good worker if he only had some motivation." But he does have motivation. People always do. The trouble is that George is not motivated in the way his boss wishes he were.

There is always unfinished business where motives are concerned. It is different with a reflex, which is an immediate reaction to a stimulus. As soon as the reflex stimulus is removed, the machine (the body) comes to rest — except in rare instances, such as an attack of hiccups, where the response acts as a stimulus for another response. Such circular reflexes require some strong stimulus, like a fright, to break the circle.

Biological needs are intermittent, coming and going as bodily conditions change. Eating allays hunger. As Seneca wrote around A.D. 30: "The stomach begs and clamors, and listens to no precepts. And yet it is not an obdurate creditor; for it is dismissed with a small payment if you give it only what you owe and not as much as you can."

Motives, in contrast, are fairly continuous and persist in the dreams of sleep. Motives last. Motivated action is ongoing action.

As the first goal is approached, motives shift somewhat, but they do not dissolve into nothingness. A young woman studied typing to earn money in congenial surroundings so that she could buy nicer clothes than an older and more favored sister was able to buy. Then she studied shorthand at night to become a private secretary and further boost her self-esteem. Then she set up her own direct-mail service to become her own boss. She expanded this business to send her children to a better school than her sister's children attended. Her motives really did not shift much, when you examine them, since in all these successive goals, the motive was to excel the older sister, of whom she was jealous.

This ongoing nature of motives merits emphasis. People have continuing wants. Their self-regard needs to be fed continuously. Sporadic attempts to feed the self-regard of others are not enough. Satisfactions need to be in the atmosphere, to be the spirit of the establishment or the home.

Good human relations cannot be retained by "kiss-'em-and-leave-'em" treatment. People always have sensitive feelings, not just on Tuesdays and Fridays. Now you can understand why employees forget about the big Christmas bonus and desert the factory on the first day of the fishing season. What counts is not how well they are treated once in a while, but how they are treated continuously.

 MODERN INDUSTRY AND THE WILL TO WORK

These considerations bring us face to face with a question that we cannot evade: Does modern industrial and business life make it more difficult for people to fulfill the demands of their inborn propensities or needs?

As work has changed through the ages, especially for recent generations, much of the spontaneous excitement and happiness has been taken out of it. This is likely a potent factor in leading many people to feel they are not getting what they want out of life, although they cannot figure out exactly what it is they want. Better than asking people what they want is looking back at mankind's development for some suggestions. In his book *The Story of Man*, Dr. Carleton S. Coon has done this, and here are his comments.[3]

> Although we will not again be hunters, our biological make-up is the same as theirs and our biological needs were determined by natural selection over hundreds of thousands of years. We can live and work most happily and efficiently if we reproduce, with modern improvements, some

3. Dr. Carleton S. Coon, *The Story of Man*, Knopf, New York, 1954, pp. 421–422. Quoted by permission.

approximation to our ancestors' living conditions. A hunter needs space to move around in. He needs trees and grass and rocks and streams; he needs the presence of birds and animals, and the opportunity for exercise and recreation. He needs a job which is at times dangerous, and at all times sharpens his wits. He needs to be able to seclude himself with a small group of intimate relatives and friends with whom he interacts face to face, and his more formal interactions with larger groups must be kept within limits which vary with the individual temperament, but which are often exceeded in modern living. Above all, he needs to be able to make decisions on his own, not to have his opinions molded into a rackful of rubber stamps.

People who have primary personal interests that are not fulfilled by their jobs need to find some expression for these interests in their off-the-job hours. The same thing is true for their propensities, or wants; they need to be satisfied on the job or off. If a man's work lets him do things that fulfill his propensities, there need be no worry about his will to work.

Dr. Frederick Herzberg, who has devoted many years to the study of motivation both in the United States and abroad, and his colleagues have made studies of employed engineers and accountants that illustrate the importance of having work that can be considered fulfilling. The men who were studied had found their work a little more satisfying after the boss gave them a pat on the back or some compliment—but only a little more, and only for a short time. What had given them the most will to produce and what had had the longest effect was satisfaction with the job itself and its details. Better than a dozen pats on the back by the boss was to have good work recognized by other workers, to be given responsibility for planning and developing the job, and to have the challenge of some nonroutine tasks.

Work does not seem fulfilling unless it also seems important. There was one chemical plant, for instance, where it was difficult to keep workers on the easy job of gauge tender. Employees were promoted to this from the wearisome job of wheeling cinders, but in a few weeks they would ask to be shifted back as laborers. As gauge tenders, they had nothing to do but turn a valve a few times a day; most of the time was spent looking at comic books.

The gauge-tending work was glamorized. Names of the chemicals were printed on the pipes in large letters. A few lengths of transparent plastic pipe were spliced in so that the different-colored solutions, which blended together at this point, could be watched. Overnight the work changed into something that seemed worthwhile. The workers could see something happening, and chemical terms on the pipes were impressive, even though they were not understood.

According to Harry A. Bullis, who started as a bookkeeper with General Mills, Inc., and gradually worked his way up through the ranks to become its chairman,

1.12

Complaints

.35

Told job was important

Told job was unimportant

Data from Dr. Harold H. Kelley

Work does not seem fulfilling unless it seems important. When two groups of high school graduates were put to work doing the same jobs, the group that was told it had the best and most important job complained only one-third as often as the others.

A good share of our personnel problems results from the very nature of our mass-production system. Under the old handicraft system, a man made an article from beginning to end. He could look at the finished product and know that his own strength and skill had made it what it was. He took pride in his work. He derived satisfaction from doing a good job.

Today, pieceworkers often do not know the use of the part they make. Is it any wonder they become bored? The worker in a monotonous, repetitive operation must have some compensation for pride in workmanship. He wants recognition of some sort if he is to get any real satisfaction from his job. It is up to management to devise ways of giving it to him.

In a number of ways, many of the conditions of modern industry do not mix with human propensities. Trying to make adjustments for this lack of "fit" brings out many puzzling characteristics. The central problem of business psychology, as the authors judge it, is to adjust human beings, whose propensities are at least 5,000 years old, to making a living in conditions that have been changed drastically, without regard for human propensities.

What can the individual himself do for himself? He may get some ideas from the advertisements. But we prefer to recommend the following sage summary that Sir Heneage Ogilvie, a famous British surgeon, gave to some of his professional colleagues:

We make a great mistake if we think that happiness consists in having a forty-hour week, a smart car, a television set, and a chromium-plated bathroom.

Happiness consists in a job that provides a succession of varied and interesting tasks that demand skill and call for individual enterprise, that is useful to the community in which we live, that offers security if we do it conscientiously and advancement if we do it well, and, if not a belief in a future life, at any rate, a confident belief in the future that this life holds for us.

All these things the craftsmen and peasants of the Middle Ages had. All, or nearly all, of them we lack today.

10 MOTIVATION OF EMPLOYEES

How do companies get employees to do what they want them to do? Dr. Frederick Herzberg has come to the conclusion that the most straightforward way to move people to action—though not the best way to keep them going in the desired direction—is to use force. According to Dr. Herzberg, many managers feel that the surest and quickest way of getting someone to do something is to kick him in the pants, a process that is politely called "KITA" (*kick in the . . .*).

He describes various forms of KITA as follows:

1 *Negative physical KITA,* the literal application of the term— a real kick
2 *Negative psychological KITA*, cruelty that is not visible, such as making the employee feel useless by assigning some of his tasks to others
3 *Positive KITA*, offering promotions or raises in return for increased output

Many of us are quick to recognize that negative KITA is not really motivation. We must agree with Herzberg that "if I kick you in the rear (physically or psychologically) I am motivated and you move!"[4]—not that you are motivated and move. But why do we assume that positive KITA is motivation? Why do so many managers feel that just because we allow ourselves to be kicked around (accepting positive KITA) instead of resisting such action, we are motivated? Until we need no outside stimulation, we aren't motivated. Unless we *want* to do whatever we must do, we aren't motivated. The shorter workweek, raises, fringe

4. Frederick Herzberg, "One More Time: How Do You Motivate Employees?" *Harvard Business Review*, Vol. 46, January–February, 1968, pp. 53-62.

benefits, human relations and sensitivity training, employee counseling, and job participation are all examples of short-term, positive KITA that will not spontaneously create the will to work.

11 FACTORS AFFECTING WORKERS' ATTITUDES

In Chapter 4, we mentioned that Dr. Herzberg's studies encouraged him to distinguish between hygiene factors and motivation factors. He and his associates asked individual employees to recall times that they felt very good about their jobs and times that they felt very bad about them. The findings of their studies and at least 16 other investigations suggest that the motivation factors involved in "feeling very good about a job" (job satisfaction) are separate and distinct from the hygiene factors, factors that help prevent "feeling very bad about a job" (job dissatisfaction).

Herzberg concluded that if certain job conditions, the hygiene factors, were absent, the situation could make an employee feel bad; however, the mere presence of these same job conditions did not necessarily make the employee feel satisfied. The employees might not be complaining, but there was no generating force within the workers to make them feel truly satisfied with their jobs — there were no motivating factors.

These studies revealed a significant paradox: factors often viewed by management as motivators (fancy personnel policy, fringe benefits, high wages) are not viewed as motivators by employees. (Look at the lists prepared by employees and employers on pages 333 and 334 in Chapter 17, and you will notice that Dr. Herzberg's views are borne out.)

Dr. Herzberg lists as hygiene factors those items that are extrinsic to the job, such as company policy and administration, supervision, interpersonal relations, working conditions, salary, status, and security.

He lists as motivation factors those items that are intrinsic to the job (that are generated by the worker rather than the job or supervisor), such as achievement, recognition of achievement, the work itself, and growth or advancement.

The graph on page 375 is based on one prepared by Dr. Herzberg. Notice the factors involved in causing job satisfaction (presence of motivators) and the factors involved in causing job dissatisfaction (absence of hygiene factors), as reported in 12 investigations including a wide range of employees.

Many companies have been appealing to their workers' motivation factors by establishing job-enrichment programs. (This concept has also been discussed extensively in Chapter 4.) Of course, the hygiene

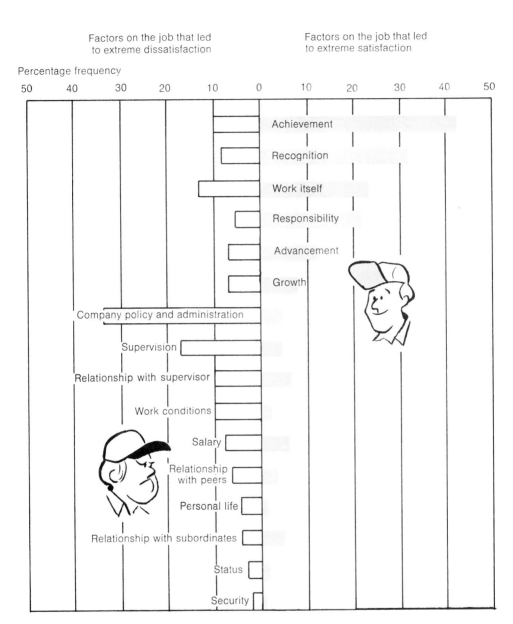

Factors on the job that led to extreme dissatisfaction

Factors on the job that led to extreme satisfaction

Percentage frequency

50 40 30 20 10 0 10 20 30 40 50

Achievement

Recognition

Work itself

Responsibility

Advancement

Growth

Company policy and administration

Supervision

Relationship with supervisor

Work conditions

Salary

Relationship with peers

Personal life

Relationship with subordinates

Status

Security

Key ☐ Hygiene factor

☐ Motivator factor

Data from Dr. Frederick Herzberg, "One More Time: How Do You Motivate Employees?" *Harvard Business Review*, January-February, 1968, p. 87

In 12 studies conducted by Dr. Frederick Herzberg, extreme job satisfaction was shown to be highly related to motivation factors, and extreme dissatisfaction was highly related to the absence of hygiene factors.

factors have not been neglected in the attempt to make the job more intrinsically meaningful and psychologically satisfying.

SUGGESTIONS FOR FURTHER READING

Argyris, Chris, *Integrating the Individual and the Organization,* New York: Wiley, 1964.

Foulkes, Fred K., *Creating More Meaningful Work,* New York: American Management Association, 1969.

Herzberg, Frederick, *Work and the Nature of Man,* New York: New American Library, 1973.

McGregor, Douglas, *The Human Side of Enterprise,* New York: McGraw-Hill, 1960.

Maslow, Abraham H., *Eupsychian Management,* Homewood, Ill.: Dow Jones-Irwin, 1965.

Vroom, Victor H., *Work and Motivation,* New York: Wiley, 1964.

TO HELP YOU REMEMBER

1. Why should a firm be interested in the social desirability of jobs it offers?
2. Give examples of biological and social or psychological needs.
3. List five psychological wants in the order of their effectiveness as motivating factors.
4. How did Dr. Cattell prepare his list of propensities, and what are six of them?
5. In your own words, compare the interrelationship between needs, urges, and wants to the structure of a tree.
6. Which parts of human nature change the most, and what usually causes the changes?
7. What point was illustrated by the story of the young women working in an embroidery factory?
8. What does it mean to move someone with KITA? What are negative physical KITA, negative psychological KITA, and positive psychological KITA?
9. Describe job enrichment.

WORKING WITH PEOPLE, DATA, OR THINGS

Donald Fancher, assistant manager of the accounting department, is worried about the morale in Anita Winkle's section. Anita is the supervisor of the payroll section. Donald has become increasingly concerned about (1) the increased number of absences of Anita's clerks and (2) a work measurement record that should be improving but is not. He believes that improvement is possible; however, he can't honestly put his finger on the real problem. Whatever it is, it is not affecting the other sections; they are performing very well. The work in these sections is always up to date and of good quality. Yet, in the payroll section overtime is required one or two nights a week. Donald feels that it is probably unnecessary overtime. There are indications that the section is not performing efficiently.

In a person-by-person analysis of the section, he comes to the conclusion that it is basically as strong as his other two sections. The supervisor, Anita, is a good one, as far as he is concerned. She knows the work as well as anyone. He does not feel that the problem is one for which she is directly responsible. As for the workers, they compare favorably with those in the other two sections. Donald has decided to conduct interviews, first with Anita and then with the other employees in the section, as opportunities present themselves. He arranges a talk with Anita for the next day on the subject of overtime.

DONALD: How did things go last night on overtime? Get caught up a little bit?

ANITA: We made some progress, but I know we're not doing as well as we should be. The girls seem to be holding back. They talk more than they should and aren't paying as much attention to the work as they should. As a group, they're not nearly as good as they were six months ago.

DONALD: Yes, I know. I'd sure like to know what happened. Do you have any idea?

ANITA: No. It's hard for me to find out what the girls are thinking lately.

DONALD: It is?

ANITA: I know it sounds funny, but the girls just aren't saying much to me. They do what I tell them to do, but they're not doing it willingly.

DONALD: That's strange. But now that you mention it, I guess I'd have to say there's been a change in their attitude, too. And you don't know what has been causing it. They all seem to be good kids. Let's see, there's Evelyn, Mary, Janet, Faith, Fran, Carol, and Elaine. Not a bad one in the bunch.

ANITA: Yes. Taken individually, each of them is a nice person. But, together . . . they can be troublesome and unpredictable.

DONALD: They get together. and their bad side comes out. huh?

ANITA: Yes. And Janet seems to be the ringleader. The other girls really like her. What she says or does has a definite effect on them. They pay more attention to her than they do to me sometimes.

DONALD: Well, we can crack the whip if you want. I'm sure I can put a stop to any visible horseplay.

ANITA: I know you can, but it may do more harm than good.

DONALD: What do you mean?

ANITA: If you talk about the way they act on the job, they'll figure I put you up to it. Anyway, I think I can handle that much.

DONALD: OK, you go ahead and see what you can do. But if they don't show some improvement in a couple of weeks, I'll have to talk with them and get them moving. (Donald thinks, "No need telling her that I intend to talk to Janet right after this meeting. It will only worry her. After all, I do have to get to the bottom of this and dangle something in front of their noses to get them producing.")

Questions

1. Do you think Donald is right in planning to talk to Janet without Anita knowing about it? Why or why not?
2. Do you think Donald's talk with Janet will get the workers moving? Why or why not?
3. What kind of motivation do you think Donald will use?
4. How would you approach this problem?
5. Would you say Donald's remarks indicate that he uses an organizational or behavioral scientist theory of management? Explain your reasoning.

THINGS TO DO

1. Look through several national magazines, and tear out three advertisements that appeal to one of the Maslow motives or Cattell propensities.
2. Collect incidents of rewards, threats, and punishments with which parents try to motivate their children. Classify these by the motive or propensity appealed to, and report on which seemed to produce the desired results on the children's conduct.
3. Discuss an incentive plan with someone you know who has a job. Does the person seem to understand the plan thoroughly? Does it seem to increase his or her will to work? Might the plan be more effective if he or she understood it better? Report to the class.
4. Interview an appropriate official in the public school system or in some large firm to find out what is done about the problem of vandalism. Has it been increasing? in what parts of town?
5. Visit either a worker who has recently taken a new job or a personnel officer, and report on what was done to help the worker get acquainted with other workers and adjust to the social conditions of his job.

DEVELOPING
A DESIRABLE
WORK CLIMATE

20

WhatThis
Chapter Is
About

1 THE HAWTHORNE EFFECT

The classic study of motivation and human relations in dealing with people was conducted in the late 1920s at the Hawthorne works of the Western Electric Company in Chicago, Illinois. This now-famous study actually got under way when the Western Electric engineers were trying to increase efficiency and production by installing better lighting.

The engineers were experimenting with the use of various levels of lighting in several workrooms and keeping track of the productivity rate in each of the workrooms. They then chose a special group of women and put them to work in a control room where the lighting was constant. The Hawthorne works study produced amazing results: no matter what the engineers did in terms of illumination, production increased in each of the workrooms, including the control workroom where the lighting had remained constant.

These amazing results encouraged the engineers to bring in a group of industrial psychologists from the Harvard graduate school headed by Dr. Elton Mayo. Dr. Mayo chose six women to continue in the control group and proceeded to continue a new series of experiments.

The team of researchers developed strong channels of communication with the women and encouraged them to cooperate in the study. Before any change or experiment was initiated, the women were informed and sold on the idea. Workers and management became committed to the experiments.

At first the workers were allowed breaks; the productivity increased. Amazingly, however, no matter how the researchers varied the breaks, productivity still continued to increase.

There was increased productivity no matter what the researchers experimented with. Even when they shortened the workday, productivity increased. A piecework program also increased productivity.

Professor Mayo could have been satisfied with the results of his studies at this point, but he wasn't. He could have listed all the factors — shorter hours, breaks, piecework program — as motivators, but he wanted to learn more. So he and his group began to pull the motivators away from the control group. The breaks were eliminated; longer hours were assigned; straight salary was restored; working conditions were forsaken. The result — still greater productivity!

Professor Mayo described this phenomenon in *The Social Problems of an Industrial Civilization* as follows:

> The major experimental change was introduced when those in charge sought to hold the situation . . . by getting the cooperation of the workers. What actually happened was that the six individuals became a team and the team gave itself wholeheartedly and spontaneously to cooperation in the experiment.

The team of researchers concluded (after 20,000 interviews) that the feeling of being important and "something special" made the women also feel different from their co-workers. As already discussed in Chapter 17, people *need* to feel like "somebody," and when and if they do, nothing can stop their efficiency and productivity. This is called the Hawthorne effect.

Many other studies resulted from the Western Electric experiment. One such experiment[1] involved maintenance workers who participated in developing their own pay incentive plan to reward good attendance on the job. These workers were part-time custodians who cleaned buildings at night. The workers were divided into three groups: the first group developed its own incentive pay program; the second group had a program *imposed* on them by management; and the third group continued as before. As it turned out, the first group's attendance was markedly improved, while the attendance of the other two groups remained the same.

An excellent example of participation by manual workers is the experience of an electronics manufacturer. When the company started production of a new navigation instrument, actual assembly time for the first few months was 138 hours, even though standard time was 100 hours. After three months of assembly experience the supervisor and the assemblers participated in a production improvement program which resulted in a goal of 86 hours for assembly. Within three months they had reduced production time to 75 hours, and at the end of nine months the time was only 41 hours.[2]

These experiments show that workers may be capable of much greater productivity than their employers expect of them. This capability can be realized if they are allowed to participate in management policy.

2 THEORIES EXPLAINING BEHAVIORAL CLIMATE

Douglas McGregor's "Theory Y," which we discussed in Chapter 4, supports the theory that the ideal behavioral work climate is one that attempts to attain simultaneously the needs of individuals and the goals of the organizations that employ them.

The following words of McGregor indicate that the real challenge of every supervisor in creating the climate necessary for getting things

1. Edward D. Lawler III and J. Richard Hackman, "Impact of Employee Participation in the Development of Pay Incentive Plans," *Journal of Applied Psychology*, December, 1969, pp. 467–471.

2. Robert I. Dawson and Dorothy P. Carew, "Why Do Control Systems Fall Apart?" *Personnel*, May–June, 1969, p. 13.

done is to integrate the *needs* of the employees with the *needs* of the organization:

> The industrial manager is dealing with adults who are only partially dependent. They can—and will—exercise remarkable ingenuity in defeating the purpose of external controls which they resent. However, they can—and do—learn to exercise self-direction and self-control under appropriate conditions. His task is to help them discover objectives consistent both with organizational requirements and with their own personal goals, and to do so in ways which will encourage genuine commitment to these objectives. Beyond this, his task is to *help* them achieve these objectives: to act as teacher, consultant, colleague, and only rarely as authoritative boss.[3]

McGregor's theory seems to be practical and in tune with Maslow's model of a priority of needs, discussed in Chapter 4. McGregor's "Theory Y" and Maslow's need priority model recognize that while human beings are unique, they must still live and act together in groups, one of which is the work group.

Unless you make some effort to study human behavior, you will never understand why people act the way they do, why people work the way they do, and why companies organize the way they do.

Thus, if you can understand some basic facts regarding the work behavior of other people, you will be in a better position to control your own work behavior. Mason Haire, in his book *Psychology in Management,*[4] summarizes three basic facts regarding the understanding of human behavior as follows:

1 The environment itself is not organized, and so people are faced with the problem of organizing their observations of their environment into a form that makes sense.

2 Human behavior depends on the way people see the world and organize their observations rather than on an organizational structure inherent in the world.

3 Human behavior is based on the way people organize their views of the world. If a person's organization fits his environment, his behavior can be successful. If not, he will fail. Therefore people are very concerned about their organization and understanding of the world.

From the foregoing studies we realize that the most satisfying work climate is also the most efficient one. This suggests that even if a person's economic needs are satisfied, he will still be dissatisfied if his work

---

3. Douglas McGregor, *The Human Side of Enterprise,* McGraw-Hill, New York, 1960. p. 152.
4. Mason Haire, *Psychology in Management,* McGraw-Hill, New York, 1964, p. 52.

environment is cold and formal. Therefore, the primary reason for presenting these studies and the ideas they reveal is to provide some underlying beliefs, assumptions, and premises on which to base some of your thinking. Perhaps you will now be able to develop your own theory regarding a desirable work climate and analyze it critically.

3 GENERATING FRIENDLINESS AT WORK

Many factors contribute to the relations that a person develops with his co-workers. Some of these factors are accidental or beyond the worker's control, but if he wants to generate a friendly work environment, he can apply his own efforts to the given situation. He can use the factors that *are* under his control to develop friendliness and help create the desired atmosphere.

The Human Climate

The human climate of an organization determines the attitudes of people who work there. Some companies have warm climates, and friendliness blossoms without coaxing. Others have cold climates that chill people's interactions.

The effects of organizational climates extend to after-hour activities, too. The Institute of Industrial Relations at the University of California found this after-hour hangover when making studies of office and laboratory workers for the Office of Naval Research. Some of the workers had a restrictive, authoritarian boss. Other workers had a permissive, democratic boss. The interactions at work were much more satisfying for those who had the permissive boss. In addition, those who worked with the permissive boss did more socializing during the evenings and over weekends.

Propinquity

We form most of our friendships with people who live or work close to us. The worker who is alone in a far-off corner will not have as many friends, as a rule, as the person who works in a group, where he has the opportunity to meet and come to know more people. Thus, *propinquity* (physical closeness) is a factor in forming most friendships.

Propinquity is usually accidental, which means that many friendships are formed on the basis of chance. Some people make propinquity less accidental by joining a lodge or moving to a neighborhood where there are people with whom they want to strike up friendships. Accidental propinquity, which is the rule, shows that friendliness can bloom between almost any people. Something may be wrong if we have to go a great distance to find friends. Potential friends are right beside us if we only are able to recognize them.

Well-Planned Work Groups

The size of the work group is another factor that is largely accidental, but it is a factor to be reckoned with. When there are only three persons in a group, there is every likelihood that they will soon divide into a twosome and a leftover member. Two become very friendly with each other, while the third person is left out in the cold. In view of this, some firms are now arranging work so that three-person teams are not necessary.

Interactions seem to be best when there are five to seven people in the group. (The evening will be a much greater success if you try to have as many as that when you invite the boss home for dinner.)

Similar Ideals

Similar ideals are a powerful factor for drawing and holding people together, according to experiments by Dr. William R. Thompson. He found that people who have similar interests and opinions and whose ideals are much the same are most likely to become close friends without trying. Authoritarians are drawn to one another, not to egalitarians, who have different ideals. High-tariff advocates are drawn to one another and "cold shoulder" the low-tariff man.

Warm Introduction

Warmth of introduction has also been found to make a marked difference in how people take to one another. It does not help initial friendliness in the least if a new worker is introduced as an expert, rich, widely traveled, or especially interesting. But it does help if the newcomer is introduced as a warm person whom others will like. The effects of the kind of introduction on women who were starting on a new job together are shown in the cartoon on page 385. These women had not met each other until they reported for work. The way the boss introduced them to one another made a great difference in their attitudes.

Personal Effort

The attempt to be friendly is often overlooked. Propinquity and the kind of introduction we get may be an accident, but efforts to be friendly to those we work with should not be.

Willingness to work together again

3.1

Cold introduction

4.0

Warm introduction

Data from Dr. Stanley Schachter

Warm introductions contribute to a pleasant work environment. In one experiment, three-woman teams were introduced negatively and positively and their reactions were reported on a scale from 1 (refusal to work together again) to 4 (enthusiastic response to working together again).

4 WHAT FRIENDLINESS DOES

An odd thing about this complex attitude called "friendliness" is that we can't take the friendliness of others for granted. We cannot even take for granted the friendliness of people we have never seen before, who surely have no reason for being unfriendly toward us. Because we can't take it for granted, we have to conduct our lives—and businesses—so that we will win friendliness.

When you and a stranger are introduced, for instance, both of you say, "Glad to meet you," or something similar. But do you really mean that you are "glad"? Dr. John W. Thibaut and Dr. John Coules tried to find the answer to this question, using young men of college age. The young men were hired for temporary work and introduced to their working partners. Conditions were arranged so that the experimenters could get information about how each of these men really felt when saying "Pleased to meet you" on this first meeting.

As the diagram shows, the majority did not have friendly attitudes on first meeting. This represents what we may expect when two new employees start work together. There is probably even more hostility lurking in the background when a new worker is introduced to some established employees, who may tend secretly to regard the newcomer as a rival.

When hostile impulses are uppermost in an individual, unfriendly feelings arise without reason. In some people, the hostility seems to be uppermost most of the time. In any of us it may be uppermost for a few minutes—when someone slights us or when we are criticized, for example.

One of the cruel facts of life is that hostility is always in the background in interpersonal relations. This is particularly significant to the business person. For instance, did you go back to buy again from that salesman who gave you an unfriendly brush-off? We all prefer to do business with friendly people.

The U.S. Air Force has also found that there is a significant relationship between friendliness on the job and the productivity of aircraft mechanics. The bar on the left in the chart on page 387 shows the strong influence between crew friendliness and output. The bar on the right shows how the friendliness between crew members and their boss had an even stronger influence on their output—not "palsy-walsiness" or backslapping, but attraction to the other person as a person.

We have had many examples of the importance of "climate" in influencing the attitudes and productivity of workers. This climate comes from human beings.

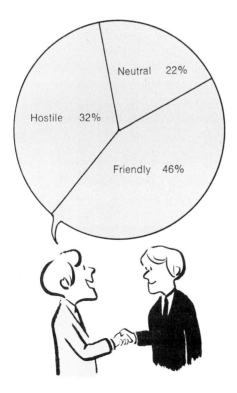

Neutral 22%

Hostile 32%

Friendly 46%

We are not always "glad to meet" the people we are introduced to. A study using young men of college age showed that fewer than half of them reacted pleasantly to people they were introduced to and almost one-third of them were actually hostile, although there was no visible reason why.

Data from Dr. John W. Thibaut and Dr. John Coules

.77

Correlation with output

.65

Rapport among crew members   Rapport between chief and crew members

Data from Dr. Hans H. Strupp and Dr. H. J. Hausman,
Human Factors Operations Research Laboratories

An Air Force study of the relationship between productivity and friendliness on the job showed that, although friendliness among crew members affected output positively, good relations between crew and chief brought even better results.

Companies sometimes spend considerable sums to furnish and decorate offices to give an atmosphere that pleases the eye. But almost always the human climate counts for much more in the long run. This is because the human climate shapes the *interactions* of people. Some people are *warm* and friendly. Others are *cold* and aloof. Experiments have shown that warm people and warm firms have the better human relations.

Morale is tied in with friendliness. Thus, absenteeism, which reflects low morale, is also tied in with the spirit of friendliness prevailing in the workplace. Managers sometimes think unnecessary absence from work is due to workers' irresponsibility. But now records show that playing hooky from work often reflects lack of friendliness at work, not irresponsibility.

Labor turnover is also influenced by the friendly spirit of the establishment. Recall that the average worker remains only 3½ years with one firm. Half of the workers leave before then, unconsciously hoping that the next place will be more friendly.

The success or failure of bargaining sessions often depends on the atmosphere in which they are held. Records show that time in sessions that failed has been spent mostly on unfriendly interactions marked by aggression, defense, or negation. How the first half-hour of one unsuccessful session was spent is pictured in the graph on this page.

Whenever we are dealing with people in any way, it is helpful to bear reciprocal action in mind; that is, we get back what we hand out. This is particularly true with friendliness, which lies so close to hostility in the deep urges. People in the lonely crowd feel frustrated trying to find friends and consequently react strongly to any show of unfriendliness. Often a person interprets as unfriendly something that was not intended that way. To be safe, we must let our friendly intentions show.

Data from Dr. Wesley H. Osterberg

The failure of one bargaining session could almost be predicted from this breakdown of how its first half-hour was spent.

5 THE BOSS IS A SURROGATE

The child wants attention, especially from his parents. When a child starts school, the teacher shares some of the authority formerly associated with parents; so teachers also become persons from whom children especially want attention.

When the individual goes to work, the boss is the person with authority and, consequently, joins parents and teachers as one of the people whose attention is much wanted. Thus it goes through life. We want to be noticed in general, but we want most of all to be noticed by those in authority as a result of our childhood conditioning.

The boss and teacher are *parent surrogates* (*sur*-o-gates), or substitutes for our parents. Any individual is especially sensitive to lack of friendliness or to signs of favoritism toward others from these surrogates. Realizing that he is a parent surrogate, the boss should make some effort to help the employees in the ways that a considerate and loving parent would help them. Most surveys have shown that workers work their hardest for the boss who, instead of prodding them to work harder, smooths the way so that they can do better work; the workers appear to expect this kind of leadership. Such bosses, needless to say, are usually considered promotable by their companies. This is the essential difference between the inspiring leader and the coercing boss.

6 THE BOSS'S "HOWDY" ROUNDS

Sometimes a boss gets too busy with "important things" to have time to get acquainted with the employees.

At a conference of some supervisors of a food-manufacturing plant that was faced with labor trouble, one could sense an uneasy attitude among the workers as the group was gathering. A whisper about it to the superintendent brought forth this reply: "It's because the general manager is in the room. It is the first time most of the workers have seen him." He had been general manager for 10 years, and conditions had been steadily going from bad to worse during that time. Some things might have been prevented if he had become acquainted with the employees.

A hundred miles away, a meeting of about the same number of supervisors for another food manufacturer took place the following week. This plant had no worry about labor trouble. The meeting was a friendly get-together, part of the educational program. The general manager of this plant looked like a battered prizefighter, but that appearance was deceptive. As the group was gathering, he introduced each man by name, told about his work, and added some individual esteem-building touch, such as, "Couldn't get along without John here." The supervisors in that second group did not feel lost in the crowd.

The higher the position, the fewer employees an executive works with directly. Top executives seldom work through more than seven department heads. Their person-to-person acquaintances usually are more extensive outside the company than inside. This puts psychological distance between higher executives and the rank and file, an unfavorable situation for human relations inside the business.

On the other hand, supervisors and foremen work directly with anywhere from 17 to 70 people. These immediate supervisors are usually so beset with duties that they seldom notice workers as individuals—until something goes wrong. Yet it has been shown time and time again that supervisors will have fewer troubles and fewer things will go wrong if they make an effort to notice employees as individuals.

Some 20,000 supervisors and executives of General Motors Corporation, for instance, were given a training course in human relations on the job. Conferences and individual interviews were held to stimulate these surrogates to make the "howdy" rounds—to visit each worker on the job for two minutes just to say "Howdy, how're things going?" to give each worker individual notice systematically, to get acquainted, and keep acquainted. A brief visit with *each* employee avoids signs of favoritism.

The boss who is too busy to notice individual workers when things are going smoothly is not establishing the kind of relations that will stimulate them to pull with him when there is rough going. The strong, silent person who knows the business from A to Z often makes the poorest boss because he fears his dignity will suffer if he notices people. The silent treatment is a prison form of discipline.

7 LEARN NAMES AND USE THEM

"Imagine! The old grouch! I've been here for 11 months, and he still doesn't know my name." So that worker has a hostile attitude because he feels slighted when his name is "You at the Third Desk."

Seeing your name in print in the company magazine may be flattering, but hearing it from the lips of others touches a deeper spot.

When a new worker comes to your department, introduce yourself to him at the first opportunity. Learn his correct name, and make an effort to remember it. Be brief, but do tell him that he will find the office a good place to work after he gets acquainted. New workers usually are confused and need the encouragement of such a positive attitude and a suggestion that their jobs have prestige.

Learn the names of the bus drivers, librarians, fountain clerks, and newsstand boys with whom you are in daily contact. It will help you take an interest in people as individuals, and they will give you friendlier service.

Before applying for a job, learn the employment manager's name so that you can mention it in conversation. To learn the manager's name, simply telephone the day before and ask the switchboard operator for it.

The direct-to-the-home salesman asks each housewife the names of her neighbors and uses their names when calling on them. The industrial salesman tries to learn the prospect's name early and use it frequently. The store salesperson makes regular customers of those whose names he learns and greets by name.

Friendliness rather than hostility is gained by successful trial lawyers when they refer to a client by name, not as "the defendant." As one veteran lawyer said, "Juries will hang an anonymous defendant, but it is harder for them to hang John Brown or Jim Smith."

Individually written letters that start with "Dear Sir" are cold. It is better psychology to start with a person's name, even though the letter may be to an impersonal corporation. People are not indifferent to the sight of their own names; indeed, it makes for a friendly reaction.

THE MARKS OF A GOOD COMPANION

We are in agreement with those who say that the priceless ingredient missing from modern life is satisfying companionship. Although we are engulfed by people, loneliness is rampant and causes much anxiety and bizarre behavior. Suggestions for achieving satisfying companionship are quoted from *How to Get Along With Automation*:[5]

> A built-in weakness that causes many to flounder in their pursuit of companionship is that nothing whispers to them that it is sincere companionship they are after. The propensity pushes them in the general direction of being with people, so they hurry to where people are—to the cocktail lounge or night club, if they can afford them, where the alcoholic haze makes people seem companionable until the morning after.
>
> Or, for free pseudo-companionship, to the airport to join the crowd waiting the arrival of some entertainment celebrity. A person can see and hear much there, and can feel a tinge of excitement, and perhaps exchange a few words with strangers beside him.
>
> But merely being with people gives scarcely more than a pseudo-companionship. It does not provide the deeper human relationships that

5. Donald A. Laird and Eleanor C. Laird, *How to Get Along With Automation*, McGraw-Hill, New York, 1964, pp. 341–343.

the inner man seeks in companionship. What satisfies this propensity most fully is a spontaneous and warm interaction between kindred spirits without pretense on either side—mutuality; it is like the difference between being with the crowd of strangers at the airport and one's brethren at a lodge meeting.

Not just occasionally, as at the lodge meeting one night a week, but through much of the day, in the home and on the job.

Merely working beside someone all day long in a modern organization seldom provides companionship, because he is more likely to be a rival for promotion in the system than a companion. And you are not working with him as a team toward some goal the team has set, but as the job sheet has set it.

Five guides to satisfying companionship can be extracted from the many recent researches in the field of group dynamics. These can tell you what to look for in the quest of satisfying companionship. And at the same time they can tell you what you yourself must be like, or do, to achieve it . . .

INGREDIENTS OF SATISFYING COMPANIONSHIP

Ingredient	Satisfies	Does Not Satisfy
Sincerity	Spontaneous attraction to the person or people; "I like them"	Pretended, forced attraction; questionable motives
Similarity	People with same beliefs, tastes, etc., as you; "My kind of people"	Divergences in beliefs, etc.
Agreeableness	People who do not criticize, boss, nag, outshine you; "Comfortable to be with"	Disagreeable, competitive, intolerant people
Continuity	Frequent association; "People who wear well"	Rare association
Shared goals	Work or play together toward goals they have set together; "Kindred spirits"	Rivalry or no goals calling for teamwork

More than at any other time since man has been on earth, he needs to give intentional effort toward making his relations with other people satisfying—satisfying to the other person as well as to himself, which means being a good companion as well as searching for good companions.

That we have been neglecting this is suggested by the fact that there is no one word in English meaning good companion. The Italian and

Spanish languages do have one in the word *simpatico*; the Germans have the word *gemütlich* for it.

To live with automation and like it one needs to be *simpatico* and *gemütlich*. We've come a long way from the farm village in our living standards, but our compulsive pursuit of happiness indicates that we have yet to start on the way toward becoming good companions.

As you weave more of those five ingredients of satisfying companionship into your own life and work, you can change a mere place to eat and sleep in near luxury into a "home, sweet home" and the automated treadmill where you earn fringe benefits into "a great place to work."

MOOD SWINGS

Life has its rosy days and black days—days when we are hopeful, days when there is discouragement. Sometimes it is not just a day; moods may last a week or even longer.

These shifts in mood frighten some people into believing that they are losing control of their minds. But shifting moods are so common that they must be normal. An interesting thing about everyday mood shifts is that they often occur in regular cycles. Some people have short cycles,

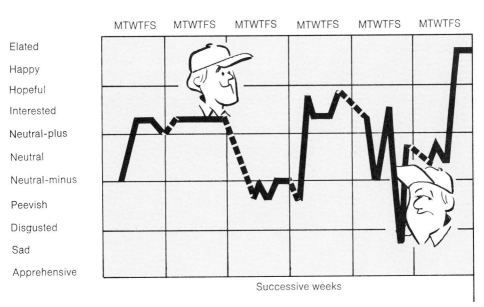

Data from Dr. Rexford B. Hershey

The mood cycle of Gus, a 36-year-old, married railroad worker, is shown on this chart, which records only working days. Dotted sections of the line indicate days Gus was absent. Note the one sad day which recurred every 6 weeks.

swinging from happy to sad and back again to happy in two-week periods. With others, the cycles are longer, and a swing takes about 6 months. With most people, however, these normal mood shifts go from happy to sad and back again to happy approximately every 4 or 5 weeks. The wise person anticipates his moods and works with them. A chart of mood shifts for Gus is shown on page 393.

These normal mood shifts are not due to the weather or good or bad news. What causes them is not yet known, though their regular rhythm in some people suggests that the cause may be physiological.

In gathering data about workers who hold rotating-shift jobs in factories, the Survey Research Center of the University of Michigan has found that, in many instances, the change in work shifts also tends to shift the worker's mood to the depressed side. We are concerned in this section, however, with the mood shifts that appear to be spontaneous and not caused by any discernible environmental factors.

Cyclothymia (si-klo-*thi*-me-ah) is a form of mental breakdown in which moods vary so greatly that the person is incapacitated. Such a person will be extremely elated, confident, happy, fast moving, talkative — until he reaches an almost maniacal pitch. After a while this cheerful mood is transformed into depression. It may take a week, perhaps a year, for him to change from the elated to the depressed period. During the depressed cycle he is sad, weepy, pessimistic, slow moving, unable to make decisions, often extremely silent. In this phase he is a picture of *melancholia* (mel-an-*ko*-le-ah).

Between the elated and dejected phases, there is usually a long period in which moods are not so marked. Since the moods come in cycles, the term "cyclothymia" is appropriate.

Each year, approximately 15,000 people in the United States have such severe attacks of cyclothymia that they have to be hospitalized. About three-fourths of them recover, though some relapses may occur. In addition, several times this number have lesser attacks that keep them from work or make them almost useless at work for a week or a month.

The most common cause of normal mood swings seems to be the ups and downs of a person's ambitions. The swing down into gloom is brought on by a person's feeling that he is balked in ambition and can do nothing. He retreats into a melancholy mood of discouragement. The swing up into joy is due to his feeling that he is not balked and can do anything — overcompensating.

People who swing high and then swing low tend to be the world's doers, not the shirkers. When in the elated mood, they are warm and make the human climate friendly. The cycloids usually have a sense of humor and high initiative and may be heavy smokers. Some become heavy drinkers when they feel a sad period coming on. Many periodic drinkers are cycloids.

10 HANDLING MOODY PEOPLE

The cycloid makeup is found in every occupation, but it predominates among salespeople. This is often the reason why a good salesperson gradually slumps and then comes back to former standards. Bosses have an inclination to criticize a worker who is slipping, but what the depressed worker needs is encouragement. The criticism may complicate the mental condition because it not only adds to the feeling of failure but also arouses hostility. It is silly to tell a person he has slumped; he already knows it only too well. It is better mental hygiene to remind him of a good job he recently did.

During the upswing in mood, the individual may be overly optimistic and take on too much work. Salespeople ask to have their quotas increased when they are in the upswing, for example. But too much work helps bring on the discouraged feeling that later causes a slip into the downswing.

The psychological moment to ask the boss for a raise or to ask a parent for the use of the family automobile is when he or she is filled with the optimism and general good feeling of the upswing. Daniel Boone made a rough-and-ready test to see whether the woman he liked was in the right mood before asking her to marry him. He cut her dress, apparently accidentally. When she took the damage in good spirits, canny Daniel popped the question. They lived happily ever after, partly because he watched her moods and conducted himself accordingly.

During the downswings of others, it is especially appropriate to pass out brief words of encouragement to them. When we ourselves are in a downswing, there is no better medicine than to keep busy at something that once seemed worthwhile and to recall some of our previous successes.

Apply for a job or a raise when in an upswing in mood. You will make a better impression then, and you will also be able to take a turndown with less damage to your ego. And if we really have to call something unpleasant to another's attention, let's wait until he is in an upswing.

11 PRAISE CAN BUILD

There have been no systematic studies of the effects of praise in business, but many studies have been made with schoolchildren. Without exception, it has been found that praise helps learning and increases the amount of work done. Praise, in short, makes people work harder and feel more cooperative—as any salesperson knows.

It has sometimes been claimed that office workers are more likely than blue-collar workers to be praised by their bosses. The available data, however, do not bear that out. *Dun's Review & Modern Industry,* for instance, surveyed several thousand secretaries and found that 70 percent of them said that their bosses often failed to praise them for a job done well. A survey by Arthur Kolstad indicates that about 60 percent of the bosses of blue-collar workers do not praise a job done well. Or to consider the figures in reverse, only 30 percent of the office workers are praised, while 40 percent of the blue-collar workers are.

This neglecting to give encouraging praise is often deliberate. The horse-trading type of boss believes a praised worker will want a raise and that faultfinding keeps the worker trying harder. This psychology is completely wrong.

The bosses of a company in the East were instructed to talk with each of the nearly 800 semiskilled workers employed and to give each one praise for some little thing. The management had expected this to bring a rash of requests for salary increases. In anticipation of such requests, a review board had been set up to handle them. But there was not a single request for a raise! Yet production increased, and rejections, absenteeism, and tardiness declined.

Praise is more effective than criticism in gaining desired results. Better than criticizing an employee for tardiness is praise for 12 days of punctuality before the tardiness occurred. Thus, praise can be used to emphasize a desirable goal or quality. Desirable actions grow best in a seedbed cultivated by praise and encouragement.

Tell the good bookkeeper that you admire the accuracy with which she can add in her head. Tell an employee that his interest in promoting safety is appreciated, not just that you appreciate his interest—period. Put a handle on praise by making it definite.

 THE VALUABLE ART OF "GOOD-FINDING"

You will not find "good-finding" in the dictionary, but it should be there. Good-finding builds human relations and individual morale. Faultfinding harms both.

Good-finding is an expression of optimism that gives others optimism. The faultfinder says, "Unpleasant weather we are having." The good-finder says, "Better than no weather at all."

The good-finder overlooks weak points and gives attention to good points. When he notices weaknesses, it is with a constructive attitude.

One manager used an object lesson to bring home the importance of looking for the good side in people. A small Oriental tapestry was hung with its face side to his office wall, leaving the unattractive underside showing. When a subordinate complained about a worker, the executive would point toward the tapestry and say, "Now, let's look at the good side of that person."

The successful executive does not think in terms of weak points. He asks, "How can we make best use of what this person has?" And good use of what he or she has makes a weak point unimportant.

The records used for the chart on this page indicate that the successful executive does not indulge in the form of faultfinding that is called "disputing" but lets the other person hold on to his faith in himself. Better yet—the other person is helped to build more faith in himself on the basis of accomplishments that count for something.

Look at a baseball player who struck out 1,300 times. That is a world's record. The same man also made 714 home runs. And that also set a world's record. Babe Ruth, who made both records, remembered and is remembered for his home runs, not his strikeouts. During his lifetime, he was the "Home-Run King"—also the "Strikeout King," if you want to emphasize failure. A sure way to fail in human relations is to emphasize faults, whether in yourself or in others.

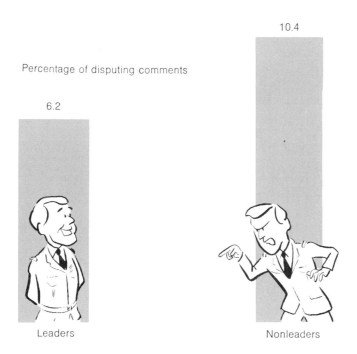

Percentage of disputing comments

6.2

10.4

Leaders

Nonleaders

Data from Dr. Thomas F. Staton, Air Command and Staff School of the Air University

One mark of leadership is the tendency not to think in terms of weak points. An analysis of conferences held among Air Force officers showed that those who had been rated as "leaders" by their colleagues were less inclined to dispute than those regarded as "nonleaders."

13 UNIONS

As we mentioned in Section 6, a corporate executive works directly with fewer employees than a foreman or a middle-management official. The executive is almost isolated from person-to-person relations with the average worker because of the size and structure of large organizations. There are, however, channels through which groups of workers can communicate with management about matters of common interest. For workers who cannot gain the boss's ear individually, unions are an important means of making themselves heard. The union can also provide social activity, political action, and educational opportunities for its members, but its main function is to influence the employer's decisions about employment conditions, particularly hygiene factors. The union's chief tools for this purpose are collective bargaining, which allows the union to participate in building the framework of employment conditions, and the grievance system, which keeps the framework in good repair by correcting actions that violate the terms of the employment contract.

Collective Bargaining

The success of unions in winning working conditions favorable to their members supports the old saying that "there is strength in numbers." The union provides the individual worker with a second formal organization, in addition to the company, through which he can communicate his ideas about the conditions of employment. Knowing that the union officer speaks for a large group of workers, the employer is likely to listen to what he has to say. The union is also an informal organization in which active members can influence the action of the group. The employee's dual loyalty to his employer and his union can complicate human relations within the company, but if the union is strong, the employer will recognize the importance of employee participation in decisions concerning employment conditions.

Unless those in management positions accept unions and their leaders, they have not fully accepted the business system. A stubborn, negative attitude could chill the human-relations climate in bargaining sessions.

Several tactics are recommended in order to make the human relations easier at the bargaining table:

1 Negotiators should delay negotiation by tabling especially troublesome issues.
2 Easier problems should be tackled first.
3 Difficult problems should be pulled out of the main bargaining session and referred to subcommittees (smaller groups).
4 Negotiators should use counterproposals to get the sides closer together.

After a contract has been negotiated, the collective-bargaining process continues as the union and company officials communicate the terms of the contract to their members and see to it that employment conditions follow these terms.

Grievance Systems

We have discussed in Chapter 16 the complaints that employees may have about their work situations, and we have considered the sources of these conditions and possible means of solution. If the problem is that the employee feels that he has suffered a personal injustice in his work situation, he has a *grievance*. A grievance system is a formal solution to this problem. When the employee files a complaint with the proper authority, the problem is brought into the open, and corrective action can be taken. The result may be that the employee has only imagined the injustice or that he is misinformed about employment conditions, but if the grievance is justified, the injustice can be corrected.

14 HUMAN RELATIONS AND EQUAL EMPLOYMENT OPPORTUNITY

Title VII of the Civil Rights Act of 1964, entitled "Equal Employment Opportunity," requires employers, labor unions, and employment agencies to treat all persons equally regardless of race, color, religion, sex, or nationality in all phases of employment.

Minority Workers

Dr. Keith Davis defines a less-advantaged person as "one whose background has deprived him of the capability to make normal behavioral responses in the culture in which he lives."[6] Often the less-advantaged person belongs to a racial or ethnic minority that is restricted to certain neighborhoods because of the discriminatory practices of the majority group in the larger community. If a person remains in his ghetto, he is unlikely to suffer discrimination from the people with whom he works and lives, but often the job opportunities of the neighborhood are limited. When the less-advantaged person, particularly the member of a minority, leaves his immediate neighborhood, he suffers a real handicap in the job market. He may be rejected solely on the basis of his background, and if he is given a chance to prove himself in a job, he may have to learn a whole new pattern of "normal" behavior — perhaps even a new language.

6. Keith Davis, *Human Behavior at Work: Human Relations and Organizational Behavior*, McGraw-Hill, New York, 1972, p. 311.

To correct this situation, federal, state, and local governments and some private organizations have set up special training programs for the less advantaged. In addition, Title VII forbids discrimination against minority-group members solely because of their background. These special considerations will probably have to be maintained for a long time to correct the deep-rooted problems that have been caused by unfair discrimination. However, minority-group employees who have found jobs in the majority community do not want to maintain their equality on the basis of special attention. In fact, special attention is unequal treatment.

The supervisor who holds each and every minority-group employee, as well as every other employee, responsible for his or her acts and work is developing the best behavioral climate for the less advantaged. One is equal only *if* and *when* "he is psychologically and socially accepted as an equal within the work environment."[7]

Women

Women constitute one-third of the work force in the United States, and they are found in nearly every business and profession; yet some occupations still do not accept women — some officially, some unofficially. We are accustomed to thinking of certain jobs as being appropriate to one sex or the other: a tailor is a man, and a seamstress is a woman. Yet these two words really identify people who perform the same job.

It wasn't until 1928 that women in the United States could vote for public officials. Even now, many stores will not give charge accounts to women without their husband's signature; many banks have the same requirement for issuing loans to women.

In some firms, when women have the same jobs as men, and the same titles, their pay scale is lower. But things are beginning to change. Various women's groups have been fighting these inequities, and civil-rights laws in many states now include prohibitions against discrimination on the basis of sex.

The role of women as homemakers has a long tradition in Western cultures. Therefore, wives who have careers outside the home are subject to pressures and assumptions that are not applied to their husbands. For example, a mother, rather than a father, may be expected to stay home from work to care for a sick child. Many employers fear that loyalties divided between home and career and the fact that many women consider their income a supplement to their husband's make women less reliable employees than men. However, absentee records of many firms contradict this belief.

The progress toward equality in employment, which has been more rapid and more widespread in the past decade than previously,

7. Ibid., p. 304.

has resulted in many generalizations about women as employees and managers being called into question. Changing conditions make it difficult to compare data and draw lasting conclusions. However, for the individual worker, male as well as female, the decline of sexual stereotypes has the great advantage of encouraging employers to hire and evaluate employees on the basis of their unique personal characteristics.

Older Workers

The Age Discrimination section of the Employment Act of 1967 adds age as a characteristic for which discrimination is prohibited. People aged 40 to 65 are covered by the law.

Since older people need to feel secure in being a "part of things," management and workers need to build a behavioral climate that accepts and integrates older workers.

Older workers' greatest adjustment comes at around age 60, or when they face the stark realization that there are no more promotions in store for them. At this time, job satisfaction tends to decline because the opportunities for self-realization are blocked.

The successful manager is compassionate toward the older workers and recognizes certain factors regarding their behavior:

Older workers may need "job engineering" (revisions in duties or procedures to make the job physically less taxing).

Older workers may be reluctant to learn new skills, realizing that they will have little time to apply them.

Older workers may be more impressed with hygiene factors — pensions, hospitalization plans, and investment plans — than with motivation factors, such as opportunity and self-realization.

Older workers may need more reassurance about the quality of their work than younger workers. A thoughtful manager reminds the older workers that they are still useful employees.

Many organizations have a rule about a mandatory retirement age. This rule protects the organization from the decline in productivity of the person who is slowed down by old age. Also, employment opportunities for younger workers are opened up by the retirement of the older ones.

These advantages do not directly benefit the older worker himself, however, and he may resent being "put out to pasture," especially if retirement is forced on him while he is still healthy and alert. There are many people who have made significant contributions to society in their later years. The English historian Arnold Toynbee was over 45 when his *Study of History* was published. Paul Gauguin, the nineteenth-century French artist, did not begin his painting career until he was past 40, and

Anna Mary Robertson Moses was known as "Grandma" Moses because she was in her 70s when she began to paint. Many judges, senators, and other government officials continue to work beyond retirement age. They simply become "elder statesmen."

With such examples before them, older workers may understandably find retirement unappealing. It is a wisely conceived company policy that provides respect and security for older employees after they leave their jobs and can make retirement a reward for their years of work.

SUGGESTIONS FOR FURTHER READING

Drucker, Peter, *The Practice of Management,* New York: Harper & Row, 1954.

Kepner, C. H., and B. B. Tregoe, *The Rational Manager: A Systematic Approach to Problem Solving and Decision Making,* New York: McGraw-Hill, 1965.

Lindgren, Henry Clay, and S. Donn Byrne, *Psychology: An Introduction to a Behavioral Science,* New York: Wiley, 1971.

Mayo, Elton, *The Social Problems of an Industrial Civilization,* Cambridge, Mass.: Harvard Business School, 1945.

TO HELP YOU REMEMBER

1. What is the Hawthorne effect, and what did it prove?
2. How do McGregor's Theory Y and Maslow's need priority model explain the need for a favorable behavioral work climate?
3. Describe five ways in which a firm can develop a friendly work climate.
4. What is the meaning and significance of the statement that the boss is a surrogate?
5. What are "howdy" rounds? What do they accomplish?
6. What are the five ingredients of good companionship?
7. Describe "mood swings" and their principal cause.
8. What are the effects of moods on business decisions?
9. What are the effects of praise on workers? How is praise best given?
10. What is the purpose of Title VII of the 1964 Civil Rights Act?

WORKING WITH PEOPLE, DATA, OR THINGS

Aaron Jackson is the first black employee on the sales force of the Western Division of the Crown Testing Bureau. Last month Jackson's supervisor, David Eden, noticed that Jackson had turned in one two call reports (reports about places he had visited to make sales) for a whole month. Eden was concerned, and so he called his boss, the sales manager, and discussed the report and Jackson's poor performance.

"Don't jump on him, Dave," said the sales manager. "After all, he's only been aboard ship six months. He needs time to learn the ropes. In fact, don't even discuss the matter with him. I just wouldn't want Jackson to get the idea that all the whites around him weren't even giving him a chance. The guy's had enough of that, don't you think?"

Eden agreed, and so he didn't talk to Jackson.

The following month, Jackson turned in four call reports. Eden looked them over and thought, "How in the world can I make my budget with one of my men making only four calls in one month? Well, I guess I can't complain. After all, he's 50 percent over last month's calls."

Questions

1. Discuss the nature of the misunderstanding that is developing with regard to human relations.
2. Would you have handled this situation as the sales manager suggested? If not, how?

THINGS TO DO

1. Interview a female manager, and discuss any human-relations problems that she may have had because she is a woman. Report to the class, and turn in a summary of your findings.
2. Interview a manager, and discuss his or her theory of management. Make sure that you tactfully probe and attempt to determine whether the manager leans toward the Theory X or Theory Y management style. Report to the class, giving examples to support your conclusions, and turn in a summary of your findings.
3. Visit a large company, and discuss any human-relations problems it may have encountered in practicing equal employment opportunity and how it is attempting to solve them. Report to the class, and turn in a summary of your findings.
4. Visit a large company that is unionized, and talk to a union leader and one member of the management team. Discuss human-relations problems with each of them, and try to determine their working relationship. Report to the class, and hand in a summary of your findings.

PART 5

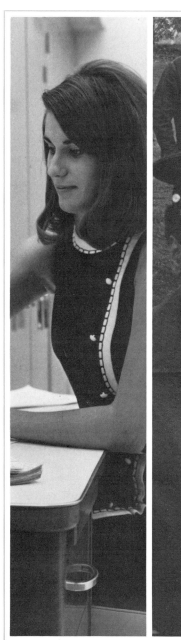

LEADERSHIP

21

What This Chapter Is About

Many people think of leadership in abstract terms — something mysterious and attainable only by extraordinary people. This may·be true for great leaders like Abraham Lincoln, Winston Churchill, and John F. Kennedy, who had an unusual ability to arouse people to do great things. They had the ability to transform the objectives of their followers into realizable goals and to inspire the sacrifice and hard work needed to accomplish these goals. This type of leadership is *charismatic*, which means "gifted."

President Kennedy's famous words in his inaugural address, "Ask not what your country can do for you, but what you can do for your country," expresses his appeal for the personal dedication of individual American citizens to the purposes of the nation. The enthusiastic response of the public to such programs as the Peace Corps is an example of the response of the followers of this charismatic leader.

Although the leaders of a business organization need the support and confidence of their followers, they do not require the gifts of charismatic leadership in order to inspire the cooperation of those who follow.

Marvin Bower, the Managing Director of McKinsey and Company, Inc., once said, "Given a chief executive with the will to manage, most system-managed companies[1] can attract a reasonable proportion of high-caliber people and from them develop the leaders they need for success. It doesn't quite come about automatically, but it is fairly likely to happen if the system is followed."[2] Bower feels that if an above-average worker is guided by the company's system, his own economic and emotional self-interest in his work will naturally bring out his leadership abilities.

At times a leader must be able to call forth feelings of personal concern from those under him in the interest of some objective to be achieved. This can be done by a personal appeal or by setting up a condition that brings out "team" effort on the part of the workers. We saw this in Chapter 20, in the discussion of the Hawthorne effect, which increased production by means of a feeling of teamwork rather than by improved lighting. The business manager has to appeal to the workers' psychological needs for esteem and self-realization to obtain his objectives. He has to show the workers that their work toward the achievement of the company's goals is in their own interest.

1. A system-managed company has an established procedure or system for conducting its business and built-in methods by which information about this system can be easily communicated to all parts of the company.
2. Marvin Bower, *The Will to Manage,* McGraw-Hill, New York, 1966, p. 251.

2 THE "BORN LEADER" THEORY

Some people seem to be "born leaders" because they were lucky as youngsters and started leading others in a way that made others want to follow. These young leaders had more practice month by month in leading—while others had more practice as followers.

Charles H. Percy, who became president of Bell & Howell Company at the age of 29, provides a good example of practice in leadership. He started his career at the age of 5 by selling magazines. This was not for boyish fun; it was a necessity. He had other boys working for him when he was 8, thus gaining practice in supervising others. Through most of his years in grade school, he captained his grade's baseball team—and this was more practice in leading others. In high school he supervised the distribution of a newspaper in his suburb and ran a parking lot at night. He started college with savings of $50, yet he went through and actually made money by using his experience in leadership to organize a purchasing agency for fraternity supplies.

In 1943, at age 23, Percy was elected to the board of directors of Bell & Howell, and 6 years later he became president of the company upon the death of President Joseph H. McNabb. By the time he ran for the U.S. Senate in 1966, Percy had some 41 years' experience as a leader in both business and civic affairs—more leadership experience than most executives twice his age.

Shirley Chisholm was the first black woman ever elected to the U.S. House of Representatives. She was born into a poor family, but she had a natural gift for leadership, and she was able to persuade people in the black community of Bedford-Stuyvesant in Brooklyn, her home, to do things to help themselves. From 1953 to 1959 she was director of the large Hamilton-Madison Child Care Center in lower Manhattan. By this time she had become an authority on childhood education and welfare. She took the initiative to learn Spanish so that she could work better with Spanish-speaking children and their parents. Her ability as a leader carried her forward and upward—she became educational consultant in the Division of Day Care of the New York City Bureau of Child Welfare. Mrs. Chisholm began to be more and more involved in community and civic activities, and this eventually led to her career in politics. She is extremely careful and thoughtful in decision making, but once she has made up her mind to do something, she works relentlessly toward her objective. Her persistence, honesty, and forthrightness are indeed true leadership qualities.

Another great among American leaders is Cesar Estrada Chavez, who was called "one of the heroic figures of our time" by the late Robert F. Kennedy. He is truly a charismatic leader who has dedicated himself to bettering the lives of his fellow Mexican-Americans, particularly those who are farm workers in California. He defied orthodox labor by orga-

Shirley Chisholm, the first black woman ever to be elected to the U.S. House of Representatives, has shown true leadership qualities.

nizing the United Farm Workers. Fred Ross, who organized the self-help Community Service Organization (CSO) in Southern California for poor Mexicans, described Chavez as "potentially the best grass-roots leader I had ever run into." Chavez has also involved himself in politics by leading voter-registration drives. He learned how to recruit members and develop leadership for the CSO. Chavez has been described as having a "messianic quality"; he is a very quiet, thoughtful man, but he evokes in his followers love, loyalty, and a sense of dedication. He has always stressed nonviolence and shuns giving people direct orders. Chavez knows his supporters intimately because he is one of them, and he has worked with them. He, probably more than anyone else, knows their needs, values, and goals.

The theory that there are born leaders was widely accepted in the nineteenth century. It seemed that leadership was passed from parents to children in certain families, along with the color of hair and eyes. Actually, environment, more than heredity, was often the source of leadership in these families. At a time when social barriers were very strong and when business was often a family enterprise, the leadership role could be passed from one generation to the next as part of the family business. The children of the wealthy and influential could be trained to lead.

As leaders from poor families and minority groups gained national prominence, the born-leader theory became less popular. Although these people seemed to be natural leaders, it was apparent that their ability was not something that "ran in the family"; it was, rather, a personal characteristic.

3 THE LEADERSHIP TRAIT THEORY

Back in the 1930s, some behavioral scientists believed that leadership could be achieved through experience, education, and training. Thus, these theorists began to compile lists of leadership traits ranging from nervous energy to superior intelligence. It seemed to them that physical and emotional qualities could be recognized in the potential leader. Although this *leadership trait theory* survived for years, it became discredited because no two lists were identical, terminology was not well defined, and the ordering of traits varied from list to list. Nevertheless, while the theory no longer stands, some general leadership characteristics have emerged, and these have been tested. These leadership characteristics are intelligence, confidence in oneself, communication skills, and sensitivity to group needs.

4 THE GROUP THEORY OF LEADERSHIP

That there are differences among lists of leadership traits suggests that there is no single set of characteristics common to all leaders. Some modern theorists have therefore suggested that leadership does not arise solely from the personality of the leader but also depends largely on the followers. The group theory of leadership takes into account the leadership needs of the group of followers at the time when the leader emerges.

The rise to power of Charles de Gaulle is a case in which the group and the leader came together at the right time. De Gaulle escaped from France to England just before France was conquered by Germany during World War II. In England he organized the Free French, and he became the head of the French Government in Exile, which was supposed to be the true French government. He was so persistent in his objective of liberating France that Winston Churchill, the Prime Minister of Great Britain, referred to him as "my *cross* of Lorraine." After the war, when the French people were depressed both spiritually and economically, de Gaulle's strong leadership was welcome. De Gaulle was, as a consequence, able to unite his and the French people's goals in a common effort to better the country.

Abraham Lincoln, another political leader, believed deeply that a united America was so important that no sacrifice, even war, was too much to achieve this goal. He was able to convince his followers in the Northern states that his aim of a unified nation was also in their interest. He was a true leader because he had an objective, he knew how to accomplish this objective, and he was able to convince others that this was also their objective and that they should follow his leadership.

In business as well as in politics, the leader must convince the group members that he is capable of directing them toward a common goal. The business leader has an advantage over the political leader in that the business group is made up of people who have certain common interests. While the potential following of the political leader consists of a large, diverse population, the business group's members have chosen to join the group because of certain common goals.

5 LEADERSHIP IN SYSTEM-MANAGED COMPANIES

Marvin Bower maintains that a system-managed company requires less initiative on the part of a leader than other groups because the system provides the guidelines that tell what the leader must do to lead. The leaders in a system-managed company will take "the steps necessary to build, articulate, support, and operate the system. These steps, in themselves, constitute adequate leadership."[3]

Bower feels that the system gives guidance and leverage for business leadership in the following ways:

1 The decision to make a company system-managed is in itself a leadership decision.
2 The philosophy of a system-managed company includes a belief in basing decisions on facts and a keen sense of competition. These are leadership attitudes.
3 The system requires management to develop strategies and goals for production and marketing and to stimulate employees to develop alternate strategies and goals.
4 In setting up its system, the leadership plans company organization, standards, and procedures.
5 The management searches for leadership personnel for various key positions in the company. The system includes plans for training these potential supervisors.
6 Orders, advice, discipline, rewards, and all other communications are transmitted in order to maintain the established system.
7 The leaders inspire others to support the system by setting an example in their own behavior.
8 The job-training program emphasizes the contribution of the system-managed company to society.
9 The system reveals opportunities and problems that face the company.
10 The leaders must be ready to act if the system is not operating properly.

3. Ibid., pp. 256–258.

Since the needs of the organization and the needs of individuals employed by it are not exactly the same, there must be some way of encouraging workers to make a conscious effort to support company goals. The purpose of a company is to earn a profit by producing certain goods or services, and when a worker joins a company he should be interested in becoming part of the overall effort of the other workers to produce these goods or services. Even if a company is run on a cooperative basis by members of the community, those who work for the company must unite their efforts in the interest of company production.

Three methods have been used to induce the cooperation of workers. These are (1) using coercion, (2) giving rewards, and (3) encouraging commitment.

Coercion

Coercion means controlling people by threatening them in some way, usually by physical punishment of some kind. This method appeals to fear; intimidation is used to enforce unquestioning obedience.

In one instance, relatively unskilled workers in a factory were paid high wages, yet they were restless and went on strike about every 18 months. One cause of this restlessness was visible. On a wall in each workroom was a sign as big as a desk top containing the shop rules displayed in type the size of newspaper headlines. This sign also gave the penalties, such as days of layoff, for breaking the rules. Hitting a foreman called for immediate discharge. This firm was trying to lead by shouting in big type, "Do as we tell you or take the consequences."

The use of coercion tends to harden workers so that they become accustomed to rough handling. The coercive leader has to bully workers to get anything accomplished, and the workers themselves will always anticipate being bullied into getting things done. Thus, coercive techniques become part of a vicious cycle that cannot be abruptly broken. A year or so of democratic leadership is usually required before workers can break their old habit of waiting until they are given stiff pushes.

Leadership methods are seldom the reason given for a strike, but resentment toward these methods may be a background cause. This was shown in a study of a West Coast strike. The workers in one company had been on strike over wages and seniority. A similar company in the same locality was not on strike. Groups of workers from both companies were interviewed individually, and their attitudes toward their bosses were recorded. As the chart on page 413 shows, many more strikers than nonstrikers were dissatisfied with the leadership they had at work.

Percentage dissatisfied with leadership

51

39

Strikers

Nonstrikers

Data from Dr. John James

Poor leadership can often be a background cause for strikes. Individual interviews with groups of workers from two neighboring companies showed that more workers from the company which was on strike were dissatisfied with their boss than were workers from the company where there was no strike.

Both groups of workers were uncertain about their bosses getting any better, although the nonstrikers were more hopeful. Both groups also thought it would be at least 4 years before their bosses showed any improvement. And both groups felt quite strongly about their bosses.

If you recall McGregor's Theory X (see Chapter 4), you should be able to relate coercive methods to this theory. Those king-size shop rules listing penalties were an example of coercive measures advocated in Theory X, based on its premise that since people inherently dislike work, management must threaten them with punishment to ensure action. You may also relate coercive measures to Herzberg's KITA technique (see Chapter 19).

Rewards

The use of rewards such as raises, bonuses, goods, or services is more subtle than coercion. In one company, the workers are given pamphlets listing rewards for good work and high production. For example, the workers are given two and one-half days' extra vacation with pay if they are not tardy for six months and an extra full week's vacation if they are not tardy for a year. You may relate this method of dealing with workers to Herzberg's concept of "positive psychological KITA" (Chapter 19). The workers move because they "kick" themselves by saying, "I am not going to be late for work for six months because I want to get those extra two and one-half days of vacation with pay."

Commitment

Commitment on the part of the workers occurs when the objectives of the company are *meshed* with those of the workers. For example, the newly appointed president of a small Midwestern firm that produced snowmobiles was able to increase his annual output by 40 percent by installing a system of group goals to be accomplished in each department. Every member of a department participated in setting the goals. Thus the challenge to achieve the goals became a *commitment*, and the goals were *achievable*. You may relate this commitment technique to McGregor's humanistic approach to management described in his Theory Y (Chapter 4). He believes that control is achieved through conviction, which is attained by uniting the needs of the workers with those of the company. You will recall that Theory Y proposed an integration of the employees' needs and the organization's aims. You may also recognize the group goal-setting approach as an example of the motivation factors, recognition and responsibility, described by Herzberg (Chapter 19).

 ## FORMAL AND INFORMAL LEADERSHIP

Amitai Etzioni wrote, "The power of an organization to control its members usually rests in a specific position, person, or a combination of both."[4] In other words, authority is carried by a specific job title, such as "President," "Manager," or "Supervisor," and by the person who assumes the title. Etzioni goes on to say that an "individual whose power is chiefly derived from his organizational position is referred to as an *official*. An individual whose ability to control others is chiefly personal is referred to as an *informal leader*. One who commands both positional and personal power is a *formal leader*."

 ## LEADERSHIP IN PRISONS

Etzioni further states that there are two kinds of activities within an organization that may require control through leadership: "instrumental and expressive." He describes the instrumental activities as those activi-

4.   Amitai Etzioni, *Modern Organizations,* Prentice-Hall, Englewood Cliffs, N.J., 1964, p. 61.

ties that relate to production within an organization and expressive activities as those activities that relate to interpersonal relations within an organization.

In prisons, where control strategy is almost always coercive or punitive, the control of work for the prisons (instrumental activities) is always the responsibility of official leadership—the guards are the officials. However, the control of inmates (expressive activities) is usually left to informal leadership—strong inmate leaders who hold no official positions but instead hold personal power over their fellow prisoners. Most prison officials rely on informal leaders to control the inmates, with little or no dependence on formal or official leaders.

R. H. McCleery studied prisons in which informal (personal) leaders supported "law and order" until prison officials, following a change in administrative personnel, underestimated the powerful influence of their informal leaders by trying to escalate the personal power of the wardens and guards. Unfortunately, the newly enforced leadership role triggered a riot.

It is relatively safe to assume from McCleery's study that coercive organizations encourage the development of informal leaders and that officials lose power when coercive means of control are enforced.

Almost all expressive activities (interpersonal relations) are controlled by the personal or informal inmate leaders. They "determine if and when it is proper to speak to a guard, which crimes are more or less prestigious (murders rank higher than rapes), and so on."[5]

Even the instrumental activities in prisons (distribution of food and work) are within the jurisdiction of the informal inmate leaders. Although food and cigarettes are initially distributed by the guards (the formal official leaders), such items are often redistributed by the informal leaders among the inmates.

LEADERSHIP IN SOCIAL ORGANIZATIONS

Social organizations are composed of people committed to the organization. Thus the leadership must appeal to commitment. Social organizations may have rewards, but these are not financial inducements, as in a business organization. However, most social organizations have some kind of formal leadership; even a bridge club sometimes has a president who is elected by the members because there are nearly always events to be planned.

The officers of a social organization are committed to taking charge of planning events and working out details. For example, a church group may plan a picnic. Leadership will be needed to decide on the date and location, collect food, arrange transportation, and obtain contributions. Churches also often have formal leaders, such as vestrymen,

5. Ibid., p. 62.

wardens, and deacons; some of these are honorary, and some plan how the money collected on Sundays will be spent, such as on the clergyman's salary or a new organ, or on singers for special events.

10 THE EFFECTS OF LEADERSHIP

Supervisors and other business leaders cannot be selected too carefully. Their influence on the workers they supervise extends to production levels, employee turnover, absenteeism, and accident rates.

Leadership Affects Production

The Industrial Health Research Board of Great Britain conducted an experiment intended to determine the efficiency of several different makes of typewriters. Experienced typists used one model for a year, and then they used another model for the next year. Toward the end of the year it appeared that the typists using a certain model were in the lead. Then they continued using the same machines, but the supervisors were switched. It seemed that under supervisor J. C., every typist improved her speed, even those using older models. But supervisor P. H. was a nervous person, and consequently the output of those who worked under P. H. was decreased. Thus, the leadership of the supervisors had more effect on output than the machines.

Leadership Affects Turnover

The records of two small factories in the same town show that the boss's leadership affects labor turnover. These competing plants made the same product, paid the same wages, and were generally very similar except for their general managers. The general manager in one of these factories inspired the workers' cooperation; labor turnover in his plant was about 15 percent a year. But the manager in the other plant was a coercive sledgehammer type of leader—he ordered and bullied with a loud voice. The turnover in his plant was 55 percent a year.

Leadership Affects Absenteeism

Absenteeism due to sickness may also be affected by the type of leadership provided by a boss. Indeed, the remark "He makes me sick," referring to the boss, may literally be true. According to research conducted by the Industrial Health Research Board of Great Britain, 80 percent of the office workers in one department of a large company were absent one Friday during an epidemic of colds. The supervisor of this department was a chronic nagger, and the employees were glad to

55

Percentage of labor turnover

15

Inspiring manager   Authoritarian manager

A correlation between leadership and turnover was found by checking the records of two small factories, similar in every way except for the personalities of their two general supervisors. Turnover was dramatically higher in the factory that was run by dictatorial methods.

have a chance to stay away from work. There were few absences in the other departments of the company during the cold epidemics.

Leadership Affects Accident Rates

At the Industrial Relations Center of the University of Chicago, accidents were studied for 5 years in a firm having 5,000 employees. At the outset it was found that departments that had autocratic supervisors had accident rates four or five times higher than similar departments that had democratic supervisors. When the supervisors were switched, the low-accident departments had increased accident rates, and the high-accident departments had decreased accident rates.

Good Leadership Can Be Developed

In former times a company had to buy whatever leadership was available, and much of it was low grade. As a consequence, many companies inherited many labor problems that were caused by old-style bosses whose leadership was inadequate. But now, many modern companies are training their own people for leadership through a variety of new programs. They have given up looking for "born leaders."

SUGGESTIONS FOR FURTHER READING

Bower, Marvin, *The Will to Manage,* New York: McGraw-Hill, 1966.

Dale, Ernest, *Management: Theory and Practice,* 3d ed., New York: McGraw-Hill, 1973.

Etzioni, Amitai, "Dual Leadership in Complex Organizations," *American Sociological Review,* October, 1965.

Haimann, Theo, and William G. Scott, *Management in the Modern Organization,* Boston: Houghton Mifflin, 1970.

Likert, R. A., *The Human Organization: Its Management and Value,* New York: McGraw-Hill, 1967.

McCleery, R. H., *Policy Changes in Prison Management,* East Lansing: Michigan State University Press, 1957.

McGregor, Douglas, *The Professional Manager,* New York: McGraw-Hill, 1967.

TO HELP YOU REMEMBER

1. Does a business leader need to possess mystical qualities in order to influence? Explain why or why not.
2. According to Bower, how does a system-managed company develop leadership skills?
3. Was Charles Percy a born leader? Explain.
4. What is the leadership trait theory?
5. Describe the group theory of leadership.
6. Name the three means of controlling the participants in an organization, and describe each briefly.
7. How does Etzioni describe the instrumental and expressive activities of organizations?
8. Describe the difference between formal and informal leaders.
9. What is the relationship between leadership and output, turnover, absenteeism, and accident rates?

WORKING WITH PEOPLE, DATA, OR THINGS

The biggest event for the employees of the Lather Company, located in a small town in Minnesota, is the company's Christmas party. The food is lavish, cocktails are served, and there is good music.

The president of the company has decided to eliminate the Christmas party because the parties seem to be getting out of hand. Last year many of the employees made fools of themselves. After the party, one of the employees slipped on some ice while getting into his car and broke his ankle. Efforts to collect medical benefits and loss of working time by the injured person are still not settled.

A memorandum was issued, stating that the Christmas party was to be terminated. The announcement was received with great disappointment. It became the topic of office gossip. Staff members criticized the decision as being a mistake and thought the president should reconsider. They brought their criticisms to John Jacobs, the plant foreman and one of the company's informal leaders. They asked him to speak to the company president, Robert Daniels, and tell him that the party has been a traditional event that is anticipated and enjoyed by the employees and that nothing could replace it. They wanted John to tell Mr. Daniels that the party should be reinstated because of the morale factor involved when he eliminated the practice without consulting the employees.

Questions

1. What kind of executive leadership is reflected in Mr. Daniels's decision to eliminate the Christmas party? Explain.
2. Do you feel the party should be continued? If so, what recommendation would you suggest to the management of the Lather Company?
3. What responsibility does John Jacobs, as a recognized informal leader, have to his fellow employees?
4. How would you have tackled the problem of eliminating a popular employee social function?

THINGS TO DO

1. Get organization charts from local firms as well as from a school, a library, and a hospital. Note the number of jobs at each level and the number of levels.
2. Study the biography of a great statesman, and make note of incidents in which the person assumed a leadership role. How did the person rise to the position of leader? Present a brief report to the class.
3. Observe a group of at least five young children who are playing together without adult supervision. Note the leadership methods. Take notes, and report to the class.
4. Clip news reports about a public figure for several days or a week, and attempt to size up the leadership methods he or she uses. Look for actions or quotations that may serve as examples of coercion, rewards, or encouragement of commitment.
5. Make arrangements to visit a mental institution, a correction institution, a religious organization, a prison, or a nonprofit charitable organization. Analyze its leadership functions, and determine if it leans toward controlling through formal or informal leadership. Present your findings in a five-minute report to class. Be prepared to support your views with good theory.

DEVELOPING A LEADERSHIP STYLE

22

What This Chapter Is About

MATTER TO BE SHAPED

> In examining the life and deeds of great leaders it will be seen that they
> owed nothing to fortune but the opportunity which gave them matter to
> be shaped . . . without that opportunity their powers would have been
> wasted and without their powers the opportunity would have come in vain.

You may recognize these words from Machiavelli's *The Prince*, since
they have been quoted often when leadership is discussed. These words
suggest that successful leadership doesn't come by chance but by
seizing opportunities as they present themselves. Most of the heads of
large companies, who didn't inherit their fathers' businesses, had to work
hard and grab opportunities to reach the top. But keep in mind the
famous General Motors message to executives and supervisors: "It
takes followers to make a leader."

2

SUCCESSFUL BUSINESS LEADERS

Fortune magazine completed a rather interesting study regarding its top
900 company executives some years ago and printed the results in the
November, 1952, issue. "The typical nine hundred man committed himself to the company he now manages when he was between twenty and
thirty." Three-fourths of the men interviewed had been working for their
companies for 20 years or more.
    The majority of men who lead the largest companies in the world
have reached their leadership roles gradually and purposefully. They
have come up through the ranks in their companies, and many of them
have been with their companies 20 years or more.
    Dun's Review and Modern Industry has reported that "the most
heavily traveled single pathway toward the presidential destination is
sales."[1] *Fortune* found that one in four reached the top through sales
and one in four through production. Other studies have shown that the
path to the top was through finance. But Ernest Dale says, "The truth
seems to be that a chief executive is picked according to the times and
the main problem a company is facing at the times."[2] Dale supports this
statement by drawing on the experiences of General Motors. William C.
Durant, the corporation's first president, famous for his "a car for every
purse" motto, was a promoter and expert at opportunities for mergers

1. Kenneth Henry, "110 Leaders of Industry Look at Their Jobs—and the Future," *Dun's Review
and Modern Industry,* July, 1957, p. 30.
2. Ernest Dale, *Management: Theory and Practice,* 3d ed., McGraw-Hill, New York, 1973, p. 746.

as well as able to capture the interest of investors. However, Durant had faults as well as virtues, and eventually in 1920 General Motors almost faced ruin under his leadership. It was really the du Pont Company, holding a large block of GM stock, that saved the corporation by appointing Alfred P. Sloan, Jr., to the presidency. Sloan was a leader-negotiator and had exactly the kind of expertise needed at General Motors at the time.

When the man who ran the war output program, William S. Knudsen, was appointed president of General Motors, an organizer and financial genius was necessary. Then, when the spark was needed to get the terrific postwar auto boom under way, supersalesman Mr. Harlow Curtice was chosen. Due to his efforts, General Motors achieved the billion-dollar profit figure.

The qualities that take one person to the top in one company at one time could ruin another company at the same time or ruin the same company at another time. All the General Motors presidents were different, and yet all were recognized as great presidents. They were chosen to do specific jobs—or, we should say, they were given the opportunity to lead. As Machiavelli so ably put it: ". . . they owed nothing to fortune but the opportunity which gave them matter to be shaped. . . ."

3 THE POWER OF OFFICE

The officeholder often wields authority by virtue of his office, even though he may not have much leadership potential. Parents, teachers, policemen, supervisors, and low-level managers have power over others chiefly because of the authority carried by their offices or social positions. But official position alone never makes a leader. The official position supports leadership, which, as we have seen, depends on more than a job title. Nevertheless, people often think that an official position will bring them into a leadership position. They are confusing leadership with authority; they do not understand that leadership involves a meaningful relation between the leader and those whom he leads, while authority, by itself, is purely arbitrary. Compare two parents. One says to a child, "Shut up and do what I am telling you to do." The other says, "Now, don't you think this is the best way to do it because. . . ." One is an "authority," but the other is a leader who encourages his child by helping him to understand why something should be done in a particular way.

An aggressive person often tries to get authority by getting an authoritative position. This type of person will be a bad boss because he just wants to "boss"; he doesn't realize that a little bossing goes a long way. He will only end up causing trouble among workers, and this will be counterproductive for his company.

4 THE POWER OF APPEARANCE

The symbols of office offer prestige to the wearers. For example, a police-man's uniform is the symbol of authority with its badge and pistol. Even doormen and elevator operators frequently wear uniforms that carry authority in their areas. And let us not forget the person with a white carnation, who has authority to take returned merchandise in the depart-ment store. Of course, there is a whole assortment of emblems of author-ity in military organizations.

In many factories, the lower-level workers wear overalls or other protective or informal garments that best suit their work, while the "bosses," if they are men, wear white shirts, ties, and suits. Thus the common businessman's dress becomes a symbol of authority in the factory. Of course, it might be difficult to detect rank among the suit wearers by determining who wears the most expensive suit.

Such badges of authority are especially needed in the lower ranks of leadership. Any slight superiority in clothes or uniform does more than give the appearance of authority. It also gives the wearer the feeling of having authority. It must be recognized that clothes affect the wearer as well as the onlooker.

Sometimes a person is given an impressive title but no authority to go with it. Will the title alone give him enough power to be an effective leader? What happens was found in a survey of some 8,000 employees of a metropolitan electric power firm. Some of the supervisors who made promises of better conditions—pay increases and such—had high-morale workers. But other supervisors who made just as many promises had low-morale workers. Further analysis showed that it was not the pro-mises but the power to make good on the promises that counted. The cartoon on page 424 shows that the supervisors who could get results with the higher-ups were generally the ones with high-morale workers.

5 CONSENT TO BE LED

By this time, you may have come to the conclusion that authority is not built into any position. The "consent to be led" is often overlooked, yet it is the real source of the power of position. Basically, most people want to be led and give their consent willingly—at first. But they will withdraw their consent if they lose confidence in and respect for those in authority or feel that authority has been overused or misused. People in various situations withdraw consent in different ways, as the following examples show:

> Teen-agers withdraw consent to their parents' leadership by running away from home or taking jobs in distant cities.

68

Percentage of cases when supervisors' promises raised employee morale

29

High-power supervisors   Low-power supervisors

Data from Dr. Donald C. Pelz, Survey Research Center

Findings from a survey of the employees of a metropolitan electric power company showed that employee morale was influenced by the power of the supervisor to carry out his promises.

Workers withdraw their consent by quitting jobs, by being absent frequently, by more or less ignoring the boss, by setting up their own leader as a steward, or by openly revolting or stalling.

Citizens withdraw their consent by voting politicians out or by ignoring unpopular laws.

Much recent research in group dynamics and social psychology has shown beyond doubt that the final power of authority comes from the group that is being led. Each work group has certain *expectations* of what its leaders should be like and especially of how these people should lead. It gives most power to—that is, follows most enthusiastically —the one who comes closest to these expectations.

These expectations are usually constructive and reasonable. For instance, workers seldom expect their leader to work beside them at the same kind of work they are doing themselves. They expect him to perform leadership functions, such as taking care of their complaints, helping to solve their work problems, and making good on promises to them; they work their best when he meets their expectations.

Seemingly slight differences between supervisors may make noticeable differences in workers' attitudes. That is, although two supervisors may apparently be quite alike on the surface, workers may readily consent to be led by one, but not by the other. The result may be a considerable difference in output. This was shown by a study of 208 office workers in a Kentucky factory. The productivity of workers who had a favorable attitude toward their bosses was contrasted with the productivity of those who had a less favorable attitude toward their bosses. The cartoon on this page shows the difference.

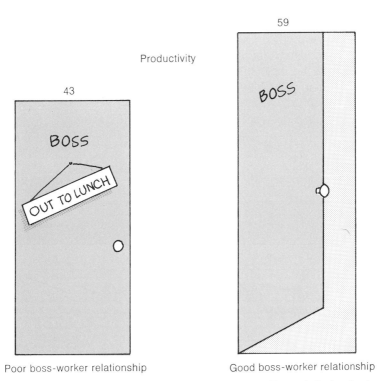

Productivity

Poor boss-worker relationship   Good boss-worker relationship

Data from Dr. Charles H. Lawshe, Occupational Research Center, Purdue Univ.

The relationship between productivity and good boss-worker relations was shown in a study of 208 office workers in a Kentucky factory.

Here are some of the favorable human-relations points that these workers sought in their bosses:

Being easy to find when workers have a problem to talk over

Not criticizing workers for things that couldn't be helped

Being prompt to take care of workers' complaints

Making good on their promises to their subordinates

Showing an interest in workers' ideas and suggestions

Giving good explanations of how to avoid errors

Giving sincere answers and no run-around

Discussing why work changes may be necessary

Having a certain position and a fancy title, a uniform, or a luxurious office does not necessarily indicate leadership. The power of position must be granted to the individual by those he is supposed to lead. Holding the official position is a help, but it is no guarantee of having real power.

Dr. John K. Hemphill analyzed 500 adult groups of various sizes, the average group having about 30 members. About one-quarter of the groups were in job situations. Dr. Hemphill found that the majority of people—more than half—thought and acted independently of the leader of the group. The percentages are shown in the cartoon on this page.

Data from Dr. John K. Hemphill

A survey of 500 adult groups of various sizes pointed out that most people do not lean heavily on their leader.

Knowledge wins consent to be led more readily than does mere position. Thus, knowledge gives force to leadership. People tend to follow those who obviously know what should be done, regardless of whether they are leaders or not. In a medium-size Pennsylvania bank, the employees virtually ignore the cashier, who is supposed to be head man. They look to a quiet woman who is a superb accountant as their real leader. There are many instances in which the person who has the position does not have leadership because he lacks knowledge.

There is the weak executive whose intelligent secretary or assistant is the power behind the throne, the one in whom actual leadership resides. The boss who is weak in knowledge or impulsive in judgment is often bypassed. The employees whom he is supposed to be leading catch on to his inadequacies and follow an unofficial leader, a level-headed person who has more background for the job and in whom they have greater confidence.

Some apprehensive executives weaken their organizations by getting rid of the unofficial leaders in order to preserve their own positions. Others try to maintain their prestige artificially by not hiring anyone who has superior technical or business training; they also weaken their organizations. Such tactics are varieties of cunning and are usually discovered.

On the other hand, knowledge alone does not make a leader. The strong leader who is going places is glad to be surrounded by people who have specialized skills and knowledge to contribute to the organization. He has knowledge sufficient to hold his position of leadership, and he knows that half-qualified yes-men can add to nothing but an executive's conceit. As Andrew Carnegie said, "The able executive is the man who can train assistants more capable than himself."

Lammot du Pont said, "There's one trick about management that I learned early. It is to surround yourself with men who know more than you do, and listen to them."

Capable assistants can push a leader up the ladder if he works with and through them. Two heads are better than one, especially when the second head has more knowledge or higher intelligence. The smart assistant pushes his boss up and follows him up.

Suppose you had the largest museum in the world and were moving its contents to a new location. How could you make the move with no labor cost? Charles Wilson Peale, a founder of the famous Museum of Natural History in Philadelphia, a painter, and a friend of Thomas Jefferson, had that problem when his specimens were to be moved into

Philadelphia Hall in 1794. Peale wrote to Jefferson about how he managed the move:

> To take advantage of public curiosity I contrived to make a very considerable parade of the articles, especially those which were large. As boys are generally very fond of parades, I collected all the boys of the neighborhood. At the head of the parade was carried, on men's shoulders, the American buffalo, the panthers, tiger cats; and a long string of animals were carried by boys. The parade from Lombard Street to the Hall brought all the inhabitants to their doors and windows to see the cavalcade. It was fine fun for the boys. They were willing to work in such a novel removal and saved me some expense in moving the delicate articles.

Empathy, as you will recall, is the ability to experience through imagination another person's feelings. Research indicating that empathy is essential to leadership is accumulating. The successful leader seems to be able to read the minds of his followers. By knowing what they want, he can coordinate their activities toward the goals in which they are interested and which support his own goals, just as Peale did. Full consent to follow him is a result.

This is illustrated by a study of some groups that voted for the members they would like to follow. One member out of five received no votes, not even his own; he was ignored by the group. Those who were voted leaders greatly excelled over the average members in the ability to know, without asking, what the others wanted from the group

Degree of superiority of leaders in judging group opinion

Compared with average member

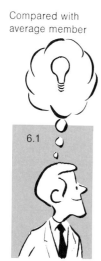

6.1

Compared with those ignored by group

9.0

Data from Dr. Kamla Chowdry and Dr. Theodore M. Newcomb

That the ability to judge group opinion is an essential leadership quality was illustrated when group members voted for members they would like to follow. Those who were voted leaders excelled in reading the members' minds on topics they took seriously.

activity, as is shown by the bar on the left of the cartoon on page 428. When the leaders' ability in this area was compared with that of those who received no votes, the leaders' superiority in "taking the pulse of the people" seemed even greater.

General recognition of the importance of knowing how people feel is shown by the widespread use of surveys. Morale surveys provide information about how a group feels, and they are often used in business and industry today. Public opinion surveys are being used by many political leaders, by some federal departments, and by many businesses to find out what the public (each follower) wants, and action is planned accordingly.

To a large extent the successful leader follows the group's aims rather than imposing arbitrary aims on the group. It sometimes happens that a labor official understands workers' aims better than management, and as a result, the labor leader often has more power over the workers than the official bosses. For this reason, many companies promote union shop stewards to managerial positions so that they will be out of the union and completely under the company's control.

THE SIX PRINCIPLES OF LEADERSHIP

It has been found that if the leader of a group employs six methods, he or she will best be able to mobilize the mental and social forces of the members of the group so that they will be motivated to work together toward the common goal of productivity with understanding and assurance. The cartoon on page 430 illustrates the six principles of leadership in order of importance.

A close look at this cartoon will reveal what you should aim for. Workers' comments, which illustrate the ways in which successful leaders function according to these principles, follow.

1   Sets group goals with the members
     "Our boss asks our opinions frequently."
     "He talks over changes with us."
     "The boss uses some of our suggestions."
     "He tells us about things that may be coming up."
     "We have frequent group confabs on work problems."
2   Helps them reach the group goals
     "My boss gives me help when I need it."
     "He shows he is proud when we do a good job."
     "He can help us on the technical details of the work."
     "He listens to complaints and takes care of them promptly."
     "He sees that we have good equipment and materials on hand when we need them."

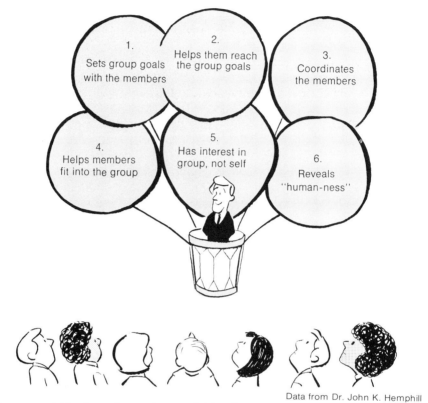

The successful leader performs six essential functions.

Data from Dr. John K. Hemphill

3 Coordinates the members
"Our boss delegates authority wisely."
"He lets us help each other."
"He gives us all a chance at choice jobs—no favorites."
"He lets us know how each of our jobs is important."
"He helps us work out things together."

4 Helps members fit into the group
"Our boss understands the way we feel about things."
"He is good at seeing that the right people work together."
"He made me feel at home with the crew."
"Our leader takes a personal interest in us."
"He gives me a chance to do the work I am best at."

5 Has interest in group, not self
"Our leader is usually pulling for us."
"My boss does not stand between me and the company."
"He is good at getting us overtime, transfers, and changes."
"He gives us sincere answers, and no run-around."
"Our leader will stick his neck out for us."

6   Reveals "human-ness"
    "Our boss is easy to see and talk to."
    "He is reasonable in what he asks, and in enforcing rules."
    "I feel free to talk over my personal problems with him."
    "He gives us a pat on the back when we do a good job."
    "I feel that I know him well."

LEVELS OF LEADERSHIP

There are about 5 million people in the United States who are in executive positions or other business leadership posts. Of this number, about one million have major responsibilities. There is one such leader for about every 10 or 12 employees.

These 5 million or so who are leaders in title, if not always in performance, are responsible for the work of others. Their responsibilities cover these three broad functions:

Getting things done

Keeping costs reasonable

Building group spirit

Business leaders of all levels, from straw boss to chairman of the board, have those responsibilities. In practice, most of them emphasize the first two and neglect the building of group spirit. When group spirit becomes so noticeably negative as to cause concern, they may blithely blame the condition on the times or on some other outside force.

The ability to meet the responsibilities of business leadership requires several competences:

Knowledge of technical details

Understanding of people

Planning and judgment

The leader at the supervisory level needs a good supply of the first two competences and some of the third. At the higher executive levels, the last two are more critical. Advancement to higher responsibility comes because of improved business judgment and ability to handle people, not because of increased technical knowledge.

Let's follow through and consider the responsibilities of the various ranks of executives, starting at the bottom of the ladder.

The Supervisor

At the bottom of the leadership ladder is the *supervisor*. Yet in many ways he has greater responsibilities than the chairman of the board. He is the immediate boss of one to a hundred workers. To these workers, the supervisor is Mr. Company.

In a contest called "My Job and Why I Like It," 47 percent of the General Motors employees who participated gave the "ability and consideration of my immediate boss" as a reason for liking their jobs. Only 2.5 percent mentioned the pension plan provided by the board of directors.

The supervisor—sometimes still called "foreman"—has a face-to-face relationship with the workers, and his decisions usually concern day-to-day problems and minor emergencies, such as rearranging work because an employee is ill, settling a complaint about poor tools, or devising some strategy to lessen horseplay. The supervisor does not set policies that affect other departments, although some of his ideas may be adopted by other supervisors.

The supervisor carries out company policies but does not originate them. He may not like a policy, but he is responsible for seeing that it is followed. Knowing the policies is part of the preparation for supervisory work; so is knowing the people who are affected by the policies.

The supervisor usually has considerable know-how concerning the operations in his department. Some supervisors persist in putting a hand in and helping out with the work. Others spend more of their time supervising—making sure that supplies will be there when needed, training workers, keeping in touch with related departments, taking a personal interest in the workers, building group spirits.

When the production records of 600 office workers were analyzed, it was found that the supervisors who lent a hand to help out with the work were mostly in the low-output offices. The supervisors of the high-output offices were much more likely to spend their time coordinating group activities and keeping the organization going as an organization, as the cartoon at the top of page 433 shows.

The supervisor has a great deal to do with the climate of his department, although he may be unaware of this fact and may not even notice whether the atmosphere in his department is tense or relaxed.

One way in which the supervisor can achieve a relaxed climate is by serving as a shock absorber for the pressures that come down from the upper levels of management. For example, when your boss's boss antagonizes your boss because production is lagging in your department, your boss should cool off before talking it over with you. Serving as a buffer and toning down the outbursts from above—and there usually are some, even in the best of places—are important functions of the supervisor, though they are often overlooked. The good supervisor should be able to "take it" without passing it along; that is, he needs to have a high tolerance for frustration.

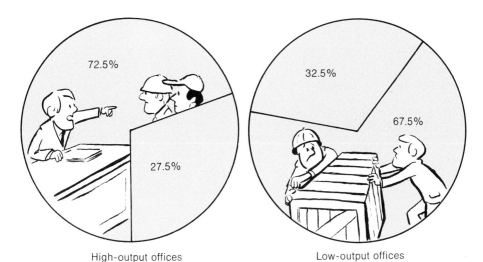

High-output offices   Low-output offices

Data from the Survey Research Center, Univ. of Michigan

In high-output firms more supervisors organize, coordinate, and keep the work going; in low-output firms more supervisors spend time doing the same work as the employees.

If the supervisor expects to have much influence on the workers, he must let them know that he is sincere in everything he does relating to them. For foremen, it is particularly important to have a reputation for being sincere and using no double talk, as the cartoon below shows.

Degree of satisfaction with conferences

Workers who believed   Workers who believed
foreman was not sincere   foreman was sincere

Data from Dr. Alvin Zander and John Gyr of the Research Center for Group Dynamics at the Univ. of Michigan

That a supervisor's sincerity improves worker morale was demonstrated by a study involving dissatisfied telephone workers. Workers rated their satisfaction with conferences on a scale of 1 to 3. Those supervisors whom the workers considered insincere were least able to relieve dissatisfaction by calling conferences.

The Executive

A wide range of positions is covered by the term *executive,* and some executives are paid ten times the salary of others. Sometimes, the title is given to a staff specialist who really does no executive work.

The executive supervises workers indirectly through the supervisors. The supervisor knows a particular department, whereas the executive is in charge of several departments and should know the business. The supervisor's job is to keep his department or section going smoothly; the executive's job is to keep the business going as an organization.

The executive usually leads by remote control. Most of his person-to-person contacts are with other executives and with supervisors. This makes many workers feel that the company is not interested in them personally. Although the executive may have personal contacts with only six supervisors, he can control several hundred employees through these supervisors. The executive talks with fewer employees but influences more of them than supervisors do.

The executive's decisions are concerned with long-range policies that affect a large number of the employees, such as a change from hand-operated to motor-powered machines, an increase in safety activities, or a longer lunch period.

The decisions made by the executive must be in harmony with the policies adopted by the company president or board of directors. The executive must also be acquainted with the policies of other divisional executives so that there is no conflict.

Some of the differences in decision making at the supervisory and higher executive levels are brought out in the table on this page. In general, the higher the executive, the more the items in the column on the right apply.

DECISION MAKING

Supervisory Level	Higher Executive Level
Many decisions each day.	Few decisions each day.
Few workers affected.	Many workers affected.
Decisions concern current problems.	Decisions deal with future problems.
Decisions made on the spot.	Decisions need months of analysis.
Decisions concern tangibles.	Decisions concern intangible policies.
Results evident immediately.	Results not evident for months.

The last item in the table reminds us that the supervisor has speedier feedback on his decisions. Usually, he knows by the end of the shift whether or not he made a good decision. The executive may not see the results of his decision for a year or more.

The executive may do some routine work and carry out some policies himself. But, if the business really needs him as an executive, he is worth more if he plans, organizes, and stimulates and lets others take care of the production.

The higher the executive climbs, the further ahead he must see and plan. As he moves into a bigger office with more bookshelves and overstuffed furniture, his face-to-face contacts with the rest of the organization diminish. His personal leadership may slump until he becomes just a name on the letterhead to most employees — until he is a forgotten man. His lack of contact with the mass of workers may lead him to overlook the human side in his decision making; his low empathy will diminish his stature as a leader. The executive should spend a definite amount of time each day maintaining his contacts in the shop and office, or he may lose his leadership position.

The Board of Directors

Questions of general business policy, such as decisions to move to another location, to discontinue a line of business, to lower wages or keep them up and skip dividends, and so on, are the concern of the *board of directors*. The president reports to the board of directors periodically. The directors of a company are trustees for the owners or stockholders.

Directors seldom have face-to-face relationships with workers, but they should have. The directors set the general tone of the business, which in turn affects the quality of leadership given the rank and file. Many of their decisions affecting workers are based on theory, unless they have visited remote corners of the business and have an acquaintance with employees and processes. Too many try to direct from a bank or club downtown. The directors tend to be a conservative force, tempering executives' enthusiasms and bright ideas.

The *president and executive vice president* are, in theory, the top officers who administer the policies determined by the directors. In practice they may be the real policy makers, while the board members are rubber stamps. In other instances they are office boys for the board.

As a president's work increases, or when he wishes semiretirement, some of his responsibilities are laid on the shoulders of an executive vice president. In such instances the title "general manager" is added.

Large companies may have several executive vice presidents, each in charge of several vice presidents. To keep a vice president from resigning, many small companies give the title "executive vice president" without making any change in duties or responsibilities. Others use the title to give prestige to an executive and make it easier for him to contact customers who may be flattered by being called on by such a high officer.

10 THE TEN CHARACTERISTICS OF TOP EXECUTIVES

In your previous study of leadership responsibility, you saw that an executive vice president might need personality qualities different from those needed by a supervisor. In a talk at the Columbia University Graduate School of Business, Chris Argyris listed ten characteristics of top executives that rated high in a study he had made. They are as follows:

1 *They have a high tolerance for frustration.* They do not "blow up"—or sulk—when things don't go as hoped. They can hold feelings in check and work enthusiastically for some long-range goal that they realize may be a gamble.

2 *They encourage participation by others.* In reaching decisions, they welcome participation by others rather than insisting on the acceptance of their own ideas. This demands the ability to both consider seriously ideas that they might not like at first and take some implied criticism of their own ideas.

3 *They continually question themselves.* They look for mistakes in their own methods or thinking but do not become upset over blunders.

4 *They are cleanly competitive.* They realize that other firms and executives are out to beat them, and they enter into the competition without a feeling of hostility.

5 *Their impulses to "get even" are under control.* They can take hostility from others without trying to get even with the instigator or showing hatred.

6 *They win without exulting.* They never get excited when they reach a goal or win a victory. They feel good about it, but they are not carried away in a spirit of triumph.

7 *They lose without moping.* They are good losers as well as considerate winners. A setback on one goal does not cause them to give up on other goals.

8 *They recognize legal restrictions.* They recognize restrictions imposed by laws and agreements that make it more difficult to reach some of their goals, but they do not feel that these limitations mean that someone is out to get them.

9 *They are conscious of group loyalties.* They are loyal to lodge, club, technical society, management groups, church, and close personal friends. They are anchored to these groups, which give them comfort when they make decisions that are unpopular with other groups.

10 *They set realistic goals.* They have realistic goals that are challenging enough so that they have to "make a fight" to achieve them, but the goals *are* achievable.

11 LEADERSHIP VARIABLES

No one "best personality" for leadership has yet been found. Studies show that many different sorts of people who have different types of personalities can be good leaders. Consider the men who built a great steel empire: Andrew Carnegie was a pint-sized "smoothie," a tactful diplomat, and a gentleman in all his relations with others; and Charles M. Schwab, his million-dollar-a-year right-hand man, was a physical giant, a hail-fellow-well-met.

Different types of work may call for different leadership methods. This is shown by observations of naval officer cadets who were given two different kinds of work—mechanical assembly and committee work. Both jobs were similar in that they required problem solving, but the assembly work dealt with tangible things, while the committee work dealt with ideas and attitudes. The interactions of the men were observed while they were doing both types of work. The same men did both jobs, but the person-to-person interactions of the men were much different for each job, as the cartoon below shows.

Not much spontaneous leadership was shown in either task. Disagreeing and arguing, included in the section labeled "miscellaneous," accounted for nearly 10 percent of the interactions in committee work, but only 2 percent in assembling. Apparently, the leader of a committee has greater need of the ability to pour oil on troubled waters than the leader of a group whose work involves things.

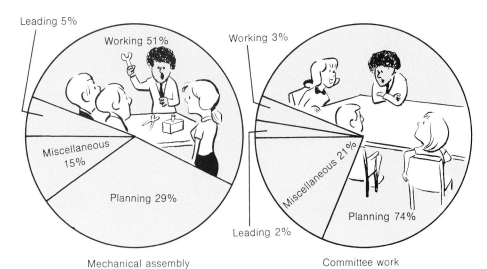

Leading 5% Working 51% Working 3% Miscellaneous 15% Planning 29% Miscellaneous 21% Planning 74% Leading 2%

Mechanical assembly Committee work

Data from Dr. Launor F. Carter and Associates

Leadership methods differ according to whether the work being done deals with tangibles or intangibles.

SUGGESTIONS FOR FURTHER READING

Bass, Bernard M., *Leadership, Psychology and Organizational Behavior,* New York: Harper & Row, 1960.
Drucker, Peter, *The Practice of Management,* New York: Harper & Row, 1954.
McKinsey & Company Inc., *The Arts of Top Management: A McKinsey Anthology,* New York: McGraw-Hill, 1971.
Newman, William H., *Administrative Action: The Techniques of Organization and Management,* 2d ed., Englewood Cliffs, N.J.: Prentice-Hall, 1963.
Rohrer, Hibler S. Replogle, *Managers for Tomorrow,* New York: New American Library, 1965.

TO HELP YOU REMEMBER

1. What is the power of office?
2. How do clothes and job titles help the power of position?
3. Who really grants a leader's authority? When is it withdrawn?
4. Explain how knowledge of the job can help business leadership.
5. Of what value is empathy to a leader?
6. Describe the six principles of leadership that Dr. Hemphill found essential for successful leadership.
7. In what ways do an executive's functions differ from those of a supervisor?
8. What is the responsibility of the board of directors? What is its relationship to the president and the executive vice president?

WORKING WITH PEOPLE, DATA, OR THINGS

A new manager was assigned to the collar and cuff department of a leading shirt factory to make some production improvements. He soon recognized that a new sewing machine attachment might reduce labor costs in one operation by at least 20 percent. He discussed his idea with the union leader and the department supervisor. Although the union leader was apathetic regarding the suggestion, the supervisor was interested and even offered suggestions for some other minor changes in work organization.

The manager, feeling he had the approval of the supervisor, decided to have the sewing machine attachment installed on one of the machines. With the help of the supervisor, the manager assigned a worker to try the new attachment. She was enthusiastic in being selected and on the first day proved that the 20-percent expectation was low.

When the manager brought the results to the attention of the union leader, she reacted negatively, saying, "You haven't proved a darn thing. Betty's the fastest operator in the department anyway; what she can do in one day is twice as much as most of the operators in the department can do!"

On the second day, the manager asked the supervisor for another operator but failed to explain to the supervisor the purpose of this request. At this time, the supervisor noticed that the work organization ideas that she had recommended to the manager were not being used. The manager ignored the sullen attitude of the supervisor, and so the supervisor became negative regarding the sewing machine attachment.

When the manager attempted to teach the second operator the way he had taught the first one, he noticed her negative attitude. She seemed to stall deliberately, and he heard her comment, "These new-fangled ideas from these big-shot bosses are a pain in the neck!" At the end of the day, the second woman's production was 5 percent below normal production (using the machine without the special attachment).

Questions

1. What are the leadership problems in this situation?
2. If the manager had been trained in the use of Dr. Hemphill's six principles of leadership, how do you think he would have handled this change in production?
3. What can be done to salvage the sewing machine attachment idea?

THINGS TO DO

1. Think of the bossiest person you know. Describe in writing, trying to use specific incidents, how that person exerts authority. Try to classify each incident, using the six principles of leadership listed in Section 8.
2. Evaluate someone you have worked for, using the list of six decision-making items for supervisors shown on pages 429, 430, and 431. Summarize specific incidents on which your evaluation is based.
3. Get organization charts from local firms as well as from a school, a library, and a hospital. Note the number of jobs at each level and the number of levels.

Labor unions, 398–399
Laird, Donald A., 39, 42,
    249, 362n., 391n.
Laird, Eleanor C., 249,
    362n., 391n.
Land, Edwin H., 353
Language barriers,
    339–340
Language development,
    career choice and,
    212–213
Lashley, Karl S., 89
Leadership, 407–439
    absenteeism and,
        416–417
    accident rates and, 417
    authoritarian, 383, 384
    authority and, 422
    "born leader" theory,
        408–409
    business, qualifications
        for, 421–422
    charismatic, 407
    consent to, 423–426
    dependence on, chart,
        426
    empathy and, 427–429
    formal, 414
    good, development of,
        417
    group theory of,
        410–411
    informal, 414
    knowledge and, 427
    labor strikes and,
        412–413
    labor turnover and,
        416; graph, 417
    leadership trait theory,
        410
    levels of responsibility,
        431–435
        board of directors,
            435
        executive, 434–435
        executive vice
            president, 435,
            436
        president, 435
        supervisor, 432–433
    nature of, 407
    organizational controls
        coercion, use of,
            412–413
        commitment,
            encouragement of,
                414
        rewards, giving of,
            413–414
    output and, 416, 432;
        chart, 433
    personal appearance
        and, 423
    power of office and,
        422
    principles of, 429–431
    in prisons, 414–415
    in social organizations,
        415–416

Leadership (continued)
    in system-managed
        companies, 411
    variables in, 437
Learning, 83–89
    advancement and, 319
    by association, 101
    curves in, 85–87
    from experts, 84–85
    memory and, 90–91
    motivation and, 83–84
    physiological limits
        and, 85
    plateaus in, 85–89
    rote, 101
    of values, 229–232
Learning theory, 12
Lee, Christopher A., 368
Lee, Dorothy E., 189n.,
    190n.
Lee, Harper, 170
Leedy, Paul D., 107–108,
    126, 127
Legibility
    of instrument panels,
        122; illus., 124
    reading and, 121–122;
        illus., 123
Lens, eye, 106; diagram,
    107
Lenses, eyeglass, 110–112
Letters, business (see
    Business writing)
Levels of Knowing and
    Existence
    (Weinberg), 174
Liars, 96–97
    pathological, 97
Libido, 11–12
Life style, values and,
    239
Lifting, techniques for,
    200–202
Lighting
    for reading, 122,
        124–125
    of work area, 37–38
Lincoln, Abraham, 122,
    248, 366, 407,
    410
Listening, 138–145
    ability in, intelligence
        and, 139
    in business, emphasis
        on, 138–139,
        143–144
    concentration and,
        140–141
    improvement of,
        suggestions for,
        140–143
"Listening to People"
    (Nichols/Stevens),
    138, 141n.
Literary Market Place, 291
Littlejohn, Vance T., 113
Locke, John, 94
Loneliness, 302, 352
LSD, 109

McCleery, R. H., 415
McConnell, James V.,
    90
McGregor, Douglas,
    65–67, 78, 79,
    381–382, 413, 414
McNabb, Joseph H., 408
Machiavelli, Niccoló, 421,
    422
Magic Island (Seabrook),
    108
Man, Medicine, and Work
    (Felton), 260
Management
    communication by,
        337–340
    scientific, 24, 187
Management philosophy,
    basic types of,
        65–67
Manifest interests, 217
Manual dexerity, 216
Market research, 42
Marshall, George C., 192
Maslow, Abraham H., 45,
    52–54, 59–61, 69,
    334, 360, 361, 382
Mass production, 34,
    259–260, 352, 372
Mathematical development,
    career choice and,
    212
Mayo, Elton, 380–381
Meaning, reading for,
    116–118
Medicine, early 6, 8
Meetings, leading of,
    179–183
Melancholia, 394
Memorizing, 90–91
Memory, 16, 89–101
    abuse of, 92–93
    aids to
        association, 98–99
        emphasis, 101
        imagination, 95
        repetition, 99–101
        self-confidence,
            graph, 94
    attitude and, 94–95
    distortions of, 96–98
    eidetic, 95
    incidental, 93
    intentional, 93–94
    interferences in,
        reduction of, 91
    learning and, 90–91
    for names, 93, 95, 99,
        101, 390–391
    nature of, 89–90
    for pleasant
        experiences,
        94–95
    recall and, 98–99
    retroactive inhibition
        and, 91
    sex differences in, 89
    short-term, 90
Mescaline, 109

INDEX 445